THE
BLACK ALMANAC

Fourth Revised Edition

By

ALTON HORNSBY, Jr.

Chairman/Department of History

Morehouse College, Atlanta, Georgia

BARRON'S EDUCATIONAL SERIES, INC.

WOODBURY, NEW YORK

Library of Congress Catalog Card No. 75-45432

International Standard Book No. 0-8120-0684-4

PRINTED IN THE UNITED STATES OF AMERICA

Library of Congress Cataloging in Publication Data

Hornsby, Alton.
  The Black almanac.
Bibliography: p.
Includes index.
  SUMMARY: A chronology of important facts concerning the role of the
Afro-American in United States history.
  Bibliography: p.
  1. Negroes—History—Chronology. [1. Negroes—History—Chronology] I. Title.
E18s.H63 1976   973'.04'96073 75-45432
ISBN 0-8120-0684-4

to the memory of

JAMES CASS HORNSBY

and

ALTON HORNSBY, SR.,

grandfather and father

Contents

List of Tables

Preface

This fourth edition of *The Black Almanac* extends the coverage of events through June, 1976, and contains several new features and revisions. Among these are new items on black contributions in music, literature, and sports. This revised edition contains many more tables, charts, and excerpts from speeches, manifestos, and documents than previous editions. Additional biographical sketches have been included and existing ones have been expanded. There is also an expanded introduction as well as an updated select bibliography.

Several persons have assisted with this first major revision of *The Black Almanac* and I wish here to express my gratitude. Professors Abraham L. Davis, and E. A. Jones of Morehouse College; Professor C. A. Bacote of Atlanta University; and Professor Robert Moran of Southern University in Baton Rouge offered helpful suggestions. My student assistants, Betty Reedy, Raymond Gordon, Leslie Pickens, and Walter Green performed numerous detailed chores. Angela Culmer and Cleta Winslow typed the manuscript. I also wish to thank the Faculty Research Committee of Morehouse College for a grant which enabled me to complete a portion of the research for this new edition.

Acknowledgments

The author gratefully acknowledges permission to reprint materials from previously published sources as follows:

The Associated Press for permission to reprint excerpts from an interview with Tom Bradley on June 22, 1975. Reprinted with permission from the Associated Press.

The Atlanta Inquirer, Inc., for permission to reprint excerpts from Boyd Lewis' interview with John Lewis. Reprinted with permission from the Atlanta Inquirer, Inc.

The National Urban League, Inc., for permission to reprint an excerpt from an article by their executive director, Vernon E. Jordan, Jr., which appeared in the January 22, 1975, edition of the *Atlanta Constitution*. Reprinted with permission of the National Urban League, Inc.

The Southern Regional Council for permission to reprint excerpts from the SRC study, "The Distribution of Southern Black Population" by Tucker and Lee. The study is available from the Southern Regional Council, 52 Fairlie Street, N.W., Atlanta, Georgia 30303, $1.25. Reprinted with permission of the Southern Regional Council.

United Press International for permission to reprint excerpts from an interview with Coretta Scott King on January 12, 1975. Reprinted with permission of United Press International.

The author would also like to acknowledge permission to reprint statements made by U.S. Senator Julian Bond regarding the 1965 Voting Rights Act. Reprinted with permission of the senator.

Introduction

The *Black Almanac* is designed to provide a convenient repository of important facts concerning the role of the Afro-American in the United States. Those occurrences which have profoundly affected the lives of black Americans, materially as well as emotionally, have been selected. The book contains important biographical data, significant events, laws, court decisions, programs, manifestos, and data on important institutions. It can thus prove valuable to students at all levels as well as to the general reader.

The many momentous occurrences in the lives of black Americans in the last 100 years have provoked enormous interest in this period of Afro-American history; hence those events after about 1870 are given in greater detail than those before 1870. The book is further subdivided into the ten most significant eras affecting Afro-Americans since their arrival in North America.

Involuntary Servitude (1619-1860)

The beginning of the history of Afro-Americans in the United States is that period of involuntary servitude from 1619 to 1860 when the large majority of blacks were chattels. Although blacks are known to have accompanied the early explorers to the New World, the first permanent settlers were the twenty blacks deposited at Jamestown, Virginia in 1619. These blacks, who had been captured in Africa and sold to the highest bidders (as many lower-class whites had been similarly captured or kidnapped and sold in Europe) were not slaves, but indentured servants.

Afro-Americans were probably indentured servants in the American colonies until 1640, and perhaps as late as 1650. After serving their period of indenture (normally seven years), some of these blacks became property holders and politically active citizens. Throughout the seventeenth century, however, the numbers of blacks, servants, slaves, or free, were still relatively small. There were about 300 blacks in the colonies by 1650. The first rapid increase came toward the close of the seventeenth century. Then, by the time of the American Revolution, almost half of the population in some of the Southern states was black. Virginia and Maryland, for example, had a total population of approximately 480,000 at the time of the Revolutionary War; about 206,000 of these people were black. South Carolina's black population was larger than the white one. Slavery was not confined to the South. The first black slaves arrived in New England probably in 1638. By 1700 there were about 1,000 blacks out of a population of 90,000 in the New England colonies, and at the time of the American Revolution there were 16,000 slaves in the region. Massachusetts and Rhode Island became great slave-trading colonies, while Connecticut was the leading New England slave colony. On the eve of the American Revolution, there were about half a million black slaves in the American colonies.

In the South, the slaves were principally employed in producing the staple crops which were the basis of the Southern economy. By 1700 they had proved to be the most reliable form of cheap labor for the Southern planters. The typical slave, however, did not work on a large plantation. He would be found more likely on a small farm, with one or two other blacks, where he worked alongside the master and his family. The majority of blacks were field slaves, and they worked under one of two systems — the Gang Plan or the Task System. Under the Gang Plan, large groups of blacks, on the larger plantations, worked long hours in the fields. In the Task System, individual blacks were given various specific chores to perform. Most urban slaves worked under the Task System, in such occupations as messengers, domestic servants, and craftsmen. A smaller group of favored slaves (selected principally because of light skin color, loyalty, or old age) worked in and around the master's house as domestic servants.

The climate and soil in New England prevented huge profits from agriculture, but skilled and unskilled labor was in much demand on small farms, and in homes, ships, factories, and shipyards, as well as on fishing and trading ships. Since Indians and indentured servants proved insufficient, black slaves were a welcome supplement. In the Middle Colonies and later states, black slaves were employed in similar occupations and in larger numbers.

Since English law did not define the status of a slave, the colonies were left to adopt their own regulations. Essentially all the colonies and states aimed first to protect the property rights of the master and second to protect white society from what was considered an alien and savage race. The codes grew out of laws regulating indentured servitude, but the slave had practically no rights, while the servant had many.

The first statutory recognition of slavery came from Massachusetts in 1641. Rhode Island passed a law regulating slavery in 1652. Virginia's regulations, which were to set the standards for the South, were passed in 1661. The status of the mother would determine whether a child was slave or free. Children born to slave mothers would become slaves. Most interracial unions and unions of slaves and free persons were of black women and white men, so the products of such unions would be mostly slaves. This practice ran counter to the English tradition which determined the status of a child according to that of his father.

Generally speaking, the slave codes prohibited the assembling or the wandering of blacks without permission from masters. Slaves could not own weapons; could not testify against white persons; received harsher punishment for some crimes, lesser for others. An attack, for example, on a white person usually meant severe punishment. Petty theft often went unpunished. A master or any white man could not kill a slave with impunity, but was likely to receive less punishment than for killing a free man. Cases involving relations between slave and master could be tried in special courts, without juries. Justices of the Peace and a selected group of planters heard the case. The strictness of enforcement of slave codes varied from region to region, from colony to colony, from state to state, and even from one plantation to another. The Massachusetts code was less restrictive than the Mississippi one, where blacks could be emancipated or manumitted only with legal approval. Urban slaves were less restricted than rural ones. Slaves on small farms enjoyed more freedom than those on huge plantations.

Physical cruelties were inflicted upon some slaves, primarily for insubordination, refusal to work, slave plots or revolts, and running away. The cruelest punishment was likely to be seen on large plantations and was received at the hands of foremen or slave drivers. Modern historians tend to indict American Negro slavery not so much for physical cruelty, but because of the harshness of the slave codes, wherein the blacks had little legal protection, and the psychological effects of the slave system. In the view of many, the slave system almost completely distorted the Negro's personality.

The historians disagree vehemently on the question of the slaves' acceptance or rejection of his status and on many related matters such as whether or not religion stifled resistance or served as a vehicle for leadership and protest. One school, commonly associated with the Southern-born historian Ulrich B. Phillips (See Bibliography), pictures a docile, contented African, naturally pliable, and logically a slave. Another school, taking its name from the New England historian Stanley Elkins (See Bibliography), assesses the psychological consequences of slavery and concludes that the blacks' personalities were so distorted by the harshness of the system that they assumed a docile, "Sambo", character. Still another school, which includes such liberal historians as Kenneth Stampp and the Marxist historian Herbert Aptheker, see the slave as rebellious and troublesome to his master.

Slaves did, in tact, protest their enslavement from the very beginning. Aside from the day to day rebellion, which took such forms as escape, destruction of property, feigned illness, and disloyalty, there were a number of plots and at least one major mutiny and one major revolt. Black slaves joined with white servants in a conspiracy in Gloucester County, Virginia in 1663; fifty-five whites were killed in the slave rebellion led by Nat Turner in Southhampton County, Virginia in 1831; and slaves mutineered on the *Amistad* off the coast of Long Island in 1839. In the final analysis, Negro slave plots, mutinies, and revolts resulted in the freeing of only a few blacks, although vicious repression often followed the acts. Many more slaves secured freedom by escape and by manumission or emancipation.

The origins of the free black population in the United States stems principally from escaped slaves, manumitted slaves, and descendants of early indentured servants. For thirty or forty years after the first blacks arrived in Jamestown, there was a free black community in Virginia which participated in political processes, owned land and even servants. The first blacks in New England included servants, who were later freed. Some few free blacks immigrated to the United States from the West Indies and some fewer African blacks paid their way in order to settle in America.

The great increase in the free black population in America came after the Revolutionary War. In appreciation of the service of some 5,000 blacks in the war for independence, and as a result of the libertarian and egalitarian spirit which the Declaration of Independence and the war inspired, many masters, especially Northerners, manumitted their slaves. Soon individual states in the North decreed the gradual abolition of the institution, beginning with Vermont's action in 1777. In 1776 the population of the United States was about two and one-half million, more than 500,000 black slaves and approximately 40,000 free blacks. More than one-half of these free blacks lived in the South. The Revolutionary leaders, including Washington and Jefferson, anticipated a continuation of the trend toward manumission and emancipation until eventually slavery would disappear from the land. This expectation was to be drowned, almost literally, by the whirling noise of Ely Whitney's cotton gin. The invention of this native of Massachusetts made cotton production increasingly profitable and caused rapid and substantial increases in the slave population, so that on the eve of the Civil War there were four million black slaves in the South.

Free blacks in the rural South worked primarily as farm workers or as independent farmers. In the urban areas, North and South, free blacks were employed in factories, such as tobacco plants and textile mills; they worked in ship yards and in railroad construction. There were some independent merchants and many personal servants and artisans. The principal professional occupation was preaching, hence the first black leader of national stature was Bishop Richard Allen of

Philadelphia, one of the founders of the African Methodist Episcopal Church.

Prior to the American Revolution, free blacks were so small in number that they did not pose a problem for whites in most of the states. Then, in the Revolutionary Era thousands were freed from Delaware north. This rapid increase in the free black population inspired more severe restrictions on the blacks. By 1790, free blacks faced regulations similar to those governing slaves. In the early history of New England, blacks could not serve in the militias as combatants (The black military hero, Peter Salem, had to beg his master's permission to serve during the American Revolution.), although they could be called to work on the roads. They could not walk on the streets at night without a pass. Free blacks could not visit a town other than the one in which they lived without passes. They could not entertain black or Indian slaves without permission. In the South, they ran the risk of being enslaved themselves if caught without proof of their status. In early Rhode Island, free blacks were not allowed to keep horses, sheep, or any other domestic animals. In Boston, they could not own hogs. The possession of weapons was severely restricted. In one New England state blacks could not possess walking sticks or canes unless demonstrably required for the actual support of the person. There was constant conflict in places like New York as free blacks and whites competed for jobs.

By 1840, the free black population in the United States was almost completely disfranchised. More than ninety percent of the American free black population lived in states which totally, or in part, restricted their right to vote. On the eve of the Civil War, blacks voted with relative freedom and safety only in Massachusetts, Vermont, New Hampshire, and Maine.

Restrictions on the political and civil rights of free blacks were motivated by racial prejudice and, additionally, in the South by beliefs that the group had a disquieting influence on the institution of slavery. Free blacks were implicated in a number of the slave plots and uprisings and their very existence pointed to a different life, although not a very radical one, for black men in America. In the final analysis, a free black in pre-Civil War America was little better off than a slave. The inferior status of this group has led historians to classify them appropriately as quasi-free Negroes.

Despite the inferior civil, social, and political status of quasi-free blacks, many managed to achieve considerable distinction in American society. Although discriminated against in employment and in other economic endeavors, a number acquired substantial wealth. Even in the pre-Civil War era, there were prosperous free black communities in Philadelphia, Baltimore, Charleston, New Orleans, and elsewhere. Individual blacks like John Jones and Paul Cuffee (See Below) acquired considerable fortunes. In military service, the arts and sciences, and religion there were free blacks who distinguished themselves and won recognition even from white America. The free black communities, especially in the North, were vociferous opponents of slavery and discrimination, and the abolition movement of the 1830's and the convention movement of the 1840's and 1850's were interrelated vehicles used by blacks to protest their status in America, whether slave or quasi-free.

War and Freedom (1861-1876)

Momentous changes in the lives of black Americans occurred in the years between 1861 and 1876. These were the years of the American Civil War, Emancipation, and Reconstruction. Four million Negroes were freed as a result of a war in which many of them participated. Then, for the first time, large numbers of blacks had an opportunity to direct their own social and economic destinies; and some, during the Reconstruction era, were able to assert political leadership. Despite the war and the resulting freedom, however, these were still very difficult years for the black masses as they struggled to survive in a hostile environment, and even the gains made during Black Reconstruction failed to provide lasting security.

After the Confederate attack on Fort Sumter, South Carolina on April 12, 1861 and Lincoln's call for 75,000 volunteers to "defend the union," many Northern blacks rushed to answer the President's appeal. The blacks erroneously interpreted the unfolding conflict as a war against slavery. They soon discovered that the President's war aims did not include interference with slavery where it already existed and that they were not to be permitted combat roles. Abraham Lincoln judged that a war against slavery would drive additional Southern and Border states into the Confederacy and that such a program and the employment of black troops would anger much of Northern white opinion. Blacks and their white abolitionist supporters, in and out of Congress, clearly expressed their opposition to a war whose aims did not include the abolition of slavery as well as the refusal to employ blacks as troops.

The first year of the Civil War was for the most part a frustrating one for Abraham Lincoln and the Union. In addition to inept military commanders, he had to contend with apathy and even disloyalty in the North; the possibility of an alliance between the Confederacy and cotton-seeking European nations; abolitionist and Negro agitation; runaway slaves entering Union lines; unauthorized slave emancipation by military leaders; and the employment of blacks in fatigue duties by the Confederacy. Then there was the continuous matter of preventing the secession of additional slave states. By the summer of 1862, the President concluded that the emancipation of certain slaves and the eventual employment of black troops had become military necessities. There were risks — the Border states might join the Confederacy; much of Northern white opinion might be alienated; morale in the Union Army might be lowered. On the other hand, England and the rest of Europe would not likely oppose a war against slavery; abolitionist sentiment in the North would enthusiastically support the effort; thousands of blacks would be lost to the Confederacy; thousands of blacks could be drawn to the Union.

The Emancipation Proclamation specifically excluded all slave states and areas loyal to the Union, hence preserving the Border States for the North and having little immediate effect in most of the South, which the Confederate Army controlled. At the same time, the Proclamation and the employment of Negro troops convinced blacks and abolitionists that the "Day of Jubilee" was at hand. Bells rang from the spires of Northern black churches and blacks rejoiced when the emancipation edict took effect on January 1, 1863.

The moral crusade known as abolitionism had sprung up during the 1830's. This new, militant movement resulted from the efforts of New England and Midwestern reformers such as William Lloyd Garrison, James Finney, Lewis Tappan, and Theodore Dwight Weld. The talents of black ex-slaves like Frederick Douglass, Henry Highland Garnett, and Harriet Tubman as well as members of the free black communities in the North were joined with the efforts of the

white reformers. These people were successors to the Quaker protestors of earlier centuries, the moderate abolitionists of the 18th and
19th centuries, and the colonizationists of the early 1800's, who
would rid the land of the Negro problem by shipping the blacks
to Africa or other foreign lands. In 1863 their long and painful efforts
finally received political sanction at the highest level when emancipation became a war aim, even though prompted not by moral
suasion or moral right, but by military necessity.

Almost 200,000 blacks fought for the Union during the Civil War.
Although they faced discrimination of one type or another throughout the conflict, many rendered distinguished service and won com-
mendations from the Commander-in-Chief himself. A few rose to
the ranks of officers. About 40,000 blacks died in the fight for
freedom — most of these deaths were disease related, reflecting the
poor medical attention received by black soldiers in the Civil War,
their proneness to front-line duty and other hazardous occupations.
The Confederacy debated the use of black troops until 1864, but
when the final positive decision was grudgingly made, the war was
nearing its end. Blacks never saw combat duty for the Confederacy.

The generous terms of surrender which General U. S. Grant offered
the Confederates in April, 1865 were symptomatic of much of Northern white opinion at the close of the Civil War. They certainly reflected the attitude of President Lincoln toward the seceded states.
They should, in his view, be returned to the Union as expeditiously
as possible in a spirit of leniency and reconciliation. Lincoln's mild
Reconstruction program was aborted by an assassin's bullet on April
14, 1865, but his successor, Andrew Johnson, a Southerner, continued
the lenient policies toward the white South. Johnson, who did not
believe in Negro equality, following Lincoln's example, supported
ratification of the 13th Amendment abolishing slavery, but did not
push Negro enfranchisement or the protection of civil rights. He
tolerated anti-Negro violence in Louisiana, Tennessee, and Mississippi, as well as the Black Codes which the Southern white or
"Johnson" governments enacted in 1865 and 1866. These codes,
reminiscent of the ante-bellum slave codes, proscribed the Negro
to an inferior status in Southern society.

Republican leaders in Congress correctly viewed the Johnson
program as an invitation to restore white Democratic supremacy

in the South. Some of these leaders motivated by a desire to institute Republican party supremacy in the region and others motivated by a sincere interest in protecting Negro civil rights combined to form a solid front of opposition to the President's programs. The "Radical Republicans" favored a harsh program of Southern Reconstruction, one which would delay the reentrance of the Southern states until Republican strength could be garnered; until the blacks could be enfranchised, in the belief that they would form a bloc of Southern Republican votes; and one which would guarantee civil rights for Negroes. Southern white Democratic agriculturists should not be allowed to regain economic and political ascendancy in the nation.

In 1866 and 1867 the Republican leadership, using the party's majorities in Congress, snatched the Reconstruction of the South out of the President's hands and instituted their own program. Their plans included an extension of the Freedmen's Bureau (originally proposed by Lincoln) to help freed blacks and poor whites eat, attain clothing and shelter, secure job protection, receive medical attention, and some education. Negroes were to be made citizens of the United States and granted all rights and privileges enjoyed by other American citizens. This was accomplished through the Civil Rights Act of 1866 and the 14th Amendment (ratified in 1868). The blacks' right to vote was to be insured through the 15th Amendment (ratified in 1870).

The Radical Republican Reconstruction program guided through the House by the Pennsylvania egalitarian Thaddeus Stevens and through the Senate by Charles Sumner, a Massachusetts humanitarian, paved the way for the first large scale participation by blacks in the political processes of the nation. Blacks attended the constitutional conventions in the South which were called in 1867 and 1868 to establish new fundamental laws to replace the pro-Democratic, anti-Negro documents instituted by the Johnson governments. In South Carolina, more blacks than whites attended these conventions, and in Louisiana the races attended in equal numbers. Elsewhere, Northern whites ("carpetbaggers"), some of them economic and political opportunists and Southern whites ("scalawags"), political and economic allies of the Northern Republicians, dominated the conventions. These same latter groups were also to exercise the greatest influence in the new Southern governments, except in South Carolina where blacks had a majority in the Legislature throughout the early years of Radical or Black Reconstruction.

Although, except in South Carolina, blacks never really controlled any part of the Southern governments during the whole Reconstruction era (1865-1877), they voted in large numbers and elected members of their own race and sympathethic whites to offices ranging from city councilman to United States Senator. There are, for example, four black lieutenant governors, twenty U. S. congressmen, two U. S. senators, three secretaries of state, a state supreme court justice, two state treasurers, and numerous other minor black officials. P. B. S. Pinchback served briefly as acting governor of Louisiana.

Black voters and elected officials tended to pursue an attitude of charity and reconciliation toward their ex-slave masters and their descendants. They refrained from passing or supporting vindictive legislation and insisted that Southern whites reap equal benefits from the reformist acts which they passed. The Black Reconstruction governments, despite examples of waste and corruption, made great strides in the physical reconstruction of the South; in providing free public schools; in eliminating anachronistic penal institutions; and in guaranteering civil rights. In these matters, black and white alike could look for a better life.

The Nadir (1877-1900)

The growing Republican strength in the Northwest, economic ties between Northern and Southern capitalists, anti-Negro intimidation and violence of the Ku Klux Klan variety, and the economic helplessness of black Americans, eventually caused the waning of Northern Republican enthusiasm for Black Reconstruction. The nadir came with the disputed election of 1876. In return for Republican pledges of federal aid for internal improvements in the South and the withdrawal of the remaining federal troops supporting Radical Reconstruction, Southern Democratic leaders allowed the Congress to proceed in certifying Rutherford B. Hayes as President of the United States instead of the Democratic contender, Samuel Tilden. Following the inauguration, Hayes removed the last federal troops from the South, and the remaining Radical or Black Reconstruction governments in Florida, Louisiana, and South Carolina toppled.

Professor Rayford Logan of Howard University and others have called the period between 1877 and 1900 the nadir in Negro life and history. Following the disputed election of 1876, and the so-called Compromise of 1877 which settled it, the Republican party abandoned the Negro and left him in the hands of Southern "redeemers," those native whites who reasserted white supremacy. From Hayes through McKinley the national government exhibited a policy of "hands-off" the "Southern problem". With little or no relief to be expected from state and local authorities, Negroes faced an environment reminiscent of slavery. Legalized segregation and discrimination and political disfranchisement became the order of the day. The U. S. Supreme Court in 1883 and 1896 conclusively stamped legality on racial separation. In the Civil Rights cases of 1883, the Court struck down the Civil Rights Act of 1875, which, among other things, had guaranteed blacks equal access to public accommodations. In 1896, in the historic *Plessy vs Ferguson* decision, the Court sanctioned the principle of separate-but-equal facilities for whites and blacks. In practice, the facilities were to be separate and unequal. Beginning with a Mississippi law in 1890, one southern state after another adopted ingenious devices for denying the ballot to blacks. These ranged from literacy tests to the infamous white primary, in which blacks were excluded from the most important state and local elections. Ku Klux Klan type violence, the most notorious form of which was lynching, continued to augment the legal oppression. Out of this nadir, however, were to come two outstanding voices who would leave large imprints upon Afro-American history — Booker T. Washington and W. E. B. DuBois.

The Age of Booker T. Washington (1901-1917)

Booker T. Washington was the only black American invited to speak at the Cotton States International Exposition in Atlanta in 1895. Most prominent Southern whites were aware of the significant work he was performing at Tuskegee Institute in Alabama, where, as principal since 1881, he had been turning out trained black agriculturists, artisans, and teachers; encouraging cleanliness and respect for hard labor; and fostering racial harmony. In his speech, later dubbed "the Atlanta Compromise," Washington admonished blacks against agitating for political power and social equality, and called on whites to assist blacks in education, principally agricultural-industrial training, and economic advancement.

The formula for racial peace and progress which Washington outlined at Atlanta met wide approval from whites, South as well as North. The *Atlanta Constitution* called it the greatest speech ever delivered in the South, and President Cleveland sent Washington a congratulatory telegram. While many blacks supported Washington's ideas, some, like the publisher William Monroe Trotter and the scholar W. E. B. DuBois, came to disagree with Washington's remarks and launched attacks against him. The best known opposition to Washington was that of W. E. B. DuBois.

The publication of *Souls of Black Folk* by DuBois in 1903 crystallized the opposition to the "accommodationist" philosophy of Booker T. Washington. A group of black "radicals," led by DuBois and Trotter, met at Niagara Falls, Canada in June, 1905, and adopted resolutions calling for aggressive action to end racial discrimination in the United States. The lynchings, riots, intimidation, and disfranchisement of the previous decade had taught them that temporizing would not guarantee security to black Americans. The Niagara group held other meetings in the United States, picking up black intellectuals as they went, and has become known to history as the Niagara Movement. Following the anti-Negro riots at Brownsville, Texas, Atlanta, Georgia, and Springfield, Illinois (1906-1908), the Niagara Movement, minus Monroe Trotter, who was suspicious of whites, merged in 1910 with a group of white progressives and produced the National Association for the Advancement of Colored People (NAACP). The NAACP became the most militant civil rights organization in the United States, as it sought to obtain racial equality for all Americans.

Despite the activities of the Niagara radicals and the NAACP, the policies of Booker T. Washington and his "Tuskegee Machine" remained in vogue, and won heavy financial subsidies from wealthy white Americans and the political endorsement of the White House, many congressmen, state and local authorities. The anti-Washington radicals were hard put in their effort to war against Tuskegee. Without a doubt, that period in Afro-American history following the

Atlanta Compromise Address to the death of Washington in 1915 was the Age of Booker T. Washington.

Between War and Depression (1918-1932)

After the death of Booker T. Washington, the NAACP-type radicals gained the ascendancy in Negro leadership, for there could be no one real successor to the Tuskegee "king-pin." White America was in no mood to accept "militant demands," and racial oppression continued to be commonplace. Legal and extra-legal discrimination in jobs, housing, and education, and political disfranchisement were the milder forms of oppression when compared with police brutality and atrocious lynchings. Tuskegee Institute kept a running count of lynchings in the United States and made annual reports — as many as eighty-three were recorded in one year, and it was 1952 before none was recorded. When the United States intervened in World War I, some seemed to feel that the participation of blacks in the conflict would prick the conscience of white Americans and lead to concessions for blacks. Such precedents, in fact, existed in the War for Independence and in the Civil War. But the contemporary story turned out to be one of harassment of black soldiers, even while in uniform, at home and abroad, and the war itself was followed by one of the worst series of racial clashes in American history. During the summer of 1919 at least twenty-five cities witnessed racial disturbances in what James Weldon Johnson called "the Red Summer".

The "Red Summer," a product of the post-war depression, financial and mental, and the growing Negro migration to large urban areas, produced a wave of disillusionment in black America. The disillusionment had positive as well as negative effects. In the early 1920's scores of black intellectuals, centered in Harlem, began producing literary and artistic works depicting Negro life in the ghettoes and crying for relief from oppression. Black nationalism was revived in the movement of Marcus Garvey. Garvey taught race pride and despaired of an equitable solution of the American race problem. He urged large-scale removals to Africa. Garvey's would-be African empire collapsed behind the cell doors of the Atlanta Federal Penitentiary where he was incarcerated after being convicted of using the mails to defraud.

The Great Depression which hit the country in 1929 stung the Negro. Most blacks were already on the lowest rung of the economic ladder, now they were in serious danger of touching ground. The depression, of course, stifled the growing militancy among the race, while doing little, needless to say, to relieve discontent. Blacks contended that even in the midst of common woes, they were still singled out and made the victims of discrimination. Their plight in the area of employment, for instance, was depicted by the slogan "the last hired and the first fired". When Franklin D. Roosevelt took office in 1933, American blacks were certainly ready for a New Deal.

A New Deal — A New Life? (1933-1940)

New Deal measures lifted blacks, like whites, out of the depths of the depression, but even here some blacks felt that they did not receive their fair share of the benefits. The precise truth is hard to discover, but many of the recovery and reform programs were administered by the state and local governments and this meant, especially in the South, all-white control. Discriminatory handling of the measures for relief, in many instances, would not be difficult to imagine. In any case, the New Deal administration was a segregated one. President Roosevelt even had a so-called "Black Cabinet," Negro advisers on Afro-American affairs. In the end, the New Deal was viewed by black as well as white Americans as an era of progress —certainly a marked advance over the depression years.

War Again (1941-1945)

The outbreak of the Second World War in Europe, like the First, encouraged a wave of emigration to the North by Southern Negroes. As the nation entered a state of defense-readiness, blacks sought to obtain a share of the increasing number of jobs in defense industries. Again, they met a good deal of frustration resulting from discrimination. Finally after blacks threatened to stage a massive protest march in Washington, President Roosevelt issued an executive order forbiding discrimination in defense related industries. After the United States entered the conflict, hundreds of thousands of black Americans served with distinction. This service, the growing black populations in the urban centers, increasing literacy, and increasing economic opportunities appeared to foster a new determination to end racial discrimination in American life. The NAACP, bolstered by the records of Negro servicemen, an increased membership, a new crop of brilliant young lawyers, and steady financial support from white philanthropists, led the way toward freedom.

The Attack Against Segregation (1945-1954)

The existence of segregation and discrimination in the most democratic nation in the world constituted an American dilemma, according to the Swedish social scientist Gunnar Myrdal, who in 1944 had concluded a year-long study of the race problem entitled *An American Dilemma*. The NAACP had long been aware of the dilemma and was deadset on resolving it by eliminating segregation and discrimination from American society. The NAACP leaders, like most Americans, revered the constitutional structure of the United States and thus sought to implement its program through legal channels. Prior to the World War, the organization's legal minds had been chipping away at the foundations of segregation and discrimination by winning important decisions from the U. S. Supreme Court. After the war, there was a virtual avalanche. From 1945 to 1954 the NAACP attacked legalized segregation and discrimination in almost every area and the foundations slowly crumbled. Ingenious devices for denying blacks the right to vote, discrimination in housing, bias in transportation, and segregation in recreation and educational facilities fell victim to NAACP sponsored suits. The Supreme Court decisions on school segregation which are highlighted by the Brown case in 1954 were so far-reaching and portended so much for the future that they inaugurated a whole new era in Afro-American history, the era of civil rights.

The Era of Civil Rights (1954-1964)

The school-house had long been considered an integral part of the democratic process. It was, in fact, a bulwark of American democracy. Its ability to socialize individuals made it, indeed, an almost sacred institution. The destruction of segregation and discrimination in the schools could, then, bring the day closer when America would boast an integrated society. The school decisions inspired a literal stampede for equality. Court actions quickly knocked down the remaining vestiges of legalized segregation. Congress, in the face of skillful lobbying and increasing black voter registrants in the North, got into the act by passing laws designed to insure Negro voting rights against extra-legal trickery in the South. Presidents issued executive orders affecting segregation in the armed forces and in housing. They established civil rights committees to investigate and report injustices. Boycotts, such as the famous one in Montgomery, Alabama, 1955-56, broke down Jim Crowism on local busses. With segregation and discrimination by law a dead letter, black groups turned to overt and covert bias in the private sector. Centering their attention on the humiliating separate lunch counters and restaurants, the sit-in technique (aided by the boycott) was revived and used massively to wipe out discrimination at the hot-dog stands and other public accommodations from hotels to cemeteries. The Civil Rights Act of 1964 acknowledged the correctness of the sit-in attacks by, among other things, outlawing discrimination in public accommodations. The American dilemma seemed to be over, all would be free at last in "the land of the free." The dream which Martin Luther King, Jr. had so eloquently described at the 1963 March on Washington seemed near fulfillment.

An Age of Disillusionment (1964-1973)

President Johnson's signature on the Civil Rights Act of 1964 had barely dried when a serious racial disturbance erupted in Harlem. That same summer several other Northern ghettoes were the scenes of violence. Then in August, 1965 the black ghetto of Watts in Los Angeles exploded, leaving many dead and injured, and property losses in the millions of dollars. For the next two summers, peaking with the equally destructive Detroit riot of 1967, scores of major racial outbursts, oft-times sparked by clashes between blacks and white policemen, occurred. The nation sought an answer. Why had these eruptions happened, particularly at this time when the millennium appeared at hand? The Presidential Commission on Civil Disorders (Kerner Commission) offered its findings in March, 1968.

In spite of all the court decisions, the sit-ins, marches and boycotts, the average black American was disillusioned with his status in American society, for he still found himself ill-housed, ill-clothed, poorly paid, if at all, and segregated and discriminated against, through covert and extra-legal means, in all walks of American life. Ingrained white racism, the Commission reasoned, blocked the legitimate aspirations of black people. The slaying of Martin Luther King, Jr., the nation's leading apostle of non-violent resistance to racism and bias, in April of 1968, increased the disillusionment and, in fact, led to some outright despair. New cries of black nationalism, black separatism, and violent resistance were heard in Afro-America.

In three and one-half centuries of life in America, the African race has seen momentous changes in the legal and social structures of the country which relate directly to its own status. The legal foundations of segregation and discrimination which kept it in a straitjacket were toppled in the last decade. The attainment of even these goals involved a long, painful, oft-times frustrating and disillusioning struggle. Yet, as the Kerner Commission Report so dramatically showed, the long fight for dignity and justice was by no means completed, for the real victory would have to involve the repression of white racism. White Americans would have to face up to their ingrained, and often unconscious, bias on the subject of race, and work consciously to erase its effects from the land.

A Return to the Mainstream (1973-1976)?

The landslide proportions of Richard Nixon's re-election to the presidency in 1972 cast a dark cloud over Black America. During his first term, the President had consistently reaffirmed his commitment to racial equality and justice, but at the end of the term many of the most prominent leaders in Black America found his record on civil rights seriously wanting. Some even claimed that there had been an erosion of the gains made under the two previous Democratic administrations. They cited, for example, the President's failure to appoint blacks to top level positions in the federal government (i.e., Under Nixon, the Cabinet returned to an all-white status); his nominations of G. Harrold Carswell and Clement Haynsworth, "conservative" Southerners, for seats on the U.S. Supreme Court; his vehement opposition to busing to achieve school desegregation; his lukewarm support for desegregated housing; and his lukewarm support for black institutions of higher education. The U.S. Commission on Civil Rights joined its voice with that of the black leaders, charging that the administration was derelict in its enforcement of existing civil rights laws.

President Nixon used several occasions, including press conferences and meetings with blacks inside and outside of government, to express concern with the disillusionment and disenchantment with his administration within Black America. Yet, he refused to alter his course. He was prone to cite the phenomenal progress of black Americans in the past decade in the areas of civil rights, economic opportunity, and political development. He seemed to suggest that the remaining problems of blacks were less a matter of race and more of initiative, self-reliance, and economic development. He talked much about the need for "black capitalism" and black entrepreneurship. As he approached the election campaign of 1972, he predicted substantial black support for his candidacy. The President did, in fact, win endorsement from several prominent blacks in his bid for re-election. But the heads of most of the major black civil rights organizations in the country urged his defeat, and on election day he amassed only about 30% of the total black vote.

The President began his second administration amid the aura of the greatest election victory in American history and with the growing cancer of Watergate still only slowly creeping into his political life. The "Watergate Affair," whose discovery was attributed to a black guard, Frank Wills, would soon bring down the presidency of Richard Nixon. Meanwhile, however, the President, re-elected overwhelmingly, but without substantial black support, continued his policies of "benign neglect" toward Black America.

The indifference of a national administration toward the peculiar problems of black Americans, combined with a growing economic recession, created a certain amount of confusion among blacks. Ironically, this was also a time of substantial political progress at the local level, particularly in the South. The problem, however, in large measure, was that the local political prowess which blacks were gaining could not be transformed or translated into influence at the national levels and could not halt the growing spiral of black unemployment and underemployment. The indifference manifested by the national administration had its impact in other facets of American life. The drive for "affirmative action" in recruiting blacks to higher paying jobs seemed to lose some of its steam, as did the preferential recruiting of black students to previously all white or majority-white schools and colleges. The economic decline was a part of the explanation; the cry by some whites of "reverse discrimination" was another part; but the complacent tone set in Washington was also of great significance. What should blacks, still the most ill-fed, ill-housed, poorly trained segment of the American population, do now? Would the disillusionment of the past become outright despair? Would there be new Watts, Detroits, and Atlantas? Would the black masses again take to the streets to vent their frustrations at still not being able to share fully in the American dream? There were, as always, voices in the black community urging such a course of action, but they were, as always, on the fringe of the black mainstream. They were without a substantial following.

The black mainstream, during the Nixon nadir, would continue to look to the leadership of the black middle class, as exemplified in the major civil rights organizations—the NAACP, the SCLC, Operation PUSH, the Urban League—for the right path to the Promised Land. That leadership, faced with the political and economic realities of the 1970's and the growing displays of overt racism in the North, could only sprout the same old shibboleths of the Civil Rights era and espouse the same old strategies. In fact, black American leaders were now faced with problems, policies, and practices which defied solutions and attack by a march in the street, a Supreme Court edict, or even a rock thrown through a plate-glass window. Black America needed influence at the highest levels of political and economic decision-making, and that it did not have.

While the Nixon administration undoubtedly exaggerated the extent of black progress in America in the 1960's, it was, nevertheless, true that all indexes, income, education, housing, etc., showed numerical, and often percentage, gains for black Americans during the 1960's. In many respects, Black America was still a colonized nation, but its colonial status was closer to that of America in the 1760's than to Rhodesia in the 1970's. These facts, together with the apparent futility of violent outbursts, seemed to suggest to Black America, the masses as well as the elite, that, after a decade of disillusionment, a return to the mainstream would best promote physical and psychological well-being. The mood of Black America suggested a harvesting of gains to prevent further erosions; to place education above demonstration; to seek whatever securities were inherent in middle-class life in America; and to acknowledge the fact that America was still a nation of two societies—one black, one white—separate and unequal.

CHAPTER

I

Involuntary Servitude

1619-1860

1619

August 20. A Dutch ship with twenty Negroes aboard arrived at Jamestown, Virginia. The twenty had been captured in Africa and sold to the highest bidders, as many impoverished whites had been similarly kidnapped in Europe. These blacks were not the first of their race to arrive in North America. Pedro Alonso Nino, of Columbus' crew, was perhaps a Negro. On Columbus' last voyage, which set out in July, 1502, Diego el Negro, a black man, was a member of the crew on the *Capitana*. Certainly as many as thirty blacks, including Nuflo de Olano, were with Balboa in the discovery of the Pacific Ocean. Blacks were with Spanish, Portuguese, and French explorers in the Americas throughout the sixteenth century. The most noted black explorer was Estevanico (Esteban). He was a member of the ill-fated Narvaez expedition that left Spain in 1527 to explore the western coast of the Gulf of Mexico. The ships were blown off coast and landed far to the east, at Tampa Bay, Florida, in 1528. Moving onward by land and boat, the expedition ship wrecked on Galveston Island, off Texas. Only four survivors, Cabeza de Vaca, Alonzo del Castillo, Andres Dorantes, and his slave Estevanico (Esteban) were able to continue the trek. Estevanico, a Moroccoan, because of his good rapport with Indians, became a valuable member of the party. The explorers reached Mexico City after 1536 and excited the officials

1

there with stories the red men had given them of seven golden cities of Cibola somewhere to the northwest. Francisco Coronado was assigned to conquer Cibola. In 1539 Coronado sent an advance party led by Friar Marcos, but guided by Estevanico. Friar Marcos sent Estevanico ahead and the black scout discovered Arizona and New Mexico. The Zuni Indians of Cibola then killed Estevanico and the rest of the party retreated. The twenty blacks left at Jamestown in 1619 were, however, the first permanent involuntary settlers of their race, hence the history of Afro-Americans in what is now the United States begins with their arrival.

1638

Negro slaves were brought into New England. Blacks had been sold in Boston prior to this date, but it is not definitely known when the first Negro slaves were brought into the region. Authorities (George H. Moore, *Notes on Slavery in Massachusetts*, p. 9; Elizabeth Donnan, *Documents Illustrative of the Slave Trade to America*, III, 4n.; Lorenzo Greene, *The Negro in Colonial New England*, pp. 15-18) who claim that Negro slaves were first brought to New England in 1638 base their contention on an entry in John Winthrop's *Journal*, recording on December 12, 1638 the return to Boston of Captain William Pierce in the ship, *Desire*, with a cargo, according to Winthrop, including salt, cotton, tobacco, and Negroes. The statement of Governor Winthrop is the first recorded account of Negro slavery in New England.

1641

Massachusetts recognized slavery as a legal institution; the first of the North American colonies to do so. Section 91 of the *Body of Liberties* of 1641 read: "There shall never be any bond slaverie, villinage or Captivitie amongst us, unless it be lawful Captives taken in just warres, and such strangers as willingly sell themselves or are sold to us. And these shall have all the liberties and Christian usages which the law of God established in Israell. . . . This exempts none from servitude who shall be Judged thereto by Authoritie."

1661

Slavery recognized by statute in Virginia; the status of the mother would determine whether a black child would be slave or free. The slave codes of Virginia, and those which followed them, were motivated by the growth of the black population and the fears of slave uprisings. They were designed to protect the property in slaves and to protect white society from an "alien and savage race." Generally, slaves were not allowed to leave the plantation, to wander, or to assemble without permission from the master. They could not own weapons, could not testify against white persons in court. Slaves found guilty of murder or rape were to be executed. For petty offenses slaves were whipped, maimed, or branded. The slave codes grew out of the laws regulating indentured servitude, but the slaves, unlike the indentured servants, had practically no rights at all.

1663

September 13.   First major conspiracy of persons in servitude in Colonial America. A plot of white servants and black slaves was betrayed by a servant in Gloucester County, Virginia.

1664

September 20.   Maryland took the lead in passing laws against the marriage of English women and black men. The preamble of the statute justified the prohibition of intermarriage because "divers free born *English* women, forgetful of their free condition, and to the disgrace of our nation, do intermarry with Negro slaves," causing, among other things, questions to arise over the status of such blacks. The law was passed to remove this problem and to deter "such free-born women from such shameful matches."

1688

February 18.   Quakers at Germantown, Pennsylvania adopted the first formal anti-slavery resolution in American history. The Society of Friends declared that slavery was opposed to Christianity and the rights of man. The sect continued its protests throughout the 17th century.

1704

————. A school for blacks, one of the first in the colonies to enroll slaves, was opened by Elias Nau, a Frenchman, in New York City.

1712

April 7. Negro slave revolt in New York City. Nine whites slain. Twenty-one blacks were executed as participants. Six other alleged participants committed suicide. The insurrection was spearheaded by twenty-seven armed slaves who met in an orchard near the center of the city. A fire was set to an outhouse of a white master. As other whites attempted to assist in extinguishing the blaze, they were shot by the blacks. The state militia was called out to pursue and capture the black rebels. New Yorkers responded by strengthing their slave code. The number of slave crimes punishable by death was increased to include willful burning of property. Conspiracy to murder was also made a capital offense.

1739

September 9. The first serious slave uprising took place in South Carolina. Twenty-five to thirty whites were slain. More than thirty blacks were killed for alleged participation. The uprising, led by a black called Cato, began about twenty miles west of Charleston at Stono. The slaves killed two warehouse guards, secured arms and ammunition, and fled south, hoping to reach Florida. They marched to the beating of two drums and killed all whites who attempted to interfere. Armed, organized whites pursued the rebels, capturing all but a dozen.

1761

December 15. Jupiter Hammon, born a slave in 1720, published

Salvation by Christ with Penetential Cries, the first known poetical work by an American Negro. Hammon's masters had given him a rudimentary education, including religious instruction. They helped him publish his verse. The verse was preoccupied with the salvation epic. Scholars do not accord much merit to his work, but he is an important figure because of his place in the chronology of black literature. Hammon is also known for his *Address to the Negroes of the State of New York*, 1787, in which he called upon blacks to be faithful and obedient to their masters. The race should endure its bondage humbly and patiently until it earned its freedom by honesty and good conduct.

1764

————. Brown University was founded at Providence, Rhode Island. The university was named for the wealthy New England shippers, the Brown Brothers, who made huge profits in the African slave trade.

1770

March 5. Crispus Attucks of Framingham, Massachusetts, an escaped slave, died together with four other Americans in the so-called Boston Massacre. After escaping slavery, Attucks worked for twenty years as a merchant seaman. He was in the forefront of the group that taunted British soldiers in Boston and is commonly said to have been the first to fall from their fire. Massachusetts has honored him with a statue in Boston.

1773

————. George Leile and Andrew Bryan organized the first Negro Baptist church in the American colonies at Savannah, Georgia. Leile and Bryan were both ex-slaves with modest education. When they first began preaching, at very young ages, there were no black denominations. Leile and Bryan preached without compensation. Leile supported himself by hiring out his labor, after being freed by his pious master. Opposition to Negro worship eventually forced Leile to flee to Jamaica. Bryan's master defended him against other whites who were alarmed over the growth of the black church, and, although Bryan bought his wife's freedom, he did not purchase his own freedom until after the master's death because of gratitude for the master's defense.

————. Phillis Wheatley, an African-born poetess, published her book, *Poems on Various Subjects, Religious and Moral*, becoming only the second American woman to publish a book.

————. Miss Wheatley, a frail black woman, was born in Senegal and was sold as a slave at Boston in 1761 to a tailor, John Wheatley. Mrs. Wheatley tutored young Phyllis, enabling her to become literate. She began writing verses in her early teens. Manumitted in 1773, she took a trip to London and was received by the Lord Mayor there. On February 28, 1776, she had an audience with General George Washington at his Cambridge, Massachusetts headquarters, in order that he might express his appreciation for her poem in his honor.

————. Jean Baptiste Point DuSable, first permanent settler of Chicago, a black man, purchased the property of Jean Baptiste Millet at "Old Peoria Fort." DuSable was born in St. Marc, Haiti in 1745. He was the son of a successful Frenchman, who had emigrated to Haiti from Marseilles, France, and a black slave. DuSable was educated in France. He arrived at New Orleans in 1765 as a representative of his father's business. When the Spanish took over Louisiana that same year, DuSable and an associate, Jacques Clemorgan of Martinique, left for the French settled areas of the upper Mississippi River. They stopped at St. Louis and carried on a successful fur trade with the Indians there for two years. Later DuSable and Clemorgan moved farther north into Indian territory and lived with the Peoria and Potawatomie tribes. At the same time DuSable participated in fur trapping expeditions which carried him to the present sites of Chicago and Detroit, and into parts of Canada. In 1772, he decided to build a fur trading post on the Chicago river near Lake Michigan. A successful trading center grew around the post and the Chicago settlement developed. After Illinois came under the jurisdiction of the United States, DuSable sold his property, returned to Missouri, and died there in 1818.

1775

April 14. The first abolitionist society in the United States was organized at Philadelphia. The group, which had many active Quaker participants, was known as the Pennsylvania Society for the Abolition of Slavery. The Society first directed its efforts toward obtaining an abolition law in Pennsylvania and protecting free blacks from being kidnapped and sold into slavery. After a successful campaign for adequate protective legislation, the Society helped to enforce the new laws through committees of correspondence and by employing lawyers to secure the conviction of offenders. The Society suspended its operations during the Revolutionary War, although individual members continued active work. The group was reorganized in 1787 as the Pennsylvania Society for Promoting the Abolition of Slavery, the Relief of Free Negroes Unlawfully held in Bondage, and for Improving the Condition of the African Race.

April 19. The War for Independence opened at Lexington and Concord. Blacks were among the minutemen who opposed the British.

June 17. Two blacks, Peter Salem and Salem Poor, were commended for their participation on the side of the Patriots at the Battle of Bunker Hill. Salem had been a slave in Framingham, Massachusetts, but was manumitted in order that he might serve in the Revolutionary Army. The Committee on Safety of the Continental Congress had decreed in May, 1775 that only free blacks could serve in the American army. During the Battle of Bunker Hill, Salem killed the British commander, Major John Pitcairn. Although the Americans did not achieve victory at Bunker Hill, the death of Pitcairn raised the soldiers' morale at the time. The Massachusetts General Court later commended Salem for the act. Poor also won commendation from the Massachusetts Court and from his officers. He was described by his officers as an excellent soldier. However, on July 9, 1775 General George Washington announced that there would be no further enlistments of blacks. The Continental Congress sanctioned this move in October (See Below).

October 23. The Continental Congress prohibited black enlistment in the American Army.

November 7. Lord Dunmore, British royal governor of Virginia, issued a proclamation promising freedom to slaves who joined the British forces in the Revolutionary War. Southerners, especially Virginians, were alarmed and angered. Virginia responded by trying to convince blacks that the British motives were purely selfish, and promising blacks good treatment if they remained loyal to the Patriot cause. On December 13, 1775 a Virginia Convention promised pardon to all slaves who returned to their masters within ten days. It is not clear how many slaves served with the British, but the war did have an unsettling effect on the institution of slavery. At least 100,000 blacks ran away from their masters during the conflict. The Dunmore Proclamation helped to bolster Southern support for the Patriots, as the British threatened slavery, at least in this respect.

December 31. General George Washington, revising his order of November 12, 1775, ordered recruiting officers to accept free Negroes in the American army. More than 5,000 Negroes, mostly Northern blacks, fought against the British. Georgia and South Carolina steadfastly opposed the enlistment of black soldiers. In 1779 the Continental Congress agreed to pay owners of slaves in Georgia and South Carolina $1,000 for each slave allowed to serve in the American army, but at the end of the war the blacks were to be freed and given fifty dollars. The two Southern states rejected the offer.

1776

July 4. The Declaration of Independence was approved in Philadelphia. A section which alleged that King George III had forced the slave trade and slavery on the colonies had been eliminated at the insistence of Georgia and South Carolina. Thomas Jefferson had charged the King with waging "cruel war against human nature itself, violating its most sacred rights of life and liberty in the persons of a distant people who never offended him, captivating and carrying them into slavery in another hemisphere, or to incur miserable death in their transportation thither." In the King's determination "to keep open a market where men should be bought and sold," Jefferson said he had suppressed "every legislative attempt to prohibit or to restrain this excerable commerce." Historians agree that this was one example of the American exaggerations in the list of grievances against George III.

1777

July 2. Vermont took the lead in abolishing slavery. By 1804 all the states north of Delaware had taken action leading to the gradual abolition of slavery.(Some slaves were seen in New Jersey as late as 1860.) Pennsylvania passed a law for gradual abolition in 1780. New Hampshire's law was passed in 1783. In 1784 Connecticut and Rhode Island took similar action. Manumission acts were passed in New York in 1785 and in New Jersey in 1786, though effective legislation stipulating gradual abolition was not achieved in the two states until 1799 and 1804 respectively. In 1783 the courts of Massachusetts upheld the contention of blacks that slavery in that state violated a section of the state constitution of 1780 which asserted that "all men are born free and equal." One immediate result of the Northern manumissions was the establishment of schools for free blacks by the early abolition and philanthropic societies. The African Free School in New York City, for example, was opened on November 1, 1787.

1787

April 12. Richard Allen and Absalom Jones organized the Free African Society, a Negro self-help group, in Philadelphia. Allen was perhaps the most conspicious Negro leader in the country before the rise of Frederick Douglass. His stature rested upon his leadership in the establishment of such organizations as the Free African Society and the African Methodist Episcopal Church (See Below). Jones was long a close associate of Allen, but the two parted when Jones, who was attracted by Anglicanism, became rector of the first separate

Protestant Episcopal congregation for blacks. Jones had been born a slave at Sussex, Delaware. His master once took him to Philadelphia to work as a handyman in a store. He was taught to write there by one of the clerks. Later he attended night school and completed his education. Saving money that visitors to his master's house had given him, together with his earnings, he purchased both his own freedom and that of his wife. He became a member of the St. George's Methodist Church in Philadelphia and was, along with Richard Allen and others, pulled from his knees there in 1787 and ordered to move to the reserved worship area for blacks in the church's balcony. Out of this incident grew the Free African Society. The Free African Society was basically a quasi-religious organization. Its program included a fund for mutual aid, burial assistance, relief for widows and orphans, strengthening of marriage ties and personal morality, cooperation with abolition societies, and correspondence with free Negroes in other areas. It was probably the first stable, independent black social organization in the United States. Among the various other joint efforts of Allen and Jones were the organization of relief measures for the black population in Philadelphia during the yellow-fever epidemic in 1793, and the raising of a company of black militia during the War of 1812.

July 13. The Continental Congress prohibited slavery in the Northwest Territory under the famous Ordinance of 1787. Specifically, there could be neither slavery nor involuntary servitude in the region northwest of the Ohio river except as punishment for a crime.

September 12. Prince Hall, a veteran of the War of Independence, received a charter for a Masonic Lodge for blacks. Hall was born in Barbados, British West Indies, in 1735, the son of an Englishman and a free black woman. He was apprenticed as a leather worker, but abandoned that training to emigrate to Boston. During the Revolutionary War, Hall and twelve other free blacks were inducted into a Masonic Lodge by a group of British soldiers stationed in Boston. When the British evacuated the area, Hall organized a Masonic Lodge for blacks. This group was chartered in England in 1787 as African Lodge No. 459. Hall, the first master of the organization, set up additional African lodges in Pennsylvania and Rhode Island during 1797. Following his death in 1807, the African Grand Lodge became the Prince Hall Grand Lodge. Hall, a self-educated clergyman, also championed the establishment of schools for black children in Boston; urged Massachusetts to legislatively oppose slavery; and urged measures to protect free Negroes from kidnapping and enslavement. The Prince Hall Masonic Lodge, Hall's principal legacy, has become a major social institution in Black America.

September   The Constitution of the United States was adopted. The "Three-fifths Compromise" which allowed the South to count three-fifths of the slave population in determining representation in the House of Representatives was incorporated. The Constitution also prohibited any legislation which might close the slave trade before 1808, but allowed a tax of ten dollars per head on each slave imported before that date, and demanded that fugitive slaves be returned to their owners.

1791

January————.   Free blacks in Charleston, South Carolina presented a petition to the State Legislature protesting laws restricting their freedoms. The blacks pointed specifically to an Act of 1740 which deprived slaves and free blacks of the right to testify under oath in the courts and of the right to trial by jury. The blacks reminded the legislators that they were tax paying citizens of South Carolina and were considered free citizens of the state, and thus, hoped to be treated as such. At the same time the blacks acknowledged that they did not "presume to hope that they shall be put on an equal footing with the free white citizens of the state *in general*." The petitioners were merely seeking the repeal of the objectionable clauses of the Act of 1740.

November 9.   Benjamin Banneker, a grandson of a white woman, a notable astronomer, inventor, mathematician, and gazeteer, was born at Ellicott, Maryland. Banneker gained a modest education from a school for free blacks near Joppa, Maryland, but was aided in scientific study by George Ellicott, a Maryland Quaker, planter and philanthropist. While still a youth, he made a wooden clock which is said to have remained accurate throughout Banneker's life. Between 1791 and 1802, he published a yearly *Almanac*, which was widely read. He was the first black man to publish astronomical materials in the United States. Other publications included a treatise on bees. Banneker is also credited with computing the cycle of the seventeen-year locust. In 1791, Banneker was appointed, upon the recommendation of Thomas Jefferson, to serve as a member of the commission to lay out plans for Washington, D.C. In August of that same year, Banneker wrote a famous letter to Thomas Jefferson appealing for a more liberal attitude toward blacks, and using his own work as evidence of Negro intellectual equality. Banneker said, in part:

> I apprehend you will embrace every opportunity to eradicate that train of absurd and false ideas and opinions which so generally prevail with respect to us [blacks]; and that your sentiments are concurrent with mine which are: that one universal Father hath given being to us all; that He not only made us all of one flesh, but that He hath also without partiality afforded us all with these same faculties and that, however diversified in situation or color, we are all the same family and stand in the same relation to Him. . . .

Jefferson accepted, then later rejected, the notion of black mental equality and even entertained doubts about the intellectual skills of Banneker.

1791

————. Newport Gardner, one of the first black music teachers in America, opened a music school in Newport, Massachusetts. Gardner, born in 1746, was a slave of Caleb Gardner, one of Newport's leading merchants. The slave taught himself to read and to sing, and later wrote music. One of his compositions, *Crooked Shanks*, was included in the collection *A Number of Original Airs, Duettos and Tiros*, published in 1803. Another song, an anthem, was performed in a Boston concert in 1825. Among Gardner's music students was his former mistress, Mrs. Sarah Ann Gardner. Newport Gardner was also active in religious affairs. He was a founder of the Newport

Colored Union Church and Society and became a missionary to Africa in 1826, the estimated year of his death.

1793

February 12. Congress passed the first fugitive slave act, making it a crime to harbor an escaped slave or to interfere with his arrest.

March 14. Eli Whitney of Massachusetts, a white inventor, obtained a patent for his cotton gin. The invention strengthened the institution of slavery.

1794

June 10. Richard Allen of Philadelphia founded the Bethel African Methodist Episcopal Church, the first AME church in the United States.

1797

January 30. Blacks in North Carolina presented a petition to Congress protesting a state law which required slaves, although freed by their Quaker masters, to be returned to the state and to the status of slavery. This first recorded anti-slavery petition by Negroes was rejected by the Congress.

August 30. A slave uprising planned by Gabriel Prosser and Jack Bowler near Richmond, Virginia was suspended because of a storm, then betrayed. Prosser was born in Virginia in 1776. In 1800, the young insurrectionist planned to seize an arsenal at Richmond, attack whites in the area, and free the slaves. It was hoped that the revolt would spread throughout the state. Perhaps as many as 1,000 slaves were prepared to participate in what would have been one of the largest slave revolts in United States history. Prosser had won such a large following by telling fellow blacks that he was their chosen leader, quoting Biblical scriptures to bolster his claim. The rebels had made or obtained swords, bayonets, and bullets, when the storm hit and two slaves, belonging to Mosby Sheppard, betrayed the plot. Governor James Monroe declared martial law in Richmond and called up 600 members of the state militia. Prosser fled, but was captured in Norfolk on September 25. He was later convicted and, with fifteen others, sentenced to hang on October 7. Another 35 blacks were executed later. Although interviewed by the governor, himself, Prosser refused to implicate others. The demeanor of the captured rebels led John Randolph of Virginia to declare that: "The accused have exhibited a spirit, which if it becomes general, must deluge the southern country in blood. They manifested a sense of their rights, and a contempt of danger."

1804

January 5. The Ohio legislature took the lead in passing "Black Laws," designed to restrict the rights and freedom of movement of free Negroes in the North. The laws indicated the steady deterioration of the legal and social status of free Negroes since the Revolutionary War. Although Northern blacks had endured severe restrictions in the Colonial period — In some areas of New England they faced curfews at night; could not visit a town other than the one in which they resided without permission; could not own certain types of property, etc. — these were somewhat relieved by the atmosphere of freedom which prevailed in the North after 1776. But by 1835 several Northern states had prohibited free Negro immigration, and severely restricted or completely disfranchised Negro voters. By 1860, according to Professor John Hope Franklin, it was actually difficult to distinguish, in terms of status, between slaves and free Negroes.

1808

January 1. A federal law prohibiting the importation of any new slaves into the United States went into effect. The law was passed in March, 1807 and stipulated that persons convicted of violating it were to be fined, anywhere from $800 (for knowingly buying illegally imported blacks) to $20,000 (for equipping a slave vessel), or imprisoned. Illegally imported blacks were to come under the jurisdiction of the state legislatures, which would decide their disposition. The coastwide trade of slaves was prohibited also if it was carried on in vessels of less than forty tons. The new law was poorly enforced.

The responsibility for the enforcement was given first to the Treasury Department, then to the Secretary of the Navy, and sometimes to the Secretary of State. Neither department put any vigor in its efforts in view of the shifting responsibility. Some Southern states passed laws disposing of the illegally imported blacks, others took no action at all. Some of the blacks were sold, the proceeds going into the state treasury. Northern commercial interests as well as Southern planters ignored the law with impunity.

1811

January 8-10.   U.S. troops suppressed a slave uprising in two Louisiana parishes near New Orleans.

1812

May 6.   Martin R. Delany, pioneer black physician, colonizationist, and Union Army officer, was born in Virginia. Delany was educated in the African Free School of New York City, the Canaan Academy in New Hampshire, the Oneida Institute in upper New York State, and at the Harvard University Medical School, where he took his medical degree in 1852. Delany tried to practice medicine in Pittsburgh, but prejudice and poor profits drove him into other areas. He became a member of the British Association for the Promotion of Social Science, published two books, *The Condition, Elevation, Emigration and Destiny of the Colored People of the United States* (1852) and *Principle of Ethnology* (1879). Earlier he had published an unsuccessful newspaper, *The Mystery* (1843) and had joined Frederick Douglass in the publication of *The North Star* (1847). He was a leader of the national convention movement of black Americans. Following the passage of the Compromise of 1850, with its new Fugitive Slave Act, Delaney became convinced that the United States was too inhospitable for persons of African descent. He turned his attention to colonization. He helped organize an expedition to Nigeria in 1858; negotiated treaties with eight African chiefs, which granted lands for prospective American black settlers; and began plans for the expanded production of cotton in the region, and the development of a cotton export trade. During the Civil War Delany was a medical officer with the rank of major in the 104th Union Regiment in South Carolina. He settled in Charleston after the war, working with the Freedmen's Bureau. He was later a justice of the peace there. He was defeated in a bid for Lieutenant Governor of South Carolina in 1874. Delany died eleven years later.

1816

April 9. The African Methodist Episcopal Church, the first all-black religious denomination in the United States, was formally organized at Philadelphia. Richard Allen was named the first bishop of the Church. Allen was born a slave in Philadelphia and was sold as a youth to a master in Delaware. He became a preacher shortly thereafter and received permission to hold services in his master's home. He preached to both blacks and whites and was allowed, at the same time, to hire himself out. He bought his freedom by hauling salt, wood, and other products, and by laboring in a brickyard. After leading the AME Church for fifteen years, he died in 1831. He was succeeded by Morris Brown, an exile from South Carolina, who had resided in Philadelphia since 1823.

December 28. The American Colonization Society, formed to ease American race problems by transporting free blacks to Africa, was organized in Washington, D. C. John C. Calhoun of South Carolina and Henry Clay of Kentucky were among its sponsors.

1817

January _____. Philadelphia Negroes, meeting in Bethel AME Church, formally protested against the American Colonization Society's efforts to exile blacks from the United States.

————. Paul Cuffee, a black New England shipbuilder and African colonizer, died. Cuffee was born in New Bedford, Massachusetts in 1758 as a free man. In 1797, he purchased a farm and built a school for the children in his hometown. An activist in the cause of civil rights, he and his brother, John unsuccessfully sued the State of Massachusetts for the right to vote. Disillusioned over the outlook for free Negroes in America, Cuffee transported a group of 38 blacks to Sierra Leone, a British colony on the West Coast of Africa in 1811. Failing health and uncertainty about the colonization scheme caused him to withdraw from the venture shortly before his death. At his death he left an estate valued at more than $20,000, making him one of the wealthiest blacks in the early United States.

1818

April 18. A force of Indians and Negroes were defeated in the Battle of Suwanne, Florida ending the First Seminole War, by United States troops under Andrew Jackson. Jackson characterized the hostilities as a "savage and negro war."

1820

March 3. The famous Missouri Compromise was approved by Congress. Slavery was prohibited north of Missouri, north and west of the 36°30′ line within the Louisiana territory. Missouri itself entered the Union as a slave state; Maine entered as a free state.

————. The black Republic of Liberia, in West Africa, was founded under the auspices of the American Colonization Society. American Negroes were encouraged to emigrate there as a means of alleviating the race problem. In the end, only about 20,000 did so. The capital city, Monrovia, was named for President Monroe.

1822

May 30. A slave conspiracy led by Denmark Vesey in Charleston, South Carolina was betrayed. Vesey, an ex-slave, had been free since 1800 and had worked as a carpenter in Charleston. He plotted his slave uprising for several years, carefully chose his associates, and collected weapons. He also sought assistance from Santo Domingo. His revolt, in which as many as 5,000 blacks were prepared to participate, was first set for the second Sunday in July, 1822, then moved up, before the betrayal. South Carolina and other states tightened their control of slaves and free Negroes as a result of the plot. Morris Brown, the preeminent A. M. E. leader in South Carolina, was one of those free blacks who became suspect. He fled to the North and eventually succeeded Richard Allen as Bishop of the A. M. E. Church.

1824

November _____. American politics were becoming democratized as the elimination of the caucus system for choosing presidential candidates was accompanied by the removal of property qualifications for voting. The way was being paved for virtual universal male suffrage in the United States. At the same time the Northern and Western states adopted measures denying blacks the right to vote.

1827

March 16. Two blacks, John Russwurm (the first American Negro college graduate) and Samuel Cornish began publication of *Freedom's Journal*, the nation's pioneer Negro newspaper, in New York City. The paper was not very successful, so two years later Cornish began a second publication, *Rights of All*, a militant but also short-lived paper. In 1836 Cornish published the unsuccessful *Weekly Advocate*, and the following year co-edited *The Colored American*. Most of the Negro newpapers founded before the Civil War were principally abolitionist propaganda sheets, Douglass' *North Star* being the most successful.

1829

March 4. Blacks attended the inaugural reception for President Andrew Jackson at the White House. A South Carolina woman observed one black female "eating jelly from a gold spoon," and disapproved.

September 28. David Walker's militant anti-slavery pamphlet calling on blacks to revolt was discovered in several areas of the country. Walker's *Appeal*, published in Boston, stirred slaveholders in several Southern states. Walker was a free black who had wandered across the South, then settled in Boston as the proprietor of a secondhand clothing store. He had become widely acquainted with anti-slavery and revolutionary literature. The *Appeal*, which was smuggled into the South probably by black seamen, was a carefully written trumpet call for mass slave uprisings, with violent reprisals against slaveowners. Although, perhaps only a few literate blacks could read it, Southern states took extreme precautions. The mails were scrutinized, ships arriving in Southern ports were searched, and black seamen were restricted. The circulation of the work became a crime and a price was put on Walker's head. Walker died under mysterious circumstances in 1830.

1830

April 6. James Augustine Healy, the first black Catholic bishop in America, was born on a plantation near Macon, Georgia. Healy was the son of an Irish immigrant and a mulatto slave. His father sent him and his brothers to the North for their education. After being rejected by several academies, the Healys entered a Quaker school on Long Island. Later they transferred to the College of the Holy Cross at Worcester, Massachusetts. James was the most outstanding pupil. In 1852 he entered the Sulpician Seminary in Paris, and on June 10, 1854 he was ordained a priest in Notre Dame Cathedral, Paris. Healy's first assignment as a priest was in a white parish in Boston. He became secretary to the Bishop of Boston, and when his superior died he became pastor of the new St. James Church. His stature in the New England Catholic hierarchy continued to rise until 1874, when he was appointed Bishop of Maine. He was consecrated in the Cathedral at Portland on June 2, 1875. Healy proved to be energetic and devoted to duty. He ministered to an all-white following, but only occasionally was subjected to racial abuse. Shortly before his death on August 5, 1900, Healy was promoted to the rank of Assistant at the Papal Throne.

September 20-24. The initial National Negro Convention met at Bethel AME Church in Philadelphia. Delegates from Delaware, Maryland, New York, Pennsylvania, and Virginia attended. The convention, under the leadership of Richard Allen (Other prominent black leaders present included James Forten, the wealthy abolitionist and shipmaker, and the journalist, Samuel Cornish.), adopted resolutions calling for improvements in the social status of American blacks. The delegates considered projects to establish a black college and to encourage Negroes to emigrate to Canada. Neither of these proposals was adopted. Opposition even arose to the idea of a Negro convention at all. Yet these ad-hoc conventions continued to meet and occasionally were attended by white abolitionists and reformers. In the ten years before the Civil War, there was a rash of conventions, meeting in Cleveland, Rochester, and New York City as well as in Philadelphia. One of the most important was held in Rochester in 1853, during which a National Council of Colored People was formed. This group issued a memorable statement denouncing racial oppression in America, but, at the same time, citing instances of black progress. These conventions were in the American tradition of assembling for redress of grievances and increased solidarity among the blacks.

1831

January 1.   William Lloyd Garrison, with financial aid and moral support from prominent blacks, including the wealthy James Forten of Philadelphia, published the first issue of the militant anti-slavery newspaper, *The Liberator*.

August 21-22.   The most momentous slave revolt in United States history occurred in Southhampton County, Virginia. It was led by the mystical black minister, Nat Turner, who had on a previous occasion run away and then decided to return to his master. Approximately sixty whites were slain. Turner was captured on October 30 and hanged on November 11. Several other blacks were implicated with Turner and thirty of these were also executed. The revolt caused near pandemonium in the South. Slave codes were vigorously enforced, slave patrols were increased, and suspicious blacks were incarcerated or killed. No other major slave revolt or conspiracy followed the Turner insurrection until John Brown's raid on the U.S. arsenal at Harper's Ferry, Virginia in 1859.

1835

June 1-5. The fifth national Negro convention met in Philadelphia and urged blacks to abandon the use of the terms "African" and "colored" when referring to Negro institutions and organizations, and to themselves.

1836

————. The infamous "gag rule" was adopted in the U.S. House of Representatives. Under the act anti-slavery petitions were simply laid on the table without any further action. This denial of the right of petition angered former President John Quincy Adams, now a congressman from Massachusetts. Adams fought vigorously against the rule, helping to rouse public opinion in the North. Anti-slavery petitions began to pour into Washington, more than 200,000 of them in a single session. In 1844 the gag rule was rescinded. Its opponents saw it as an effort to suppress the liberties of white men in an attempt to keep black men slaves.

1838

March 14. Blacks held a mass meeting in Philadelphia to protest the action of the Pennsylvania Reform Convention of 1837 which denied them the right to vote. The Convention, acting on the basis of a State Supreme Court decision (*Fogg* vs *Hobbs*, 1837) that blacks were not freemen, restricted the suffrage to white males. At the Philadelphia mass meeting the blacks, claiming to represent 40,000 of their number threatened with disfranchisement, said the denial of suffrage would make poiltical rights dependent upon the "skin in which a man is born," and divide "what our fathers bled to unite, to wit, TAXATION AND REPRESENTATION." The blacks argued that they were indeed citizens, having been recognized as such by article four of the Articles of Confederation—"The free inhabitants of each of these states, paupers, vagabonds, and fugitives from justice excepted, shall be entitled to all privileges and immunities of free *citizens* in the several states." The Constitution of the United States, according to the black petition, made no changes as to their rights of citizenship. The petitioners asked the Supreme Court to reverse its decision in

Fogg vs *Hobbs* and/or the people of Pennsylvania to reject the new Constitution. The court's action stood, however, and the new Constitution's disfranchising clauses won popular approval.

————. Frank Johnson, one of America's first black band leaders, gave a command performance before Queen Victoria at Buckingham Palace. He was presented with a silver bugle. Johnson was born in 1792, and by 1820 had established himself as a versatile musician, playing with white groups in Philadelphia. When he organized his own band, principally a woodwind group, it won national acclaim for its excellent performances at parades and dances. Frank Johnson's Colored Band, as it was called, even played on plantations as far south as Virginia. Johnson became noted for his ability to "distort a song into a reel, jig, or country dance." He also composed music, including the "Recognition March on the Independence of Hayti" (1825). Johnson died in 1844.

1839

July ————. The most famous slave mutiny in United States history took place on a Spanish ship, the *Amistad*. A group of Africans, led by Cinque, brought the captured vessel into Montauk, Long Island, where they were arrested. Former President John Quincy Adams defended the rebels before the Supreme Court, and they won their freedom.

1843

August 22. A national convention of black men met at Buffalo, New York. The black abolitionist Henry Highland Garnet called for a slave revolt and a general strike to improve the lot of blacks in the United States. Many of the delegates, including Frederick Douglass, denounced the speech. Garnet, a minister, had served as pastor to whites and blacks in Troy, New York.

1844

June 24. A mass meeting of blacks in Boston adopted a resolution declaring that segregated public schools in that city violated the State Constitution. They urged the city's School Committee to abolish separate schools and to extend to black citizens the right to send their children "to the schools established in the respective districts" in which they resided. The blacks' request was denied and the schools in Massachusetts remained segregated until 1855.

1846

August _____. Norbert Rillieux obtained his first patent for the revolutionary multiple-effect vacuum evaporation process, refining sugar whiter and grainier. The technique became the basic manufacturing process in the sugar as well as other industries. Rillieux was the son of a white engineer and a free mulatto mother. He was born in New Orleans in 1806. His father was the inventor of a steam-operated cotton-bailing press. He sent his bright Negro son to school in Paris. In 1830 young Rillieux became an instructor of applied mechanics at L'Ecole Centrale in Paris. It is believed that he developed the theory for his later invention about this time. He had built and installed a triple-effect evaporator on a Louisiana plantation in 1834. This invention had only limited success, as did a similar one installed in 1841. Rillieux reached a permanent solution in 1845 and obtained a patent the next year. Frustrated by racial discrimination in Louisiana, he returned to Paris in 1861 and died in France in 1894.

1847

June 30. Dred Scott, a slave, filed suit in the St. Louis Circuit Court claiming that his temporary residence in free territory should have made him a free man. Scott was a semi-literate man whose moves about the country, specifically into the free portions of the Louisiana Purchase, where slavery had been excluded by the Missouri Compromise of 1820, and into free Illinois, formed the basis for the case.

December 3. The black abolitionist, Frederick Douglass, began publication of his own newspaper, the famous *North Star*. Douglass, an ex-slave, became the principal black anti-slavery speaker and writer. He was born in Tuckahoe, Maryland in 1817. He was separated in infancy from his mother, and had harsh masters as a child. While still very young he became a house servant in Baltimore. There he learned to read from white playmates and a mistress. His first attempt at escape was thwarted. Later, in 1838, while working as a ship calker, he managed a successful break from slavery. Further education by anti-slavery groups in the North made him a very lucid speaker and writer. The publication of the *North Star* was one of the factors which led to Douglass' break with William Lloyd Garrison, the noted white abolitionist and publisher of *The Liberator*. Garrison saw no need for two major, rival anti-slavery publications, but Douglass and other blacks had become convinced that they must play a more leading role in the abolitionist movement, including the printing of a newspaper. In later years Douglass was appointed to several political and diplomatic posts, including unofficial advisor to Presidents Lincoln and Johnson, marshal of the District of Columbia, recorder of deeds for the District of Columbia, and minister to Haiti. He also served as president of the Freedmen's Bank in 1874 (See Also Below).

1848

February _____. The Treaty of Guadalupe Hidalgo was concluded between the United States and Mexico ending the two years of combat between the countries. Under the terms of the treaty, the present states of New Mexico and California were ceded to the United States. Many pro-slavery Southerners had supported the war, anticipating that new lands would be opened to slavery. Many anti-slavery Northerners had opposed the war, fearing that it was the result of a pro-slavery conspiracy designed to open new territory to slavery. Shortly after the war started in 1846, Democratic Representative David Wilmot of Pennsylvania introduced an amendment to a pending bill in Congress. This "Wilmot Proviso" sought to prohibit slavery in any territory acquired as a result of the Mexican War. The Proviso passed in the House of Representatives, but was defeated in the Senate. The Mexican Cession and the status of slavery there precipitated bitter debate between North and South in the years from 1848 to 1850. One proposed solution was offered by President Zachary Taylor. He suggested that California and New Mexico bypass the territorial stage of government and apply directly for statehood, thus nullifying the question of slavery in the Mexican Cession territories. This proposal was unacceptable to the South, for both New Mexico and

California would enter the Union as free states, thus upsetting the precarious sectional balance in the United States Senate which now stood at fifteen states each. The grounds were laid for the famous Compromise of 1850 (See Below).

1849

July ————. Harriet Tubman escaped from slavery in Maryland. Miss Tubman, the best known black female abolitionist, then returned to Maryland and Virginia at least 20 times, and is credited with freeing more than 300 blacks. The daring abolitionist was born in Dorchester County, Maryland in 1823. As a young girl, while working as a field hand, she was injured on the head by a weight that an enraged overseer had thrown at another slave. The damage from that blow caused her to suffer from "sleeping seizures" for the rest of her life. In 1844, she married a free black, John Tubman, but remained a slave. When in 1849, her master died and rumors emerged that his slaves were to be sold into the Deep South, Miss Tubman, along with two of her brothers, escaped. Fearing capture and punishment or death, the brothers returned to the plantation, but Miss Tubman, with the North Star for directions, marched on until she reached Philadelphia. In 1850, she returned to Maryland for a sister and a brother. The next year she led a party of eleven blacks from the South into Canada, but failed to secure her husband who had married another woman. In 1857, she made one of her last trips into Maryland, rescuing her parents and three additional brothers and sisters. The family, then settled in Auburn, New York. The family home, purchased from anti-slavery senator William H. Seward, was later turned into a home for elderly and indigent blacks. After serving in the Civil War as a nurse and as a spy, Miss Tubman devoted all of her energy and earnings to this home during the twilight of her life. The little black woman, often called "the Moses of her People," died at Auburn in 1913.

————. Benjamin Roberts, a black parent in Boston, sued his city for denying his daughter admission to a "white" public school. The Massachusetts Supreme Court rejected the suit, but, instead, established the "separate but equal" doctrine.

————. Elder Peter Lowery became pastor of a black church in Nashville, Tennessee, making him, probably, the first black pastor of a church in the South. Lowery, who was born a slave, had managed to purchase his freedom and that of other members of his family, including his mother, brothers, and sisters, over a period of more than forty years. In his endeavor, he was substantially aided by his wife, Ruth, a free woman of color. Lowery was the father of Samuel Lowery, the first black lawyer to practice before the U.S. Supreme Court (See Also Below).

1850

September 18. Congress enacted the famous Compromise of 1850. Senator Henry Clay of Kentucky and other "moderate" statesmen from both sections drew up this omnibus solution to the problem of slavery in the Mexican Cession as well as other outstanding differences between North and South or the free states and the slave states. The provisions of the Compromise relating to slavery included the outlawing of the slave trade in Washington, D. C., but the retention of slavery itself; the passage of a new, tougher fugitive slave law to replace the poorly enforced act of 1793, and the admission of California as a free state (See Also Above).

1851

————. Elizabeth Taylor Greenfield, "The Black Swan," made her debut at a concert sponsored by the Buffalo Musical Association. Ms. Greenfield, a soprano, was born a slave in Natchez, Mississippi in 1809. As an infant, she was taken to Philadelphia and adopted by a Quaker woman named Greenfield who arranged for her to study music and to sing at private parties. After her debut in Buffalo, Ms. Greenfield toured the northern states between 1851 and 1853. She toured England in 1854 and gave a command performance before Queen Victoria in Buckingham Palace. A contemporary critic described her voice as one with "amazing power," "flexibility," and xecution." America's leading historian of black music, hern says that "Miss Greenfield was the best known black ist of her time."

1852

March 20.   Uncle Tom's Cabin, a novel by a Norther
woman, Harriett Beecher Stowe, was published in Boston. The   ⌐,
which exaggerated the cruelties of slavery, evoked sympathy for the
blacks in the North and greatly angered the South.

1853

July 6–8.   The National Council of Colored People was founded
in Rochester, New York. An outgrowth of the ante-bellum Negro
Convention Movement, the new organization was formed as a permanent body to advance the cause of blacks. A notable feature of the
Rochester convention was a proposal to erect a national industrial
school for the race. The institution was to be financed by the issuance
of $50,000 worth of stock in shares of $10 each, through the sale of
scholarships "at judicious rates," and by the raising of a $100,000
endowment. The school was to be co-educational and was to be gov-
erned by a board of trustees, residents of the state wherein the institution was located. The sponsors of the measure, which was never
implemented, hoped that the education of black youth would "give
them means of success adapted to their struggling condition; and ere
long, following the enterprise of the age, . . . see them filling everywhere positions of responsibility and trust, and, gliding on the triple
tide of wealth, intelligence, and virtue, reach eventually to a sure
resting place of distinction and happiness."

————.   William Wells Brown, an ex-slave, abolitionist, and
physician of sorts, published *Clotel* in London. The book about a
black daughter of an American president was probably the first novel
written by an American Negro. Brown was born to a slave mother
and a white father in Lexington, Kentucky in 1816. He was educated
in St. Louis, where he served as an apprentice to the martyred abolitionist editor, Elijah P. Lovejoy. Between 1850 and 1854, in addition to *Clotel*, he published *Three Years in Europe* (based upon his
experiences in France and England) and *Sketches of People and
Places Abroad* (in which he gave his impressions of notables such as
Richard Cobden, Victor Hugo, and Alexis de Tocqueville). Brown
was also a regular contributor to *Frederick Douglass' Paper*, the *Lib-*

erator, the London *Daily News*, and the *National Anti-Slavery Standard*. His reputation as an historian rests largely upon such works as *The Black Man* (1863) and *The Negro in the American Rebellion* (1867). Brown's Principal anti-slavery work was as a "Conductor" on the Underground Railroad and as an anti-slavery lecturer. He died in 1884.

1854

January 1.   Lincoln University, the first Negro college, was chartered as Ashmum Institute at Oxford, Chester County, Pennsylvania.

May 30.   The Kansas-Nebraska Act was approved by Congress and President Franklin Pierce. In addition to providing formal organization for the two territories of Kansas and Nebraska, the act repealed the Missouri Compromise of 1820, thus removing anti-slavery restrictions north and west of 36°30′ in the Louisiana Purchase. According to the bill's author, Senator Stephen A. Douglas of Illinois, Congress, in the Compromise of 1850, had abandoned all efforts to protect or to prohibit slavery in the territories. It was only consistent, therefore, he reasoned, that the new principle be applied in the Louisiana Purchase as elsewhere. Southerners viewed Kansas as ripe for slavery. Northern anti-slavery men opposed the prospects of a slave Kansas and the repeal of the Compromise of 1820. The contest for control of Kansas between the pro- and anti-slavery forces led to several years of bitter, often bloody, strife in the territory and in Congress. In fact, Kansas came to be known as "Bleeding Kansas." The most significant acts of violence were (1) the sacking of the anti-slavery town of Lawrence, Kansas in May, 1856 and the subsequent retaliation by John Brown. Brown and his followers slaughtered five pro-slavery men at Pottawatomie Creek; (2) the beating of anti-slavery Senator Charles Sumner of Massachusetts by Congressman Preston S. Brooks of South Carolina on the floor of the U.S. Senate, also in the spring of 1856. Sumner had denounced the South and some of its representatives for the "crime against Kansas," the rape of a virgin territory by slaveholders. His remarks against Senator Andrew P. Butler of South Carolina led to the attack by Brooks, Butler's nephew. The acrimony and political confusion in Kansas prevented the territory from being admitted by Congress until just before the Civil War. On January 29, 1861 Kansas came into the union as a free state, representing the will of the majority of the *bona fide* residents.

June 3.   Anthony Burns, a fugitive slave, was arrested in Boston. His master refused an offer of $1,200 made by Boston citizens for his freedom. Burns was escorted through the streets of Boston, past angry residents, by United States troops to be returned to the South. The incident was indicative of a growing anti-slavery sentiment in the North, especially following the passage of the Kansas-Nebraska Act.

1855

————.   John Mercer Langston was elected clerk of Brownhelm Township in Lorain County, Ohio, making him the first black to win an elective political office in the United States. Langston was born to a white man and a black slave on a Virginia plantation in 1829. His white father having provided for his education, he was sent to Ohio, after the father's death, where he was reared by one of his father's friends. He attended school in Cincinnati and then Oberlin College. By 1854, he was engaged in an active law practice in Chillicothe, Ohio. In 1855, as the only black attorney in Brownhelm, he was elected clerk. The next year he won a seat on the Brownhelm City Council, a post he held until 1860. In 1865, he was named president of the National Equal Rights League and in 1867 a member of the Board of Education of Oberlin, Ohio. After his return to the South during Reconstruction he was variously inspector general of the Freedmen's Bureau Schools (1868-1869); teacher, dean of the law school, and acting vice-president of Howard University (1869-1876); minister to Haiti (1877-1885); president of the Virginia Normal and Collegiate Institute (1885-1888); and congressman from Virginia (1889-1891). Langston, who died in 1897, was one of the last blacks elected to the U.S. Congress in the 19th century (See Also Below).

1857

March 6.   The Supreme Court rendered its decision in the case of *Dred Scott versus Sandford*, declaring that Negroes were not citizens of the United States, and denying to Congress the power to prohibit slavery in any federal territory. Scott was eventually freed by new owners. Meanwhile, he remained as a slave, albeit a famous one, in St. Louis where he worked as a porter. The Dred Scott decision, a clear-cut victory for the South, alarmed anti-slavery men in the North and fueled the fires leading to the Civil War.

June ————. The California legislature defeated by the narrow margin of 32 to 30 an attempt to prevent the immigration of blacks into the state. The opposition to the measure was lead by Representative G. A. Hall. Despite the defeat of the immigration measure, California blacks continued to protest instances of racial discrimination against them. Excerpts from a protest of two black businessmen in 1857 are quoted below:

During a residence of seven years in California, we, with hundreds of other colored men, have cheerfully paid city, state and county taxes on real estate and merchandise, as well as licenses to carry on business, and every other species of tax that has been levied from time to time for the support of the government, save only the 'poll tax'—that we have persistently refused. On the day before yesterday, the Tax Collector called on us, and seized and lugged off twenty or thirty dollars' worth of goods, in payment, as he said, of this tax. . . . Now, while we cannot understand how a 'white' man can refuse to pay each and every tax for the support of government, under which he enjoys every privilege—from the right to rob a negro up to that of being Governor of the State—we can perceive and feel the flagrant injustices of compelling 'colored men' to pay a special tax for the enjoyment of a special privilege, and then break their heads if they attempt to exercise it. We believe that every voter should pay poll-tax, or every male resident who has the privilege of becoming a voter; but regard it as low and despicable, the very quintessence of meanness, to compel colored men to pay it, situated as they are politically. However, if there is no redress, the great State of California may come around annually, and rob us of twenty or thirty dollars' worth of goods, as we will never willingly pay three dollars as poll tax as long as we remain disfranchised, oath-denied, outlawed colored Americans. . . .

1859

March 7.   The Acting Commissioner of General Lands for the United States, J. S. Wilson, stated that blacks were not citizens of the United States "as contemplated by the preemption law of September, 1841" and, therefore, were "not legally entitled to preempt public lands."

October 16.   John Brown, a mystical white abolitionist from Kansas, attacked the United States Arsenal at Harpers Ferry, Virginia. Brown, who had unsuccessfully sought the aid of leading abolitionists including Frederick Douglass, was accompanied by a dozen white men and five blacks. The raid, which was to be a prelude to a general slave uprising, was foiled by local, state, and federal forces. Two blacks were killed for their part in the affair. Brown, himself, was executed on December 2.

————.   The last slave ship, the *Clothilde*, to stop at an American port landed at Mobile Bay, Alabama.

————.   The U. S. Supreme Court in *Ableman* vs *Booth*, overruled an act by a Wisconsin state court declaring the Fugitive Slave Act of 1850 unconstitutional. The new Fugitive Slave Act, and its methods of enforcement (See Above), were increasingly opposed by Northern residents. Many Northern cities and states passed Personal Liberty Laws, denying the use of Northern jails for the housing of fugitive slaves and prohibiting local law enforcement officers from assisting in their capture, in an attempt to offset the Fugitive Slave Act. The Wisconsin case arose when a newspaperman was arrested for rousing a mob to free a captured runaway. The state court ordered him released on a writ of *habeas corpus* and declared the federal statute unconstitutional.

1860

January 1.   A law went into effect in Arkansas which prohibited the employment of free blacks on boats and ships navigating the rivers of that state.

November 6. Abraham Lincoln, viewed by Southerners as an abolitionist, was elected President on a platform opposed to the further expansion of slavery into the territories.

December 17. South Carolina, partly because she felt Lincoln's victory threatened slavery, seceded from the Union.

————. The Pony Express began operations in the West. Eastern mails went by railroad to St. Joseph, Missouri, then were picked up by professional riders who, working in relays, delivered letters as far west as San Francisco. Two of the earliest black Pony Express riders were George Monroe who rode from Merced to Mariposa, California and William Robinson who rode from Stockton to the gold mines.

CHAPTER

II

War and Freedom

1861-1876

1861

April 12. The Confederates attacked Fort Sumter, South Carolina. President Lincoln called for 75,000 volunteers to defend the Union. The Civil War began. Many blacks viewed the conflict as a war for freedom. Some rushed to join the Union forces, but were refused.

August 6. Congress passed the Confiscation Act providing that any property used by the owner's consent and with his knowledge in aiding or abetting insurrection against the United States could be captured wherever found. When the property consisted of slaves, they were to be forever free. President Lincoln refused to order vigorous enforcement of the law.

August 23. James Stone, a very light complexioned fugitive slave, enlisted in the First Fight Artillery of Ohio. Stone, whose wife was a white woman, was taken for white himself. Having fought for the Union in Kentucky, where he had been a slave, Stone died from a service related illness in 1862. After his death some blacks revealed his true racial identity. Thus, Stone was actually the first black man to fight for the Union during the Civil War—almost two full years before blacks were authorized to join Union forces.

September 25. The Secretary of the Navy authorized the enlistment of blacks in this branch of the armed forces.

————. General John C. Fremont proclaimed military emancipation in Missouri. President Lincoln countermanded the order.

1862

March 6. President Lincoln proposed to Congress a plan for gradual, compensated emancipation of slaves. Lincoln urged the congressional delegations from Delaware, Kentucky, Maryland, Missouri, and West Virginia to support his proposal. They opposed it, as did Northern abolitionists who felt slaveholders should not be paid for property which they could not rightfully own. Congress, however, passed a joint resolution on April 10, 1862, endorsing the concept of gradual, compensated emancipation.

April 16. The U. S. Senate passed a bill abolishing slavery in the District of Columbia. Slaveowners were to be compensated at the rate of $300 per slave. One hundred thousand dollars was also allocated for the voluntary emigration of these freedmen to Haiti or Liberia.

May 9. General David Hunter issued a proclamation emancipating slaves in Georgia, Florida, and South Carolina as "contrabands of war." President Lincoln overruled the order.

May 13. Robert Smalls, a black pilot, later a South Carolina congressman, sailed the Confederate steamer, the *Planter* out of Charleston, South Carolina, and turned the ship over to the United States as a booty of war. Smalls, an ex-slave, had received some education through the indulgence of his master. He was a member of a crew in the Confederate Navy when he performed his Civil War heroics. His Civil War fame aided his rise in South Carolina politics and business. He served five terms in the U. S. House of Representatives.

June 19. President Lincoln signed a bill abolishing slavery in the federal territories.

July 17. Congress authorized President Lincoln to accept Negroes for service in the Union Army. The blacks were to receive less pay than white soldiers. A white private was paid thirteen dollars a month and $3.50 for clothing, but blacks of the same rank were to receive seven dollars and three dollars respectively. Eventually more than 186,000 blacks served in the Union army; some 38,000 lost their lives. Many of the deaths were non-combat related, due principally to overwork and poor medical care.

August 14. President Lincoln called in a group of blacks for the first discussion by a U. S. President with Negroes on public policy. He urged Negroes to emigrate to Africa or to Latin America. Many blacks denounced the President's suggestion.

September 22. President Lincoln issued a preliminary Emancipation Proclamation, giving rebellious states and parts of states until January 1, 1863 to abandon their hostilities or lose their slaves.

1863

January 1. President Lincoln signed the Emanicipation Proclamation. Based upon military necessity, it declared slaves free in all states and parts of states then in rebellion against the United States.

May 1. The Confederate Congress passed a resolution calling Negro troops and their officers criminals, thus permitting captured black soldiers and their officers to be murdered or enslaved.

May 27. Two Louisiana Negro regiments made six unsuccessful charges on the Confederate fortification at Port Hudson, Louisiana.

July 9. Eight Negro regiments played a vital role in the siege of Port Hudson which, with the capture of Vicksburg, allowed the Union to control the Mississippi River.

July 13-16. Four days of rioting in New York City, protesting the Union's Draft Law, left more than 1,000 persons, mainly blacks, dead or wounded, and resulted in approximately $2 million in property damage. The riot grew out of the Civil War Draft Law's provision which allowed men to pay $300 for a substitute draftee. Since poor white laborers, many of them Irish and German immigrants, could not afford to buy substitutes, they bore the brunt of the draft. Blacks were ineligible, at the time, for the draft. In venting their frustrations over the draft law, the poorer laborers turned on the blacks, especially, as they saw them as the principal inheritors of the jobs they would have to leave behind to enter the army. During this period of racial tension, similar riots occurred in Boston, where 20 persons were killed or wounded, and in Troy, New York, where a ship with black servants aboard was diverted to avoid an attack on it.

July 30. President Lincoln warned of retaliatory action if the Confederates continued to murder or enslave captured Negro soldiers.

————. The Fifty-Fourth Massachusetts Negro Regiment served a year without pay rather than accept discriminatory wages.

1864

April 12. Confederate forces under General Nathan Bedford Forrest captured Fort Pillow, Tennessee. Following the surrender, the Union's black troops were massacred.

June 15. Congress passed a bill equalizing salaries and supplies for Negro troops.

June 19. A Negro sailor, Joachim Pease, won the Congressional Medal of Honor for his role in the famous naval battle between the USS *Kearsage* and the CSS *Alabama* off the coast of France.

October 4. The *New Orleans Tribune*, a black newspaper, began daily publication, in French as well as English.

————. Black Sergeant William Walker of the Third South Carolina Regiment was shot under orders of a court martial for leading a protest against discriminatory pay for black soldiers.

1865

————. The "Black Laws" of Illinois were repealed. These laws, like similar ones in other Northern states, restricted the freedom of movement, and limited the civil and political rights of free blacks. John Jones, one of the wealthiest blacks in America, led the fight for repeal. Jones had been born free in Greene City, North Carolina in 1816. He was self-educated and became a tailor's apprentice, first in Memphis, Tennessee. In 1845 he moved to Chicago. He opened a tailoring business there, from which he amassed a fortune. Using his wealth and influence he led the successful fights against the prohibition of the immigration of free blacks into Illinois (1853), the "Black Laws," and school segregation in Chicago. He was elected a Cook County Commissioner in 1875 and served for two terms. He was the first black elected to the Chicago Board of Education. Prior to the Civil War he had also been active in the abolitionist movement, his home being used as a station on the Underground Railroad. Jones died in 1879 leaving an estate valued at more than $100,000.

January 11. Robert E. Lee, with his armies at low tide, recommended the employment of blacks in the Confederate forces because it was "not only expedient but necessary."

February 1. John S. Rock, a black man, became the first of his race to practice before the United States Supreme Court.

March 3. Congress established, within the War Department, a Bureau of Freedmen, Refugees and Abandoned Lands. The Freedmen's Bureau was to help freed blacks survive, aid them in their contractual relationships, and begin educating them. The Bureau, in its five years of existence, issued more than twenty million rations, more than five million going to whites; established about fifty hospitals; resettled more than 30,000 persons; set up 4,330 schools, enrolling 247,000 students; aided in the establishment of such colleges as Atlanta University, Fisk University, Hampton Institute, and Howard University.

March 3. The United States government chartered the Freedmen's Bank at Washington to encourage financial responsibility among the ex-slaves. On April 4, 1865 the headquarters of the Freedmen's Bank opened in New York. Shortly thereafter branches were started in Louisville, Nashville, New Orleans, Vicksburg, and Washington. By 1872 there was a total of thirty-four branches, all in the South, except the New York and Philadelphia offices. Incompetency and inefficiency in the Bank's operation appeared almost immediately. By the time Frederick Douglass was made president in March, 1874, the bank was already a failure. It closed its doors on June 28, 1874.

March 13. President Jefferson Davis signed a bill authorizing the use of blacks as soldiers in the Confederate Army. The law culminated a long period of dispute in the South over the use of blacks as soldiers. While Southerners willingly used blacks for fatigue duties and personal service, the idea of black combat soldiers was generally repugnant. It seemed to invite slave violence and to make a mockery of the concept of Negro inferiority. The war ended before any blacks faced combat.

April 11. President Lincoln again conceded that Negro veterans and "very intelligent" blacks might be given the right to vote. He had suggested in a letter to Governor Hahn of Louisiana in 1864 that the "very intelligent" and those who had "fought gallantly in our ranks" should be considered for the franchise. At the time of Lincoln's death no serious efforts had been made to grant suffrage to freed Negroes.

April 14. Abraham Lincoln, who had favored a mild plan for readmitting the South to the Union (one which would not have guaranteed Negro suffrage), was shot. He died early the next morning.

May 29. President Andrew Johnson announced his program of Reconstruction. It required ratification of the 13th Amendment, but did not guarantee Negro suffrage.

December 18. The Thirteenth Amendment, prohibiting slavery or involuntary servitude, except as punishment for a crime, was adopted.

————. All-white legislatures, under the Johnson Reconstruction program, began enacting Black Codes which restricted the rights and freedom of movement of Negroes. The laws were patterned after the Ante-Bellum slave codes. Newer aspects of the laws imposed heavy penalties on vagrant blacks; penalties for "seditious speeches," "insulting gestures," and curfew violations.

1866

January 9.   Fisk University, one of the most prestigious black colleges in the nation, opened in Nashville, Tennessee. The school was distinguished early by the music of its Jubilee Singers.

April 9.   The Civil Rights Bill of 1866, granting to Negroes the rights and privileges of American citizenship, was passed by Congress. The law formed the basis for the 14th Amendment to the U. S. Constitution. It was passed over the veto of President Johnson.

May 1-3.   A tragic race riot took place in Memphis, Tennessee. Forty-eight persons, mostly blacks, were killed. Negro veterans were special targets. At least five black women were raped during the disturbances. Schools and churches were burned.

July 30.   A serious race riot occurred in New Orleans. At least thirty-five were killed; more than 100 wounded. Anti-Negro attitudes and actions on the part of policemen allegedly sparked the outbreak.

————. The first blacks to sit in an American legislative assembly, Edward G. Walker and Charles L. Mitchell, were elected to the Massachusetts House of Representatives.

1867

January 8.   Congress enacted a law giving the suffrage to blacks in the District of Columbia.

February 7. A delegation of Negroes, led by Frederick Douglass, visited President Johnson and urged that the suffrage be given to all qualified blacks.

February 18. An institution was founded at Augusta, Georgia which was to become Morehouse College, after removal to Atlanta. Morehouse College is one of the most prestigious black colleges in the nation.

March 2. The Congress began passing a series of Reconstruction Acts which were to lay the basis for Negro political participation in the South. The ex-Confederate states were required to ratify the 14th Amendment, guaranteeing civil rights to blacks, before being readmitted to the Union.

April 1. The first national convention of the Ku Klux Klan, a violently anti-Negro hate group, was held in Nashville, Tennessee.

May 1. Howard University, "the capstone of Negro education," opened in Washington, D. C. The school was established under the auspices of the Freedmen's Bureau and named for General Oliver O. Howard, head of the Bureau.

————. Atlanta University, the first all-black American graduate school, received its charter. The University began as an undergraduate institution, but became strictly graduate in 1929.

————. The National Association of Baseball denied admission to any club with black players. Excerpts from the official statement are quoted below:

> It is not presumed by your committee that any clubs who have applied are composed of persons of color, or any portion of them; and the recommendation of your committee in this report are based upon this view, and they unanimously report against the admission of any club which may be composed of one or more colored persons. . . . If colored clubs were admitted, there would be in all probability some division of feeling—whereas by excluding them, no injury could result to anybody.

1868

January 14. The new state constitutional convention met in Charleston, South Carolina. Negro delegates were in a decided majority. Louisiana had an equal number of blacks and whites in its convention. All other Southern states had white majorities. The magnanimity of the Negro delegates at Charleston can be seen in the words of black representative Beverly Nash: "I believe, my friends and fellow-citizens, we are not prepared for this suffrage. But we can learn . . . We recognize the Southern white man as the true friend of the black man . . . In these public affairs we must unite with our white fellow-citizens. They tell us that they have been disfranchised, yet we tell the North that we shall never let the halls of Congress be silent until we remove that disability." The state constitutions drawn up by the Southern constitutional conventions with black members in 1867 and 1868 included among their progressive features the abolition of property qualifications for voting and holding office, abolition of imprisonment for debt, and state abolition of slavery.

April _____. Hampton Institute, for a time the leading agricultural-industrial college for blacks and now the most affluent Negro college, opened in Virginia. Samuel Chapman Armstrong, an ex-Union officer and an advocate of agricultural-industrial training for the freed blacks, was one of the founders and first head of the institution.

June 13. Oscar J. Dunn, a freedman, became Lieutenant Governor of Louisiana, the highest elective office held by an American black to that time. Dunn was an apprentice to a plasterer and house painter until age 15, when he escaped. Born in New Orleans in 1826, Dunn took a job with the Freedman's Bureau there at the close of the Civil War. (He had served as a captain in the Union Army during the War.) As an agent of the Freedman's Bureau, Dunn checked the employment practices of planters who hired black laborers. He found that the freedmen were often cheated of their minimum $15 a month earnings. He reported these and other abuses of the Freedman's Bureau wage-contract system. Dunn was one of the 49 blacks who attended the Louisiana Constitutional Convention, 1867–1868. As lieutenant governor, Dunn presided over the state senate and signed some of the laws emanating from the new state constitution. In 1871, he was named chairman of the Republican State Convention. Since Dunn was a skillful politician, some consideration was given to nominating him for Governor or U.S. Senator before his untimely death in 1871. Two other Negroes, C.C. Antione and P.B.S. Pinchback, served in the same office in Louisiana. Antoine was a freeborn Creole Negro, whose father fought under Andrew Jackson at New Orleans in 1814 and who himself organized a black regiment in Louisiana during the Civil War and served as its captain. After the war he became a grocer and later a politician in Shreveport. Prior to becoming Lieutenant Governor, he served in the Constitutional Convention of 1867–1868, and the state senate. (For a biographical sketch of Pinchback, see below.) Blacks also served as Reconstruction lieutenant governors in Mississippi and South Carolina.

July 6. The South Carolina Legislature met at Columbia. More than half of the lawmakers were black (87 Negroes and 40 whites). This was the only state legislature in American history to have a black majority. The whites, however, controlled the state senate, and by 1874 there was a white majority in the lower house. At all times there was a white governor. There were two black lieutenant-governors, Alonzo J. Ransier in 1870 and Richard H. Gleaves in 1872. Two blacks, Samuel J. Lee and Robert B. Elliott, served as Speakers of the House between 1872 and 1874. One of the most accomplished South Carolina black officeholders was Francis L. Cardozo. Cardozo, educated in London and Glasgow, served with distinction as secretary of state, 1868–1872, and state treasurer, 1872–1876.

July 28. The Fourteenth Amendment, which made blacks American citizens and gave them constitutional guarantees, was adopted. All persons born or naturalized in the United States were defined as American citizens as well as citizens of the states in which they resided. No state could make or enforce laws denying such persons the rights and privileges of citizens or to fail to give them the equal protection of the laws.

September 22-October 26. A series of serious race riots occurred in Louisiana. One riot occurred in New Orleans on September 22; another at Opelousas, September 28; another in St. Bernard Parish on October 26.

1869

June 7. Marie Laveau, Queen of the Voodoos, was dethroned because of old age. Marie, the most famous and most powerful of all of the Voodoo queens, was born in New Orleans about 1796 as a free woman. A beautiful mulatto, Marie, a professional hairdresser, worked in the homes of some of New Orleans most prominent white women. She was also reportedly a procuress for white men. She became a member of the Voodoo cult about 1826 and by 1832 had become queen succeeding the old Sanite 'Dede.' Marie subsequently dominated Voodooism in New Orleans for nearly forty years. Under Marie, Louisiana Voodooism was a mixture of West Indian fetishism and a distorted form of Catholicism. This unusual mixture served to increase the popularity of Marie's cult and to give it a degree of legitimacy. Marie's unusual power lay in her ability to convince blacks and whites alike that she could produce "good fortune" and stave off evil. Marie died in 1879 and was succeeded by Malvina Latour.

1870

February 2. Jonathan Jasper Wright, a well-educated Pennsylvanian, became Associate Justice of the South Carolina Supreme Court. Wright served for seven years as the highest black judicial officer in the nation. Although Wright was one of only three members of the Court, he exercised no influence on behalf of Negro rights. Yet white Democratic leaders sought constantly to have him removed, charging him with corruption. Wright left the Bench in 1877 as Black Reconstruction toppled in the state.

February 25. Hiram R. Revels of Mississippi took Jefferson Davis' former seat in the United States Senate, becoming the only black in the United States Congress. Revels, an ex-barber and preacher, was a reluctant politician. It is said that his fervent prayer before the Mississippi legislature in 1870 persuaded many to vote for his election to the Senate. Revels was a free-born mulatto and as such disappointed many white Democrats. Many of these Democrats opposed his selection to the Senate and argued vainly that he could not be legally seated, not having been a citizen before the Civil War. (Constitutionally, senators must be citizens of the U.S. for at least nine years.) After retiring from politics, leaving an undistinguished legislative record, Revels became president of Alcorn College for Negroes in Mississippi.

March 30. The 15th Amendment, forbidding the denial of the right to vote to American citizens, was ratified.

May 31, 1870-October 17, 1871. Congress and President Grant made efforts to prevent Ku Klux Klan intimidation of Negro voters. The Enforcement Acts (Ku Klux Klan Acts) and a Presidential Proclamation were the most important measures.

December 12. Joseph H. Rainey of South Carolina was seated in the U.S. House of Representatives. Rainey was born to slave parents in Georgetown, South Carolina in 1832. His own freedom was purchased before the Civil War by his father, a barber. A rather well educated mulatto, Rainey himself became a barber in Charleston, having learned much from listening to and observing his better educated, white customers. Even though a respected member of the Charleston black community, he was called to work on fortifications by the Confederates during the Civil War. Rainey refused and exiled himself in the West Indies, where he remained until the end of the Civil War. During Reconstruction, he returned to South Carolina and served as a delegate to the Constitutional Convention of 1868. In 1870 he was elected to the state senate, but soon resigned to accept the seat in the U.S. House vacated by B. Franklin Whittimore of South Carolina. Rainey was then elected to the four succeeding congresses. As a member of the House, he frequently spoke in favor of education and other social advances for blacks. The House's first black member was also a consultant to President Hayes and once received the President's personal commendation for sobriety and attention to duty. After returning from Congress in 1879, Rainey served as an Internal Revenue Service [IRS] agent in South Carolina and then entered business in Washington, D.C. He returned to Georgetown, South Carolina in 1886 and died there a year later.

1872

December 11. P. B. S. Pinchback, an ex-Union officer and Lieutenant Governor of Louisiana, became temporary Governor of the state. He served for forty-three days as the incumbent was impeached. No other black American has served as governor of an American state. Pinchback was the son of a white Mississippi planter and an army officer, and a mulatto woman, who bore him nine other children. The father took all of the children north for manumission. Young Pinchback received private tutoring at home and then formal schooling in Cincinnati, Ohio. After his father's death he became a cabin boy on Mississippi river boats. During the Civil War he organized a company of Union volunteers at New Orleans and became their Captain. He held sundry political offices during the Reconstruction of Louisiana, including United States Senator (See Below). He earned a reputation as a shrewd, aggressive politician.

1873

November _____. The first black graduate of Harvard University, Richard T. Greener, was appointed to the faculty of the University of South Carolina. The university's white students and faculty left the college when it was integrated.

1874

July 31. Father Patrick Francis Healy, a black priest, became president of Georgetown University, the oldest Catholic college in the United States. Healy, brother of James Augustine Healy — the only black American to become a Roman Catholic bishop, headed the institution until 1883.

1875

March 1. A Civil Rights Bill was passed by Congress which prohibited discrimination in places of public accommodation. Inns, public conveyances on land or water, theaters, "and other places of public amusement" were included among those accommodations to which "all persons within the jurisdiction of the United States" were entitled to enjoy, regardless of any previous condition of servitude. Because of economic deprivations and prickly legal arrangements, few blacks were able to take advantage of the law's provisions. In any case, the U. S. Supreme Court overturned the law in 1883 (See Below).

March 15. Mississippi's second black senator, Blanche K. Bruce, took his seat. He was the only Afro-American to serve a full term in the U. S. Senate until the mid-twentieth century. Bruce was only thirty-five at the time. He had been born a slave in Virginia. As a body servant for the son of a wealthy planter, he was allowed some education. When his young master took him to the Confederate Army as a valet, Bruce escaped into Missouri. There he established a school for blacks. Later he entered Oberlin College, where he spent two years in study. After the Civil War he became a modestly wealthy Mississippi planter, taught school occasionally and held minor political office (as a Republican) before being elected to the Senate. Bruce's good reputation even won him a few votes from white Democrats in the Mississippi legislature. However, when Bruce's fellow Senator (a white) from Mississippi refused to escort him to be sworn, as was the custom, dapper Senator Roscoe Conkling of New York took the Negro's hand and led him to the front of the chamber. It was a well-publicized event and an historic moment.

1876

March 8. The United States Senate, following three years of debate and controversy, refused to seat P. B. S. Pinchback of Louisiana. In the fall of 1872 Pinchback had been elected to the U.S. House of Representatives; then in the winter of 1873 he was elected to the U. S. Senate. Pinchback sought to take the Senate seat. During the long debate over Pinchback's case, including almost the whole of an extra session of Congress, the affable Pinchback became a national political figure as well as a prominent name in Washington society. Opponents of Pinchback argued that he had not been properly elected or that he was not qualified, but the real reason, some authorities insist, was that many senators' wives were opposed to social intercourse with Mrs. Pinchback and influenced their husbands' negative votes.

July 8-October 26. Serious racial disturbances in South Carolina resulted in President Grant's ordering federal troops in to restore order. At Hamburg, five blacks had been killed in July.

————. Undoubtedly the first Doctor of Philsophy degree to be awarded to an Afro-American by a major university was bestowed upon Edward A. Bouchet, a physicist, by Yale University.

————. Meharry Medical College, the first all-black medical school in the United States (and still one of only two), was established in Tennessee. In the beginning Meharry was a branch of the Central Tennessee College. In 1915 it became a separate corporate entity at Nashville.

CHAPTER

The Nadir

1877-1900

1877

February 26. A conference was held in black-operated Wormley Hotel in Washington, D. C. between representatives of Presidential candidate Rutherford B. Hayes and representatives from the South. A complicated agreement was reached which led to the election of Hayes as President, and the removal of the last federal troops supporting Black Reconstruction in the South.

March 18. Despite opposition within his own party as well as much Southern opposition, President Hayes appointed Frederick Douglass Marshal for the District of Columbia.

1879

————. Large numbers of Southern blacks frustrated with discrimination and poverty in the South, emigrated to the West. Most were disappointed in the "Exodus of 1879" as they met white and red hostility in the West. The most prominent leader of the exodus, principally to Kansas, was Benjamin "Pap" Singleton. He was an ex-slave who, after a number of unsuccessful attempts, made his way to freedom in Canada. An unlettered mulatto, Singleton favored racial separatism, and encouraged industriousness among blacks.

Many of the better educated blacks were hostile to Singleton's movement, especially to his concept of a black community apart from white influence.

1880

February 2. Samuel Lowery, a Huntsville, Alabama lawyer, became the first black person admitted to practice before the U.S. Supreme Court. Lowery, the son of an ex-slave father and a free woman of color, was born in Nashville, Tennessee in 1832. He enrolled at Franklin College at the age of twelve. After the Civil War, Lowery began studying law and won the right to appear in the Supreme Court of Tennessee and various courts in Northern Alabama. In 1875 Lowery moved to Huntsville, where he started a school. In that school, his daughters, Ruth and Anna, introduced sewing, knitting, and needlework among the poor black girls. During part of their leisure time, the Lowerys cared for silkworms. In 1878, Lowery, himself, appeared before several agricultural and scientific societies in the South as well as the North, showing specimens of the silk which had been made at his school. The Lowery silk won prizes at international fairs. Lowery's law practice and the early death of his daughter, Ruth, however, made the industry a short-lived one.

1881

April 11. Spelman College, a Rockefeller-sponsored school, opened for Negro women in Atlanta. It became the Radcliffe and the Sarah Lawrence of Negro education.

May 17. Frederick Douglass became Recorder of Deeds for the District of Columbia. This second important appointment for Douglass was made by President Garfield.

May 19. President Garfield appointed ex-Senator Blanche K. Bruce of Mississippi Register of the Treasury.

July 4. Booker T. Washington opened the famed Tuskegee Institute in Alabama. The school was to become the leading Afro-American agricultural-industrial institution.

————. Tennessee took the lead in requiring segregation in railroad cars. By 1907 all of the Southern states required segregation in public accommodations.

1883

March 20. Jan E. Matzeliger, a black Lynn, Massachusetts shoemaker, invented a complicated machine that manufactured an entire shoe. The invention, which was sold to the United Shoe Company, revolutionized the industry. Matzeliger was born in Paramaribo, Dutch Guiana, the son of a black woman and a Dutch engineer, in 1852. He began working in his father's machine shop at the age of 10. Later, he worked his way to the United States as a sailor. Stopping at Philadelphia, he soon moved to Lynn, Massachusetts where he learned the shoemaking trade. By 1880 machines were able to cut and stitch the leather, but not to shape and attach the upper portion of the shoe to the sole. This had to be done by hand, a slow and tedious process. Working in secret, Matzeliger tackled the "lasting" problem for 10 years. In 1883, he received the patent for his perfected product, a "lasting machine," which could hold the shoe on the last, grip, and pull the leather down around the heel, set and drive the nails and discharge the completed shoe. A shoemaker to the end, Matzeliger died in 1889.

October 15. The United States Supreme Court ruled that the Civil Rights Act of 1875 was unconstitutional. The Reconstruction Amendments, the Court reasoned, did not extend into the area of public accommodations.

November 26. Sojourner Truth, the second best known black female abolitionist, died at Battle Creek, Michigan. Miss Truth was born a slave, with the name Isabella, in Hurley, New York in 1797. The mother of five children, she was separated from her husband prior to her freedom in 1827. After her statutory emancipation in New York in 1827, she went to work for a "religious fanatic" named Pierson in New York City. By 1843, she had become disillusioned with Pierson and left, proclaiming that her name was no longer Isabella, but Sojourner. She said that, "the Lord gave [her] Truth, because [she] was to declare the truth to the people." She, thus, became a legendary "sojourner," as she travelled about espousing abolition, women's rights, and other reforms. She held steadfastly to the belief that she was a chosen messenger of God. Though unlettered, she made a substantial impression upon her audiences. On one occasion when Frederick Douglass was speaking at Faneuil Hall in Boston, he said that blacks could not hope to find justice in America. Miss Truth sought to counter this pessimism. She asked: "Frederick, is God dead?" A more hopeful atmosphere then pervaded the meeting. Miss Truth played a prominent role in the Second National Women's Suffrage Convention in Akron, Ohio in 1852. During the Civil War, she supported the arming of the slaves and helped to care for wounded soldiers and freedmen. In the Reconstruction era, and until the end of her life, she urged property ownership and education as keys to black advancement.

1884

————. T. Thomas Fortune founded *The New York Age*. Fortune, born in Florida in 1856 to mulatto parents, was the leading Afro-American journalist until the First World War. After the Civil War, he attended a Freedmen's Bureau school. His father, a tanner and shoe merchant, served several terms in the Florida Black Reconstruction legislature and secured for his son an appointment as page boy in the state senate. The family's political activities and close social contacts with some whites created racial animosity among other whites that eventually forced the family from the capital to Jacksonville, where the father became town marshal. Fortune himself, went to Washington, where he attended Howard University, partly from earnings secured as a special customs agent in Delaware. After leaving Howard, he taught briefly in Florida, but soon left for New York. In 1879 he began his long newspaper career in New York City. His first paper was the *New York Globe*, which was succeeded by the more successful *Age*. Fortune later became an editorial writer for the *New York Sun*, one of the city's leading newspapers. He published three books — the well known *Black and White*, an historical essay on land, labor, and politics in the South, as well as *The Negro in Politics* and *Dream of Life*. He was active in Republican politics after the Civil War and an exponent of civil rights for blacks. He closely identified with Booker T. Washington and his ideas, but in later years edited some of Marcus Garvey's black nationalist publications. During World War I, Fortune had helped to establish the 369th black regiment. He died in 1928.

1886

June 12. The Georgia State Supreme Court sustained the will of the late David Dickson, thus making Amanda Eubanks the wealthiest Negro in America. Dickson, an ex-slaveholder, willed more than half a million dollars to Miss Eubanks. White relatives of Dickson, a bachelor, had contested the will on the grounds that it was illegal for a white man to leave property to his black illegitimate children. The Supreme Court disagreed.

1890

August 12-November 1. A constitutional convention in Mississippi adopted the literacy and "understanding" tests as devices to disfranchise Negroes. A poll tax of two dollars and a provision excluding voters convicted of bribery, burglary, theft, arson, murder, bigamy, and perjury were also included in the amendment. Before the convention black delegates from forty countries had met and protested to President Harrison their impending disfranchisement. The President declined to interfere. To avoid a fight over ratification the white proponents of the disfranchising measures declared the amendment to be in effect after passage by the convention.

————. The Colored Farmers' Alliance, a socio-economic-political organization dedicated to improving the lot of the black farmer, reached a membership of one million. The Alliance, founded in 1886, included twelve state organizations and there were local chapters wherever black farmers were sufficiently numerous. There was for a time cooperation between the black group and the white farmers alliance, but this was ruptured when the black group called for a strike of Negro cotton pickers. Leonidas L. Polk, president of the National Farmers' Alliance, accused the blacks of attempting to better their condition at the expense of whites.

1891

January 22. The Lodge Bill, aiming to prevent infringements on the Negro's right to vote, was killed in the U. S. Senate.

July 10. A black jockey, "Monk" Overton won six straight horse races at the Washington Park race track in Chicago. In 1907, another black jockey, Jimmy Lee also won six straight races at Churchill Downs in Louisville. Prior to 1907, only two other jockeys had equalled the feats of Overton and Lee. They were both Englishmen, Fred Archer and George Fordham.

————. Isaac Murphy, a black jockey, riding "Kingman," became the first man to win three Kentucky Derbys. Murphy won his first derby in 1884 on "Buchanan" and his second in 1890 on "Riley." Other black jockeys winning the derby were:
Oliva Lewis, 1875, "Anstides"
Billy Wakers, 1877, "Buden Baden"
Babe Hurd, 1882, "Apollo"
Enoch Henderson, 1885, "Joe Cotton"
Isaac Lewis, 1887, "Montrose"
Alfie Clayton, 1892, "Azra"
"Soup" Perkins, 1895, "Haima"
Willie Sims, 1896, "Ben Brush"
Willie Sims, 1898, "Plaudit"
Jimmy Winkfield, 1901, "His Eminence"
Jimmy Winkfield, 1902, "Alan-a-Dale"

1892

————. The Populist Party, which at first welcomed black support, became a viable political organization in the South.

————. Sissieretta Jones, the "Black Patti," performed for President Benjamin Harrison at the White House. Miss Jones, a soprano, was born in Virginia, spent her childhood in Providence, Rhode Island, and studied at the New England Conservatory. She first attracted the attention of critics in 1892 when she appeared at the Jubilee Spectacle and Cakewalk at Madison Square Garden in

New York. One critic called her the "Black Patti," a comparison with the Italian prima donna Adelina Patti. According to some authorities (including Eileen Southern, *The Music of Black Americans*, 1971), "Black Patti" was sought for roles in *Aida* and *L'Africaine* by the Metropolitan Opera, but the project was dropped, reportedly because the "musical world was not ready to accept black prima donnas." Miss Jones made her grand tour of Europe in 1893. After which she organized an all-black company, "Black Patti's Troubadours," in which she was the featured soloist. Miss Jones died in 1933.

1895

January 14.   Blacks organized the National Steamboat Company in Washington, D.C. The company sailed a steamboat, *The George Leary,* between Washington and Norfolk, Virginia. The luxury boat had three decks, 64 state rooms, 100 berths, and a dining room. It had a capacity of 1,500 passengers.

February 20.   Frederick Douglass died in Anacostia Heights, D. C.

June _____.   W. E. B. DuBois became the first Afro-American to receive a Harvard Ph.D. He immediately embarked upon a successful career of teaching and research, principally at Atlanta University.

September 18.   Booker T. Washington, the ex-slave principal of Tuskegee Institute, delivered his controversial "Atlanta Compromise" speech to the Cotton States International Exposition in Atlanta. Washington called for black emphasis on economic and educational progress, and white help, and de-emphasis on political power and social equality.

1896

May 18.   The U. S. Supreme Court upheld the concept of separate but equal public facilities for blacks in the case of *Plessy versus Ferguson* stemming from a dispute over transportation facilities in Louisiana. The segregation of the races thus won the sanction of the highest national tribunal. Justice John Harlan in a prophetic dissent pointed out that segregation laws fostered ideas of racial inferiority and would increase attacks against the rights of blacks.

June _____. Booker T. Washington received the honorary Master of Arts degree from Harvard University.

July 21. The National Association of Colored Women, led by Mary Church Terrell, was organized in Washington, D. C. Mrs. Terrell was born in Memphis, Tennessee at the close of the Civil War. She was the daughter of wealthy and well-educated parents. Mrs. Terrell herself inherited a substantial fortune and received an Oberlin education. As Mary Church, she married Robert Terrell, a prominent D. C. educator, attorney, and judge. She probably would have become a teacher, but her father considered the occupation beneath her station. She did become a feminist leader and a close associate of a number of white feminist leaders. She remained wedded to the goal of racial integration despite numerous disappointments.

—————. W. E. B. DuBois' *The Suppression of the African Slave Trade to America*, his Harvard dissertation, was published as the first volume in the Harvard Historical Studies Series. This work, along with *Souls of Black Folk*, *The Philadelphia Negro*, and *The Atlanta University Studies*, helped to establish DuBois' scholarly reputation.

1897

November 15. John Mercer Langston, Virginia soldier, educator, diplomat, and U. S. congressman died.

1898

March 17. Former United States Senator Blanche K. Bruce died in Washington, D. C. After leaving the Senate, Bruce had been Register of the U. S. Treasury and a successful banker.

July 1. Four black regiments participated in fighting around Santiago during the Spanish-American War. Approximately twenty Afro-American regiments served in the conflict. Most of the black outfits had been activated shortly after the end of the Civil War for action against the Indians in the West. In reality, the blacks, like many of their white counterparts, were ill-prepared in terms of experience, equipment, and training for combat in a tropical zone. Yet, in the end, the blacks won the praises of almost all their officers. At the beginning of the Spanish-American conflict, there was only one Negro commissioned officer, Captain Charles Young. At the close of the war, there were more than one hundred officers, including Young, now a Brevet Major and commander of the Ninth Ohio regiment.

July ———. At least 25 black soldiers, members of the U.S. Tenth Colored Cavalry, participated in the famous charge up San Juan Hill in Cuba. The assault was a major engagement of the Spanish-American War.

———. Will Marion Cook directed the sensational musical-comedy sketch, *Clorindy, the Origin of the Cakewalk* on Broadway. Disregarding warnings that Broadway audiences would not listen to blacks singing black opera, Cook composed music to lyrics written by the famed black poet, Paul Laurence Dunbar, and assembled a company of 26 black performers. The performances of the first Negro musical-comedy sketch in New York were held at the Casino Roof Garden. Cook was born in Washington, D.C. in 1869. The son of a Howard University law professor, he was sent at age thirteen to the Oberlin Conservatory to study the violin. Later, in Berlin, he studied with the violinist Joseph Joachim, and at the National Conservatory of Music, he studied with John White and with Dvořak. Cook made additional theatrical history with *In Dahomey* (1902), a satire on the American Colonization Movement's efforts to promote black emigration to Africa, when it opened on Times Square on Broadway. Other Cook successes were *In Abyssinia* (1906) and *In Bandana Land* (1907). Cook's lively shows left his audiences whistling and patting their feet and helped to popularize the Cakewalk both in the United States and Europe. Cook died in 1944.

1899

————. Charles Waddell Chestnutt published a volume of tales called *The Conjure Woman*, which helped to establish him as the foremost Afro-American novelist of his time. *The Conjure Woman*, based upon the superstitions of North Carolina blacks, was probably his best work. Chestnutt was born in North Carolina in 1858, but spent much of his adult life in Ohio. After the Civil War, he taught in the public schools of North Carolina, then was principal of the Fayetteville (North Carolina) State Teachers College. As segregation and discrimination intensified in the South in the 1880's, Chestnutt returned to the North, first to New York where he worked as a journalist; then to Cleveland where he was a clerk and an attorney. Prior to the publication of *The Conjure Woman*, he had contributed several short stories to American magazines, including *The Atlantic Monthly*. Following the highly successful *Conjure Woman*, he published *The Wife of His Youth* and *The House behind the Cedars* (1900); *The Marrow of Tradition* (1901); and *The Colonel's Dream* (1905). In recognition of his literary and other achievements, the NAACP awarded him its prestigious Spingarn Medal in 1928. Chestnutt died four years later.

1900

April 30. The famed steam locomotive driven by John "Casey" Jones collided with another train. The incident inspired the writing of the popular song, "Casey Jones." Two black men, Wallace Saunders and Sim Webb, were members of Jones' crew. At the time of the collision, Jones ordered Sim Webb to jump, but remained with the train himself. When Jones' body was recovered, it was discovered that he had kept one hand on the airbrake and the other on the whistle. Saunders took the occasion to write a song immortalizing the noted engineer and his train.

July 24-27. Another serious race riot broke out in New Orleans. Black schools and homes were destroyed.

August 23-24. The National Negro Business League, sponsored by Booker T. Washington, was formed at Boston. More than 400 delegates from thirty-four states had answered Washington's call to stimulate black business. Washington himself, was elected the first president of the organization. After only one year of the League's existence, Washington reported a large number of new black businesses and by 1907 the national organization had 320 branches. Though service-related concerns were by far the most numerous, blacks engaged in various types and sizes of business enterprises. The North Carolina Mutual Insurance Company, founded in 1898, became the largest of black-owned concerns.

CHAPTER

IV

The Age

of

Booker T. Washington

1901-1917

1901

January 16. Hiram R. Revels, ex-United States Senator from Mississippi, died at Holly Springs.

March 4. George H. White left Congress. It would be more than 20 years before any other Afro-American served in Congress. White was first elected to the Congress from North Carolina in 1896 and had been re-elected in 1898. In a moving valedictory address, White attacked Jim Crowism and predicted that the Negro would return to the United States Congress.

October 16. Booker T. Washington dined with President Theodore Roosevelt at the White House. The dinner meeting was viewed by many whites, especially Southerners, as a marked departure from racial etiquette and was bitterly criticized. In the previous year, the publication of Washington's autobiography, *Up From Slavery*, had been hailed by Southern and Northern whites for its "reasonable" and non-vindictive attitude towards the South and the previous slave system. The book has become one of the classics in American biography primarily because of the prominence of Washington.

————. William Monroe Trotter, a Phi Beta Kappa graduate of Harvard University, founded the *Boston Guardian*, a militant newspaper which opposed the accommodationist policies of Booker T. Washington and demanded full equality for blacks. Trotter was born in Boston in 1872. After achieving a Harvard B.A. degree, he returned for his Master's which was awarded in 1895. He opened the *Guardian* offices in 1901 in the same building where William Lloyd Garrison had published the *Liberator* and where Harriet Beecher Stowe's *Uncle Tom's Cabin* had been printed. Trotter announced that "propaganda against discrimination based on color" was a principal aim of his publication. In publishing the *Guardian*, Trotter abandoned a promising career as an insurance executive because, as he said, "the conviction grew upon me that pursuit of business, money, civic or literary position was like building a house upon sands; if race prejudice and persecution and public discrimination for mere color was to spread up from the South and result in a fixed caste of color . . . every colored American would be really a civil outcast, forever an alien, in the public life." Trotter confronted his foe, Booker T. Washington at the Columbus Avenue African Zion Church in Boston on July 30, 1903. He and his followers heckled the preeminent black leader and the police were called in. Trotter was arrested and sentenced to jail for 30 days. Trotter explained that he had to resort to a public confrontation with Washington because the "Tuskegee kingpin" held a monopoly on the American media and opposing views could not be heard. The treatment of Trotter in Boston inspired W.E.B. DuBois to become more active in the opposition to Washington. Trotter collaborated with DuBois in the organization of the Niagara Movement, but declined a position of leadership in the NAACP because of his distrust of whites.

Yet, Trotter continued his career as an agitator and protester in the cause of civil rights. In 1906, he protested President Theodore Roosevelt's discharge of the black soldiers involved in the Brownsville, Texas riot. In 1910, he led a demonstration against a performance of the anti-Negro play, *The Clansman* in Boston. In 1913, he confronted President Woodrow Wilson at the White House, accusing the President of lying when he [Wilson] denied that he was responsible for segregation in the government cafeterias of Washington, D.C. In 1915, Trotter, again, landed in jail for picketing the showing of the anti-black film, "Birth of a Nation."

When the Paris Peace Conference convened in 1919, Trotter applied for a passport to attend in order to present the grievances of American blacks to this world forum. When the U.S. government denied his visa, Trotter obtained a job as a cook on a transatlantic ship and managed to reach Europe. As a representative of the National Equal Rights League and of the Race Petitioners to the Peace Conference, Trotter supported the Japanese motion to include a prohibition against discrimination in the Covenant of the League of Nations. The Western Allies, including the United States, opposed such a proviso. In his remaining years, his money and energy dwindling, he continued to agitate for equal rights. He died in 1934.

1903

———. *The Souls of Black Folk* by W. E. B. DuBois was published. The book crystallized black opposition to the policies of Booker T. Washington.

1905

July 11-13. A group of black intellectuals from across the nation met near Niagara Falls and adopted resolutions demanding full equality in American life. The meeting has become known to history as the beginning of the Niagara Movement. W. E. B. DuBois and William Monroe Trotter spearheaded the movement.

———. The Atlanta Life Insurance Company was founded by Alonzo F. Herndon in Atlanta. It was once the first, and now the second, largest black-owned business in the United States. The distinction of largest black-owned business was later acquired by the North Carolina Mutual Insurance Company of Durham, founded in 1898-99 by John Merrick, C. C. Spaulding, et al.

———. Robert S. Abbott began publication of the militant

Chicago Defender. It became one of the most widely read and influential black newspapers. Abbott was the son of a slave butler and a field woman who purchased their son's freedom. After his father's death, Abbott's mother married John Sengstacke, educator, clergyman, and editor. Young Abbott worked on his step-father's newssheet. He received his education at Hampton Institute where he came under the influence of the same General Samuel C. Armstrong who had molded Booker T. Washington. In Chicago, Abbott began his newspaper with a staff of former barbers and servants as well as a few recently educated blacks. He attracted good journalists like Willard Motley, and printed the early poems of Gwendolyn Brooks. His scathing attacks on Southern racism coupled with his appeals for Northern migration enhanced the *Defender's* prestige.

1906

February 9. Paul Laurence Dunbar, the black poet who made dialect an accepted literary form, died at Dayton, Ohio. Dunbar was born in Dayton in 1872, the son of an ex-slave. Although he was senior class poet at Dayton's Central High School, and editor of the school paper and yearbook, he began his career as an elevator boy. In 1893, he compiled a book of his verses, "Oak and Ivy," which he sold to passengers on his elevator, which he operated for four dollars a week. In 1895, he published "Majors and Minors," which received a very favorable review by William Dean Howells in *Harper's Weekly*. That review brought Dunbar national recognition. The next year, Dunbar's "Lyrics of Lowly Life" appeared. Many of these earlier works were published by Orville and Wilbur Wright who were experimenting with printing newspapers on a homemade press. In 1897, Dunbar became an assistant at the Library of Congress, a post which he held for only one year. During the last ten years of his life, he produced eleven volumes of verse, three novels, and five collections of short stories.

Critics generally agree that Dunbar's poetry is the most lasting of his work and that his best poems were those written in Negro dialect. Despite his midwestern origins, Dunbar's poems dealt nostalgically with the pathos and humor of the Old South. The *Encyclopaedia Britannica* for 1911 described Dunbar's poetry "as a distinct contribution to American literature, and entitles the author to be called preeminently the poet of his race in America." William Dean Howells described him as the first Afro-American to feel an aesthetic appreciation of the life of his people and to express it lyrically. Dunbar's biographer, Benjamin Brawley said Dunbar:

> soared above race and touched the heart universal. He came on the scene at a time when America was being launched on the machine age and when the country was beset with problems. . . . In a world of discord, he dared to sing his song about nights bright with stars, about the secret of the wind and the sea, and the answer one finds beyond the years. Above the dross and strife of the day, he asserted the right to live and love and be happy. That is why he was so greatly beloved and why he will never grow old.

No black writer before him had been so widely hailed by white and black Americans. The conflict between his genius and the limitations of American racism probably drove him to drink. Whiskey and tuberculosis brought him down at age thirty-four.

April 13. Serious racial disturbances involving white civilians and black soldiers occurred at Brownsville, Texas. The black soldiers who had retaliated for racial slurs, killing and wounding at least three white men, were dishonorably discharged by President Theodore Roosevelt. The President's handling of the matter convinced many blacks that there could be no appeal to him in the wake of increasing anti-Negro assaults. When Congress met in December some Northern solons led by Senator Joseph B. Foraker of Ohio protested that a full investigation and trial should have preceded the President's action. In January, 1907, such an investigation was launched by the Senate. After several months, the Senate Committee's majority report upheld the President. Finally in 1909 Senator Foraker won approval for a court of inquiry to pass on the cases of the discharged soldiers and to allow re-enlistment for those deemed eligible.

June ——. John Hope assumed the presidency of Morehouse College. Hope, one of the most militant of early black educators, was the school's first Negro head and began many of the programs which resulted in the institution's favorable reputation. Hope was born in Augusta, Georgia in 1868 to prosperous parents, a white father and mulatto mother. His relatively secure childhood was shaken by his father's death in 1876 and the subsequent loss of much of the family's inheritance at the hands of callous executors and prejudiced whites. In the same year, Hope witnessed a violent racial clash in Atlanta. This incident, together with the infamous Atlanta riot of 1906, probably influenced his militancy. Hope denounced Booker T. Washington's Atlanta Compromise and was the only black college president to join the militant Niagara Movement. Hope was the only college head to attend the founding meeting of the NAACP in 1909 (See Above and Below). Hope was a founder and later president of the South's first bi-racial reform group, the Commission on Interracial Cooperation (the forerunner of the Southern Regional Council). The group was organized in 1919. Hope became president in 1932. Hope ended his career as president of the Atlanta University Center from 1929 until his death in 1936 (See Also Below).

September 22-24. A major race riot at Atlanta left twelve, mostly blacks, dead. An irresponsible press and moves to disfranchise blacks had increased racial tensions in the city. On September 22, newspapers reported four successive assaults on white women by black men. Many of the city's whites, joined by country-folk in town for Saturday shopping, formed Negro-seeking mobs, bent upon retaliation. Blacks who sought to arm themselves for defense were quickly arrested. The state of panic existed for several days until a group of level-headed blacks and whites could get together and plead for calm. The Atlanta Civic League, an interracial organization, dedicated to racial harmony, was formed in the wake of the riot.

1907

———. Alain Locke, one of the most brilliant of American Negro intellectuals—a philosopher, critic, and author—received a Rhodes Scholarship. No other Afro-American recevied this distinguished award for more than half a century. Locke was born in Philadelphia in 1886. He obtained his Ph.D. degree from Harvard in 1918. As a Rhodes Scholar, he studied at Oxford University in England from 1907 to 1910. He continued his European studies at the University of Berlin from 1910 to 1911. He became Professor of Philosophy at Howard University in 1912, a post he held until his retirement in 1953. He published *Race Contacts and Interracial Relations* in 1916. His fame as a literary and art critic and interpreter of black culture rests largely on his publication of the book *The New Negro*, one of the major syntheses of the Harlem Renaissance. Locke died in 1954, prior to completing *The Negro in American Culture*. This work was completed by Margaret Just Butcher and published in 1956.

1908

August 14-19. A serious racial disturbance at Springfield, Illinois. The shock of the riot near Lincoln's home prompted concerned whites to call for a conference which led to the founding of the NAACP.

1909

February 12. The National Association for the Advancement of Colored People (NAACP), for many years the nation's pre-eminent civil rights organization, was founded at New York City. White progressives and black intellectuals were the group's first leaders. Among these were Jane Addams, John Dewey, W. E. B. DuBois, Mary White Ovington and Oswald Garrison Villard. Moorfield Storey of Boston was named president.

April 6. Matthew H. Henson, a black servant, accompanied Robert E. Peary to the North Pole. Henson, a Washington, D. C. mulatto, received a modest education, worked as a cabin boy, then later as a stock boy in a Washington clothing store. There he met Commodore Peary and was hired as his servant. After sharing Peary's great feat, Henson served for many years as a messenger in the New York Customs House. Finally, in 1945, he received a medal for "outstanding service to the government of the United States in the field of science."

1910

April _____. The National Urban League, an organization design-
to assist black emigrants to the North, was established in New York
City. It soon became a social relief organization for black urban
dwellers, North and West and later South.

————. The NAACP organ, The *Crisis*, began publication.
W. E. B. DuBois was the first editor.

1912

September 27. A revolution of sorts occurred in the music world
when W. C. Handy published a blues composition, *Memphis Blues.*

1913

March 10. Harriett Tubman, "the Moses of her People," died in
Auburn, New York.

1915

June 21. The U. S. Supreme Court, in *Guinn vs the United States*
outlawed the "grand-father clauses" used by Southern states to deny
blacks the right to vote. The clauses, which originated in Louisiana,
were actually parts of the state constitutions. They restricted the ballot
to descendants of the qualified voters as of January 1, 1867 — prior
to Black Reconstruction.

September 9. Professor Carter G. Woodson founded the Association for the Study of Negro Life and History. The group stood virtually alone for a while in attempting to properly portray the role of
the Afro-American in United States history. Woodson, the son of
ex-slaves, had a Harvard Ph.D. He is sometimes called "the father of
modern Negro historiography," having edited for many years *The
Journal of Negro History* and other publications of the ASNLH, and
having published a number of works on the Negro.

November 14. Booker T. Washington, the most noted black American between Frederick Douglass and Martin Luther King, Jr., died at Tuskegee. He was succeeded by Robert Russa Moton of Hampton Institute. Moton was born just after the Civil War in Virginia. He was reared as a houseboy on a Virginia plantation, receiving secret instruction from his literate mother. Moton taught at Hampton Institute, his alma mater, before taking over at Tuskegee. He was one of the sponsors of the Committee on the Welfare of Negro Troops sponsored by the Federal Council of Churches during World War I. While continuing, in the main, the policies and practices of Booker T. Washington, both in education and race relations, Moton expanded the academic-classical curriculum at Tuskegee, and fought the efforts of white bigots to prevent black control of the Tuskegee Veterans Hospital.

————. The NAACP led the black outcry against the showing of the controversial movie, *Birth of a Nation*. The movie, based on the racist writings of Thomas Dixon, was the most technologically advanced motion picture produced to that time. It told an obviously distorted story of emancipation, Reconstruction, and black immorality. It glorified anti-Negro elements, like the Ku Klux Klan.

————. Bishop Henry McNeal Turner, black Pan-Africanist leader and A. M. E. churchman died. Turner had been born free in Abbeville, South Carolina in 1833. At an early age he was hired out to work in the field with slaves. His first learning came from a white playmate. Making his way to Baltimore at fifteen, he worked as a messenger, and then as a handyman at a medical school, where he had access to books and magazines. He continued his self-education here until an Episcopal bishop consented to teach him. This was one of the influences which led him into the church, where he became an A. M. E. minister. During the Civil War, President Lincoln appointed Turner as Chaplain of the 54th Massachusetts Negro regiment. After the war he worked with the Freedmen's Bureau in Georgia and became actively involved in Republican politics. He served in the Georgia constitutional convention of 1868 and then was elected to the state legislature. Turner vehemently opposed the successful attempt of white Georgia lawmakers to expel the Black Reconstruction legislators. These and other experiences convinced him that the black man had no future in the United States. He became a colonizationist and Pan-Africanist. Turner was one of the sponsors of an ill-fated expedition of some 200 blacks to Liberia in 1878. In spite of the failure of this venture, he continued his support of colonization. Prior to his death in 1915, he also served as director of the A. M. E. publishing house, editor of denominational periodicals, and chancellor of Morris Brown College, an A. M. E. school in Atlanta.

————. The war-time migration by blacks to Northern industrial centers began. Millions of blacks left the South for better economic and social security.

1917

April 6. The United States entered World War I. Approximately 300,000 blacks saw service during the conflict. One thousand and four hundred blacks were commissioned as officers. Three Negro regiments received the Croix de Guerre for valor. Several individual blacks were decorated for bravery.

July 1-3. A serious race riot occurred in East St. Louis, Illinois. At least forty blacks were killed. Martial law was declared. The riot resulted from the employment of blacks in a factory which held a contract with the federal government. In one of the most tragic incidents, a small black child was shot down and then thrown into a burning building. The Germans seized upon the riot in their campaign to attract Negro sentiment in the World War.

July 28. Some 10,000 Negroes participated in a silent march down Fifth Avenue in New York City to protest racial oppression. The march, organized by the NAACP, was largely motivated by the East St. Louis riot. The protestors asked prayer for East St. Louis, and asked the President "Why not make America safe for Democracy?"

August 23.   A serious racial disturbance erupted at Houston, Texas, involving black soldiers and white civilians. Two blacks and seventeen whites were killed. Thirteen blacks were executed as participants.

November 5.   The Supreme Court, in *Buchanan vs Warley*, ruled unconstitutional a Louisville law which forbade blacks and whites from living in the same block.

————.   Emmett J. Scott, formerly secretary to Booker T. Washington, was appointed special assistant to the Secretary of War. Scott was to serve as "confidential advisor in matters affecting the interests of . . . Negroes of the United States and the part they are to play in connection with the present war." Specifically, Scott was to work for non-discriminatory application of the Selective Service Act; to formulate plans to build up morale among blacks, soldiers and civilians; and to investigate complaints of unfair treatment of blacks. He also disseminated news concerning black soldiers, as well as various related activities on the home front. In June, 1918 Scott called a conference of some thirty black newspaper publishers, who pledged their support of the American war effort, but denounced anti-Negro violence and discrimination at home, called for black Red Cross nurses, asked for the appointment of a black war correspondent, and requested the return of black Colonel Charles Young to active duty. Most of these requests were granted.

————.   Harry T. Burleigh was awarded the Spingarn Medal, the NAACP's highest award, for excellence in the field of creative music. Burleigh was born in Erie, Pennsylvania in 1866. Although he showed an interest in music as a child, he did not receive formal training until many years later. In 1892, he began his studies at the National Conservatory of Music in New York where he majored in orchestral as well as vocal music. During his sophomore year, he studied under the famed Czech composer Dvořak, who took the young black student as a protégé. In his senior year, Burleigh became an instructor of voice at the Conservatory, a position he held for two years after his graduation. Two years after entering the conservatory, Burleigh was well on his way in a singing career. He became the first black soloist at St. George's Episcopal Church in New York and at the Temple Emanu-El. His European tours included a command performance before King Edward VII in England.

About 1900 Burleigh began to shift his attention from singing to composing. His first compositions were sentimental ballads; then he branched out into choral pieces, spirituals and miscellaneous works. Among his better known compositions are: *Six Plantation Melodies for Violin and Piano* (1901); *Southland Sketches* (1916); *The Prayer* (1915); *Little Mother of Mine* (1917); *Deep River* (1916); and *The Lovely Dark and Lonely One* (1935). Contemporary critics lauded his "imagination" and his "masterly musicianship." Of his spiritual compositions, Burleigh, himself, wrote: "My desire was to preserve them in harmonies that belong to modern methods of tonal progression without robbing the melodies of their racial flavor." His determination "to capture the spirit of Negro folksong in composed music," according to Eileen Southern, "makes him a true disciple of his teacher, Dvořak. It was as an arranger of spirituals for the solo voice that Burleigh made a unique contribution to the history of American music."

In addition to the Spingarn Medal, Burleigh was the recipient of honorary degrees from Atlanta University and Howard University. The Harry T. Burleigh Association, a black performing company, was founded in his honor. Burleigh died in 1949.

CHAPTER

V

Between War and Depression

1918-1932

1918

July 25-29. Serious racial disturbances occurred at Chester and Philadelphia, Pennsylvania, with approximately ten killed and more than sixty injured.

July 29. The National Liberty Congress of Colored Americans asked Congress to make lynching a federal crime.

February 19-21. The First Pan-African Congress, led by W. E. B. DuBois, met in Paris. The Congress met at the same time as the Paris Peace Conference, ending World War I. There were about sixty delegates, including West Indians, Africans, and American blacks. The meeting focused attention on the fact that blacks all over the world were materially interested in the Paris Peace Conference and specifically how they might benefit from it — the democracy for which many of them fought, they now said, should indeed become a reality. While this Congress accomplished very little, it stimulated subsequent and more fruitful assemblages of black people in later years.

July 13-October 1. Major race riots occurred across the nation in what James Weldon Johnson called the "Red Summer." More than 25 riots left more than 100 dead, more than 1,000 wounded. Federal troops had to suppress the disorders in some areas. Washington, D. C., Chicago, Illinois, and Longview, Texas were among the scenes of the disturbances.

————. Eighty-three lynchings were recorded during the year.

1920

August 1-2. The national convention of the Universal Negro Improvement Association met in New York City. Marcus Garvey, the founder of the organization, spoke to some 25,000 blacks during a rally at Madison Square Garden. Garvey-type black nationalism was reaching its zenith. Garvey had begun his organization in his native Jamaica in 1914. In 1916 he arrived in the United States to organize a New York chapter of the U. N. I. A. By the middle of 1919 there were thirty branches of the organization in the United States, principally in the Northern ghettoes. Garvey founded a newspaper, *The Negro World*, to disseminate his ideas of race pride and a return to Africa. His other auxiliary organizations included the Universal Black Cross Nurses, the Universal African Motor Corps, the Black Star Steamship Line, and the Black Eagle Flying Corps. In 1921 Garvey formally organized the Empire of Africa and appointed himself Provisional President. He appealed, unsuccessfully, to the League of Nations for permission to settle a colony in Africa and negotiated towards that end with Liberia. After these failures, he began planning a military expedition to drive the white imperialists out of Africa. This campaign, however, was never launched. In 1923 Garvey was arrested for fraud in raising money for his steamship line.

————. Robert Nathaniel Dett, black composer, arranger, and conductor, was awarded the Bowdoin Prize by Harvard University for an essay, entitled, "The Emancipation of Negro Music." Dett was born in 1882 in the community of Drummondville, Quebec, which had been established by fugitive slaves before the Civil War. Inspired, as a child, by the Negro spirituals, he studied music at the American Conservatory of Music in Chicago, Columbia University, Harvard University, the Oberlin Conservatory, the Oliver Willis Halstead Conservatory in Lockport, New York, and the University of Pennsylvania. During his early career, Dett performed as a concert pianist, while also teaching and doing further study. Dett taught at Lane College, Tennessee (1908-11); Lincoln University, Missouri (1911-1913); Hampton Institute, Virginia (1913-1931); Sam Houston College, Texas (1935-1937); and at Bennett College, North Carolina (1937). Under the leadership of Dett, the Hampton Institute Choir became internationally known, giving performances at the Library of Congress, Carnegie Hall in New York, and Symphony Hall in Boston. In 1930, the choir toured seven European nations. Meanwhile, Dett took some time off to study with Arthur Foote in Boston and with Nadia Boulanger at the American Conservatory at Fontainebleau. Among Dett's many notable compositions are *Magnolia* (five piano suites, 1912); *Music in the Mine* (1916); *The Chariot Jubilee* (an oratorio, 1921); *Enchantment* (1922); and *The Ordering of Moses* (1937). In addition to the Bowdoin Prize Dett was the recipient of the Francis Boot prize for composition; the Palm and Ribbon Award of the Royal Belgian Band; the Harmon Foundation Award; and honorary degrees from the Eastman School of Music, Oberlin and Harvard Universities. Dett died in 1943.

1921

———. Eubie Blake, along with Noble Sissle, produced the historic musical *Shuffle Along*. Blake was born in Baltimore in 1883. He began practicing music at age six. As a youngster, he played music in department stores and in "bawdy" and "sporting" houses. In 1899, he composed his first rag, *The Charleston Rag*. Others which followed, included *Chevy Chase* (1914), *Fizz Water* (1914), and *Bugle Call Rag* (1926). Even as late as 1970, Blake was still composing rags. Blake is often called "the leading exponent of the eastern school" of ragtime music.

1922

January 8. Colonel Charles R. Young, one of the highest ranking blacks in the United States Army, died in Nigeria. Young, the son of an ex-slave soldier in the Union Army, was born in Kentucky. He entered West Point in 1884, served with distinction in Cuba, Haiti, and Mexico, but always labored under the burdens of racial discrimination. During World War I he was called up for a physical examination and then retired due to "poor health." The move was an apparent subterfuge to prevent Young's promotion to general. After black protests (See Above), he was recalled, but assigned only to relatively obscure duty in Illinois, and then in Liberia.

1923

September 4. George Washington Carver of Tuskegee Institute received the Spingarn Medal, the NAACP's highest award, for distinguished research in agricultural chemistry. In 1939, Carver was awarded the Roosevelt Medal for distinguished achievement in science. Carver was born a slave at Diamond Grove, Missouri in 1864. He attended undergraduate school in Iowa and received a Master of Science degree from Iowa State College. In 1896, he was appointed to the faculty of Tuskegee Institute, where he began a program of research in soil conservation and crop diversification. Often called by fellow blacks "the greatest chemist in the world," his scientific fame rests largely in the 400 different products he produced from peanuts, potatoes, and pecans. He was a Fellow of the Royal Academy of England. A foundation and a museum have been established in his honor at Tuskegee Institute. Carver died there in 1943.

October 24. Black migration to the North continued as the Department of Labor estimated that some half-million Negroes left the South within the last year.

————. Garrett A. Morgan, a black inventor, developed the automatic traffic light. Morgan had earlier invented the gas mask used by American troops duiring World War I. The black inventor was born in Paris, Tennessee in 1875. In 1895 he moved to Cleveland, Ohio where he produced, in 1901, a belt fastener for sewing machines. In 1914 Morgan won the First Grand Prize at the Second International Exposition of Sanitation and Safety for the invention of a smoke inhalator. This inhalator was used in a successful rescue of workers trapped in a tunnel under Lake Erie in 1916. The city of Cleveland awarded Morgan a gold medal following the rescue. The patent rights to the traffic light were sold by Morgan to the General Electric Company for $40,000. Morgan died in 1963.

1924

July 1. Roland Hayes, born in a Georgia cabin in 1887, was named a soloist with the Boston Symphony Orchestra. Earlier he had received the Spingarn Medal for "so finely" interpreting the beauty of the Negro folk songs.

1925

January 10. Adelbert H. Roberts was elected to the Illinois state legislature — the first black to serve in a state assembly in at least 25 years.

May 8. The Brotherhood of Sleeping Car Porters, the trailblazing black labor union, was organized by A. Philip Randolph. Randolph, often called the dean of Negro leaders, was reared in Florida. He was the son of a minister and a seamstress, both ex-slaves. He attended Cookman Institute in Florida and City College in New York. His intellectual interests and his practical experiences in Harlem evoked an intense hatred of racial bias, and a zeal for economic and social justice. He joined the Socialist Party and attempted to organize black students and workers. He founded the socialist periodical, the *Messenger,* which became one of the best magazines in the history of black journalism. In later years he was prominent as an opponent of American intervention in foreign wars; an outspoken opponent of military segregation; the central figure in the 1941 "March on Washington;" an humanitarian; and a consultant to Presidents on matters of civil rights (See Below).

1926

June 30. James Weldon Johnson was honored for his careers as secretary of the NAACP, U.S. consul, editor, and poet by the NAACP in New York. Johnson was born in Florida in 1871 and was educated there, at Atlanta University, New York City College, and Columbia University. He started out in Florida as a school teacher, journalist, and lawyer before joining his brother J. Rosamond in New York as a writer of musical comedies. He is best known as a writer of prose and verse. His most notable works include *God's Trombones*, *The Book of American Negro Poetry*, *Black Manhattan*, *The Autobiography of an Ex-Colored Man* (a novel), and his own autobiography, *Along This Way*. Johnson's poem "Lift Every Voice and Sing," when set to music by his brother J. Rosamond, was so inspiring to blacks during the 1930's that it became known as "the Negro National Anthem." The song still retains that characterization among blacks today (See Below). In New York, Johnson moved widely in interracial circles. These moves, together with his success as a writer and a diplomat and his "moderate" opposition to racial discrimination, made him a likely choice as the NAACP's first executive secretary. In this capacity he led the campaign to outlaw lynching in the United States, culminating in the Dyer anti-lynching bill of 1921 (which passed the House but died in the Senate). Before his death in 1938, Johnson also devoted a part of his career to a teaching assignment at Fisk University in Nashville, Tennessee. He has been called an "American Renaissance Man" in recognition of his multiple talents.

"Lift Every Voice and Sing," James Weldon Johnson and J. Rosamond Johnson—*"The Negro National Anthem"*

Lift every voice and sing, till earth and heaven ring,
ring with the harmonies of liberty; Let our rejoicing
rise, high as the list'ning skies, let it resound
loud as the rolling sea.
Sing a song full of the faith that the dark past
has taught us; Sing a song full of the hope that
the present has brought us. Facing the rising
sun of our new day begun, let us march on till
victory is won.
Stony the road we trod, bitter the chastening rod
Felt in the days when hope unborn had died;

Yet with a steady beat, have not our weary feet
Come to the place for which our fathers sighed?
We have come over a way that with tears has been
watered; We have come treading our path through the
blood of the slaughtered; Out from the gloomy past,
til now we stand at last
Where the white glean of our bright star is cast.
God of our weary years, God of our silent tears,
Thou who hast brought us thus far on the way; Thou
who hast by Thy might led us into the light, keep
us forever in the path, we pray.
Lest our feet stray from the places, our God, where
we met thee, Lest our hearts, drunk with the wine
of the world, we forget Thee; Shadowed beneath
Thy hand, may we forever stand, True to our God,
true to our native land.

1927

March 7. The U. S. Supreme Court, in the case of *Nixon vs Herndon,* struck down a Texas law which excluded blacks from the Democratic primaries in that state. Texas managed, however, to erect new defenses against Negro voting.

December _____. Marcus Garvey, after having been convicted in 1925 for using the mails to defraud, was released from the Atlanta Federal Penintentary and deported as an undesirable alien. Garvey had tried, unsuccessfully, to keep his black nationalist movement alive from his cell.

_____, *1922-1927.* A period of unusual activity on the part of Afro-American artists and writers, centered principally in Harlem and called the Harlem or Negro Renaissance took place. The writings of the poets, Claude McKay, Langston Hughes, Countee Cullen, James Weldon Johnson, and the novelists, Jean Toomer, Walter White, Wallace Thurman, and Nella Larsen, among others, drew attention even from whites. James Weldon Johnson produced in these years his celebrated *Book of American Negro Poetry,* an anthology of the works of outstanding contemporary black poets; *God's Trombones*, black sermons in verse; and *Autobiography of an Ex-Coloured Man*. Claude McKay, the first important figure in the Renaissance, was noted for *Harlem Shadows*, a group of bitter, but eloquent, poems on the condition of the Negro in post-war America, and *Home to Harlem*. Jean Toomer's *Cane* certainly ranked with McKay's *Harlem Shadows* in its significant portrayal of Negro life. Among Countee Cullen's better known works was his volume of poems, *Color*. Its appearance in 1925 pushed the Renaissance to a new high. Other notable works were Langston Hughes' "The Negro Speaks of Rivers": Walter White's *Fire in the Flint*; Nella Larsen's *Quick-Sand* and *Passing*, depicting the plight of young black women; and Wallace Thurman's *The Blacker the Berry*.

1928

November 6.   Oscar de Priest was elected congressman from Illinois. De Priest was born in Alabama shortly after the Civil War to ex-slave parents. He was reared in Kansas, where he worked as a painter, but after removing to Chicago he became involved in real estate and interested in politics. He was Chicago's first black alderman. De Priest became deeply involved with Republican ward politics in Chicago and was rewarded by local politicians with the House nomination in 1928. When he first assumed office, some blacks felt him to be an unscrupulous politician and an' accommodationist on racial matters, but at the end of three terms in office he had won a reputation for outspoken militancy. De Priest was the first black from a non-Southern state to sit in Congress and the only Afro-American to serve in that body since George White left in 1901.

1929

January 15.   Martin Luther King, Jr., called by many the greatest American of the twentieth century, was born in Atlanta. King's parents were members of the city's "black establishment," his father being one of the city's leading Negro ministers and his mother the daughter of a prominent preacher. King was educated at Morehouse College, Crozier Theological Seminary, and Boston University. He began his ministerial career as pastor of the Dexter Avenue Baptist Church in Montgomery, Alabama in 1954. (See Below).

October 29. The New York stock market crashed, signaling the beginning of the Great Depression. During the Depression decade blacks complained that they were "the last to be hired and the first to be fired."

————. Albon Holsey of the National Negro Business League organized the Colored Merchants Association in New York. The group planned to establish stores and to buy their merchandise cooperatively. Blacks were urged to make their purchases from these merchants as a means of providing jobs for members of the race. The Depression forced the stores out of business within two years. By 1931 the "Jobs-for-Negroes" movement began in earnest in St. Louis, Missouri. The Urban League there launched a boycott against a white chain store whose trade was almost exclusively black but employed very few Negroes. This movement spread to Chicago, Cleveland, New York, Pittsburgh, and other major cities. New York became the center of an intensive, sometimes bitter, campaign. The Citizens League for Fair Play launched a drive in 1933 to persuade white merchants to employ black sales clerks. They adopted as their motto: "Don't Buy Where You Can't Work." The campaign led to the employment of hundreds of blacks in Harlem stores and with public utility companies.

————. Lynchings were reported decreasing in the United States; ten were recorded for the year.

————. The New York City Board of Education issued a directive that the word Negro should be spelled with a capital "N."

1930

March 31. President Hoover appointed Judge John J. Parker of North Carolina, a known racist, to the Supreme Court. The NAACP launched a successful campaign against confirmation.

June 7. Respecting Negro demands, the *New York Times* announced that the "n" in the word "Negro" would be henceforth capitalized in its pages.

June 22. Mary McLeod Bethune, a Florida Afro-American educator, feminist leader, and civil rights spokeswoman, was named one of America's fifty leading women by the historian Ida Tarbell. Mrs. Bethune was born in Maysville, South Carolina in 1875. She studied at Scotia Seminary in North Carolina and at the Moody Bible Institute in Chicago. In 1904, she founded the Bethune-Cookman College at Daytona Beach, Florida. A recipient of the Medal of Merit from the Republic of Haiti and the NAACP's Spingarn Award, Mrs. Bethune was president of the National Council of Negro Women and the Association for the Study of Negro Life and History. She was a principal advisor as well as a friend to President and Mrs. Franklin D. Roosevelt (See Below).

1931

April 6. Nine black youths accused of raping two white women of dubious reputation on a freight train went on trial for their lives in Scottsboro, Alabama. The case became a *cause célèbre,* with Afro-American organizations, liberal whites, and the Communist Party all vying to defend "the Scottsboro boys." The defendants were hastily convicted, but by 1950 all were free — by parole, appeal, or escape.

August 4. Daniel Hale Williams, pioneer heart surgeon and founder of Provident Hospital, a largely black institution, died in Chicago. Williams had been born in Pennsylvania to a black mother and a white father. He received a medical education through the generosity of an ex-Surgeon on General U. S. Grant's staff at the Chicago Medical College. In 1913, Williams became the first black member of the American College of Surgeons. After withdrawing from Provident Hospital because of internal bickerings, he became the only black doctor on the staff of Chicago's St. Luke Hospital. His withdrawal from Provident Hospital and his marriage to a white woman subjected him to bitter attacks from fellow blacks in the latter years of his life. Prior to his death, he was seen as a bitter, frustrated man.

1932

November _____. Franklin D. Roosevelt was elected President of the United States, promising a "New Deal" to all in the depression-ridden nation.

CHAPTER

VI

A New Deal—
A New Life?

1933-1940

1933

March 15. The NAACP opened its attack on segregation and discrimination in the schools. On behalf of Thomas Hocutt, the NAACP sued the University of North Carolina. A black educator responsible for certifying the academic record of the applicant refused to do so, and the case was lost.

1934

November 7. Arthur L. Mitchell, a Democrat, defeated Republican Congressman Oscar de Priest of Chicago, becoming the pioneer black member of his party in Congress. Mitchell, like his predecessor, was born in Alabama, the son of ex-slaves. He received his education at Tuskegee Institute, where he was Booker T. Washington's office boy, and at Talladega College in Alabama. He taught school in rural Alabama, and then he was an assistant law clerk in Washington. When he moved to Chicago, he became involved in Republican ward politics, but joined the Democrats with the shifting black party preference in the Depression years. In Congress, he professed to be a "moderate," thus drawing the ire of the black press and the NAACP. He did, however, sponsor the long and costly suit that led to an end to Jim Crowism in Pullman railroad cars. Mitchell served four terms in the Congress (See Also Below).

———. Elijah Muhammad succeeded W. D. Fard as leader of the Black Muslim movement in the United States. Muhammad was born Elijah Poole in Sandersville, Georgia in 1897. His father was a Baptist preacher, sawmill worker and tenant farmer. Muhammad was a deeply religious and race conscious youth. While Muhammad was employed as a laborer in Georgia in 1923, a white employer cursed him and he decided to move north. While on relief in Detroit during the Depression, he came under the influence of W. D. Fard or Wallace Fard Muhammad, a mysterious black silk peddler, who had been teaching blacks that they were members of a superior race, descendants of Muslims of Afro-Asia. He claimed to be a messenger from Allah to reclaim his lost people, to save them from the inferior race of white devils who had made their lives so miserable. Christianity, he said, was a false religion used by whites to keep blacks in subjection. Elijah Poole soon became Fard's closest associate and when Fard mysteriously disappeared in 1934, Poole or Elijah Muhammad took control of the group as "The Messenger of Allah to the Lost-Found Nation of Islam in the Wilderness of North America." Muhammad and his followers refused to bear arms for the United States during World War II. Muhammad was convicted of encouraging resistance to the draft and served three and a half years on a five year sentence in a federal prison before his release in 1946. Meanwhile Muslim membership dropped from a high of about 8,000 under Fard to 1,000 (See Also Below).

1935

June 25. Afro-Americans received an emotional boost when the fighter Joe Louis defeated Primo Carnera, a white man, at Yankee Stadium in New York. Louis then began his great boxing career in earnest. Louis (actually Joe Louis Barrow) was born in Lafayette, Alabama in 1914. Shortly thereafter his family moved to Detroit where Louis attended, for a short time, the Duffield Grammar School. After leaving school, he worked at an automobile plant and, in his leisure time, boxed. Louis became the heavyweight champion of the world in 1937 and held the title until 1949, interrupting his career only to serve in World War II. A series of unsuccessful marriages and business ventures left Louis almost penniless after his retirement from the ring (See Also Below).

1936

July 3. John Hope, now President of the Atlanta University Center (A loose combination of Morehouse College, an undergraduate school for men, Spelman College, an undergraduate school for women, and Atlanta University, a co-educational graduate school which was organized in 1929. In later years three other black colleges in Atlanta — Clark, Morris Brown and a theological seminary, all co-educational, joined the complex making it the largest educational center for Negroes in the world.) was honored in New York by the NAACP as an educational and civil rights leader.

August 9. Afro-Americans reacted warmly to the news that Jesse Owens, a black track star, had won four gold medals at the Berlin Olympics. Owens' victories embarrassed Adolph Hitler who championed the theory of Nordic racial superiority. Owens was born in Ohio in 1913. He began running at the Fairmont Junior High School in Cleveland and continued through Ohio State University. He was a student at Ohio State when he won the 100-meter dash, the 200-meter dash, the broad jump, and anchored the victorious 400-meter relay at the 1936 Olympics. The Associated Press has designated him "the outstanding track athlete of the first 50 years of the 20th century."

December 8. The case of *Gibbs vs Board of Education* of Montgomery County, Maryland was filed by the NAACP. The decision set the precedent for equalizing the salaries of black and white school teachers.

———. President Roosevelt, continuing to organize his unofficial "Black Cabinet", appointed Mary McLeod Bethune director of the Division of Negro Affairs of the National Youth Administration.

1937

March 26. A black lawyer William H. Hastie was confirmed as the first Afro-American federal judge. He served for two years on the District Court of the Virgin Islands. Hastie entered governmental service as an Assistant Solicitor in the Department of the Interior in the early part of the New Deal. His judicial appointment was supported by the NAACP and influential whites at the Harvard Law School. His nomination was approved over the vigorous opposition of Southern senators who labeled him a "leftist," primarily because of his support of civil rights activities. After his service in the Virgin Islands, he returned to Howard University Law School as Dean, but was soon appointed to the "Black Cabinet" as a civilian aide to the Secretary of War by President Roosevelt. In 1941 Hastie resigned in protest against the failure of the War Department to move against segregation in the armed services.

June 22. Afro-Americans rejoiced as Joe Louis defeated James J. Braddock for the heavyweight championship of the world.

July 2. Walter F. White, an Atlanta-born writer and civil rights leader, was honored by the NAACP in New York for his work as executive secretary, his investigations of lynchings, and his lobbying for a federal anti-lynching law. (In the latter instance he continued the notable work of his predecessor James Weldon Johnson who actually persuaded Representative L. C. Dyer of Missouri to introduce an anti-lynching bill in the House in 1921. The bill passed the House but was killed by a Southern filibuster in the Senate.) White was successful in getting anti-lynching measures introduced in 1935 and 1940, but they died in the Senate. White, though blond of hair and with blue eyes, cast his lot with the black race after the 1906 Atlanta race riot. His pale complexion enabled him to investigate atrocities against blacks in the South and later expose the perpetrators.

————. Isaac Lane, Bishop and patriarch of the Colored Methodist Episcopal Church, and founder of Lane College in Tennessee, died. Lane was born a slave on a Tennessee plantation in 1834. While a slave, he was licensed to preach, but, even after emancipation, had to supplement his income by raising cotton and selling firewood. He founded Lane College in 1882.

1938

December 12. In the case of *Missouri ex rel Gaines*, supported by the NAACP, the Supreme Court declared that states must provide equal, even if separate, educational facilities for blacks within their boundaries. The plantiff, Lloyd Gaines, mysteriously disappeared following the decision.

1939

March _____. Marian Anderson, whose voice Toscanini described as appearing once in a century, was refused permission to sing in Constitution Hall in Washington by the Daughters of the American Revolution. Miss Anderson, a Philadelphia black contralto, had just completed a successful European tour. Mrs. Eleanor Roosevelt, the first lady, resigned from the D. A. R. in protest. The Secretary of the Interior then provided the Lincoln Memorial for the Anderson concert. It drew 75,000 people on Easter Sunday, 1939. Miss Anderson was awarded the Spingarn Medal that year.

October 11. The NAACP Legal Defense and Educational Fund, pledging itself to an all-out war on discrimination, was organized. Charles H. Houston, a brilliant Amherst and Harvard-trained black lawyer, spearheaded the effort to consolidate some of the nation's best legal talents in the fight against bias sanctioned by law.

1940

February _____. The deeply-moving novel reciting the effects of racial oppression on black Americans, *Native Son* was published by Richard Wright, and became a best-seller.

April _____. The Virginia Legislature adopted James A. Bland's, a black man, "Carry Me Back to Ole Virginny" as the state song.

June 10. Marcus Garvey died in London. He was never able to revive his UNIA movement.

October 16. Benjamin O. Davis, Sr., was appointed Brigadier General in the United States Army, becoming the highest ranking black officer in the armed services. Davis was born in Washington, D.C. in 1877 and studied at Howard University. He entered the Army, as a first lieutenant, in 1898 and served with the 8th Infantry during the Spanish-American War. Prior to the Second World War, Davis saw service in the Philippines, in Liberia, and in Wyoming. He also taught military science at Wilberforce (Ohio) University and Tuskegee Institute. In World War II, he served in the European Theater of Operations as an advisor on problems of black servicemen. He helped to implement the desegregation of armed forces facilities in Europe. At the time of his retirement in 1948, Davis was an assistant to the inspector general in Washington, D.C. His awards and decorations include the Distinguished Service Medal, the Bronze Star, the Croix de Guerre with Palm, and an honorary doctorate from Atlanta University. Davis' son, Benjamin, Jr., also had a distinguished military career (See Below).

1932-1940

————. Faced with agricultural distress and racial oppression in the South, and seeking war-related jobs in the North, a new wave of black migration began into the major industrial centers.

————. During the New Deal period the black population in the United States benefited from the amelioration of the suffering of the total population, but still faced discrimination on account of race. For instance, (1) the New Deal housing program aided blacks in their efforts to retain and upgrade old homes, to acquire new ones, and to gain employment in constructing housing projects. In many communities, however, banks would not lend money to blacks in order that they might build homes, even though such loans were to be guaranteed by the Federal Housing Authority. The most successful federal housing program for Negroes was the construction of low-cost housing projects. Local authorities were able to build these apartments with subsidies from the U. S. Public Housing Authority. (2) The National Industrial Recovery program, which sought to stimulate industry, required a minimum wage scale of twelve dollars per week, a forty hour work week, and prohibited child labor under the age of sixteen. Few blacks attended the NIRA hearings. Cost-of-living differentials discriminated against the employment categories in which most black workers were to be found. When wages were raised, in compliance with NIRA requirements, employers often dismissed black workers and paid the higher wages to whites. (3) In the crop reduction program of the Agricultural Adjustment Administration farmers received cash benefits for plowing under their crops and for killing livestock. The farmers' cash benefits rose to billions of dollars, but many of the grants intended for black farmers were misappropriated. Some landlords took advantage of the illiterate black agriculturists and kept money which belonged to the blacks. (4) The National Youth Administration and the Civilian Conservation Corps provided relief for America's youth. Aubrey Williams, the white Mississippian who headed the NYA, sought to prevent bias against blacks. Mrs. Mary McCleod Bethune was named head of the Negro division of the NYA (See Above). Young blacks were able to continue their education and make some money through the student-work programs. Illiteracy among blacks was reduced and delinquency lowered. (5) Under the Social Security program assistance was granted to the elderly and to certain categories of unemployed. Since agricultural and domestic laborers were among the excluded categories, large numbers of blacks failed to qualify for social security benefits. There was also a tendency, especially in the South, to grant lower sums for the aged blacks than for the aged whites.

VII

War Again

1941-1945

1941

April 28. The Supreme Court ruled in a case brought by black Congressman Arthur Mitchell that separate railroad car facilities must be *substantially* equal.

June 18. George Washington Carver was awarded an honorary Doctor of Science degree by the University of Rochester.

June 18. President Roosevelt held an urgent meeting with A. Philip Randolph, head of the Brotherhood of Sleeping Car Porters, and other black spokesmen and urged them to call off a march against discrimination and segregation in the national defense program, principally in employment, scheduled for July 1. Randolph refused, and pledged that 100,000 Negroes would march.

June 25. President Roosevelt issued an Executive Order forbidding racial and religious discrimination in defense industries and government training programs. A. Philip Randolph then called off the march on Washington.

July 19. President Roosevelt established a Fair Employment Practices Committee to monitor discrimination against Negroes in defense industries. Blacks hailed the Committee and the preceding Executive Order 8802 of June 25 as revolutionary developments, perhaps the most significant executive action affecting them since the issuance of the Emancipation Proclamation. They were soon disappointed, however, when discrimination continued in spite of the Committee. The Committee became entangled in bureaucratic inefficiency and politics, and faced opposition in the South.

August 6. The first in a series of serious racial disturbances involving white soldiers and black soldiers, and black soldiers and white civilians, occurred aboard a bus in North Carolina.

December 7. The Japanese attacked Pearl Harbor. President Roosevelt prepared to ask for a declaration of war. Doris (Dorie) Miller, a 22-year-old black messman from Waco, Texas, aboard the USS Arizona, downed four Japanese planes with a machine gun, after having moved his captain from the bridge to a place of greater safety. The next year, Admiral Chester W. Nimitz presented the Navy Cross to Miller. In 1943, he was listed as missing in action, and presumed dead, in the Pacific.

————. The U. S. Army established a school for black pilots at Tuskegee, Alabama. Some blacks opposed the establishment of segregated Air Force facilities, but most others seemed to view the move as a forward step, since no training schools had hitherto existed. While the pilots began their work at Tuskegee, ground crews were prepared at Chanute Field in Illinois. By the end of the year the 99th Pursuit Squadron was ready for action. About 600 black pilots received their wings during World War II.

1942

June ————. A group of blacks and whites organized the Chicago Congress of Racial Equality (CORE). They committed themselves to direct, non-violent action. Their first major effort was a sit-in against discrimination at a Chicago restaurant. The national CORE was founded in June, 1943.

September 29. The *Booker T. Washington*, commanded by a black captain, Hugh Mulzac, was launched at Wilmington, Delaware.

November 3. William L. Dawson, for two decades the dean of black congressmen, was elected to the U. S. House of Representatives from Chicago. Dawson was the son of an Alabama barber. He received his education at Fisk University and at a Chicago law school. After service in the First World War, he opened a law practice in Chicago and became interested in politics. He began as a precinct worker and soon won favor with the Thompson Republican machine. He won five terms (1933-43) in the City Council as a Republican, before switching to the Democrats with the New Deal tide. Dawson became an important member of the Kelly and Daley Democratic machines during the Second World War. He was "ward boss" in five Chicago districts, precinct captain, committeeman, vice-chairman of the Cook County Democrats, and vice-chairman of the Democratic National Committee during his long political career. He won a reputation as a shrewd political strategist. Dawson did not run for reelection in 1970 and died a year later.

1943

January 5. George Washington Carver died at Tuskegee. A museum and a foundation were established there in his honor.

May 12-August 2. A series of serious race riots occurred across the nation; approximately forty persons were killed. U. S. troops were called out in Mobile and Detroit (where the clashes threatened defense production). Other incidents were in Beaumont, Texas, and in Harlem.

1944

April 3. The U. S. Supreme Court ruled, in *Smith versus Allwright*, that the white primary, which had excluded Negroes from voting in the South, was unconstitutional. The decision paved the way for blacks to increasingly participate in Southern politics for the first time since Reconstruction, although many states were to enact new extra-legal devices to frustrate Negro voting.

April 24. The United Negro College Fund (UNCF) was founded to coordinate the fund-raising efforts of the private all-black institutions of higher learning in the nation. Many were facing extinction due to inadequate finances.

August 1. Adam Clayton Powell, Jr., one of the most flamboyant and controversial politicians of the twentieth century, was elected Congressman from Harlem. Powell was the son of a famous Harlem minister and political leader. After being expelled from City College of New York, Powell received his education at Colgate University. After graduation, he became a minister and a publisher, assuming the role of a vociferous militant. He led Harlem ministers in a jobs-for-Negroes campaign in the 1930's. He began his political career in 1941 as the first black member of the New York City Council. Powell, the first black member of the House from the East, chaired the powerful Education and Labor Committee from 1960 to 1967. He became famous for his Powell Amendments which aimed to deny federal funds for the construction of segregated schools. In 1967 he ran afoul of congressional ethics and was temporarily denied his seat in the House. Re-elected by Harlem in 1968, despite the Congress's censure, he was defeated in 1970 by another black, Charles Rangel.

August 20. The SS *Frederick Douglass*, first ship named in honor of a black man, was lost in European waters.

December 13. Black women were permitted to enter the Women's Naval Corp (WAVES).

1945

March 12. New York established the first state Fair Employment Practices Commission to guard against discrimination in jobs.

June _____. The United Nations Charter was approved in San Francisco. Several blacks, including Mary McLeod Bethune, W. E. B. DuBois, Walter White, Ralph Bunche and Mordecai Johnson, attended the San Francisco conference. Johnson, a minister and educator, was about to complete twenty years as the first black head of Howard University. He is credited with establishing the school's prestigious position in the nation.

September 2.   The Japanese surrendered and the Second World War ended. More than one million blacks served in the conflict, again distinguishing themselves for valor, and paying the supreme price for devotion to duty.

September 18.   A huge anti-integration protest took place in the schools of Gary, Indiana. One thousand white students walked out of classes. This massive walk-out, unparalleled at the time, would be a precedent for the integration troubles of the next two to three decades.

CHAPTER

VIII

The Attack Against Segregation

1945-1954

1946

May 1. Former federal judge William H. Hastie was confirmed as governor of the Virgin Islands. Hastie became the only Afro-American to govern a U. S. state or territory since Reconstruction.

May 1. Emma Clarissa Clement, a black woman and mother of Atlanta University President Rufus E. Clement, was named "American Mother of the Year" by the Golden Rule Foundation. She was the first Afro-American woman to receive the honor.

June 3. The Supreme Court in *Morgan* vs *Virginia* prohibited segregation in interstate bus travel. The case originated when Irene Morgan, a black woman, was arrested and fined ten dollars for refusing to move to the back of a bus running from Gloucester County, Virginia to Baltimore. She appealed her conviction. In practice the case had little immediate effect; buses in Southern states continued segregation practices.

June 10. Jack Johnson, the first great Afro-American boxing hero, died in Raleigh, North Carolina. Johnson, a pitch-black stevedore from Galveston, Texas, gained pugilistic fame when in 1908 he became the first nationally prominent black champion.

August 10-September 29. Serious racial disturbances occurred at Athens, Alabama, and Philadelphia, Pennsylvania; nearly 100 blacks were injured.

December 5. President Truman appointed a national Committee on Civil Rights to investigate racial injustices and make recommendations.

1947

April 9. The Congress of Racial Equality (CORE) sent "freedom riders" into the South to test the Supreme Court's June 3, 1946 ban against segregation in interstate bus travel (See Above and Below). CORE, which was organized in 1942, had pioneered in the sit-in tactic at segregated restaurants (See Above), but gained national attention with the "Freedom Rider" demonstrations. CORE is best known for the wave of "freedom rides" which began in May, 1961. These latter demonstrations eventually led to a firm anti-discrimination policy in interstate transportation (See Below).

April 10. Jackie Robinson, a Georgia-born athlete, joined the then Brooklyn Dodgers. Robinson, the first Negro baseball player in the major leagues, became an outstanding player and a hero in the eyes of many Afro-Americans. He was the first black player to enter the Baseball Hall of Fame.

June 27. Percy Julian, a distinguished black research chemist who made important breakthroughs in the area of human reproduction, was honored in New York by the NAACP. Julian, the son of a Montgomery, Alabama railway clerk, graduated Phi Beta Kappa at DePauw University and did advanced work at Harvard and the University of Vienna. He taught at Howard and DePauw universities before becoming an industrial chemist in Chicago. He later established his own Julian Laboratories and earned a reputation for soya products, hormones and pharmaceuticals.

September 1. Charles Spurgeon Johnson began his administration as president of Fisk University. He was the first black man to head the Nashville institution. Johnson was born in Bristol, Virginia, in 1893. He was educated at Virginia Union University and the University of Chicago. He directed the division of research for the Chicago Urban League from 1917 to 1919; was an investigator of Negro migration for the Carnegie Foundation in 1918; and a member of the Chicago Committee on Race Relations, 1923-29. When he took over the presidency of Fisk, after having directed its social science department, he had already become an eminent sociologist. His major works include *Shadow of the Plantation*, 1934; *Collapse of Cotton Tenancy*, 1934; *The Negro College Graduate*, 1938; and *Growing Up in the Black Belt*, 1941. Johnson died in 1956.

October 29. The President's Committee on Civil Rights formally condemned racial injustice in the United States in its celebrated report called "To Secure These Rights." The bi-racial group also called for a positive program to eliminate segregation from American life.

1948

January 12. The U. S. Supreme Court ruled, in *Sipuel vs. University of Oklahoma*, that a state must provide legal education for blacks at the same time it is offered to whites. The case stemmed from the application which Ada Sipuel filed in 1946 to attend the University of Oklahoma Law School. Miss Sipuel sought relief in state and then federal courts after the University denied her admission. Despite the Supreme Court's decision, Miss Sipuel did not enter the University of Oklahoma immediately. There were further legal proceedings, but meantime the University of Oklahoma failed to establish a law school for blacks. Finally, Miss Sipuel (now Mrs. Ada Fisher) did enter the University of Oklahoma and became one of its first black law graduates.

March 31. Negro labor leader A. Philip Randolph told a committee of the United States Senate that he would counsel black youths to refuse military induction unless segregation and discrimination were prohibited in the selective service system. In June Randolph formed the League for Non-Violent Civil Disobedience Against Military Segregation.

May 3. The U. S. Supreme Court decided, in *Shelley vs Kraemer*, that the courts could not enforce restrictive housing covenants. This case was brought to the Court by J. D. Shelley and his wife Ethel who bought a home in St. Louis, Missouri in August, 1945. It was located in a tract whose owner in 1911 had signed an agreement under which it was restricted against use and occupancy by "people of the Negro or Mongolian Race." The agreement provided that failure to comply with this restriction should result in the owner's loss of title to the property. Other owners in the tract led by Mr. and Mrs. Louis Kraemer sued the Shelleys and won an order from the Missouri Supreme Court which forced the blacks out of their home and forfeited their title because of their violation of the agreement. In 1947, the Shelleys appealed to the United States Supreme Court.

June 9. A modern breakthrough in Negro office-holding occurred in the South when Oliver W. Hill was elected to the City Council in Richmond, Virginia.

July 14. Some Southern delegates walked out of the National Democratic Convention after a strong civil rights plank was adopted. South Carolinians and Mississippians were in the vanguard of the movement which formed the "Dixiecrat" party.

July 26. President Truman issued an Executive Order which called for equality of treatment and opportunity for all Americans in the armed forces. This order was to pave the way for the gradual elimination of discrimination in the armed services.

September 13. Professor Ralph J. Bunche, a noted black political scientist, was confirmed by the United Nations Security Council as temporary UN mediator in Palestine. Bunche was born in a Detroit ghetto and reared by relatives, after his parents' death, in Los Angeles. He was educated at the University of California and at

Harvard. He began his career as a teacher at Howard University. He identified early with civil rights programs and became a staunch supporter of the NAACP. After receiving the Nobel Peace Prize (See Below), he was elected president of the American Political Science Association and a member of the Board of Overseers at Harvard University.

October 1. The Supreme Court of California ruled that the state law prohibiting interracial marriages was unconstitutional. Two decades later, the United States Supreme Court sanctioned interracial marriage in all the states.

1949

October 3. The pioneer black-owned radio station, WERD, began operations in Atlanta.

October 15. William H. Hastie, former District Court judge and governor in the Virgin Islands, was appointed a Judge of the Third U. S. Circuit Court of Appeals.

1950

April 1. Charles R. Drew, pioneer Afro-American hematologist, often called the father of the "Blood Bank," died in Burlington, North Carolina. Drew was born in Washington, D.C. in 1904. A football and track star at Amherst College, he studied medicine at McGill University in Canada. He began his research into the properties of blood plasma while holding a General Education Board Fellowship at the Columbia University Medical School. During World War II, after discovering the method of preserving blood plasma in banks for emergencies, he organized a blood-collection system for the British and U.S. governments. He served as a member of the faculty of the Howard University Medical School and was chief surgeon and chief of staff at Howard's Freedman's Hospital at the time of his death in 1950. Previously, he had been awarded the NAACP's Spingarn Medal for outstanding contributions to human welfare.

April 3. Carter G. Woodson, pioneer black historian and one of the founders of the Association for the Study of Negro Life and History, died in Washington, D. C.

May 1. Gwendolyn Brooks was awarded the Pulitzer Prize for poetry in Chicago. She is the only Afro-American to have received the honor. Ms. Brooks was born in Topeka, Kansas in 1917, but soon moved to Chicago, where she attended Wilson Junior College. Some of her earliest works appeared in the Chicago *Defender*. Later works have appeared in periodicals such as *Harpers, Common Ground, Mademoiselle, Poetry*, and the *Yale Review*. Her first volume of poetry, *A Street in Bronzeville* won the Merit Award from *Mademoiselle*. *Annie Allen*, which was her second volume, captured the Pulitzer Prize.

June 5. The U. S. Supreme Court ruled, in *Sweatt vs Painter*, that equality in education involved more than identical physical facilities. Heman Sweatt of Houston was ordered admitted to the Law School of the University of Texas, the largest university in the South. Sweatt never attended.

June 5. The Supreme Court decided, in *McLaurin vs Oklahoma*, that once a black student is admitted to a previously all-white school no distinctions can be made on the basis of race. McLaurin had been segregated within the University of Oklahoma.

June 27. The United States intervened in the Korean conflict. Once again thousands of blacks were among those fighting in the war.

September 22. Ralph J. Bunche was awarded the Nobel Peace Prize for mediating the Palestinean dispute.

1951

April 24. The University of North Carolina joined a growing list of major Southern and Border state universities in admitting black students.

May 10. Blacks continued to make political advances in the South with the election of Z. Alexander Looby, an attorney, to the city council in Nashville, Tennessee.

May 24. The Municipal Appeals Court in Washington outlawed segregation in D. C. restaurants. Mary Church Terrell, the black feminist leader, had been in the vanguard of the local anti-segregation movement.

June 21. Pfc. William H. Thompson of Brooklyn, New York received the Congressional Medal of Honor posthumously for heroism in Korea, the first such award to an Afro-American since the Spanish-American War. Private Thompson died at his machine gun after having refused to withdraw in the face of overwhelming Communist forces.

July 12. Governor Adlai Stevenson of Illinois ordered the National Guard to put down a riot in Cicero, Illinois, as more than 3,000 whites protested the attempt of a black family to occupy a home in an all-white neighborhood. The riot was called by some the worst racial disturbance in the North since 1919.

October 1. The last all-Negro army unit, the 24th Infantry, was de-activated by Congress.

December 25. A new era of racist assassinations began with the bomb-death of Harry T. Moore, a Florida NAACP leader in Mims, Florida.

———. Ralph J. Bunche, educator, diplomat, and Nobel Prize winner, was appointed Undersecretary of the United Nations, the highest ranking American in the UN Secretariat.

———. The NAACP argued cases in Kansas and South Carolina against the discriminatory effects of public school segregation.

1952

January 12. The University of Tennessee became the latest major Southern university to admit black students.

December 7. The Southern Regional Council, an interracial civil rights reporting agency, announced that racist bombings were increasing in the nation, about forty had been reported since January, 1951.

December 30. Tuskegee Institute reported that no lynchings occurred during 1952, the first such year in the 71 years the Institute had kept such tabulations.

1953

April 5. Fisk University received a chapter of Phi Beta Kappa, the prestigious scholastic honor society. In later years, only two other all-black schools, Howard and Morehouse, were awarded chapters.

June 8. The U. S. Supreme Court affirmed the opinions of lower courts that D. C. restaurants could not refuse to serve blacks. In the case of *District of Columbia vs John R. Thompson Co., Inc.* the Court said that well-behaved blacks must be served. It upheld an 1873 law that made it a criminal act for proprietors of public eating places to refuse to serve any person solely because of race or color.

June 19. Negroes protesting discriminatory treatment began a bus boycott in Baton Rouge, Louisiana.

August 4. Another serious riot erupted in Illinois in protest of integrated housing. One thousand law enforcement officers were called into the Trumbull Park apartments at Chicago.

December 2. The latest instance of black progress in Southern politics came with the election of Rufus E. Clement, president of Atlanta University, to the Atlanta Board of Education.

December 31. Hulan Jack, a native West Indian, was inaugurated as president of the Borough of Manhattan, the highest municipal executive post to be held by an Afro-American to that time.

1954

March 4. President Eisenhower named J. Ernest Wilkins, Jr. of Chicago, Assistant Secretary of Labor. Wilkins, a member of Phi Beta Kappa who took a Ph. D. at Chicago at twenty, had the distinction of being the top-ranking black in the executive branch of the federal government.

CHAPTER

IX

The Era of Civil Rights

1954-1964

1954

May 17. The U. S. Supreme Court, in *Brown vs Board of Education* of Topeka, Kansas, ruled unanimously that racial segregation in public schools was unconstitutional. The historic decision overruled the findings in *Plessy vs Ferguson* (1896) and declared that separate educational facilities were inherently unequal. The NAACP lawyers, headed by chief counsel Thurgood Marshall, won their greatest in a series of recent judicial triumphs.

July 24. Mary Church Terrell, a long-time leader of Negro clubwomen and civil rights activist, died in Washington, D. C.

September 7-8. Massive school desegregation began in the public schools of Washington, D. C. and Baltimore, Maryland. This was the first widespread school desegregation since the Supreme Court decision of May 17.

October 27. Benjamin O. Davis, Jr., commander of the 15th Air Force bombers in their important attacks on Rumanian oil fields during World War II, became the first Negro general in the U.S. Air

Force. Davis, son of the army's General B. O. Davis, Sr., was born in Washington, D.C. in 1912. He was educated at Western Reserve University, the University of Chicago, and West Point, graduating from the latter institution in 1936—only the fourth black man to do so. He received his wings from the Tuskegee Advanced Flying School in 1942 and became commander of the 99th Fighter Squadron at the Army Air Field at Tuskegee. He was ordered to North Africa in 1943. During and since the World War, he has seen service in Italy, Korea, Japan, Formosa, Germany, and several U.S. mainland installations. He was commander of the 51st Fighter-Interceptor Wing during the Korean conflict. Davis' awards and decorations include the Distinguished Service Medal, the Silver Star, the Legion of Merit with two oak leaf clusters, and the Distinguished Flying Cross.

October 30. Desegregation of the U. S. Armed Forces was completed as the Defense Department announced the final abolition of all-Negro units.

November 2. Charles C. Diggs, Jr., at 33, was elected to the U. S. House of Representatives from Michigan. Diggs, the first black congressman from the state, joined Congressman William Dawson of Chicago, re-elected in 1954 for a seventh term, and Congressman Adam Clayton Powell, Jr. of Harlem, re-elected in 1954 for a sixth term. It marked the first time in the 20th century that as many as three blacks served in Congress. All were Democrats.

1955

January 7. Negro contralto Marian Anderson made her debut as Ulrica in Verdi's *Masked Ball* at the Metropolitan Opera House. She was the pioneer black singer in the company's history.

March 21. Walter F. White, the second Afro-American to serve as executive secretary of the NAACP and leader of the organization during most of its judicial triumphs, died in New York.

April 11. Roy Wilkins of St. Louis, Missouri became the third executive secretary of the NAACP. Wilkins, a newspaperman, had served as editor of the NAACP's magazine, the *Crisis*, and as assistant executive secretary of the organization. Wilkins, a native of St. Louis, was born in 1901. He studied at the University of Minnesota and was editor of the *University Daily* there. Racial violence in Duluth, Minnesota during his student days influenced his decision to work actively against discrimination. Further experiences in Kansas City, where he was managing editor of the Kansas City *Call*, further inspired him to seek a career fighting for equal justice. He joined the staff of the NAACP in 1931. Within the NAACP, he played a leading role, representing the interests of blacks in the Philadelphia transit strike in 1943; presided over the NAACP's efforts to implement the Brown school desegregation decision of 1954; and to meet challenges after 1960 from more "militant" black organizations, who claimed the NAACP's legalistic approach to combat racial bias was outdated. An articulate lecturer and prolific writer, Wilkins, by 1975, had become one of the elder statesmen of the Civil Rights movement.

May 18. Mary McLeod Bethune, noted black female educator and political leader, died at Daytona Beach, Florida. She was one of the founders of the Bethune-Cookman College there.

May 31. The U. S. Supreme Court decreed that its May 17, 1954 school desegregation decision should be implemented "with all deliberate speed." The vagueness of the phrase permitted school segregation to continue in the South for several more decades.

August 28. Lynchings were renewed in the South with the brutal slaying of a fourteen year old Chicago youth, Emmett Till, at Money, Mississippi. Till was alleged to have made indecent advances toward a white woman.

November 7. The Supreme Court prohibited segregation in recreational facilities in a Baltimore, Maryland case.

November 25. The Interstate Commerce Commission (ICC) prohibited segregation in public vehicles operating in interstate travel. The order also extended to waiting rooms.

December 1. Rosa Parks, a black seamstress in Montgomery, Alabama, refused to surrender her seat when ordered by a local bus driver. Her arrest, for violating jim crow ordinances, led to a city-wide bus boycott by blacks which began on December 5. Despite terroristic attacks, including the bombing of the homes of boycott leaders, and legal harassment, massive arrests and civil suits, the boycott continued until December 13, 1956, when the U. S. Supreme Court ruled that segregation on public busses in Montgomery was illegal. Another significant result of the boycott movement was the emergence of Martin Luther King, Jr. as a national leader.

December 5. Two black labor leaders, A. Philip Randolph and Willard S. Townsend were elected vice-presidents of the AFL-CIO.

1956

January 30. The home of Dr. Martin Luther King, Jr. was bombed in Montgomery, Alabama.

February 3. The desegregation of major Southern universities continued with the admission of a black coed, Authurine Lucy, under court order, to the University of Alabama. Miss Lucy was suspended after a February 7 anti-Negro riot at the school, and expelled on February 29 for making "false" and "outrageous" statements about the university officials.

April 11. Racial feelings in the South continued to be explosive as witnessed by an attack on the popular Negro singer Nat "King" Cole in Birmingham.

June 30. Mordecai Johnson retired as president of Howard University. Johnson was born in Paris, Tennessee in 1890. He was educated at Morehouse College, The University of Chicago, the Rochester Theological Seminary, and Harvard University. Upon his receipt of a Master of Sacred Theology degree from Harvard in 1923, he attracted national attention for a speech entitled "The Faith of the American Negro." After teaching at Morehouse and

Howard, he was named the first black head of the latter institution in 1926. When Johnson took over the presidency, Howard, often called "the capstone of Negro education," consisted of a cluster of unaccredited departments. In 1928 Johnson was successful in getting a Congressional act allocating annual appropriations for the support and development of Howard University. At Johnson's retirement, Howard had ten schools and colleges; was a fully accredited institution; had an enrollment of more than 6,000 students, a few of them whites; and its School of Medicine was producing about half of the black doctors in the United States. Johnson was succeeded by James M. Nabrit, Jr. a law professor and civil rights attorney (See Also Above).

August 30-September 17. Anti-Negro protests and violence accompanied efforts to desegregate schools in Mansfield, Texas, Clinton, Tennessee, Sturgis and Clay, Kentucky.

November 13. The Supreme Court upheld the decision of a lower court outlawing segregation on busses in Montgomery, Alabama.

December 20-21. The Montgomery bus boycott ended. Public busses in Montgomery were desegregated.

December 25-26. The home of a black minister and civil rights activist F. L. Shuttlesworth was bombed in Birmingham, Alabama. The city's Negroes responded with a massive defiance of bus segregation regulations, at least two score were jailed.

December 27. Segregation was outlawed on busses in Tallahassee, Florida. Blacks had boycotted the vehicles for more than six months.

1957

February 14. The Southern Christian Leadership Conference (SCLC) was organized at New Orleans. Atlanta was chosen as the site of the national headquarters. Martin Luther King, Jr. was elected president.

May 17. More than 15,000 Americans, mostly black, gathered at the Lincoln Monument in Washington to demonstrate support for a voting rights act. Martin Luther King, Jr. led the speakers crying: "Give us the ballot!" It was the first large-scale Negro protest in Washington since the Second World War.

June _____. Blacks in Tuskegee, Alabama began an all-out boycott of white merchants protesting an act of the state legislature which crushed their incipient political power by gerrymandering them out of the city. Charles G. Gomillion, a Tuskegee Institute sociologist, took the lead of the movement through his Tuskegee Civic Association. The U. S. Supreme Court later ruled, in *Gomillion vs Lightfoot* (1960), the gerrymander illegal, and blacks subsequently took political control of the town and Macon County.

August 29. The Congress passed the Voting Rights Act of 1957, the first major civil rights legislation since 1875.

September 9. Violence aimed at preventing school desegregation continued in the South. A Nashville school was bombed and the Reverend F. L. Shuttlesworth was attacked in Birmingham while trying to enroll his children in school.

September 24. After unsuccessfully trying to persuade Governor Orval Faubus of Arkansas to give up his efforts to block desegregation of a Little Rock school, President Eisenhower ordered federal troops into the city to halt interference with court orders. It was the most serious state-federal clash in modern times. Faubus, and a mob of whites, gave way before the military power permitting nine black children to attend school on September 25. The regular army troops left Little Rock on November 27. The National Guard remained until May, 1958.

December 5. New York City took the lead in local efforts against discrimination in housing by passing the Fair Housing Practice ordinance.

1958

June 30. The state of Alabama's attempt to cripple the NAACP by imposing a $100,000 contempt fine against it was stymied by the U. S. Supreme Court. In *NAACP vs Alabama* the Court declared that it would not tolerate denial of constitutional rights through evasive application of obscure procedural rules. The fine had been imposed because of the NAACP's failure to produce its membership lists to an Alabama judge. Through various legal maneuvers the NAACP was kept out of Alabama until a new order was received from the Supreme Court in 1964.

August 19. Members of the NAACP Youth Council began a new series of sit-ins at segregated restaurants. Oklahoma City lunch counters were the current targets.

September 20. Martin Luther King, Jr., autographing copies of his story of the Montgomery bus boycott, *Stride Toward Freedom*, was stabbed by a crazed black woman in Harlem. King successfully recovered from the serious wound.

1959

March 11. "Raisin in the Sun", a play depicting a part of black life in the ghetto, by the Afro-American playwright Loraine Hansberry, became a Broadway hit. Lloyd Richards, the play's director, was the first such black to appear on Broadway in more than fifty years.

April 25. Another Mississippi lynching was recorded with the death of Mack Parker at Poplarville.

1960

February 1. A wave of sit-ins at segregated lunch counters, led principally by black college students, began at Greensboro, North

Carolina. Four students from North Carolina A and T College initiated the new movement. In less than two weeks the drive spread to fifteen cities in five Southern states, and within two years had engulfed the South. The sit-ins were met by physical violence and legal harassment, including massive jailings, but most restaurants eventually desegregated voluntarily, under court order, or by legislation. The success of the sit-in technique encouraged blacks to use the method of non-violent direct action in other areas where discrimination persisted. Martin Luther King, Jr, assumed leadership of the widened movement.

February 25. Black students from Alabama State University conducted a sit-in demonstration at the County Courthouse in Montgomery. This was the first protest of this type in the capital of the Old Confederacy. Sheriff Mac Sim Butler and his deputies kept close watch on the demonstrators in the Courthouse's lunchroom while groups of white men, some armed with baseball bats, patrolled outside. On February 27, a black woman was struck on the head and injured by a club-wielding white man. No arrests were made in either incident. Two days later, Alabama Governor John Patterson warned that there were not enough policemen in the country to prevent disturbances and offer protection if blacks continued "to provoke whites."

February 27. Black and white lunch counter sit-in demonstrators were attacked in Nashville, Tennessee. The violence occurred in two of five stores where students had staged non-violent lunch counter sit-ins. Police arrested about 100 persons, mostly black demonstrators. Seventy-six of those arrested declined to pay fines or bonds pending trial. Those who chose jail were mainly black. Their attorneys said their decision was based on their reluctance to support "the injustice and immoral practices that have been performed" in their arrest and conviction.

February 29. Martin Luther King, Jr. spoke to a crowd of more than 1,000 students in Montgomery, Alabama following three days of racial tensions occasioned by student sit-ins (See Above). King urged continued passive resistance to segregation. The students pledged to withdraw from their college, Alabama State University, en masse if any were expelled for previous as well as future sit-in activity. On March 1, the blacks marched to the old Confederate capitol building in Montgomery, where they prayed and sang the "Star Spangled Banner" during a non-violent demonstration against segregation. The next day, the State Board of Education expelled nine of the participating students from the Alabama State University.

On March 6, State, county, and local police stopped a march of nearly 1,000 blacks enroute to a protest meeting at the Alabama state capitol in Montgomery. There were scattered fist fights between blacks and a mob of taunting whites, but police prevented large scale violence. Two days later, Montgomery police broke up another protest demonstration on the campus of Alabama State University and arrested thirty-five students and at least one teacher. Thirty-three of the blacks were subsequently found guilty of disorderly conduct and fined $200 each.

March 4. Lunch counter sit-ins reached the Southwest as about 100 black students from Texas Southern University conducted non-violent protests in Houston. Three days later four masked white men, in apparent retaliation, kidnapped black Felton Turner, beat him, and carved the letters KKK on his chest and stomach.

March 16. President Dwight D. Eisenhower told a press conference that he was "deeply sympathetic" with the efforts of any group to enjoy Constitutionally guaranteed rights. The President did not endorse the lunch counter sit-in movement, which was then sweeping the South, but called for biracial conferences in "every city and every community of the South" to help settle racial problems.

April 15-17. The Student Non-violent Coordinating Committee (SNCC) was founded in North Carolina. The group became the nation-wide liaison for student sit-in activities.

April 19. The home of Z. Alexander Looby, a black Nashville city councilman and attorney for the NAACP, was demolished by a dynamite bomb. Looby and his family escaped injury. The bomb damaged several homes belonging to Looby's neighbors and blew out hundreds of windows at the black Meharry Medical College. Several medical students were injured by flying glass. Looby had been chief counsel for more than a hundred students arrested in Nashville sit-ins since demonstrations began in the college town in February, 1960 (See Also Above). More than 2,000 blacks marched on the Nashville City Hall on the same date, protesting the police's failure to halt the racial violence. A black minister, the Reverend C. T. Vivian, accused Nashville mayor Ben West of encouraging the violence by permitting the police to use their authority with "partiality." West denied the accusation claiming that he favored desegregation of lunch counters, but said that businessmen practicing segregation were acting within their rights.

May 6. President Eisenhower signed the Voting Rights Act of 1960. The law was designed to bolster the Act of 1957 which granted additional protection to blacks trying to obtain the suffrage. Under the new law federal courts would be authorized to appoint "voting referees" who would be empowered to register blacks in areas where racial discrimination against voters had been proven. Referees would be appointed only after (1) the Justice Department sued under the Civil Rights Act of 1957 to obtain an order requiring the registration of such persons unjustly disqualified by local registrars on racial grounds, (2) the Justice Department won the suits and then asked the judge to declare that a "pattern or practice" of discrimination had blocked the Negroes from voting. The referees could register all blacks who could establish their qualifications under state law. but who had been previously denied registration. The new law was invoked in the South for the first time on May 9.

July 31. Elijah Muhammad, leader of the Black Muslims, a religious-nationalist group, called for the establishment of an all-black state. Such a state, or group of states, later became a rallying cry for supporters of black nationalism.

September 8. New York Governor Nelson A. Rockefeller told the annual meeting of the National Urban League in New York that the lunch counter sit-ins were an "inspiring example" to the nation and said that the sit-in demonstrators personified the moral force and the "appeal to human conscience" which could solve civil rights problems.

October 19.   Martin Luther King, Jr., and some fifty other blacks, was arrested for sitting-in at an Atlanta department store restaurant. The arrest caused a Decatur, Georgia judge to revoke King's previous parole for conviction on a minor traffic violation. King was sentenced to four months in Georgia's maximum security prison. Robert F. Kennedy and John F. Kennedy, the latter then a presidential candidate, assisted King's family in obtaining his release. Some analysts feel the incident swung the Negro vote in the 1960 Presidential election to Kennedy and thus secured his victory.

November 10.   Andrew Hatcher was named associate press secretary by President-elect Kennedy. Hatcher was for a time the highest ranking black appointee in the executive branch of the federal government.

November 14.   Desegregation crept into the major industrial centers of the South with the admission of Negro children to schools in New Orleans. On November 10, U. S. District Judge J. Skelley Wright had prohibited implementation of Louisiana's anti-school-integration laws. On the same day the New Orleans school board approved plans to admit five black children to two previously all-white schools. On November 13 the state legislature took control of New Orleans schools, fired the school superintendent, and ordered all schools closed on November 14. At the same time Judge Wright issued a new order prohibiting interference by the state with the schools. Amid the jeering of angry white parents, four black children enrolled in the two schools on November 14. White protests, accompanied by a boycott, continued for much of the school year.

————.   Membership in the Black Muslim cult reportedly reached 100,000. In 1959, the movement reported thirty temples and about 12,000 members. (Because of the secrecy of the organization, membership can only be estimated.) The rapid rise in membership can be attributed to the work of dynamic ministers like Malcolm Little or Malcolm X (See Below) and publicity from the mass media.

1961

January 11. An anti-Negro riot resulted in the suspension of two recently admitted black students at the University of Georgia. The duo were reinstated under court order on January 16.

February 11. Robert Weaver, a black housing expert with a Harvard Ph.D., took over as Administrator of the Housing and Home Finance Agency, the highest federal post ever held by an Afro-American.

May 4. A contingent of white and black youths, sponsored by CORE, set out for a bus trip through the South to test desegregation practices. Despite court rulings and ICC decrees, many Southern states refused to sanction non-discriminatory transportation. The biracial group was subjected to physical violence, including savage beatings and arson, and legal harassment. In the fall, the ICC reaffirmed its orders prohibiting discrimination in transportation. Such discrimination gradually disappeared on vehicles themselves, but lingered in waiting-rooms and other facilities, especially in the rural South.

August 9. James B. Parsons was appointed by President Kennedy as Judge of the District Court of Northern Illinois, the first such position for an Afro-American in the continental United States. Parsons, a fifty year old Chicago attorney, was serving as a judge on the Cook County Court at the time of his appointment.

September 1. Four high schools were peacefully desegregated by ten black children in Atlanta, Georgia. The orderly desegregation in the Deep South's largest city won praise from President Kennedy, who hoped it would set a new precedent. Previously desegregation had been marked by violence.

September 23. Thurgood Marshall, of Baltimore, chief counsel for the NAACP, was appointed by President Kennedy as a Judge of the Second Circuit Court of Appeals (New York, Connecticut and Vermont.) Marshall was fifty-three and had been with the NAACP for more than twenty years.

December 12-16. Martin Luther King, Jr. and his forces launched an all-out attack against segregation and discrimination in Albany, Georgia. The effort was frustrated by mass arrests and political maneuverings. The Albany debacle taught civil rights leaders valuable lessons for future massive direct-action assaults on segregation.

1962

January 18-28. Student protests at Southern University in Louisiana, the largest all-black state college in the South, resulted in the closing of the institution, a precedent for handling future student disturbances. Southern students had protested the expulsion of sit-in demonstrators. These expulsions were used by administrators at publicly supported black colleges to meet the demands of state authorities to quell sit-in and related activities.

September 9. Two Negro churches were burned in Sasser, Georgia, in the southwest part of the state. Burnings and bombings of black churches, especially those used for civil rights meetings, became common during the decade.

September 30. Supreme Court Justice Hugo Black ordered the admission forthwith of a black student, James H. Meredith, to the University of Mississippi. The governor of Mississippi, Ross Barnett, tried unsuccessfully to block Merideth's admission, but a tragic riot occurred on the day that U. S. marshals escorted the black student on the campus. Federalized National guardsmen subsequently restored order on the riot-torn campus at Oxford. Meredith graduated in 1963.

November 7-8. Edward W. Brooke, an Afro-American lawyer from Boston, was elected Attorney-General for Massachusetts, the highest-ranking black official in New England. Leroy Johnson, a black Atlanta lawyer, was elected to the Georgia State Senate, the state's only black legislator since Reconstruction. Augustus Hawkins became the first black to represent California in Congress.

November 20. Racial discrimination in federally-financed housing was prohibited by President Kennedy. The order applied principally to housing projects and apartments. It would have little effect on homes which were not in commercially developed neighborhoods. Federal Housing Authority insured loans for home improvements were also excluded. The order was effective immediately. In the event of violations, the government would first seek to obtain voluntary compliance. Administrative or court action leading to cancellation of loans or contracts would be taken in the event voluntary compliance could not be obtained.

1963

April 3. Civil rights forces, led by Martin Luther King, Jr., launched a drive against bias in Birmingham, Alabama. Police, led by Commissioner Eugene "Bull" Connor used high powered water hoses and dogs against demonstrators. The brutality of the repression and the legal harassments, including massive arrests, aroused public opinion, especially in the North. President Kennedy hoped to use the new public awareness to garner support for his civil rights proposals presented to Congress on March 1. The Birmingham protests continued until May 10 when an agreement was signed calling for gradual desegregation of public accommodations. The desegregation agreement was followed by bombings at the homes and businesses of black leaders, which led to hours of Negro rioting.

June 11. Two black students were admitted to the University of Alabama after an unsuccessful attempt by Governor George C. Wallace to block their entrance. President Kennedy ordered federalized National Guardsmen to insure the Negroes' enrollment. In a television address that night Kennedy made an impassioned plea for an end to discrimination in the nation, through moral suasion and legislative action. Congress continued to take no action on the President's civil rights proposals.

June 12. Medgar W. Evers, NAACP field secretary in Mississippi, decorated in World War II, became the latest victim of assassination resulting from civil rights activity. Evers was guned down by a sniper in Jackson. His alleged assailant, a white segregationist, was acquitted by a hung jury.

June-August. Civil rights demonstrations, protests, and boycotts occurred in almost every major urban area in the country. Boston and Harlem, for instance, were the scenes of protests in June by blacks demanding an end to discrimination in the construction industry and *de facto* segregation in the schools. Limited martial law was declared in July at Cambridge, Maryland after black demonstrators and white segregationists clashed.

August 17. W. E. B. DuBois, one of the most brilliant Afro-American intellectuals and a founder of the NAACP, died in Accra, Ghana, disillusioned with American racial attitudes and the democratic-capitalist system.

August 28. The largest single protest demonstration in United States history occurred at the Lincoln Monument in Washington; 250,000 blacks and whites gathered to lobby for passage of sweeping civil rights measures by Congress. Martin Luther King, Jr. thrilled the crowd with his memorable "I have a dream" oration. President Kennedy received a delegation of civil rights leaders at the White House and promised to push ahead for anti-discrimination legislation.

September 15. Racial tensions were renewed in Birmingham when four small Negro girls died in the bombing of a church. No serious disturbances followed the incident and the culprits were never brought to justice.

October 22. A massive boycott, involving nearly a quarter of a million students, was staged in Chicago to protest *de facto* school segregation.

November 22. Black Americans joined the world in mourning the assassination of President John F. Kennedy, who many blacks believed, in the early hours following the tragedy, had been killed because of his advocacy of civil rights. Kennedy's civil rights measures were still being debated in Congress when he died.

December 7.   Ralph J. Bunche and Marian Anderson were awarded Medals of Freedom, the highest civilian decoration, for outstanding contributions to the ideals of freedom and democracy by President Lyndon Johnson.

1964

January 21.   Black newspaperman Carl T. Rowan of Minnesota was appointed Director of the United States Information Agency by President Johnson, one of Johnson's first of several high-ranking appointments of blacks.

January 23.   The 24th Amendment to the Constitution, prohibiting the denial or abridgement of the right to vote by "reason of failure to pay any poll tax or other tax" was adopted. The poll tax had been used by several Southern states as a means of discouraging black voters.

February 4.   Austin T. Walden, a veteran civil rights lawyer and political leader, took the oath as a municipal judge in Atlanta, the first black jurist in Georgia since Reconstruction.

March 12.   Malcolm X, one of the most noted of Black Muslim ministers, announced his withdrawal from Elijah Muhammad's Nation of Islam. Malcolm was born Malcolm Little in Omaha, Nebraska in 1925. His father was a Baptist minister from Georgia who had come to support Marcus Garvey. His mother was a West Indian. Three of Malcolm's uncles had been slain by whites and his father took him to Garvey rallies in Michigan. By the time he was 13, Malcolm's father had been killed and his mother committed to a mental institution; Malcolm himself was in a detention home, having gotten in trouble for stealing. A school drop-out, he made his living principally by illegal means. In February, 1946 he was sentenced to ten years in prison for burglary in Boston. Upon his release from prison, where he was converted to the Black Muslims, in August,

1952, Malcolm drew closer to the movement. In the summer of 1953, he became Assistant Minister of the Detroit temple. In 1957 Malcolm founded the Muslim newspaper, *Muhammad Speaks*, and by 1959 had become one of the leading spokesmen for the Muslims. As Malcolm's charisma brought him a larger following, Elijah Muhammad reportedly labelled him ambitious and dangerous. In November, 1963 Malcolm referred to President Kennedy's assassination as an example of "chickens coming home to roost." Muhammad suspended Malcolm from his Muslim duties for the intemperate statement. This was the beginning of the end for Malcolm X. He left the movement on March 12, 1964, carrying only a few defectors with him. He was assassinated on February 21, 1965 (See Below).

April 13. The selection of Sidney Poitier to receive an "Oscar" as best actor for his role in "Lillies of the Field" was widely hailed by blacks. Poitier has been the only Afro-American actor to receive the coveted award.

July 2. Congress passed a sweeping civil rights act, including provisions prohibiting discrimination in public accommodations and discrimination in employment. The "most important" civil rights law since 1875, passage was made certain after the Senate on June 10, for the first time in such a case, ended a Southern filibuster by imposing cloture. President Johnson signed the bill in the presence of civil rights leaders, including Martin Luther King, Jr., immediately after its adoption.

CHAPTER

X

An Age of
Disillusionment

1964-1973

1964

July 18-August 30. Serious racial disturbances occurred in a number of American cities, beginning in Harlem. The Harlem riot followed the shooting of a black teenager by a white police officer. Several of the other riots were sparked by clashes between blacks and policemen. Other areas witnessing riots included Brooklyn, Rochester, Jersey City, Chicago, and Philadelphia. Injuries in the disturbances exceeded 100, property losses ran into the millions of dollars, and national guardsmen had to be employed.

August 4. The bodies of three civil rights workers, two white and one black, were discovered buried near Philadelphia, Mississippi. The FBI accused nearly two dozen white segregationists of complicity in the murders. Included among them were law enforcement officers.

December 10. Martin Luther King, Jr., the champion of non-violent resistance to racial oppression, was awarded the Nobel Peace Prize in Oslo, Norway. King, at 35, became the youngest man in history and the second Afro-American to receive the coveted award.

December _____. The U. S. Supreme Court upheld the constitutionality of that section of the 1964 Civil Rights Act dealing with public accommodations.

————. Reports from civil rights groups indicated that three persons had been killed, three wounded, eighty physically assaulted, over 1,000 arrested, and thirty buildings bombed in Mississippi during the course of a year's civil rights activity.

————. Congress passed the Economic Opportunity Act in the nation's "War on Poverty." The scheme was later to be severely criticized by proponents and antagonists for inefficiency, but many blacks benefitted from it, especially through the Head Start, Upward Bound, and college work-study educational programs.

1965

January 2-23. Civil rights forces, led by Martin Luther King, Jr., opened a voter registration drive at Selma, Alabama. Dr. King was attacked as he registered at a formerly all-white Selma hotel, but was not seriously injured. On January 19, Dallas County law enforcement officers began arresting would-be black voters and their supporters. A federal court issued an order on January 23 prohibiting interference with those seeking the right to vote.

February 1-March 25. The drive to register black voters in Alabama developed into a nation-wide protest movement as local whites in Dallas County stiffened their resistance and civil rights leaders intensified their efforts. More than 700 blacks, including Martin Luther King, Jr., were arrested on February 1. On February 26 a black demonstrator, Jimmie L. Jackson, died as a result of wounds received at the hands of state troopers in Marion, Alabama. On March 7 several hundred protestors were routed by "billy-clubs," tear gas, whips, and cattle prods as they attempted a march across the Edmund Pettis bridge in Selma. President Johnson, sympathizing with the demonstrators, denounced the March 7 incident. A Boston white minister, the Rev. James Reeb, assisting in the voting rights drive, died as a result of wounds received at the hands of three white men on March 11. On March 17 a federal judge enjoined Alabama officials from interfering with a proposed march from Selma to Montgomery, designed to dramatize the denial of voting rights. The fifty mile Selma to Montgomery march, under the protection of federal troops, occurred from March 21-25, 1965. Perhaps as many as 50,000 persons appeared before the Alabama state capitol at Montgomery on March 25 to hear Martin Luther King, Jr. and others denounce Alabama leaders for interfering with voting rights. Alabama Governor George C. Wallace received a petition from the crowd. Viola Gregg Liuzzo, a white civil rights supporter from Michigan, was killed on that same night. As a result of the murder, three Ku Klux Klansmen were convicted of conspiracy to violate civil rights on December 3, 1965.

February 21.   Malcolm X, a black nationalist leader, and one-time member of the Black Muslim hierarchy, was assassinated in New York City. Three Afro-Americans were convicted of the murder in March, 1966. Malcolm X, an ex-convict, was largely a self-educated man, but was a persuasive orator with a fiery tongue. In recent years a sort of cult has been built around his memory by bitter young blacks. Malcolm's *Autobiography* (1965) has become a minor classic of twentieth century black America.

May 26.   A new voting rights bill was passed by Congress. The bill contained an anti-poll tax amendment designed to prevent certain states from using that tax to deny or abridge the right to vote. The bill also extended the right to vote to those who were unable to read or write English, but could demonstrate that they had an eighth grade education in a school conducted under the American flag. Federal registrars could enroll voters who had been denied the suffrage unjustly by local officials.

June 4.   President Johnson delivered a memorable speech at Howard University's commencement, in which he pledged an all-out effort to bring Negroes into the mainstream of American life. He again quoted the title of a civil rights anthem, "We Shall Overcome," as a motto for action.

June 10-16. Blacks in Chicago staged another round of demonstrations against school segregation. Entertainer Dick Gregory and CORE director James Farmer were among those arrested. A specific target of the demonstrators was School Superintendent Benjamin C. Willis who blacks viewed as a segregationist. Willis was given a new one-year contract on May 27. The next day a united front of civil rights groups, dissatisfied with the slow pace of school desegregation, announced that a public school boycott would be held to protest the rehiring of Willis. A federal judge issued an injunction on June 9 against the boycott. Nevertheless, the demonstrations began on June 10. On June 11 arrests began. Among the 225 arrested on that day were Farmer, Gregory, and nine clergymen. The protests continued through June 15, when Mayor Richard Daley sanctioned a downtown march and agreed to negotiate with civil rights leaders.

June 18-July 19. Civil rights demonstrations, marked by massive arrests, occurred at Jackson, Mississippi and Bogalusa, Louisiana. In Bogalusa, the state's governor John J. McKeithen, intervened in an attempt to bring peace.

July 13. Thurgood Marshall, now an Appeals Court judge, was nominated as Solicitor General of the United States by President Johnson, the highest law enforcement position ever held by an Afro-American.

August 11-21. The most serious single racial disturbance in American history, to that time, erupted in the "Watts" section of Los Angeles, California. Again, a clash between blacks and white policemen triggered the riot. National guardsmen assisted in quelling the disorders which left 34 dead, almost 900 injured, more than 3,500 arrested, and property losses near 225 million dollars. In the wake of the riot federal, state, and local authorities sought ways to improve black living conditions in the 20 square mile ghetto of 100,000 people.

August 20. President Johnson denounced the Watts rioters, refusing to accept "legitimate grievances" as an excuse for the disorders.

December 3-10. An Alabama jury convicted Collie L. Wilkins for conspiracy to violate civil rights in the death of voting rights supporter Viola Liuzzo. Another Alabama jury freed the whites accused in the murder of the Rev. James Reeb, a Boston minister, also slain in the Selma demonstrations.

1966

January 3. Floyd McKissick, a militant black civil rights leader from North Carolina, succeeded James Farmer as director of CORE. McKissick was to guide CORE into an agressive, mostly black group, dedicated to black liberation even if by separatist routes. McKissick, a forty-three year old Durham attorney, had served as CORE's national chairman since 1963. McKissick's announced plans included a program of community organization to help disadvantaged blacks living under "feudalism." He served for three years as national director and was succeeded by Roy Innis.

January 10. Julian Bond, a young black Atlantan, son of an ex-college president, and a leader of SNCC, was denied his seat in the Georgia legislature, after being duly elected, for opposing the U. S.'s involvement in Vietnam. The Supreme Court later ordered Bond seated (See Below). The vote against Bond in the Georgia House was 184-12. Bond, on January 6, had told newsmen that he supported an SNCC policy statement that advocated civil rights and social service alternatives to the draft. Many white Georgia legislators interpreted his statements as reflecting an "un-American attitude." The seven other black members of the House voted to seat Bond.

January 13. Robert C. Weaver of Washington, D. C., one of the nation's leading authorities on urban housing, was appointed the first Secretary of the new Department of Housing and Urban Development by President Johnson. Weaver has been the only Afro-American to serve in a presidential cabinet in U. S. history and the highest ranking black in the executive branch of the government. The appointment climaxed a long, successful career for Weaver who had previously served as housing director for New York, a member of President Roosevelt's "Black Cabinet," and the highest ranking black in President Kennedy's administration as head of the HHFA.

January 25. A black woman, former NAACP attorney Constance Baker Motley was appointed a federal judge by President Johnson, the second Negro woman to hold such a post. Marjorie Lawson had been previously appointed by President Kennedy.

March 1. Wyatt T. Walker of Brockton, Massachusetts, once a top aide to Martin Luther King, Jr., was appointed Special Assistant to Governor Nelson Rockefeller of New York, making Walker the closest black adviser to the governor of America's largest state.

March 7. The Supreme Court upheld the voting rights law of 1965.

May 10. The California State Supreme Court ruled that a state constitutional amendment nullifying California fair-housing laws violated the United States Constitution. The state amendment, known as Proposition 14, had been placed on the general election ballot in November, 1964 and was approved by a 2-1 margin. It provided that no state or local agency could interfere with a real estate owner's "absolute discretion" in the sale and rental of property. The State Supreme Court's 5-2 decision held that it was "beyond dispute" that the 14th Amendment's Equal Protection Clause secured the "right to acquire and possess property of every kind," without racial or religious discrimination. The Court overruled a lower court's rejection of a complaint by Lincoln W. Mulkey, a black man, against apartment owners in Orange County. The lower court had ruled that the California open housing acts on which Mulkey's petition was based had been rendered "null and void" by the passage of Proposition 14. Six companion cases were also covered by the state court's order. Governor Edmund G. Brown, who had announced in March, 1966 that $200 million in federal unban-renewal funds had been withheld from California because of

Proposition 14, promptly announced that the state court's decision would be appealed to the U. S. Supreme Court and that until then he would "continue to enforce" Proposition 14. State Attorney General Thomas C. Lynch said, however, that he would resume enforcement of the open-occupancy laws of 1959 and 1963 which Proposition 14 had invalidated (See Also Below).

May 16. Stokely Carmichael, an articulate West Indian-born youth, was named head of SNCC. Carmichael was to guide SNCC into a more militant organization, bent on achieving racial liberation, even if by a separatist route.

June 6. James Meredith, the black student who broke the color bar at the University of Mississippi in 1962, was shot, but not seriously injured, shortly after starting a one-man pilgrimage "against fear" from Memphis to Jackson, Mississippi. A white segregationist was arrested for the attack.

June 7-June 26. The march begun by James Meredith resumed with civil rights leaders, including Martin Luther King, Jr. and Stokely Carmichael, taking the initiative. The demonstration ended with a rally of 15,000 persons at the state capitol in Jackson. Dr. King, Carmichael, Meredith, and others addressed the crowd. It was during this march and rally that Carmichael and others began to freely employ the phrase "black power." The slogan was interpreted to mean many things, but all agreed that it denoted a more aggressive posture for its supporters.

June 9. The California State Supreme Court partially reversed a May 10, 1966 decision which invalidated a state constitutional amendment that had voided state open-housing laws. The new decision was based on a reconsideration of one of the seven cases covered by the earlier ruling. It declared that the owner of a single-family home not financed by federal funds was not covered by state open occupancy legislation and thus could refuse to sell or lease his home to blacks. The new ruling did not in any other way affect the earlier invalidation of the controversial constitutional amendment known as Proposition 14.

July 1-9. The national convention of CORE endorsed the "black power" concept. SNCC was also to adopt the slogan, while SCLC shyed away from it, and the NAACP disassociated itself from the concept.

July 10. Martin Luther King, Jr. addressed a largely black crowd of 45,000 in Chicago and launched a drive to rid the nation's third largest city of discrimination.

July 12-15. A dispute between police and Negro children over the use of a fire hydrant for recreation resulted in rioting in one of Chicago's black ghettoes. Two blacks were killed, scores of both races were injured, and 370 were arrested. On July 15, Chicago mayor Richard Daley and Dr. Martin Luther King, Jr, announced new programs in recreation for Chicago blacks, a committee to study police-citizen relations, and closer cooperation between community residents and police.

July 18-23. A serious racial disturbance occurred in Cleveland, Ohio. The toll: four dead, fifty injured, 160 arrests, widespread property damage. Shootings, firebombings and looting were prevalent throughout the black ghetto of Hough on Cleveland's East Side. The incident which touched off the riot took place in a neighborhood bar. One version was that the bar's white management had refused to serve water to blacks; another was that a woman soliciting money for a friend's funeral had been ejected. Bands of blacks began roaming in the area after the incident. At least ten buildings were destroyed by fire.

August 5-6. Martin Luther King, Jr., was stoned in Chicago while leading a demonstration against discrimination in the city. King was not seriously hurt, but left the city shortly thereafter. The Chicago campaign had been only partially successful.

September 8. Julian Bond, denied his seat in the Georgia legislature for anti-Vietnam views, resigned from the publicity staff of SNCC.

October ——. The Black Panther Party was founded in Oakland, California. The two principal founders were Huey Newton, a native of Grove, Louisiana and Bobby Seale, a native of Dallas, Texas. The two youths grew up in California and met in 1960 while students at Merritt Junior College in Oakland. Inspired by examples of police brutality and other forms of white racism and the teachings of Malcolm X, the duo was very active in the college's Afro-American association, but later withdrew and organized the Black Panther Party (Already Newton had run afoul of the law several times, having been arrested for theft and sentenced to jail for assault). The Black Panther party adopted a ten-point program; full employment; restitution for past exploitation and oppression; education relevant to black needs and aspirations; release of all black prisoners; decent housing; exemptions from military service for blacks; trial of blacks only by black juries; an end to police brutality; and black political and economic power. The Panthers insisted on "power to the people"; advocated self-defense; called for a socialistic economy; provided food and lectures to young children; and published their own newspaper. They drew wide admiration, if not a large following, from young blacks in the Northern and Western ghettoes and as their numbers and influence increased, so did clashes with law enforcement officers (See Below).

November 8. Edward W. Brooke, the black Attorney General of Massachusetts, was elected United States Senator from Massachusetts. Brooke, a Howard University graduate from Washington, became the first Afro-American to sit in the U. S. Senate since Reconstruction.

1967

January 8. Following a decision by the U. S. Supreme Court, Julian Bond was seated in the Georgia General Assembly.

January 9. Adam Clayton Powell was ousted as Chairman of the House Education and Labor Committee and denied his seat in the U. S. House.

April 4. Martin Luther King, Jr. announced unalterable opposition to the Vietnam War. Dr. King spoke first to a press conference at the Overseas Press Club in New York. Later that day at the Riverside Church he suggested the avoidance of military service "to all those who find the American course in Vietnam a dishonorable and unjust one." King compared the use of new U. S. weapons on Vietnamese peasants to the Nazis' testing of new medicines and new tortures in the concentration camps of Europe during World War II. He proposed that the United States take new initiatives to end the war "in order to atone for our sins and errors in Vietnam." Many of King's supporters disagreed with his strong anti-war stand.

May 1-October 1. The worst summer of racial disturbances in American history occurred. More than forty riots were recorded, and at least 100 other incidents. The most serious outbreaks were in Newark, New Jersey (July 12-17) where 26 died and in Detroit (July 23-30) where 40 died. New York City, Cleveland, Washington, Chicago, Atlanta, and others were also scenes of trouble. President Johnson appointed a National Advisory Commission on Civil Disorders to investigate them and make recommendations. The Commission, headed by Governor Otto Kerner (the Kerner Commission) of Illinois conducted a series of hearings and investigations and reported to the President in March, 1968.

May 12. H. Rap Brown, a militant youth, was appointed the new chairman of SNCC. Brown was to have numerous brushes with the law. He disappeared in 1970 while awaiting trial on a charge of inciting a riot in Cambridge, Maryland.

July 1. Benjamin E. Mays retired as president of Morehouse College. Mays, the son of South Carolina tenant farmers, was educated at Bates College in Maine and at the University of Chicago. An ordained Baptist minister, Mays taught at Howard University and at Morehouse College, among other places, before becoming president of Morehouse in 1940. He continued and expanded the programs began by John Hope and the college produced an outstanding list of black business and professional men and civil rights leaders. Mays, like Hope, also became known as militant civil rights advocate for his membership on the NAACP Board of Directors and his forthright speeches and writings demanding racial equality. In April of 1968 Mays delivered the eulogy at the funeral of Dr. Martin Luther King, Jr., in which he blamed America's racist society for the assassination. Mays was elected president of the Atlanta Board of Education in 1969 (See Below). Mays was succeeded by Hugh M. Gloster, Academic Dean at Hampton Institute and a scholar in Afro-American literature.

September 21.   President Johnson named Walter Washington, an Afro-American, as the first mayor of Washington, D. C. (the nation's largest predominantly black metropolis). Washington, a fifty-five year old member and chairman of the New York City Housing Authority was officially "commissioner" of the newly reorganized municipal government of the District of Columbia. One interesting opponent of Washington's confirmation by the Senate was black militant Aketi Kimani. Kimani stated that "any number of militant white men" could do a better job than "a house nigger" such as Washington.

November _____.   The steady growth of the black population in the larger cities of the nation was reflected in the number of Afro-Americans holding important public offices. While the blacks had substantial majorities in only a few cities, their numbers were large enough to, in conjunction with some whites, elect Afro-Americans in several localities. In 1967 Floyd McCree was elected mayor of Flint, Michigan, Carl B. Stokes mayor in Cleveland, and Richard B. Hatcher mayor in Gary, Indiana.

1968

January 16.   Lucius D. Amerson took over as sheriff of Macon County, Alabama, the first black sheriff in the South since Reconstruction. Three newly appointed deputies, one white and two blacks, were sworn in with Amerson. In February, 1971 Amerson was indicted by a Grand Jury in Alabama for beating a prisoner in the Tuskegee jail.

February 8.   Three black students died, several others were wounded, as a result of bullets fired by South Carolina law enforcement officers, during a disturbance on the campus of South Carolina State College at Orangeburg. The protests had begun against segregation at a local bowling alley and had led to the mobilization of the National Guard and the closing of the school for two weeks. Some of the students had been jailed on charges of trespassing. The firing on February 8 was preceded by an injury to a state trooper. The officer was knocked down by a piece of wood. The Justice Department began an investigation of the incident on February 10. Later a suit was filed against the owners of the segregated bowling alley charging them with violation of the Civil Rights Act of 1964. At the same time action was filed against segregation and discrimination in Orangeburg hospital facilities. The courts upheld the anti-segregation complaints in both instances. Attempts to indict and prosecute the officers involved were unsuccessful.

March 2.   The Kerner Commission reported that "white racism" was the principal cause of the disturbances that rocked the nation in 1967, and that the United States was headed toward two communities, one white, one black, "separate and unequal."

April 3.   Martin Luther King, Jr. addressed a rally of striking garbage workers and their supporters in Memphis, Tennessee. King repeated his defiance of would-be assassins.

April 4.   Martin Luther King, Jr., the most important black man in American history, was assassinated in Memphis, Tennessee. The assassination was followed by a week of racial rioting in at least 125 localities.

April 9.   Hundreds of thousands attended the funeral of Martin Luther King, Jr. in Atlanta. President Johnson decreed a day of national mourning. It was the most stately funeral ever accorded a civilian American.

April 11.   President Johnson signed the Fair Housing Act, prohibiting racial discrimination in the sale and rental of most housing units in the country.

May 11. Ralph David Abernathy, successor to Martin Luther King, Jr. as head of SCLC, led a motley array of blacks, poor whites, Indians, and Mexican-Americans to Washington for a Poor Peoples Campaign. The drive, originally an idea put forth by Martin Luther King, Jr., included lobbying and the erection of a camp-site known as Resurrection City.

June 25. Resurrection City was disbanded, admittedly a failure. Poor weather, insufficient discipline, and an unreceptive Congress, preoccupied with Vietnam, limited the campaign's effectiveness.

July 23-24. A serious racial disturbance in Cleveland left eleven dead. A small band of armed "Black Nationalists" fought Cleveland police in the Glenville ghetto. This was followed by burning and looting which resulted in an estimated $1.5 million in property damage. Three white policemen and eight blacks died during the riot.

August 29. The name of Channing Phillips, an Afro-American minister from Washington, D. C., was put forth for the Democratic nomination as President. Phillips received only a handful of votes. The name of Julian Bond, the black Georgia legislator, was put forth for the Democratic nomination as Vice President. He received several votes before he withdrew his name, being too young to occupy the office.

September 8. Another result of the 1967 riots was the strengthening of militant black self-defense groups such as the "Deacons" in the South and the "Black Panthers" in the North and West. The Panthers, an avowedly revolutionary group, drew the ire of law enforcement officers, clashed with officers, and with others. Several of their leaders have been arrested, exiled, and killed. Huey C. Newton, a Black Panther leader, was convicted of manslaughter on September 8.

November 5. Shirley Chisholm, an Afro-American from New York, defeated James Farmer, ex-head of CORE, for a House seat, becoming the only black woman ever to sit in Congress.

November 5.   Eighty more blacks were elected to political office in the South. There were now nearly 400 elected black officeholders in the eleven states that made up the Confederacy. By comparison only 70 blacks held political office in these states in November, 1965, just after the Voting Rights Act took effect. Most of the successful black candidates ran in districts with predominantly black constituencies. In primaries as well as in the general election most black candidates lost when they challenged whites in districts with many white voters; voters generally balloted along racial lines. To black Southerners the highlight of the November elections was the election for the first time this century of black candidates to the legislatures in North Carolina, Florida, and Tennessee. Henry Frye, a Greensboro lawyer, won a seat in the North Carolina house. Joe Lang Kershaw, a Miami school teacher, was elected to a seat in the Florida house. J. O. Patterson of Memphis and Avon Williams of Nashville were elected to the Tennessee senate. Across the South at the time there were more black city councilmen — 126 — than in any other single type of office. Second highest was school-board member, a position held by 75 blacks. According to the figures of the Voter Education Project of the Southern Regional Council, Alabama led all of the South with 72 elected black officials. Arkansas had 45; Louisiana 43; Mississippi 43; Georgia 38; Texas 19; North Carolina 19; and Florida 17. More than 3 million Southern blacks were eligible to vote in the November election.

December 31.   President Johnson ended his last full year in office. Johnson made more appointments of blacks to high level federal posts than any previous Chief Executive. Before leaving office, he appointed five black ambassadors, promoted Wade McCree from the U. S. District Court to the Circuit Court of Appeals, appointed Hobart Taylor to the Board of Export-Import Bank, and named Andrew Brimmer as a Governor on the Federal Reserve Board.

1969

January-March.   President Richard Nixon, elected without substantial black support, made only three top-level appointments of Afro-Americans to the Washington bureauracracy — James Farmer as Assistant Secretary of Health, Education and Welfare; Arthur A. Fletcher as Assistant Secretary of Labor; and William H. Brown, III as Chairman of the Equal Employment Opportunities Commission. He retained Walter Washington as mayor of Washington, D. C.

January 8. The latest example of black student unrest on a predominantly white campus occurred at Brandeis University in Waltham, Massachusetts. Sixty-five black students invaded Ford Hall, the Brandeis headquarters and communications center, and barricaded themselves in the building. They presented a "nonnegotiable" list of demands. The demands called for, among other things, an African studies department; year-round recruitment of black students by blacks; black directors of the Upward Bound and Transitional Year programs; the hiring of black professors; establishment of an Afro-American student center; and ten full scholarships for blacks. Morris B. Abram, the recently selected Brandeis president, offered temporary amnesty to the blacks and agreed to communicate with the barricaded students.

January 25. A mistrial was declared in the Mississippi murder trial of Ku Klux Klan leader Samuel H. Bowers, Jr. Bowers was one of thirteen men indicted in the fire-bomb slaying in 1966 of black civil rights leader Vernon Dahmer. The thirteen were tried separately. Four have been convicted of murder; three of these were sentenced to life imprisonmnt, the fourth to ten years in prison. Including the Bowers case, there were five mistrials when juries were unable to reach a verdict. A mistrial was also reached in Bowers' trial for arson in connection with the Dahmer slaying in May, 1968. These efforts to prosecute white men who have done violence to whites was cited by *The Christian Science Monitor* and other sources as an important factor in deterring Klan violence in Mississippi and the rest of the South (See Also Above and Below).

January 27. The Supreme Court ruled that cities — like states — cannot enact ordinances or charter provisions which have the effect of establishing discrimination in housing. The Court's decision involved a case filed by Mrs. Nellie Hunter, a black housewife from Akron, Ohio. In 1965 Mrs. Hunter tried to buy a home in Akron's all-white West Side, but she was turned down by a real-estate company on account of color. Mrs. Hunter filed a complaint with City Hall, requesting the protection of a 1964 ordinance which banned racial discrimination in housing. But city officials replied that local real-estate interests had successfully staged a drive to amend the charter, nullifying the ordinance and requiring that any future fair-housing proposal be approved by a vote of the people. The Supreme Court held that the Akron Charter amendment "is no more permissible than denying racial minorities the vote on an equal basis with others." The city had placed, unconstitutionally, the court reasoned, a "special burden" on its black residents by requiring bans against housing discrimination to have the approval of the majority of the city's voters. In effect, then, the court's decision struck down the offending charter amendment and restored the original fair-housing ordinance. The decree also reversed the results of an effort in November 1968 to repeal the amendment. Voters then balloted 45,148 to 42,419 to retain it, despite an intensive drive by fair-housing advocates to defeat it. Justice Hugo L. Black cast a lone dissenting vote in the decision. Black agreed that there was no Constitutional basis for the extension of the fair-housing principle. This Supreme Court ruling became a companion to the 1966 decision on Proposition 14 in California (See Above). The Court then, ruled that California voters could neither amend their Constitution to repeal a fair housing law nor prohibit, at the same time, future enactment of such laws.

March 10. James Earl Ray, a white vagabond, was sentenced to 99 years in prison for the assassination of Martin Luther King, Jr.

June 27. The U. S. Department of Labor issued guidelines for minority employment on federally-assisted construction projects. The guidelines which have become known as "the Philadelphia Plan" (The plan was first imposed on the city of Philadelphia.) required contractors on federally-assisted construction work exceeding $500,000 to hire a specific number of workers. Secretary of Labor George P. Shultz said on July 3 that the Philadelphia Plan was a "fair and realistic approach" toward eliminating racial discrimination in the construction industry. He added, however, that no contractor who failed to meet the standards set by the Labor Department would lose a federal contract if the contractor showed he had "made a good faith effort" to recruit the required number of minority workers. On July 16, Laurence H. Silberman, solicitor of the Department of Labor announced that the Philadelphia Plan was legal under Executive Order No. 11246 which required equal employment clauses in all federal contracts. Republican minority leader Senator Everett Dirksen (R., Ill.) had asked President Nixon on July 8 to hold up the plan because he though it imposed a quota system in violation of the 1964 Civil Rights Act. Silberman said the arrangement, known as the Philadelphia Plan, did not run counter to existing federal laws.

August 19. Black Panther leader Bobby Seale was arrested for murder by the F.B.I. Seale was accused of the torture murder of Alex Rackley. Rackley had been allegedly disloyal to the Panther organization and was burned to death on May 19 in New Haven, Connecticut. Francis J. McTernan, Seale's attorney, charged that the arrest was part of an organized campaign by the Justice Department to harass the Black Panther party. McTernan said that his staff had information that the Department had prepared a special file in connection with a program "of harassment against leaders of the Black Panther party all over the country." Seale was arrested in California and later extradited for trial in Connecticut. In the spring of 1970, Yale University students staged a protest demanding fairness in the upcoming trial (See Below).

September _____. Harvard University moved to establish an Afro-American Studies Program. An eight-man Faculty Committee on African and Afro-American Studies concluded in January that an Afro-American studies program was needed in addition to the already-established African studies program. The committee's report said: "We are dealing with 25 million of our own people with a special history, culture, and range of problems. It can hardly be doubted that the study of black men in America is a legitimate and urgent academic endeavor." Although Harvard was not the first to establish an Afro-American studies program, a program at Harvard was viewed as lending impetus to the establishment of such a field of study at other universities.

October 29. The U. S. Supreme Court ruled unanimously that school districts must end racial segregation "at once" and must "operate now and hereafter only unitary schools." The Court rejected the Nixon administration's appeal for delay in desegregating 30 Mississippi school districts. The new ruling indicated that the Court had abandoned its fourteen year old standard of allowing desegregation to proceed "with all deliberate speed." In the current decision the Court declared that "continued operations of segregated schools under a standard of 'all deliberate speed' for desegregation is no longer constitutionally permissible." The case has become known to history as *Alexander* vs *Holmes* (Mississippi). It was the first major decision delivered by the Court under President Nixon's appointed Chief Justice, Warren E. Burger.

October 31. The U. S. Fifth Circuit Court of Appeals in New Orleans moved to implement the Supreme Court's October 29 decision on school desegregation by directing 33 school districts in Mississippi to file desegregation plans by November 5, 1969. Meanwhile, NAACP attorneys said they would file motions in some 100 other school segregation cases pending in federal court to press for "immediate integration."

November 4. Carl Stokes, the black mayor of Cleveland was re-elected. In other elections, a mostly white community, Chapel Hill, North Carolina elected Howard N. Lee, a Georgia-born educator, as mayor, and Fayette, Mississippi, a mostly black community, chose Charles Evers, veteran NAACP leader and brother of the slain Medgar Evers, as mayor. Blacks took political control of counties in Alabama and Georgia and of the city of Tuskegee.

December 4. Mark Clark and Fred Hampton, Black Panther leaders, were killed by policemen in Chicago. The raid which resulted in their deaths was later labelled "excessive" by a Grand Jury. The pre-dawn raid on an apartment near the Illinois Black Panther headquarters resulted not only in the deaths of Hampton,

Illinois party chairman, and Clark, Peoria, Illinois leader, but the wounding of four others, two of them women. The raid, according to police reports, was carried out on information that Hampton's apartment was being used to stockpile weapons. Police claimed that their knock on the door was answered by shotgun fire from a woman. They said about 200 shots were fired during the ten minute altercation. On December 5, spokesmen for the Black Panthers denied the police accounts of the raid. They claimed the Panther leaders were "murdered" in bed by police. They purported to show that the only shooting in the apartment was done by policemen. State, federal, and congressional investigations were held. Neither Panthers nor policemen were brought to trial in the wake of the controversial encounter. It did serve, however, to heighten tensions between the Panthers and the law and to gain some additional sympathy for the plight of party members.

1970

January _____. Blacks gained a degree of political control over the city of Atlanta. Five blacks were elected or re-elected to the 18 member Board of Aldermen (city council), three were elected or re-elected to the 10 member Board of Education. A young black lawyer was elected Vice Mayor and President of the Board of Aldermen (Maynard Jackson). The venerable black Atlanta educator, Benjamin E. Mays, was named head of the School Board.

January 2. F. B. I. Director J. Edgar Hoover in his annual report said that black militant groups were "encouraged and inflamed from without" in violent attacks upon the government. In his report of F. B. I. operations in 1969, Hoover said also that there were more than 100 attacks on police by "extremist, all Negro, hate-type organizations, such as the Black Panther Party" during the previous six months. He reported that seven police officers had been killed and 120 injured during attacks by black militants.

January 3. Governor John Bell Williams of Mississippi announced in a statewide telecast that he would seek to help build a Mississippi private school system as a "workable alternative" to school desegregation. Williams also urged white parents to peacefully accept the ruling of the Fifth Circuit Court of Appeals on November 6, 1969 which ordered thirty Mississippi school districts to desegregate. The governor said it was "a time when reason must outweigh emotion and calm must prevail over hysteria." The governor announced later that he would resubmit to the state legislature a proposal to authorize income tax credits of up to $500 a year for those who donate to educational institutions. The legislature had previously rejected that request.

January 5.   Statistics released by the U. S. Bureau of the Census confirmed earlier reports that nonwhite as well as white families were fleeing poverty areas in the cities. The bureau said that whites had been been leaving the urban poverty areas for years, but the non-white migration seemed to have occurred chiefly since 1966. The bureau citied as factors behind the exodus: crime, educational problems, land clearance resulting from urban renewal, and the increased availability of low-income housing outside of poverty areas. Between 1960 and 1968, minority group families living in urban poverty areas declined by nine percent. In 1968 2.5 million whites and 1.6 million blacks lived in urban poverty areas.

January 5-7.   Black children were enrolled in formerly all white public schools in three districts in Mississippi on January 5 under the watch of federal marshals. The federal officers had been sent to Mississippi to prevent violence and to look for signs of non-compliance as the government moved to implement the November 6, 1969 decision of the Fifth U. S. Circuit Court of Appeals which ordered thirty Mississippi districts to desegregate. Three of the 30 districts under the desegregation order reopened classes for the second semester on January 5. The others were to reopen between January 7 and 12, 1970. There was no violence on January 5, but many white parents picketed the newly desegregated schools. Other white parents boycotted the institutions. In Woodville, only two white children attended the district school where 1,400 black pupils had been registered. Two more Mississippi school districts reopened for the second semester on January 7, 1970 with desegregated student bodies. In Yazoo City, where white business leaders had asked parents to accept the school arrangements, nearly 1,500 white students attended desegregated schools. In Petal, 4,000 white and 1,000 blacks went to classes together for the first time, despite a peaceful sit-in by 300 white parents at an elementary school. The whites were protesting a desegregation plan that assigned their children to classrooms as far as 13 miles away.

January 6.   Robert H. Finch, Secretary of Health, Education, and Welfare (HEW) expressed concern about the South's new private schools. He announced that there was a move, which he supported, within the Nixon administration to end tax exemptions for private schools established to avoid desegregation in public schools. Finch said he would request the Treasury Department to "reconsider the present policy" of granting tax-exempt status to such private schools. He estimated that as many as 400 private schools had opened in the South since the passage of the Civil Rights Act of 1964.

January 8.   The Tennessee Supreme Court refused to consider a plea for a new trial for James Earl Ray, the white vagabond serving a 99 year sentence for the murder of Dr. Martin Luther King, Jr. The Court reasoned that there could be no legal basis for granting a new trial for the defendant who had pleaded guilty and fully understood what he was doing.

January 13.   A three judge federal district court in Washington, D.C. ordered the Internal Revenue Service to stop granting tax-exempt privileges to segregated private schools in Mississippi. The order did not affect the all-white private schools that had already been granted tax-exemptions. The newly chartered all-white private academies were being set up by white parents to avoid complying with the school desegregation taking place in Mississippi's public schools (See Above and Below). Under the court order, the IRS was to stop granting tax exempt status to schools with applications now pending or yet to be filed, unless the private schools could show they were enrolling black children. Also on January 13, Mississippi Governor John Bell Williams asked the state legislature to grant financial assistance to the private academies in the form of state tax deductions to those who donated money to the all-white schools. He said his program would "strengthen the hands of Mississippians" in facing the government's desegregation orders.

January 14. The U.S. Supreme Court, in a brief unsigned order, overruled a decision by the U.S. Fifth Circuit Court of Appeals on December 1, 1969 which set September, 1970 as a deadline for student desegregation in the public schools of the South. The Court thus rejected a Justice Department request that the September deadline be approved. The Court acted on an appeal filed by the NAACP involving fourteen school districts in five Southern states. The NAACP requested a February 1, 1970 deadline and the Supreme Court's action affirmed this request (See Also Above).

January 15. Blacks and whites across the nation celebrated the 41st anniversary of the birth of Dr. Martin Luther King, Jr., as the movement to make the day a national holiday gained momentum. Several governors, including Kenneth M. Curtis of Maine, Frank Licht of Rhode Island, and Nelson Rockefeller of New York declared "Martin Luther King, Jr. Day" in their states. In some cities, including Baltimore, Kansas City (Mo.), New York, and Philadelphia, public schools were closed in tribute. In Atlanta, 400 persons heard the city's new mayor, Sam Massell, eulogize King at a memorial service. Following this service King's widow, Coretta Scott King, dedicated Atlanta's new Martin Luther King, Jr. Memorial Center which is to include King's birthplace, church, and crypt.

January 19. Governor Claude R. Kirk, Jr. of Florida personally told the U.S. Supreme Court that his state was "financially and physically unable" to meet the court's January 14, 1970 decree ordering immediate school desegregation. Kirk announced that he had instructed Florida school districts not to change their school calendars during mid-term. Kirk also asked the court for a re-hearing of its January 14 order and requested a delay in the February 1 school desegregation deadline. The governor said that Florida stood ready to comply with the court's orders, but was presently simply unable to do so. Attorneys for two Louisiana school districts also appeared before the court with similar pleas. The court listened to the arguments, then ordered the desegregation to proceed as scheduled (See Also Above).

January 20. Federal district judge Manuel L. Real in Los Angeles ordered the Pasadena, California school district to submit a desegregation plan for its public schools by February 16, 1970. The plan, covering all the schools in the suburban Los Angeles district, would take effect in September. The Pasadena case was the first of the federal government's suits against non-Southern school districts to be acted upon. The judge ruled that the plan submitted by the school officials should not produce any school with a majority of non-white students. Judge Real also ordered that the plan should cover new teaching assignments, hiring and promotional practices, and the construction of new school buildings.

January 21. A coroner's jury in Chicago found that the deaths of Black Panther Party leaders, Fred Hampton and Mark Clark, slain by a police raiding party on December 4, 1969, were justifiable. The special inquest was convened on January 6 after Panther party leaders had charged that Hampton had been "murdered in his bed." The foreman of the six-man jury said the verdict was reached "solely on the evidence presented." Chicago detectives who participated in the predawn raid had testified that one or more persons in Hampton's apartment opened fire on the police. Seven other members of the Black Panther party were arrested following the raid. The attorneys representing the families of the two slain Panthers did not call any witnesses during the hearing. They indicated that they did not want to reveal their plans for the defense of the seven Panthers who faced possible trial for attempted murder. A Cook County Grand Jury was also investigating the incident (See Above and Below).

January 24. In a report released in Saigon, army investigators found that "all indications point toward an increase in racial tension" on military bases throughout the world. The report of the investigation, ordered by General William C. Westmoreland, Army Chief of Staff, had been presented to the Joint Chiefs of Staff in Washington in the fall of 1969 and then sent to congressmen and to military commanders in the U.S. and abroad. The report said that "Negro soldiers seem to have lost faith in the Army system," and predicted increased racial problems unless "aggressive command action, firm but impartial discipline and good leadership can prevent physical confrontation of racial groups." The study concluded that the Army had "a race problem because our country has a race problem." Yet there were conditions within the Army that possibly contributed to unrest among black soldiers. For instance, according to the report, the number of black junior officers had been decreasing although there were more black non-commissioned officers of lower rank, and on bases in Europe, where one of every eight soldiers was black, one of every four non-judicial punishments (minor penalties fixed without trial) was imposed on a black soldier.

January 27. Judge G. Harrold Carswell of Florida told the U.S. Senate's Judiciary Committee: "I am not a racist. I have no notions, secretive or otherwise, of racial superiority." Senators questioned Carswell during the first day of confirmation hearings on his nomination to the U.S. Supreme Court on a "white supremacy" speech that he made during a political campaign in Georgia back in 1948. Carswell said that "the force of 22 years of history" had changed him as well as the South. On January 21, the NAACP had urged the Senate to reject Carswell because of his pro-segregation record. NAACP Board Chairman Bishop Stephen G. Spottswood noted that the NAACP and 124 other national organizations had opposed Carswell's appointment to the U.S. Court of Appeals for the fifth Circuit in May, 1969. On January 23, Ralph David Abernathy, president of S.C.L.C., announced that he had sent a telegram opposing Carswell to Senate leaders. Abernathy said the rejection of Carswell "would provide some reassurances to the black community that there is still some understanding and support among government officials for our needs." The Senate later rejected the Carswell nomination (See Below).

January 29. President Richard M. Nixon expressed concern over his administration's failure to gain the confidence of the nation's black citizens. The President said that he could improve his standing in the black community by using phrases and slogans, but that he eschewed such tactics because it would only serve to widen the gap between the government and blacks. Nixon said he was more concerned with deeds than words, and that approval of his legislative proposals against crime and for increased job opportunities would serve to end the performance gap and inspire trust in his administration.

February 1. Southern school officials in twenty districts in Alabama, Georgia, and Mississippi defied federal court orders calling for total school desegregation and refused to implement federally-designed desegregation plans. Some administrators closed their schools temporarily, while others supported boycotts by white parents and students. In two Alabama districts the court orders were ignored. The February 1 deadline for desegregation had been set by the Supreme Court on January 14. Of the 40 school districts under court orders, only a few implemented desegregation plans. These included three in Louisiana, two in Mississippi, and one in Florida. Many of the officials in the twenty districts that disobeyed the orders arbitrarily closed their schools to await further rulings on their appeals for delays. In Bessemer, Alabama, school officials stated flatly that they would not comply with the desegregation orders. Black lawyers filed a suit on February 1 requesting that the Bessemer school board be found in contempt of court. In Burke County, Georgia, the schools reopened under a "freedom of choice" arrangement, even though the courts had previously invalidated such a scheme. Panama City, Florida, was one of the few districts to fully comply with the court orders. About 1,000 of its 17,500 students were transferred to new schools to achieve a more racially balanced system.

February 26. According to a *New York Times* report, efforts to increase black enlistments in the National Guard had proved largely unsuccessful. A survey conducted by the Guard revealed that there were 5,487 blacks in the Air and Army units at the end of 1969 out of a total enlistment of nearly 500,000 men. Blacks constituted 1.15% of guardsmen in 1969 as compared to 1.18% in 1968. Congress refused a request for $6.5 million to recruit blacks into the Guard in 1969, and the Defense Department did not renew the request in 1970.

February 28. A confidential memorandum from Daniel P. Moynihan, domestic adviser to the President, to President Nixon in which Moynihan proposed that "the time may have come when the issue of race could benefit from a period of 'benign neglect'" was made public. Moynihan, a "liberal" Democrat, explained on March 2, 1970 that all he meant was that blacks could fare better if extremists on both sides of the political spectrum would lower their voices. He asserted that his memorandum had been written with a twofold purpose: to bring the President up to date on the "quite extraordinary" progress of the Negro in the last decade, and to suggest ways in which these gains could be "consolidated" in the future. On March 5, 1970, twenty black civil rights leaders, authors, legislators, and educators issued a statement describing Moynihan's memorandum as "symptomatic of a calculated, aggressive and systematic" effort by the Nixon administration to "wipe out" nearly two decades of civil rights progress. The signers included Dr. Nathan Hare, Rep. John Conyers, Jr. (D. Mich.), and Bayard Rustin.

March 3. A mob of angry whites, wielding ax handles and baseball bats, stormed buses transporting black school children to a formerly all-white school in Lamar, South Carolina. About 100 South Carolina State policemen dispersed the mob with riot clubs and tear gas, after the crowd of some 200 whites, men and women, rushed the buses and smashed their windows at Lamar High School. Thirty-nine black students were aboard the buses. Several children received minor injuries from flying glass and the effects of the tear gas. Although no one was arrested at the scene, state and federal officials later moved to apprehend the mob's leaders (See Below).

March 13. The Senate voted to extend the Voting Rights Act of 1965. The measure extended the 1965 act to 1975, incorporated a five-year nation-wide ban on literacy tests and eased residence requirements for voting in Presidential elections by permitting one to cast a ballot if he had established residence in a locality at least a month before election day (See Also Above).

March 14. U.S. District Court Judge Charles R. Weiner in Philadelphia upheld the constitutionality of the Labor Department's controversial Philadelphia Plan which sought to increase minority employment in the construction industry. Judge Weiner rejected a request for an injunction against the plan which was requested in a suit filed on January 6, 1970 by the Contractors Association of Eastern Pennsylvania. Judge Weiner said the pilot job program did not in any way violate the Civil Rights Act of 1964 which forbade racial quotas in employment. The jurist reasoned that "it is fundamental that civil rights without economic rights are mere shadows." The Philadelphia Plan did not violate the Civil Rights Act of 1964 because it "does not require the contractor to hire a definite percentage of a minority group." The contractors had only to make "good faith" efforts to hire a certain number of blacks and other minorities.

May 12. Six black men died as a result of racial rioting in Augusta, Georgia. All died at the hands of local policemen.

May 14. Mississippi law enforcement officers killed two black youths during a racial disturbance at Jackson State College, Jackson, Mississippi.

May 29. The conviction of Black Panther leader Huey Newton for manslaughter was reversed by a California Court of Appeals. Newton had been convicted in September, 1968 in the fatal shooting of an Oakland, California policeman. Newton was also implicated in the wounding of another policeman and the kidnapping of a black motorist. In his 1968 trial, Newton was prosecuted by Deputy Prosecutor Lowell Jensen and defended by Charles A. Garry. A major contention of the defense was that Newton lay unconscious from a gunshot wound at the time the Oakland policeman was shot. The California Court found procedural errors in the original trial and ordered the conviction overturned.

June _____. Charles Rangel, a black Harlem politician, defeated Adam Clayton Powell, Jr. for his long-held House seat. Eight Afro-Americans sat in the House during 1970. In addition to the defeated Powell and the venerable William L. Dawson of Chicago (on the verge of retirement), they were veteran Congressman Charles C.

Diggs of Michigan, A. F. Hawkins of California, Robert C. Nix of Pennsylvania, the youthful John Conyers of Michigan, Shirley Chisholm of Brooklyn, and Louis Stokes of Ohio.

June 29. The Chairman of the NAACP's Board of Directors, Bishop Stephen Gill Spottswood, in a keynote address to the NAACP annual convention in Cincinnati, charged the Nixon Administration with being "anti-Negro" and accused it of a "calculated policy to work agaist the needs and aspirations of the largest minority of its citizens." Spottswood indicted the Administration for, among other things: retreat on school desegregation; the nominations of "conservative" Southerners Clement Haynsworth and G. Harrold Carswell to the U.S. Supreme Court; and the Administration's memo calling for "benign neglect" of blacks. The statement marked a significant break between the largest and oldest black civil rights organization and the national Administration. Because of this fact, and the NAACP's reputation as a "moderate organization," the administration quickly responded, calling the charges "unfair" and "disheartening," and, at the same time, pointing out positive contributions such as the extension of the Voting Rights Act of 1965.

July 1. Kenneth Gibson took over as mayor of Newark, New Jersey, the only Afro-American mayor of an Eastern City. Gibson's, a city engineer, election was the latest political victory for Afro-Americans. By 1970 there were more than 500 elected black office-holders in the nation.

July 7-31. Racial rioting occurred in several Northern cities. On July 7 a curfew was applied in Asbury Park, New Jersey, following four days of violence; 43 persons were shot during the rioting. The curfew was lifted on July 10. Calm was restored in the New Jersey resort town after Mayor Joseph Mattice agreed to consider a list of demands presented to him by a coalition of black organizations. William Hamm, spokesman for the black commuity leaders, presented the mayor with a list of 22 demands, including requests for better housing, more jobs, and increased efforts at halting narcotics traffic. A curfew was imposed on New Bedford, Massachusetts on July 12, following four nights of racial disturbances. On July 31 a curfew was imposed on Hartford, Connecticut, following three days of rioting by Negroes and Puerto Ricans.

July 10. The Internal Revenue Service (IRS) announced that the tax-exempt status of private schools practicing racial discrimination in their admission policies would be revoked. The action came as the government sought to respond to the growing number of private all-white schools in the South. Most of these schools had sprung up in the wake of increasing desegregation of the public schools (See Above and Below).

July 29. Federal District Judge Frank M. Johnson, Jr. ordered seven Alabama state agencies to stop discriminating against blacks in their hiring practices and to give immediate job consideration to 62 black applicants denied poisions earlier. The federal judge directed state authorities to take steps to eliminate all future racial discrimination in hiring practices. He ordered them to submit a report to the court within 30 days on what had been done to comply with his order. In reviewing the case, which was filed by the Justice Department in 1968, Johnson noted that Alabama was the only state that had still refused to adopt a resolution formally prohibiting racial discrimination and providing for a system of redress in such cases. Johnson also directed the seven agencies to hire Negroes and to appoint them to positions other than custodial, domestics or laborers, when such applicants were listed as qualified and eligible.

August 1. The Defense Department reported that the percentage of black soldiers killed in Vietnam combat had declined substantially the first three months in 1970. The Pentagon report said that for the first time the percentage of black soldiers killed in action in Southeast Asia had fallen below the percentage of blacks among U. S. forces there. The Government's data showed that as of March 31, 1970, blacks serving in Indo-China represented about ten percent of the total American military presence in the area. During the same three months black battle fatalities accounted for 8.5% of the combat deaths in Southeast Asia. In 1969, blacks represented 9.5% of the total American force in the area and accounted for 13.5% of the battle deaths. The Defense department citied no specific effort to decrease the casualty rates among black servicemen in Indo-China.

August 7. Four persons died as a result of a courthouse shootout in San Rafael, Marin County, California. The incident resulted from the attempted escape of three black convicts. A judge, two convicts, and another black youth who attempted to free the convicts, were killed. On October 13, Angela Davis, an ex-professor at the University of California in Los Angeles, was arrested after a two-month nationwide search for her alleged role in the incident. Miss Davis, who was suspended from the University of California for being an "avowed Communist," was said to have supplied the weapons used in the ill-fated attempt at escape. She was charged with murder, kidnapping, and criminal conspiracy. Miss Davis was arraigned for trial in California on January 5, 1971 (See Below).

August 17. Chicago detective James A. Alfonso, a member of the police force gang-intelligence unit, died from wounds he incurred on August 13 when a rifleman fired a shot into his unmarked police car on the city's South side. Alfonso, 30, was the fourth Chicago policeman slain by riflemen in the city's black districts since mid-June. Chicago police said on August 18 that they had arrested four members of the "Main 21," the ruling body of the Black P. Stone Nation, a confederation of sixty black street gangs centering around the old Blackstone Rangers. One of those held, Charles E. Bey, 23, identified himself as the vice-president of the "Nation" and a member of the "Main 21." Chicago blacks contended that the recent wave of violence grew out of a widespread pattern of police brutality and a series of incidents in which the police had slain blacks, including Black Panther leader Fred Hampton.

August 19. The Nixon administration announced that it would soon terminate a contract with a Pennsylvania contractor for failure to comply with its "Philadelphia Plan" designed to train and employ blacks and other minority workers on construction jobs. It was the government's first enforcement action against a contractor charged with violation of a job agreement. Secretary of Health, Education, and Welfare (HEW) Elliott L. Richardson notified Edgeley Air

Products, Inc. of Levittown, Pennsylvania that his Office for Civil Rights intended to cancel a contract and bar the company from future federal contracts on the ground of noncompliance with the job accord ordered into effect by President Nixon. The government's contract with the Edgeley Company was for sheet metal work on a building at the University of Pennsylvania. Leonard Nucero, the president of Edgeley's, denied that the company practiced discrimination and said the company would appeal the termination of the contract.

August 26. A federal court in Washington refused a request by the Nixon administration to dismiss a suit pending against federal tax exemptions for the private all-white academies in the South. The court also denied a request by civil rights groups who brought the suit that all such academies have their tax-exempt status revoked immediately. The administration's lawyer told the court that the IRS would no longer grant tax exempt status to private schools practicing a policy of racial discrimination in admissions policies, but that for now the government had relied on the word of the schools in determining whether they were willing ot desegrate.

August 27. David L. Rice, minister of Information for the National Committee to Combat Fascism, surrendered to police in Omaha, Nebraska in connection with the August 17 death of a local policeman. Rice, a black man, had been sought in the slaying of Patrolman Larry D. Minard, 29, who was killed when he touched a satchel that police said had been filled with an explosive and rigged as a booby trap. Seven other Omaha policemen were injured. The eight policemen were called to a vacant house in Omaha's predominantly black Near North Side district to investigate a report of a woman in distress. Rice was charged with illegal possession of explosives.

August 29. Poindexter E. Williams, a black soldier killed in Vietnam during a mortar barrage, was buried in a formerly all-white cemetery in Fort Pierce, Florida. The cemetery had refused to bury the soldier since August 20. On August 27, a U. S. judge ordered the cemetery to accept Williams' body for burial. Williams was buried in a grave-site donated to his family by a white woman. Other whites, citing the Caucasians-only clause in lot purchase contracts, opposed the burial. Following Williams' interment, some whites who owned plots in the Hillcrest Memorial Gardens threatened to remove their relatives' bodies.

August 31. More than 200 school districts across the South that had resisted desegregation since it was ordered by the Supreme Court in 1954 reopened peacefully with newly desegregated classrooms. Nearly 300,000 black children from Virginia to Louisiana began classes with whites as threatened school boycotts by white parents failed to materialize. Despite the "massive" compliance, 175 other districts continued to hold out for segregation. Most of these were involved in litigation on the controversial issue of student busing and other problems. Some were involved in negotiations with governmental officials aimed at ending segregated school systems. Chief Justice Warren E. Burger announced, also on August 31, that the Supreme Court would consider the broad aspects of remaining school desegregation problems as the first order of business when the new court term began October 12. Many blacks and whites had raised questions concerning the legality of busing, the concept of racial balance, and the definition of a unitary school system.

August 31. Lonnie McLucas, the first of eight Black Panthers to stand trial for the 1969 slaying of a New York party member, was convicted of conspiracy to murder by a jury in New Haven, Connecticut. McLucas, 24, was acquitted on three other charges involving kidnapping resulting in death, conspiracy to kidnap, and binding with intent to commit a crime. He faced a maximum sentence of fifteen years in prison. The three other charges on which McLucas was acquitted all carried heavier penalties, including the death sentence for kidnapping resulting in death. McLucas and seven other Panthers, among them National Chairman Bobby Seale, were charged with conspiracy to kill Alex Rackley, whose body was found near Middlefield, Connecticut in May, 1969. The state had charged in the original indictments that Rackley had been slain because he had been suspected by the party of being a police informant (See Above and Below). McLucas' attorney, Theodore I. Kossoff, contended that the order for Rackley's murder originated entirely with one of the Panthers, George Sams Jr., who, the defense alleged, was responsible for the torture and slaying of Rackley.

August 31. The superintendent of public schools in Jackson, Mississippi, John S. Martin, resigned, citing the federal courts and the pressures of school desegregation. According to the New York *Times*, Martin joined at least 200 other school superintendents in the South who had quit their positions in the past two years because of the problems and tensions resulting from desegregation in their districts. William Dunn, superintendent of schools in Louisiana, predicted that the federal government's latest attempt to desegregate schools in the South would lead to a wave of resignations from experienced educators. The rate of turnover among superintendents in Alabama, Louisiana, and Georgia since 1968 was nearly 40%, almost double the rate in any previous two-year period. Louisiana led the South in the rate of turnovers. In two years, there had been 39 turnovers among the 66 district superintendents.

August 29-31. In Philadelphia one policeman was killed and six others were wounded in a series of gun battles between policemen and members of black militant organizations, including the Black Panthers. Police Commissioner Frank L. Riuzzo blamed the incidents on a group called "The Revolutionaries," which he said had plotted to murder policemen, and the Black Panther party of Philadelphia. The altercation with the Panthers resulted from a raid at dawn on August 31 at the Panther Information Center on Philadelphia's North Side. Police said they were searching for a suspect in connection with an earlier shooting.

August _____. Huey P. Newton, one of the founders and leader of the Black Panther party, was released from jail on $50,000 bail after serving more than two years in a California prison for a manslaughter conviction in the death of an Oakland, California policeman. Earlier the California Court of Appeals reversed the conviction on the grounds that the trial judge erred in instructing the jury and opened the way for Newton's release pending a new trial (See Above and Below). Charles Garry, Newton's attorney, charged that the bail was excessive, but acquiesced. Newton was greeted by a crowd of about 300 upon his release. He shouted: "The people have the power! All power to the people!"

September 1. A federal grand jury in Augusta, Georgia indicted two white city policemen on charges of violating the civil rights of two black men who were shot May 12 during a night of racial rioting that left six blacks dead and sixty other people injured (See Above). Officer William S. Dennis was accused of the fatal shooting of John W. Stokes, and Officer Louis C. Dinkins was accused of wounding Louis N. Williams. The grand jury began its inquiry into the shootings on August 24 and found cause for indictment in only one of the six deaths. After the bi-racial jury handed down the indictments, the action was denounced by Georgia governor Lester Maddox. The "national government, from the President on down," he said, "is only worrying about agitators."

September 1. The Justice Department in Washington announced that a federal judge in Cleveland, Ohio had issued a consent decree requiring Roadway Express Company, the nation's third largest trucking concern, to implement an equal employment program. The order ended the department's first effort to enjoin job discrimination throughout a company's nationwide operation. Judge Thomas D. Lambros specifically enjoined Roadway from engaging in any act or practice that had the purpose of denying blacks equal employment opportunities in hiring, upgrading and promotions. The decree also ordered Roadway, which had freight terminals in 28 states, to offer job opportunities on a first available vacancy basis to 105 individuals with seniority and other benefits for forty-five of them. The Justice Department had filed suit against Roadway in May, 1968, charging that blacks had been discriminated against in job placement and other opportunities.

September 2. U. S. District Judge Frank A. Kaufman, in Baltimore, rejected the appeal of William H. Murphy, Jr., a Black Muslim who contended that he should be exempted from military service as a conscientious objector. Kaufman ruled that the Black Muslim faith represented a political rather than a religious objection to war.

September 3. Representatives of nine black colleges charged the Nixon administration with failure to support black higher education. The educators, meeting in Detroit under the leadership of president Lucius H. Pitts of Miles College, Birmingham, called for increased government and private funds to strengthen the more than 100 black colleges and universities. Vivian Henderson, president of Clark College, Atlanta, accused the Nixon administration of an "utter lack of sensitivity" to the needs of black colleges and that this fed "the flames that already roar in the hearts of many black students." About two billion dollars was cited by Vernon Jordan, head of the United Negro College Fund (UNCF), as the minimum aid necessary to maintain black colleges. White House Press Secretary Ronald L. Ziegler, in a letter to Dr. Pitts, reminded the blacks of a July 23 pledge by the administration to increase support for their colleges.

September 5-7. The Black Panther party and members of the Women's and Gay Liberation movements held the first session of their "Revolutionary People's Constitutional Convention" in Philadelphia. Despite tensions over the August 29 slaying of a Philadelphia policeman and the subsequent arrest of fourteen persons at three Black Panther offices, the three-day conference went off peacefully. The Panther party had called the convention to rewrite the U. S. Constitution, which according to the group, did not go far enough in protecting the rights of oppressed people. Some 6,000 persons participated in the meeting. Among the Panther party's delegation were co-founder Huey P. Newton and Panther Chief-of-Staff David Hilliard. The second session of the convention was slated for November 4, 1970 in Washington, D. C.

September 9. Another round of school desegregation in the South began and was marked by stiffening white resistance to federal orders and confusion over new student assignments. More disruptions were recorded with the reopening of schools than had occurred when most of the South's schools desegregated peacefully on August 31. White parents in Mobile, Alabama resisted desegregation efforts by enrolling their children in their formerly segregated schools and by boycotting their newly assigned schools. On September 10 the NAACP charged that the Mobile school board had discriminated against black children in the inner city in the deployment of 225 school buses. The board replied that it had neither the time nor funds to buy more busses to handle inner city children. On September 14 the Justice Department accused the same school board of repeated violations of desegregation orders. Federal judge Daniel H. Thomas commanded the board to cease circumventing the school orders. There was little resistance in the Charlotte-Mecklenburg, North Carolina school system, one of the largest in the South, as the system reopened under a court-ordered desegregation plan that required extensive busing of children. The plan had aroused much community opposition in Charlotte. School officials said 80% of the high school students reported to their classes. The school superintendent in Bogalusa, Louisiana closed the public schools on September 14 after police used tear gas to end a fight between black and white students at a recently desegregated school. Police Chief Thomas Mixon, Jr. estimated that 600 high school students were involved in the two hour altercation. Fourteen students were arrested.

September 11.   The Internal Revenue Service (IRS) revoked the tax-exempt classification of five all-white private academies in Mississippi after the schools refused to enroll black children. The cancellations brought to sixteen the number of all-white academies in the South that had lost their tax-exempt status since the IRS prohibited tax deductions for segregated schools (See Above). The sixteen schools, and the five in Mississippi, were among several in the South, forty-one of them in Mississippi, named in a court order directing governmental officials to revoke tax-exempt status for all-white private schools practicing racial discrimination in admission policies.

September 12.   Governor Ronald Reagan of California signed into law a bill prohibiting the busing of students "for any purpose or any reason without the written permission of the parent or guardian." The law was to take effect in November. The California branch of the NAACP announced that it would test the constitutionality of the measure in court.

September 13.   Eldridge Cleaver, exiled Black Panther party leader, presided over the opening of the party's first "international section" in Algiers. The Algerian government, which had broken off diplomatic ties with the U. S. in 1967, had formally accorded the Panther party the status of a "liberation movement."

September 14-15.   One black youth was killed and 21 other persons injured during a day-long gun battle between police and blacks in a New Orleans housing project. The incident began September 14 when two black undercover policemen who had infiltrated the National Committee to Combat Fascism (NCCF), an off-shoot of the Black Panther party, were discovered and beaten. They escaped when the NCCF turned them over to a crowd of about 100 blacks for a "people's trial." Later, police returned to the project to investigate reports of a burning automobile. Policemen and firemen were fired upon and the melee broke out in full force. Fourteen blacks, most of them from the NCCF, were arrested during the disturbance and charged with attempted murder.

September 18.   Lonnie McLucas, the first of eight Black Panther party members to stand trial for the slaying of Alex Rackley, was sentenced to 12-15 years in prison by a New Haven, Connecticut court. McLucas had been convicted of conspiracy to murder in the Rackley case on August 31 (See Above and Below). Superior Court Judge Harold M. Mulvey assessed the maximum term allowed under Connecticut law for the crime of conspiracy to murder. McLucas' attorney, Theodore I. Kossoff, immediately filed notice of appeal.

September 28.   For the first time, an H.E.W. hearing examiner ruled that a Northern school district was illegally segregating its pupils according to race. The Ferndale, Michigan school district was deprived of $275,000 in federal aid because of its segregated elementary schools.

September 28.   Cleveland L. Sellers, Jr., a black activist, was convicted by a bi-racial jury in Orangeburg, South Carolina of participating in a riot on the campus of South Carolina State College in 1968, in which three black students were killed by state highway patrolmen (See Above). Sellers, a former national program secretary fo. SNCC, was sentenced to the maximum term of one year in prison and a fine of $250. Sellers was released on a $5,000 appeal bond by State Circuit Court Judge John Grimball, who said that the young black activist could leave the state in order to attend college. On September 26, Judge Grimball had ordered a directed verdict of acquittal of two other riot charges against Sellers, citing the fact that the prosecution had failed to prove that Sellers had incited the Orangeburg students to riot. During the 1968 riot, 27 blacks were wounded, including Sellers, in addition to the three students slain.

September 30. The Race Relations Information Center in Nashville, Tennessee reported that there were only three black executives among the 3,182 senior officers of the largest fifty American corporate firms. These were Robert C. Weaver of the Metropolitan Life Insurance Co., Clifton R. Wharton, Jr. of the Equitable Life Assurance Society, and Thomas A. Wood of the Chase Manhattan Bank. All of these men held the position of corporate director.

October 1. J. Stanley Pottinger, director of the Office of Civil Rights of the Department of Health, Education and Welfare (HEW), reported that federal school monitors in the South had found extensive in-school segregation of black pupils. Pottinger said his office had investigated 120 desegregated school districts since the fall term began and found patterns of in-school segregation in at least half of them. The matter of segregation by classrooms received much attention from Senator Walter F. Mondale's (D.,Minn.) Select Committee on Equal Educational Opportunity throughout the summer of 1970. Pottinger announced that the Nixon administration intended to move against the new form of segregation but only after it had solicited the advice of educators. He promised to develop guidelines by the spring semester of 1971.

October 1. A federal court in Buffalo, New York ruled unconstitutional a New York statute that had made it illegal for appointed school boards to reshuffle pupil assignment plans to achieve racial balance without the consent of parents. The law, which was enacted in May, 1969, was challenged by a group of black and white parents in Buffalo. School administrators in the South had hailed it as a means of forestalling school desegregation. The court found the law contrary to the 14th Amendment, in that it served to continue segregation in the schools and involved the state in racial discrimination.

October 1. Secretary of Health, Education, and Welfare Elliot L. Richardson announced a thirty percent, or $30 million, increase in federal aid to predominantly black colleges. This increased the total aid from HEW to $129 million a year. Secretary Richardson noted that the increase was in response to recent appeals by black educators for more aid. Blacks complained that matching provisions of the fund grants and early deadlines for applications made it difficult for most Afro-American institutions to qualify.

October 5. The Internal Revenue Service reported that nine all-white private academies in Mississippi had agreed to admit black students. In the same announcement, the IRS said it had removed fourteen other all-white academies from its list of schools eligible for tax-exempt status. These suspensions brought to 38 the number of private schools in the state which had lost their tax-exempt status.

October 5-November 8. Violent racial clashes connected with school desegregation occurred in three cities, North as well as South. Four white boys and one black youth were shot and wounded in two apparently related incidents on October 5 and 7 outside a desegregated high school in Pontiac, Michigan. A second black student was struck down by a car near Pontiac Central High School on October 7 as white and black students continued their two day battle with rocks and bottles. Tensions had run high in Pontiac following a recent court decision ordering desegregation of Pontiac's public schools. Trenton, New Jersey's public schools were closed for two days, October 29-30, due to racial disorders stemming from the school board's decision to implement a student busing plan. On November 1, the board voted to reopen the schools, and a dusk-to-dawn curfew that had been imposed on the city on October 29 was ordered relaxed by mayor Arthur J. Holland. The trouble started on October 29 when fighting began between 100 black and white students in a predominantly Italian section of the city. Fighting spread into the downtown area when bands of black youths surged into the district hurling bottles at policemen and breaking windows. More than 200 persons were arrested during the three days of disorders. The fighting was apparently triggered by the school board's decision to implement a busing plan to achieve racial balance in the schools. The plan called for the cross-town busing of 55 black and 100 white students. Four days of sporadic sniper fire and burnings erupted in Henderson, North Carolina, November 5-8, in the aftermath of a dispute over the county's school desegregation policies. Police jailed 101 persons during the violence. Blacks in Henderson had been engaged in a long protest over a decision by school officials to reopen an all-black school in the community. The blacks charged that the board of education was trying to evade desegregation by reopening the school. National guardsmen were called to help restore order. By November 9, the school board had agreed to close the school in contention and bus its pupils to desegregated schools. The National Guard remained on duty.

October 12. The U.S. Commission on Civil Rights reported that there had been a major breakdown in the enforcement of the nation's legal mandates prohibiting racial discrimination. The Commission urged President Nixon to use "courageous moral leadership" and, within the White House, to establish Committees to oversee enforcement of court decrees, executive orders and legislation relating to civil rights. Rev. Theodore M. Hesburgh, the Chairman of the Commission, said the findings were based on a six-month study of the executive departments and agencies charged with enforcing the nation's civil rights laws. The report, entitled "The Federal Civil Rights Enforcement Effort," asserted that "the credibility of the government's total civil rights efforts" had been "seriously underminded." Hesburgh warned that "unless we get serious about this, the country is on a collision course."

October 12-14. The Supreme Court heard arguments on student busing and racial balance in the schools of the South. The arguments were heard by the court as part of appeals filed by attorneys representing school districts in Charlotte, North Carolina and Mobile, Alabama. Attorneys for the NAACP Legal Defense and Educational

Fund, Inc., representing black children, argued on October 13 that each black child had a constitutional right to be enrolled in a school that was not recognizably black. The lawyers contended that any desegregation plan that did not eliminate every all-black school should be adjudged as inadequate. The NAACP lawyers told the court that the *Brown* vs *Board of Education* decision of 1954 would be undermined if the court now permitted some Southern school districts to maintain some recognizably black schools. Solicitor General Ervin N. Griswold, representing the Justice Department, rebutted the NAACP argument on October 12 and 14. The Solicitor General contended that the NAACP's petition amounted to a demand for racial balance in the schools, something which the Constitution did not require. Lawyers for the school districts told the court on October 13 that the Brown decision is violated by court-ordered desegregation plans that assigned children to schools by race, and that the busing of school children to increase the incidence of desegregation was unconstitutional. The court promised a ruling during its present term.

October 13. Angela Davis, the 26 year old black professor, who had been the object of a two-month, nationwide search because of her alleged role in the slaying of a California judge in August (See Above) was seized by agents of the FBI in a New York City motel. She was arraigned October 14 in federal court on a charge of unlawful flight to avoid prosecution on the California charges. The federal charge was later suspended when the California warrants charging her with the capital offenses arrived in New York. Federal authorities announced that it was cusomary in such cases for the state warrants to take precedence. Miss Davis' Attorney, John J. Abt, refused to waive extradition to California. Since the black woman was being held for capital offenses, no bail was permitted. David R. Poindexter, Jr., a 36 year old black companion, was released from jail on October 16 on $100,000 bail, having been arrested with Miss Davis and charged with harboring a fugitive.

October 19. The NAACP and the Washington law firm of Rauh and Silard filed suit against the Department of Health, Education, and Welfare (HEW) charging it with "general and calculated default" in its enforcement of federal school desegregation guidelines.

The suit accused the federal agency of laxity in applying the cut-off of federal school funds to force recalcitrant school districts to comply with the law. It was the second time in two weeks that the government's enforcement of civil rights had been questioned. The U.S. Commission on Civil Rights reported October 12 (See Above) that there had been a "major breakdown" in the enforcement of the nation's laws forbidding racial discrimination. Elliot L. Richardson, HEW Secretary, replied that his department was "committed faithfully to carry out both the letter and the spirit of the 1964 Civil Rights Act."

October 19. U.S. District Court Judge Julius J. Hoffman dismissed the government's conspiracy charges against Bobby G. Seale, Chairman of the Black Panther Party, at the request of the U.S. Attorney in Chicago. William J. Bauer told the Judge that "it would be inappropriate to try Seale alone on a conspiracy charge." Seale was one of eight defendants charged with conspiracy to cross state lines with intent to riot at the 1968 Democratic National Convention in Chicago. Judge Hoffman had severed Seale's case after the Black Panther leader had bitterly denounced the manner in which the jurist handled the trial. Seale's co-defendants, all whites, were subsequently acquitted on the conspiracy to riot charge. Seale still faced a four year prison term on contempt of court charges in Chicago as well as charges of kidnapping and murder in the slaying of a New York Black Panther Party Member (See Above and Below).

October 24-25. Violent clashes between blacks and policemen continued in Northern ghettoes. On the night of October 24-25, several car loads of armed blacks riddled the police station at Cairo, Illinois with hundreds of rounds of gunfire three times in six hours. No policemen were wounded and the attackers were repulsed after each assault. It was the first outbreak in racially-tense Cairo since September, 1969, when disturbances broke out in the all-black Pyramid Housing Project. The October attacks began the evening of the 24th shortly after a grocery store owned by whites and located across from the Pyramid Housing Project was burned. Cairo Mayor A. B. Thomas called the incident an "armed insurrection." In Detroit, on October 24, one black policeman, Edward Smith, 26, was killed and another wounded in an altercation with members of the National Committee to Combat Fascism. The policemen were felled by shotgun blasts from the NCCF's headquarters, according to police accounts. Fifteen blacks were arrested after a day-long confrontation around the NCCF offices. The seven men and eight women were charged with murder and conspiracy. The disturbance was triggered by an incident involving the sale of Black Panther Party literature on a Detroit street corner. The NCCF claimed that two policemen beat two youths distributing the literature and that police fired the first shots in the melee.

October 28. Edward A. Poindexter and David L. Rice, leaders of the National Committee to combat Fascism, were ordered to stand trial in Omaha, Nebraska on murder charges in connection with the August 17 slaying of an Omaha policeman (See Above). The two blacks, who had been in custody since August, were to remain in jail without bond.

November 20-22. More than 500 inmates reportedly took part in a racial disturbance at the sprawling 16,000 acre Cumming prison farm, 90 miles southeast of Little Rock, Arkansas. The fighting stemmed from inmates' demands for separate quarters for black and white prisoners. Commissioner of Corrections Robert Sawer reported that state troopers were called in after the violence reached riot proportions; some of the prisoners had armed themselves with knives, pipes, and broomstick handles. Prison guards broke up the fighting with tear gas.

December _____. Captain Curtis R. Smothers and six other black Army officers petitioned Secretary of the Army Stanley R. Resar for a court of inquiry to have an investigation of alleged racial bias against black soldiers in West Germany. The seven black servicemen complained of widespread housing discrimination. They charged that the bias was going unchallenged because the U.S. government failed to press the West Germans to enforce the laws against discrimination. According to the blacks, "only an open court of inquiry convened by the Secretary of the Army could adequately determine the facts, assess the feasibility of alternative solutions and inquire into factors motivating the long-standing noncompliance with applicable laws and regulations." Under military procedures, a court of inquiry was usually convened when the issues involved were so complex that normal proceedings would not go far enough into them, or when charges were levied against high-ranking officers. Smothers, a military circuit judge in West Germany, was joined in the petition by Major Washington C. Hill, Lieutenant Edwin Dorn, Sergeant Willie Payne and three Specialists, 4th Class, Gregory Jones, Bobby Metcalf, and James Wilder. On March 13, 1971, Pentagon officials returned to Washington after discussing the December petition with Smothers in West Germany. Smothers was then summoned to Washington for further discussions. This latter event was seen by some sources as an attempt to persuade Smothers to withdraw his petition. On June 3, 1971 the black members of the U.S. House of Representatives announced that they were sending a staff member to Germany, Greece, Italy, and Turkey to investigate complaints of racism and discrimination in the U.S. armed forces abroad. Rep. Shirley Chisholm (D., N.Y.), Chairman of the Black Caucus' Military Affairs Committee said racial tension between the Germans and black enlisted men was reported very critical.

December 11. The Justice Department filed suit in a federal district court in Alabama charging that the United States Steel Corporation, the United Steelworkers of America, the AFL-CIO and twelve union locals had violated the Civil Rights Act of 1964, which prohibits discrimination in employment. U.S. Steel operates plants in the Birmingham area. On December 14, the Chairman of the Board of U.S. Steel Corporation announced that the Justice Department had demanded that the company allocate fifty percent of its office and clerical jobs in its Fairfield, Alabama plant to blacks in the next five years and that blacks make up forty percent of all those promoted to management positions during the next five years.

December 11. A federal grand jury investigating the killing of two black youths at Jackson State College, Mississippi, on May 14, 1970 (See Above) concluded its deliberations without returning any indictments. The jury also failed to submit a report.

December 27. The U. S. State Department invited fourteen leading Soviet scientists to attend the forthcoming murder trial of Angela Davis, former UCLA professor and avowed communist (See Above), to assure themselves that she would receive a fair trial. The invitation was personally sanctioned by President Nixon. The offer was an apparent response to a Cablegram sent by the fourteen scientists to the President asking him "to safeguard the life of Angela Davis and give her an opportunity of continuing her scientific work." According to U. S. officials, the government's quick response was due to the high regard in which the scientists were held by professional colleagues in the U. S. Among the fourteen scientists were Igor P. Tamm, a Nobel Prize winning physicist, and Pyotr L. Kapitsa, the dean of Soviet physicists. It was the first time that Soviet personalities had been invited to observe American judicial proceedings.

December 30. The U. S. Court of Appeals for the Third Circuit in Philadelphia ordered the Department of Housing and Urban Development (HUD) to "affirmatively promote fair housing" in considering applications for support of housing projects. The case involved HUD mortgage insurance and rent supplements in a predominantly black neighborhood in Philadelphia. The court ruled that HUD must determine, through public hearings or other means, whether such projects would increase or maintain segregation. According to the court, HUD could not support such housing unless it determined that the need for urban renewal or increased minority housing "clearly outweighs the disadvantages of increasing or perpetuating racial concentration." The court reasoned that after the passage of the 1964 and 1968 Civil Rights Acts, HUD could no longer "remain blind to the very real effect that racial concentration has had in the development of urban blight." Edwin D. Wolf, executive director of the Philadelphia office of the Lawyers Committee for Civil Rights, said on January 4, 1971 that the ruling was a landmark decision which could have an impact comparable to the Supreme Court's 1954 school desegregation decision.

1971

January 1. James A. Floyd was named mayor of Princeton Township, an affluent, predominantly white suburban community in west central New Jersey. Floyd became the first black mayor in the township's history. He was selected unanimously by the five-member Township Committee, Princeton's governing body. In December of 1970, the same committee had named Frederick M. Porter, a black police lieutenant, Chief of Police.

January 4. The Reverend Leon Howard Sullivan, a forty-eight year old Philadelphia black minister, was elected to the Board of Directors of the General Motors Corporation. Sullivan, pastor of Philadelphia's largest Protestant church — Zion Baptist, was the founder of Opportunities Industrialization Centers of America, a job-training program for blacks and other minorities, and a director of the Girard Trust Bank in Philadelphia. His election to the GM Board was interpreted as a move to placate demands that the company, the world's largest industrial corporation, give the public and minority groups a voice in corporate decision-making. At GM's annual stockholders meeting in May, 1970, a reform group, the Project on Corporate Responsibility, had criticized GM for not having a black director on its board.

January 5. A federal labor panel charged the Bethlehem Steel Corporation, the second largest steel producer in the United States, with discriminating against blacks through its seniority system. A report compiled by the panel was sent to Secretary of Labor James D. Hodgson who would decide what sanctions, if any, to impose on the firm. The three member federal panel reached a unanimous decision against Bethlehem, but disagreed on what corrective measures should be taken. In a statement which accompanied the report, Bethlehem denied the charge but agreed to set new hiring, promotion and training quotas for blacks while studying the government's report. The action against Bethlehem was the second taken against one of the nation's major steel corporations. On December 11, 1970 the Justice Department had filed a suit against the U. S. Steel Corporation accusing it of bias against blacks at its Fairfield, Alabama steelworks (See Above).

January 5. Angela Davis was arraigned on charges of murder, kidnapping, and criminal conspiracy in a Marin County, California courtroom for her alleged participation in the August incident at the San Rafael Courthouse which resulted in the deaths of four men (See Above). Flanked by her attorney, Howard Moore, a black Atlantan, Miss Davis declared her innocence and said she was the "target of a political frame-up."

January 6. F. B. I. Director J. Edgar Hoover issued his annual report in which he stated that the number of racial incidents in schools had declined during the year, but attacks on police by blacks had increased. The F. B. I. chief said racial disorders in secondary schools declined from 299 in the first months of the 1969-70 year to 160 in the corresponding period of the new term. Hoover warned, however, that "the number of incidents of racial disorder that did occur in our cities and in secondary schools, along with the many unwarranted attacks on police, strongly indicated that we are far from the realization of racial harmony in the nation." Hoover said there was a "marked increase" in attacks on policemen by persons identifying themselves as Black Panthers. He said such persons were responsible for the deaths of six policemen and the wounding of 22 others and that in the previous two years, five policemen were killed and 42 wounded under such circumstances.

January 11. The United States Supreme Court agreed to review the 1967 draft evasion conviction of former heavy-weight boxing champion Muhammad Ali. The action assured that Ali, who won the championship under the name of Cassius Clay, would be free to fight the recognized title holder, Joe Frazier in March. (Frazier defeated Ali on March 8 in New York.) Ali had been convicted when the courts rejected his contention that he should be exempted from the draft because of his religious status as a Black Muslim Minister. The current appeal was based largely on the Supreme Court's ruling in 1969 that conscientious objectors could base their claims on philosophical or moral objections rather than strictly religious grounds.

January 14. The U. S. Supreme Court ruled that Southern states must obtain federal approval before making any changes in their election laws that might affect the rights of black voters as provided by the 1965 Voting Rights Act. The order came in a case brought by two black voters and six defeated black candidates in the 1969 municipal elections in Canton, Mississippi. The plantiffs contended that the city in shifting polling places, annexing neighborhoods with white majorities and changing to at-large elections of aldermen had discouraged and diluted the black vote. The Supreme Court returned the case to the district court to decide if the election should be reheld.

January 14. Secretary of Health, Education and Welfare Elliot L. Richardson announced in Washington that the Nixon administration would soon turn its attention to the task of increasing the rate of school desegregation in the North. The report citied a survey showing the percentage of blacks attending desegregated schools in the North and West rose from 27.6% to 27.7% in the period since 1968. This compared with a two year increase from 18.4% to 38.1% in the South. The administration concluded that a Northern drive was necessary because there was now more desegregated school systems in the South than in the North (See Also Below).

January 14. The Oregon Court of Appeals ruled that mental anguish was one of the effects of racial discrimination and could be compensated by a cash award. The court sustained the contention of Beverley A. Williams, a young black woman, who had charged she had been discriminated against when Margaret C. Joyce refused to rent her an apartment in Portland. Miss Williams' charge had been earlier upheld by the Oregon state Bureau of Labor which assessed Mrs. Joyce $200 for humiliating Miss Williams and $140 to pay for her moving expenses, but the cash award for humiliation was overthrown by the state circuit court on appeal by Mrs. Joyce. The Court of Appeals, in setting aside the circuit court's ruling said that compensation for humiliation was proper.

January 16. Preliminary studies of the 1970 U. S. Census indicated very little racial integration of American suburbs during the 1960s, according to a *Washington Post* report. Specialists at the Census Bureau predicted that early trends showing little suburban integration would hold true even as more detailed analyses were completed. Meyer Zitter, assistant chief of the Bureau's population division, estimated that about 15% of the nation's blacks lived within metropolitan areas and outside the central cities. The figures for whites was nearly 40%. Census officials said that if the preliminary reports were sustained, it would again illustrate that whites were fleeing the inner cities to the suburbs. During the 1960s there was a reported net loss of about 2½ million whites from the inner city areas and an increase of about three million blacks. Two-thirds of the rise in the number of black inner-city dwellers was attributable to births. These preliminary reports came at a time when the Nixon administration was still shaping its policies regarding suburban desegregation.

January 17. A jury in Chicago acquitted seven members of the Black P. Stone nation, a confederation of sixty black street gangs, of murder in the August, 1970 sniper slaying of a Chicago detective. All were acquitted of charges of murder and conspiracy to murder in the death of Detective James A. Alfonso, Jr. (See Above). The acquittal came three days after the bi-racial jury had begun deliberations. Those freed were Edward Bey, Lamar Bell, Tony Carter, Dennis Griffin, Ronald Florence, William Throup, and Elton Wriks. The alleged involvement of the black gangs in the murder had exacerbated tensions between the black community and Chicago police. Concomitantly, Chicago black leaders, including the S. C. L. C.'s Operation Breadbasket head, the Rev. Jesse Jackson, had criticized the black gangs for terrorizing the black communities.

January 20. The North Carolina Supreme Court sustained the state's policy of providing school buses for urban children involved in desegregation programs. As long as state funds were used to transport children from rural areas to their schools, the court reasoned, city dwelling children must have the same rights. The ruling struck down a lower court's prohibition on the use of state funds for busing. In effect, the Supreme Court's decision gave the state legislature the choice of continuing busing for all children who required it or discontinuing the practice altogether. An assistant state attorney general expressed the view that the court's decision could not be appealed because it did not involve any constitutional issue.

February 1. Howard Jordan, Jr., the president of Savannah (Georgia) State College, assumed duties as vice-chancellor of the Georgia State Board of Regents, becoming the first black so named. Dr. Jordan has been president of Savannah State College since 1963. His new duties involved handling administrative matters for all state-run colleges and universities in Georgia.

February 1. The U.S. Court of Appeals for the Fifth Circuit in New Orleans ruled that local governments must provide public services, such as road paving and sewers, on a racially equal basis. The suit was filed by black residents of Shaw, Mississippi. According to the court, no compelling interests "could possibly justify the gross disparities in services between black and white areas of town."

February 4-5. Eight black federal employees charged in a suit filed February 4 in the U.S. Court in Washington, D. C. that the Federal Service Entrance Examination, the principal test that must be passed by qualified college graduates for civil service posts, was "culturally and racially discriminatory." The eight plaintiffs, employees of The Department of Housing and Urban Development's (HUD) Chicago regional office, alleged that the examination violated the equal opportunity guarantees of the Fifth Amendment. They also charged that it violated, among other things, the 1964 Civil Rights Act. The suit asked the court to prevent the use of the examination until its alleged discriminatory aspects were eliminated, and that the use of other testing procedures be stopped until a determination could be made of their relation to specific job requirements. According to the plaintiffs, about 49% of the 100,000 persons who took the test in 1969 finished with scores above 70 [the passing percentile] with "a disproportionately low percentage" of blacks and other minority group members passing. In another development involving blacks and examinations, Edward F. Bell, president of the National Bar Association (NBA), a predominatly black lawyers' group, asked other lawyers' organizations on February 5 to ascertain whether bar examinations should be abolished as racially descriminatory. Bell said recent studies seemed to indicate that bar examinations discriminated against black law school graduates. The Detroit attorney cited lawsuits that had been filed in several states by law students seeking to abolish the bar examinations because they did not test a graduate's legal knowledge.

February 5. The Justice Department filed a suit in the U. S. District Court in Atlanta charging the Clayton County, Georgia, school board with maintaining a dual public school system. The Clayton system was described by the department as one of 50 remaining recalcitrant school districts in the South. According to the suit, Clayton officials assigned its 1,479 black and 25,220 white pupils as well as their teachers to different sets of schools. The department requested a court order demanding that the county submit a desegregation plan immediately.

Judge Oren Harris of the U. S. District Court for the Eastern District of Arkansas issued an ultimatum to the officials of the Watson Chapel, Arkansas School District No. 24, warning them that they faced stiff jail terms if they continued to defy a court-ordered desegregation ruling. Harris said a fine of $350 a day would also be levied for each day they remained in contempt of court by ignoring the school order. Watson Chapel District, which included part of Pine Bluff, Arkansas, as well as the town of Watson Chapel, had about 4,000 students, almost half of them black. Judge Harris had ordered all children in grades one through four to attend three elementary schools, all of which would retain a substantial white majority.

The Justice Department, also on February 5, charged the Henry County, Virginia, school district with failing to execute a desegregation arrangement that it had earlier agreed to implement. In a suit filed in the federal district court in Danville, Virginia, the department accused the Henry County system of continuing to assign its high school pupils on a freedom-of-choice plan in violation of the 1964 Civil Rights Act. Henry County, according to the suit, had used the freedom-of-choice scheme to assign nearly 800 black pupils to an all-black high school.

February 6-9. National guardsmen patrolled the streets of Wilmington, North Carolina, in the wake of four days of racial violence in which two persons were killed. The unrest was linked to a boycott of Wilmington's high school by black students. Blacks were protesting the city's desegregation plans. The first of the two slayings took place on February 6 when a black youth was killed by a policeman who said the boy pointed a shotgun at him. Blacks in Wilmington asserted the youth was shot as he helped move furniture from a home threatened by a nearby fire. The second victim was a white man who was shot later outside of a black church which was being used as headquarters by the boycotting blacks. The white man was armed with a pistol. Local officers, aided by the 600 National guardsmen restored order on February 8, but remained on alert.

February 10. The Gallup Poll reported that American blacks continued to disapprove of the way President Nixon was handling his job by a 2-1 ratio, the same ratio recorded in surveys the previous spring (See Above and Below).

February 11. Scores of white high school students walked out of their school near Pine Bluff, Arkansas, to protest a court-ordered desegregation plan. They were greeted by their parents and other adult supporters. The mostly peaceful dmonstration was the only incident on the day the school district began operating under the desegregation order. Watson Chapel School District No. 24 reluctantly implemented the plan after a federal judge warned the school board members that they faced stiff jail terms and fines if they continued to defy his orders (See Above).

February 16. Twenty-two whites were indicted by a county grand jury in Darlington, South Carolina on riot charges in connection with a March, 1970 incident in which a mob of angry whites overturned two school buses transporting black children to desegregated schools in nearby Lamar (See Above). Charges against 21 other whites, including a state legislator, were dropped by the grand jury.

February 17. Lucius D. Amerson, sheriff of Macon County, Alabama and the state's first black sheriff since Reconstruction, and one of his black deputies were arrested on a federal indictment accusing them of beating a black prisoner. Amerson and his deputy, Richard Coleman, Jr., posted bonds of $1,000 each on the charge of violating the civil rights of a prisoner, Wilbert D. Harris, while acting under the cover of the law. Harris had been arrested in Tuskegee, County-seat of Macon County, in August, 1970 and charged with driving while intoxicated. The prisoner reportedly used a pistol to disarm two deputies and was also accused of firing at Amerson. Harris was subdued and charged with assault with intent to murder. The alleged beating by Amerson and Coleman reportedly took place after Harris was subdued. Conviction on the federal charge carried a penalty of up to a year in prison and a $1,000 fine (See Also Above and Below).

February 17. The Carnegie Commission on Higher Education called for a tripling of federal aid to the nation's 105 black colleges and universities. In a report, entitled "From Isolation to Mainstream: Problems of the Colleges Founded for Negroes," the Commission also urged increased funds from states, corporations and foundations to allow black colleges to double their current enrollment of 150,000. The commission, headed by Dr. Clark Kerr, said that the black colleges were faced with special difficulties at a time of major transition as they emerged from their "historic isolation" into the mainstream of U.S. education. The report pointed out that at a time, when other institutions were enlarging black enrollment and developing black studies programs, the black colleges had to compete for students, faculty and financial resources. In addition, black colleges had to meet the special expenses of remedial training for poorly prepared students and financial aid for the 70% of their students who required some type of scholarship assistance.

March 3. The U.S. Census Bureau announced that contrary to earlier reports the rate of black migration from the South to the North during the 1960's had remained unchanged from the pace of the two previous decades. Earlier statistics had indicated that the number of Southern blacks moving North had dropped sharply during the 1960's to about half the levels of the prior 20 years. The new figures from the 1970 census showed that the migration pace through the 1960's was nearly the same as the high levels of the 1940's and 1950's. According to the Bureau's analysts more than three-fourths of the 1.4 million blacks who left the South during the decade settled in five large industrial centers. New York had a

Southern black influx of 396,000; California 272,000; New Jersey, Michigan and Illinois each gained about 120,000. The analysts said there were indications that the migration rate would continue to be high and might increase in the 1970's. The Bureau also reported an increased movement of whites to the South. This dual movement of blacks to the North and whites to the South was reportedly a continuation of a long-term trend toward distribution of black population throughout the U.S. According to the Bureau's report, the South still contained 53% of the nation's blacks, compared to 77% in 1940. Since 1940, the percentage of blacks in the Northeast and North Central states had risen from about 11% to 20%. Bureau analysts said that each of the eleven states of the Confederacy had lost residents. Mississippi and Alabama lead, with 279,000 and 231,000 respectively. Secretary of Commerce Maurice H. Stans speculated that the continued black Northern migration was due in part to the "higher welfare benefits" of the Northern states. He added, however, that he assumed that "greater job opportunities (in the North) would be the chief motivating factor." The Bureau statistics showed that there were about 22,672,570 blacks in the United States or about 11.2% of the population. In 1960 the figures were 18,871,-831 or about 10.6%.

March 8. The U.S. Supreme Court ruled that employers could not use job tests that had the effect of screening out blacks if the tests were not related to ability to do the work. According to the Court, the employment bias section of the 1946 Civil Rights Act involved the consequences of employment practices, not simply whether the practices were motivated by racial bias. The Court imposed limits on the use of general educational and aptitude tests and said that "any tests used must measure the person for the job and not the person in the abstract." The case stemmed from the application for promotion by 13 black workers at the Duke Power Company's generating plant in Draper, North Carolina. The NAACP, the Justice Department and the federal Equal Employment Opportunity Commission had sought the ruling.

March 8. F.B.I. files stolen from a Bureau office in Media, Pennsylvania, and released to the public revealed several documents relating to black activist groups. One of the F.B.I. memoranda was a November 4, 1970 dispatch from Director J. Edgar Hoover ordering an investigation of all groups "organized to project the demands of black students." The dispatch said that "increased campus disorders involving black students" posed a definite threat to the nation's "stability and security" and indicated need for an increase in both the quality and quantity of intelligence information on Black Students Unions and similar groups. The memorandum went on to say that such groups were targets for influence and control by "violent-prone Black Panther party and other extremists." (Black Student Unions and other such groups had sprung up on mostly predominantly white campuses during the past five years. Their origins stemmed from the increased enrollment of black students at such schools and the bias which they allegedly encountered on the campuses. Sometimes their organized protests bordered on violence. See, for instance, the entry for January 8, 1969 above. The memoranda also contained a report of a 1970 convention of the National Association of Black Students at Wayne State University in Detroit, reports of surveillance of black student activities at Swarthmore College in Pennsylvania, of the Philadelphia Black Panthers, and the National Black Economic Conference held in Philadelphia during 1970. Muhammad Kenyatta, who headed the Philadelphia conference, was mentioned prominently in several of the F.B.I. documents. Kenyatta said on March 24 that he had received copies of the memoranda relating to him before they were published. He would not identify his sources. On March 23 Attorney General John Mitchell denounced the thefts and the publication of the records. He warned that the information could "endanger the lives" of "persons engaged in investigative activities on behalf of the United States."

March 11. Whitney M. Young, Jr., executive director of the National Urban League, died while on a trip to Nigeria. Young and a group of other Americans, white and black, were in Lagos attending an Afro-American conference designed to bridge the gap between Africans and Americans, particularly black Americans. Young drowned while swimming with a party which included former U.S. Attorney General Ramsey Clark. Young left his position as Dean of the School of Social Work at Atlanta University in 1961 to become head of the nation's leading black economic and social reform agency. He made the organization more effective and increased its influence. During the height of the Civil Rights Era, Young became, with Martin Luther King, Jr., Roy Wilkins and James Farmer, one of the "Big Four" leaders. President Nixon expressed personal sorrow at the news of his death. The President said: "I have lost a friend, Black America has lost a gifted and commanding champion of its just cause . . . ."

March 23.   The Rev. Walter E. Fauntroy, a Baptist minister and a Democrat, was elected the District of Columbia's first non-voting Congressional delegate in this century. Fauntroy polled 58% of the vote to defeat Attorney John A. Nevins, a white Republican, Julius W. Hobson, a black independent, and three minor independent candidates. Fauntroy's salary, $42,500 per year, would equal that of other members of the House of Representatives and he would be permitted to sit on the House District Committee, vote in other committees, but could not vote on the House floor. The black members of Congress immediately selected Fauntroy as the thirteenth member of the so-called Black Caucus.

March 24.   The NAACP filed a suit challenging the legality of zoning laws that prohibited the construction of apartment buildings in suburban communities. It was the first time the NAACP had gone to court against suburban zoning laws. The action was taken in the federal court in Brooklyn, New York, against the town of Oyster Bay, New York. It charged that the town's zoning laws had "foreclosed black and other non-white minorities from obtaining housing in the town," with results that "intensify and harden patterns of racial ghetto living" in the city of New York. Roy Wilkins, executive secretary of the NAACP, said black workers employed in Oyster Bay often could not find suitable housing. He said 45 new industries had located in Oyster Bay since 1965, but that workers earning less than $17,000 a year could not afford to buy houses in the town because of the minimum lot sizes prescribed by the zoning laws.

March 24.   The Southern Regional Council issued a report in Atlanta which said that for the first time desegregation in the South's public schools was the rule rather than the exception. This transformation had occurred, the Council said, despite the proliferation of all-white private academies in the region and the continued operation of some all-black schools. At the same time, the Council accused the Nixon administration of "playing a deceptive game of numbers by using misleading figures about the extent of actual desegregation. Despite the recent gains, the Council asserted that the South was "a far cry" from "the final dismantling of the dual [school] system." Desegregation in 1970 and in 1971, according to the Council, was less successful than the administration asserted in its figures, but "more successful than policies of [the] government gave it any right to be." The Council's report was entitled "The South and Her Children: School Desegregation, 1970-71."

March 25. President Nixon met with a group of black members of the U.S. House of Representatives to receive a list of sixty grievances presented on behalf of black Americans. The so-called Black Caucus asked for reforms in welfare, job discrimination and job placement, social justice, school desegregation, etc. The President appointed five White House staff members to work on the list of recommendations. The meeting, first proposed in 1969, was set up soon after the black members of the House boycotted the President's State of the Union Address in January. The group charged that the President's failure to meet with them up until that time constituted a flagrant disregard for the opinions of black Americans (See Also Below).

March 31. Admiral Elmo R. Zumwalt, Jr., Chief of Naval Operations, announced the formation of a six-man team, including three admirals, to oversee a five-year program to recruit more black officers and enlisted men for the Navy. The aim of the recruiting drive was to bring the numbers of black Navy personnel up to the level of the nearly 12% black representation in the total U.S. population. Black recruiters were added to the staffs of the 37 recruiting stations across the nation. New Navy Reserve Officer Training Corps units were added at Savannah State College in Georgia and Southern University at Baton Rouge, Louisiana. These were to supplement the sole existing black Navy ROTC unit at Prairie View A and M College in Texas. The Navy said it would also increase the number of black midshipmen at the Naval Academy at Annapolis, Maryland. On June 2, 1971 Samuel L. Gravely, Jr. was named the first black Admiral in the Navy. Vice Admiral Raymond Peet performed the ritual known as "frocking" which promoted Gravely from Captain to Admiral. Gravely became director of naval communications in Washington, D.C.

April 6. Warren Widener, a Berkeley, California black city councilman, was elected mayor of the city. Widener defeated Wilmont Sweeney, described as a moderate black, by 56 votes. Widener was considered to be aligned with the so-called radical coalition which sought to take political control of the town. Two black lawyers, also called "radical," D'rmy Bailey and Ird T. Simmons, were elected to the city council. Bailey said a description of their politics as "radical" was misleading and suggested instead the term "progressive." The election results pointed to a "radical - moderate" control of the city council.

April 6-13. In other Spring municipal elections, James E. Williams, Sr. was elected the first black mayor of East St. Louis, Illinois, on April 6; and John Franklin, a Chattanooga, Tennessee, educator and businessman, was elected the first black commissioner in the city's history on April 13.

April 12. A federal jury in New York City acquitted David R. Poindexter of harboring and concealing the identity of black militant Angela Davis while she was the target of a nationwide police search. Poindexter was arrested in New York in October, 1970 along with Miss Davis, who was at that time one of the F.B.I.'s ten most wanted fugitives. She was being sought in connection with the murder of a California judge during a courtroom shootout in August, 1970 (See Above and Below). During the trial, the prosecution presented more than 40 witnesses in an effort to prove that Poindexter had moved through several cities with Miss Davis under assumed names and must have known that she was being sought under federal warrant. The defense summoned no witnesses, relying on the argument that the prosecution had failed to prove its case beyond a reasonable doubt. Following the verdict, Poindexter commented that his trial "was a minor skirmish in a big war. The major battle is in California over Angela."

April 13. The Internal Revenue Service (IRS) announced that the Fayette Academy in Somerville, Tennessee, had been notified that contributions for its operation were no longer tax deductible because it had failed to adopt non-discriminatory admissions policies. The action was the first time the IRS had suspended tax privileges for an all-white private school outside of Mississippi.

April 15. Some 2,000 black and white students gathered at the home of the president of the University of Florida at Gainesville protesting what they called the school's "racist" policies and demanding the resignation of President Stephen C. O'Connell. Earlier the same day, sixty-seven blacks, members of the school's Black Student Union, had been arrested during a sit-in outside O'Connell's office. The blacks and their white allies, called for increased black enrollment at the university by recruiting 500 new students. There were, at the time, about 300 blacks out of a 22,000 total enrollment. President O'Connell, in a television address to the students, said "we have made remarkable racial progress," but he rejected the black recruitment demands calling them "a racial quota" and "racism in reverse." Nearly 100 black students subsequently withdrew from the university in further protest of the school's policies.

April 16. Carl B. Stokes, the first black mayor of Cleveland, Ohio, announced that he was leaving office at the end of his current term in 1971. He said he would help develop a "people's lobby" to bring pressure on the two major political parties toward "responsive" presidential candidates in 1972 and toward a reordering of the nation's priorities. Stokes was first elected in 1967 as the first black mayor of a major American city, then re-elected in 1969.

April 19. The U.S. Census Bureau released a study, compiled from federal and private sources, which revealed that black women, on the average, had fewer illegitimate births in the late 1960's than they did in the earlier part of the decade. Meanwhile, the white illegitimacy rate was climbing. According to the report, the black illegitimacy rate, which was ten times higher than the white rate in 1961, had dropped to about seven times in 1968, the last year considered in the study. The raw figures for 1968 alone were 184,000 black and 155,000 white illegitimate births. The report, entitled "Fertility Indicators: 1970," was developed by Campbell Gibson of the Census Bureau.

April 20. The U.S. Supreme Court, in a series of unanimous decisions, told the Charlotte-Mecklenburg County, North Carolina joint school system and all the other school districts of the nation that busing children as a means of dismantling a racially dual school system was constitutional. The rulings ended the final legal efforts by Southern school boards to prevent the busing of students to achieve more desegregation in schools. Chief Justice Warren E. Burger wrote the opinions of the Court in the four cases on which it ruled. In addition to upholding the school desegregation plan, which included busing, for the Charlotte-Mecklenburg district, the Court struck down an anti-busing law enacted by the North Carolina Legislature, ordered Mobile, Alabama, school officials to use "all available techniques" to correct segregation in their schools and overruled a Georgia Supreme Court order that had said certain desegregation efforts in the city of Athens were unconstitutional. The Court reasoned that "desegregation plans cannot be limited to the walk-in school." The justices held that busing school children was proper unless "the time or distance is so great as to risk either the health of the children or significantly impinge on the educational process." The Court added that at times busing was an indispensable method of eliminating "the last vestiges" of racial segregation. The Court made it clear, however, that the rulings did not apply to *de facto* segregation caused by neighborhood housing patterns, as is found most often in the North. The landmark decision has become known to history as *Swann* vs *Charlotte-Mecklenburg.*

April 23. The U.S. Court of Appeals for the Third Circuit upheld the legality of the Nixon administration's pilot job plan for minorities, known as the "Philadelphia Plan." The plan, devised by the Labor Department in 1969, required contractors building on federal or federally-assisted projects to hire a fixed number of minority group members by a certain date (See Above). A number of groups, foremost among them building and construction organizations, had sought in a number of courts to stop the plan on the grounds that it was unconstitutional. In this case the Court of Appeals was asked by the Contractors Association of Eastern Pennsylvania to declare the plan illegal because it denied the group equal protection of the laws and violated the 1964 Civil Rights Act because it required racial "quotas." The Court reasoned that the plan did not violate the 1964 Civil Rights Act because the contractors were not, in fact, required to hire a "definite percentage" of a minority group.

April 28. The Joint Center for Political Studies in Washington reported that the number of black elected officials in the U.S. rose 22% during 1970. Despite the gains, however, black public officials still represented only about .3% of all officeholders in the nation. The center's director, Frank D. Reeves, commented that the 22% rise showed that "blacks are gaining clout more and more in the nation's electoral systems." The report also revealed that 1,860 blacks held office as of April, 1971. By comparison in 1967, only 475 blacks held elective offices. Nearly three-fifths of the blacks in office were Southerners. According to the report, 711 blacks held office in the eleven states of the old Confederacy, a 26% rise above the 1970 figure of 563.

May 4. In another spring election, Richard B. Hatcher was renominated to a second four-year term as mayor of Gary, Indiana. Hatcher won 59% of the vote cast and was heavily favored to win the general election over the Republican nominee, Theodore Nering. In the primary Hatcher, who was first elected as a big city black mayor in 1967, defeated Dr. Alexander Williams, the black Lake County Coroner, and John Armento, the president of the city council.

May 4. U.S. District Judge William P. Gray ordered David Hilliard, Chief of Staff of the Black Panther Party, released from federal custody after the government had refused to divulge wiretap logs of conversations involving Hilliard. Hilliard had been charged with threatening the life of President Nixon during an anti-war speech in November, 1969. When U.S. Attorney James Browning told the Court that he was not authorized to make the wiretap logs available to Hilliard's lawyers, Judge Gray ordered the indictment dismissed and the case dropped.

May 5. A riot of mostly black youths occurred in the Brownsville section of New York City. Hundreds of youths set scores of fires and fought police. One policeman was shot and 14 others were injured during the melee. Police arrested 25 persons on charges of larceny or malicious mischief. At the height of the rioting, marauding bands of young people looted stores and battled police with rocks, bricks, and bottles. The rioting began after thousands of angry Brownsville (Brooklyn) residents closed off dozens of streets in their neighborhood with abandoned cars and trash piles to protest state budget cuts affecting welfare assistance, anti-narcotics programs, medicaid, educational facilities and the food stamp program. The legislation had been signed by Governor Nelson A. Rockefeller on April 15. Organizers of the peaceful protest disavowed the actions of the rioting youths. The disturbance was brought under control by late evening.

May 5. The U.S. Labor Department announced that it would impose mandatory racial hiring quotas on federally-sponsored construction projects under way in San Francisco, St. Louis and Atlanta. The established plans for the three cities varied slightly in their formats. Overall, however, they required contractors bidding on federal or federally-sponsored projects to agree to hire a fixed percentage of minority group members by a certain date. Washington and Philadelphia were the only other two cities to have such job plans (See Also Above and Below).

May 10. The U.S. Commission on Civil Rights reported that the Nixon administration had shown some signs of progress in enforcing civil rights laws, but still considerable strides needed to be made. The new commission report came seven months after it issued a harsh indictment of the administration asserting that there had been a "major breakdown" in the enforcement of the rights laws (See Above). The commission singled out for praise George P. Shultz, director of the Office of Management and Budget and Leonard Garment, a presidential counselor, for what it termed were their efforts at "active intervention" in seeking compliance with Civil Rights laws. The report also cited other signs of progress:

1) President Nixon, in his fiscal 1972 budget recommendations, had sought more funds for the Office of Federal Contract Compliance and the Equal Employment Opportunity Commission.

2) The Army, among other departments, had set up a program to establish goals for minority employment in its own offices.

3) The Justice Department had announced that it would add six lawyers to its office to coordinate efforts to enforce Title VI of the 1964 Civil Rights Law, which forbade discrimination in federally-assisted programs.

May 13. The Army announced that it had nominated three black colonels for promotion to the rank of brigadier general. The three black officers were among 80 colonels approved by President Nixon for promotion to the one-star rank. The three blacks promoted were Colonels Alvin W. Dillard, James F. Hamlet, and Roscoe C. Cartwright. Their nominations would bring the number of black Army generals to four. The Air Force also had one black general, while the Navy nominated its first black admiral on April 28, 1971 (See Above and Below).

May 14. The Department of Health, Education and Welfare (HEW), complying with the Supreme Court's ruling which upheld school busing to achieve greater desegregation, recommended "extensive" crosstown busing as part of a plan to desegregate the public schools in Austin, Texas. The desegregation proposal was the first made by the government since the Supreme Court in *Swann* vs *Mecklenburg* (April, 1971) rejected the administration's objections to busing and declared the method constitutional as a means of dismantling dual school systems. Austin, the sixth largest city in Texas, had about 56,000 students in 56 elementary schools, 19 junior high schools and eight high schools. About 15% of the students were black and about 20% Mexican-American. The city had two high schools and seven elementary schools with virtually all-black enrollments.

May 17. An all-white jury in Opelika, Alabama, acquitted black Macon County Sheriff Lucius Amerson and his deputy, Richard Coleman, Jr. of a federal charge that they had beaten a prisoner in their custody (See Above). Amerson commented that the verdict reaffirmed his belief that he could receive a fair trial at the hands of an all-white jury in the South.

May 18. In a 115-page report, President Nixon told the Black Caucus of the House of Representatives that his administration would continue to support "jobs, income and tangible benefits, the pledges that this society has made to the disadvantaged in the past decade." The President was responding to a list of sixty grievances the black congressmen had asked him to consider in a meeting on March 25, 1971 (See Above). The President announced that he agreed with the Caucus' welfare reform proposals but limited his guaranteed annual income figure to $2,400, compared to the $6,500 a year figure proposed by the blacks. In almost all of the recommendations, the President differed with the blacks in amounts and scope of reform programs. For instance, the black legislators suggested one million summer jobs for youths. The President promised 500,000 with some 300,000 more being made available through private sectors. The Black Caucus received the report through the office of its Chairman, Representative Charles C. Diggs, Jr. (D. Mich.). After studying the report, the Caucus issued a 76-page reaction. The blacks expressed "deep disappointment." They called the President's message "a mere codification of slim efforts" rather than "massive immediate aid for minorities and the poor." In the end, the blacks charged, the administration "lacked a sense of understanding, urgency and commitment in dealing with the critical problems facing black Americans." It was pointed out that only one of the sixty demands was fully agreed on by both sides — the formation of a task force to study the problems of black soldiers and veterans.

May 21-26. Racial violence erupted in Chattanooga, Tennessee, after a black musician failed to perform at a "rock" concert in the city auditorium. When some of the black youths did not get refunds for their admission fees, they began vandalizing the building. The disorders later spread to the streets. On May 24, Governor Winfield Dunn ordered 2,000 National Guardsmen into the city after local police were unable to contain the arson and sniping which was centered in the black neighborhoods located on the outskirts of the downtown area. On May 25, a young black man was killed by police who said they fired after the man hurled bricks at them. Black witnesses said the victim, Leon Anderson, was apparently drunk and charged that police shot him without provocation. The incident increased tensions, but did not lead to heightened violence. On May 26, a rigid dusk to dawn curfew was lifted in the city and Governor Dunn announced that guardsmen would be gradually withdrawn.

May 25. Racial tension was sparked anew in Mississippi as Jo Etha Collier, an 18 year old black girl, was shot dead in Drew, Mississippi. Miss Collier was felled by a bullet from a passing car as she stood with other young blacks on a street corner in her hometown. The incident occurred less than an hour after the young black girl graduated from desegregated Drew High School and had been designated the student with the best school spirit. Three white men were arrested and charged with the killing on May 26. On June 14, the trio, Allen Wilkerson of Memphis, Wayne and Wesley Parks, brothers, of Drew, Mississippi, were arraigned on charges of murder before circuit Court Judge Arthur B. Clark in Indianola, Mississippi. The three pleaded innocent. The swift arrests and arraignments, and the sympathetic attitude of local white officials served to help calm tensions in the community.

May 25. Judge Harold H. Mulvey of the Connecticut State court in New Haven dismissed all charges against Black Panther Party members Bobby Seale and Mrs. Ericka Huggins. The two had been on trial for six months accused of murder in the May, 1969 slaying of former Panther, Alex Rackley (See Above). Judge Mulvey ordered the charges dropped after the jury in the case told him it was hopelessly deadlocked. The judge declared a mistrial and announced that the "massive publicity" about the case had made it too difficult to select an unbiased jury to try the pair again. Seale was Chairman of the Black Panther Party; Mrs. Huggins was a party member from Connecticut. Throughout the trial the state, led by State's Attorney

Arnold Markle, had sought to prove that Seale had ordered a group of party members to kill Rackley, after the former Panther was accused of treason against the party. The state's principal witness, George Sams, Jr., testified that Seale had given him the orders. Seale's defense counsel, Charles R. Garry, countered consistently that Sams ordered Rackley's death. Sams, a member of the Black Panther Party, had already pleaded guilty to second-degree murder in the case. The dismissal of charges brought to an end another chapter of violence and legal proceedings connected with the Black Panther Party.

May 30.   Three policemen were injured in a gun battle at Cairo, Illinois, one of the most racially tense cities in America. Cairo mayor Albert B. Thomas blamed the shootings on the United Front, a predominantly black organization that had led a boycott of the town's white merchants. The United Front declined to comment on the incident (See Also Above).

June 4.   Arthur A. Fletcher, assistant secretary of labor, announced that the Labor Department was withdrawing its support of Chicago's voluntary equal hiring plan for federal construction projects and would impose mandatory racial quotas on federally-assisted projects throughout the city. Chicago's voluntary plan failed after being in operation for 18 months. The plan called for the hiring and training of some 4,000 minority group members. But by June 4, 1971 only 885 blacks and Spanish-Americans had been enrolled for training, and only a few had obtained membership in the city's construction unions. The Labor Department said it would replace the Chicago plan with the now standard formula known as the Philadelphia Plan, under which a certain number of minority group members should be employed on federal projects exceeding $500,000.

June 4-22.   Racial tensions in Columbus, Georgia, the state's second largest city, erupted into violence. The trouble began on May 31, 1971 when seven members of the Afro-American Police League, including its executive director, were fired from the police department for picketing police headquarters and removing the American flag shoulder patches from their uniforms. The blacks were protesting alleged racial discrimination in the police department. Police department officials accused the black patrolmen of conduct unbecoming an officer and said they "ripped" the flag from their uniform. The blacks said they gently removed the emblems. On June 3 the Muscogee County Grand Jury announced that complaints of discrimination against black officers were unfounded. The jury said it found no basis for charges of the use of unnecessary force in the arrests of blacks but, instead, criticized both the Afro-American Police League, which made the charges of discrimination and police brutality, and the Fraternal Order of Police, a union. On June 19, Hosea Williams, national program director for the Southern Christian Leadership Conference and Chairman of the Georgia statewide Black Leadership Coalition, led more than 500 blacks on a 15-block march in Columbus, then issued a five-point ultimatum to city and county officials. The blacks demanded the reinstatement of a total of 13 black policemen, promotion of the 38 blacks still on the force, desegregation of jail facilities, a biracial "citizens police review board," and increased hiring of black policemen. On June 21, Mayor J. R. Allen of Columbus declared a state of emergency following a weekend of racial strife. A total of 26 fires attributed to arsonists were set in the city and a black man was fatally wounded by police. The City Council gave the mayor broad powers to order a curfew, shut down stores selling alcoholic beverages, stop the sale of firearms, and curtail gasoline sales. Meanwhile, the Afro-American Patrolmen's League called for a city-wide boycott of white businesses.

June 7. The U.S. Supreme Court ruled that the states are not required to carve out separate legislative districts for urban blacks or any other racial or ethnic group. The court held in an apportionment case from Indiana that core-city blacks may be lumped with more populous suburban white voters into one large district that is represented by a number of legislators elected at large. The 5-3 ruling upset a federal district court's finding that Indianapolis blacks were the victims of racial gerrymandering and were entitled to their own district with state legislators elected by and responsible to them. The five-man judicial majority, led by Justice Byron R. White, said there was no evidence that the Indianapolis blacks did not have an equal say in choosing legislative candidates or that they were not allowed to register or vote. The majority reasoned that "the mere fact that one interest group or another concerned with the outcome of Marion County elections have found themselves outvoted and without legislative seats of its own provides no basis for invoking constitutional remedies." No explanation was given of the different result that was reached on May 31 when the Court ordered Hinds County, Mississippi, which included the capital city of Jackson, to be divided into single-member districts so that black voters would have a chance to elect their own representatives (See Above). Had the Supreme Court established the Jackson principle consistently, blacks and other inner-city residents would have been assured of larger representation in state legislatures (See Also Below).

June 11. Black legislators from nine Southern states met in closed sessions in Atlanta to talk about black representation in re-apportioned legislatures. The major problem concerning the group centered around recent decisions of the U.S. Supreme Court, which, black lawmakers feel, point in opposite directions. In one decision, the Supreme Court ruled that one-representative legislative districts are allowable in Mississippi. In another decision, the Court declared that multi-member districts are allowable in Indiana. The black legislators said that they were confused and concerned about what the Supreme Court intended. The blacks felt that they had a better chance for election in the South if they were candidates in districts where more than one representative is elected. There were forty black legislators in the eleven Southern states. Only Arkansas was without a black lawmaker.

June 11. President Nixon promised to enforce federal laws prohibiting racial discrimination in housing but said the government would not force introduction of low cost housing for blacks or whites into suburban communities that don't want it. The President's fifteen page report sharply distinguished between economic segregation and racial segregation, and the government's authority to deal with each situation. Nixon said that his administration would seek to carry out all requirements of federal law and judicial decisions involving housing but that it would take no action to go beyond them. "Racial discrimination in housing is illegal and will not be tolerated," the President affirmed. But, according to the President, the issue of public housing projects for the poor was another matter. Although predominantly white and affluent suburbs will be encouraged to accept them, the ultimate decision about the location of projects will be made at the local level.

June 12. Charles Evers, the black mayor of Fayette, Mississippi, opened his campaign for governor on the eighth anniversary of the murder of his brother, Medgar (See Above). Ringed by a personal security guard of ten armed blacks, Evers returned to his childhood hometown of Decatur, in East Central Mississippi to campaign as an independent. Evers was the first black to seek the governorship since Reconstruction. He told a crowd of 300 supporters at the Newton County Courthouse that it was time for members of both races to work together for common goals.

June 12. David Hilliard, Chief of Staff of the Black Panther party, was found guilty of assault but innocent of attempted murder in connection with a 1968 shootout with police. Hilliard had contended that he was not involved in the Panther-police altercation on April 6, 1968. That gun battle resulted in the death of Panther party member Bobby Hutton, the wounding of two policemen, and criminal charges against Panther Minister of Information Eldridge Cleaver, who later jumped bail and fled to Algeria (See Above). Hilliard was charged with two counts of attempted murder and two of assault on a policeman. The trial was held in the Alameda County Superior Court in Oakland, California before Judge William J. Hayes. Frank Vukota prosecuted Hilliard, who was defended by Attorney Vincent Hallinan.

June 13. The latest in a series of race riots on military forts and bases occurred at Sheppard Air Force Base, Texas. A midnight battle between white and black airmen left twenty injured. According to a military spokesman, the two-and-one-half hour fight started when a black and white airman clashed in the base's club. The fight spread all over the club along racial lines, mostly among young trainees, and was eventually halted by base police. Major General Jerry Page, the base commander, said no arrests would be made until the completion of an investigation of the incident.

June 14. The Justice Department announced the filing of a suit in St. Louis against Black Jack, Missouri, a St. Louis suburb, charging the town with illegally blocking a desegregated housing development. The action came on the heels of President Nixon's policy statement on housing issued on June 11, 1971 (See Above). The issue arose when a nonprofit corporation made detailed plans in late 1969 to build a housing development for persons of limited income. It was widely known that the project would be desegregated. The federal suit charged that the residents of Black Jack incorporated their community to gain zoning power and then used that power to block construction of the project. This action, the suit said, violated federal civil rights laws and the Constitution.

June 14. The U.S. Supreme Court ruled 5 to 4 that officials may close swimming pools and other public facilities to avoid desegregating them. The closings are not unconstitutional since blacks and whites are treated equally, Justice Hugo L. Black reasoned in the court's rare recent setback for blacks. The ruling went against blacks in Jackson, Mississippi, who tried to force the city to reopen public swimming pools. They were closed after a district court ruled they could not remain segregated. In announcing the majority opinion, Justice Black cautioned that the decision did not signal approval of any subterfuge for desegregation. "We want no one to get any hope that there has been any retreat," he said. In one of three dissenting opinions, Justice Thurgood Marshall reasoned that the Jackson action was unconstitutional and that "the fact that the color of [a Negro's] skin is used to prevent others from swimming in public pools is irrelevant."

June 14. Owen B. Kiernan, executive secretary of the National Association of Secondary School Principals, told the U.S. Senate's Equal Educational Opportunity Committee that a survey of eleven Southern and two border states had revealed that more than 1,200 black school principals lost their jobs to whites after public school desegregation began in the South. Dr. Kiernan said the problem of the elimination, displacement and demotion of black public school principals had reached such serious proportions that it required the intervention of the federal government.

June 15. Vernon E. Jordan, Jr., former Atlanta attorney and executive director of the United Negro College Fund, was named executive director of the National Urban League. Jordan succeeded Whitney Young, Jr. who drowned in March, 1971, while swimming at Lagos, Nigeria (See Above). Jordan was director of the Voter Education Project of the Southern Regional Council in Atlanta until 1969. As head of the VEP, he helped organize massive voter registration campaigns across the South to help blacks win political power. In January, 1970, he became head of the UNCF, which raises funds for more than thirty black colleges across the country.

June 16. The Race Relations Information Center (RRIC) of Nashville, Tennessee, announced that predominantly black public colleges were in "imminent danger of losing their identity through integration, merger, reduced status or outright abolition." In a report, entitled "The Black Public Colleges — Integration and Disintegration," the RRIC said "the prevailing pattern is one of racially separate and qualitatively unequal higher education." The 1970-71 term marked the first time in their history that the nation's 33 black state-supported colleges enrolled more than 100,000 students. During the past decade, enrollment at the institution increased 75%. The report said the figures suggested thriving institutions, "but a closer look tells another story." In fact the death knell of the black state-supported colleges has already been sounded, according to the report. There were originally 35 public colleges created for blacks — two of them are now predominantly white. Those two, Maryland State College and Bluefield (W. Va) State College, were joined by two more, West Virginia State and Lincoln Universty (Mo.). The RRIC said three other institutions — Delaware State, Bowie State (Md.), and Kentucky State — "appear likely to become majority-white before long." Of the 26 remaining schools fourteen were in direct competition with a white college. The RRIC speculated that most of these would eventually lose their identity, perhaps even be completely abolished.

June 17. The U.S. Fifth Circuit Court of Appeals ordered complete desegregation in 81 Southern school districts. The Court reversed a U.S. District Court decision of April 22, 1970, which exempted some districts, mostly in Georgia, from full desegregation compliance on the grounds that such compliance would produce educationally unsound school systems. The Appeals court said that the District Court must apply the Singleton decree to the 81 school districts in the areas of faculty and staff desegregation, school construction, site selection and school attendance outside the system. The Singleton decree, issued in 1970 by the Fifth Circuit Court in the case of *Singleton* vs *Jackson,* required that the faculty of each school have approximately the same racial ratio as the entire school system, and that decisions regarding school construction and selection of school sites be made without evidence of racial discrimination. The New Orleans based court also said the 81 school systems must comply with the U.S. Supreme Court's decision in *Swann* vs *Charlotte-Mecklenburg (N.C.)* (See Above), which held that busing could be used as a tool to dismantle a dual school system. The 81 school districts have been under federal court jurisdiction since December, 1969. The latest appellate ruling in the case stemmed from the intervention by Charley Ridley, Jr., a black student from Gray, Georgia, in the blanket desegregation suit filed against Georgia and the State Board of Education in 1969.

June 17. Police, armed with riot equipment, dispersed a crowd of 400 black youths in a second night of racial violence at Jacksonville, Florida. Three youths were arrested and charged with looting. Several policemen were slightly injured by rocks and bottles during the melee. Sheriff's Captain E. W. Hartley said police went into the black neighborhood to protect its many elderly black residents in the wake of the rock and bottle hurling. Deputies reported that two supermarkets in the black business district had been looted and set afire, but there was no gunfire. Black youths had been angered by an earlier slaying of a young black man by Jacksonville police.

June 17. NAACP Executive Secretary Roy Wilkins called the Nixon administration's policy on housing discrimination a "timid tightrope walking act of the greatest kind." Wilkins challenged President Nixon to exert more "positive federal power" to help blacks move to the suburbs in search of employment. "The issue of the 1970's now appears to be whether the black population will be able to move into the suburbs in pursuit of jobs that are moving to the suburbs," Wilkins declared. "The 15-page statement issued last week by the White House has done nothing to solve that problem." President Nixon had announced on June 11 that he would enforce federal laws preventing racial discrimination in housing, but would not force communities to accept low-cost housing for blacks or whites (See Above). According to an *Atlanta Constitution* report, Wilkins also said that "Mr. Nixon ought to stop going around saying he does not want to enforce integration of the suburbs, because he is using the language and nomenclature of those who simply do not want Negroes in the suburbs." Wilkins made his criticisms of the President at a panel discussion on "The Status of Civil Rights in 1971" at the annual meeting of the black National Newspapers Publishers Association in Atlanta.

June 18. The Department of Health, Education and Welfare completed and released the most detailed study of school desegregation in the nation's history. According to the report, the only significant gains in school desegregation in the nation's largest school districts during the past two years have occurred in the South. The 38 Southern school districts among the country's largest districts accounted for almost all of the desegregation gains in urban areas while 26 of the 63 districts in Northern and Western states showed a decrease in desegregation. The figures reflected the amount of desegregation based on the number of black children in majority-white schools, the statistical yardstick favored by most civil rights groups. Of the 756,000 black pupils who moved from largely black into majority white schools during the past two years, a total of 690,000 lived in the South. The national desegregation comparison was the result of an eight-month survey conducted by HEW. The preliminary results of the study were revealed in January, 1971 (See Above).

June 22. The Department of Health, Education and Welfare (HEW) announced that letters had been sent to 39 school districts in 11 Southern and border states suggesting that they must further desegregate by the fall of 1971. HEW had been attempting to bring all school districts in line with the Supreme Court's ruling in the Swann case in North Carolina (See Above). Recent action was taken in Nashville, Tennessee, Norfolk, Virginia, and Austin, Texas. The latest action included such diverse localities as Wilmington, Delaware, Paducah, Kentucky, Gulfport, Mississippi, Fayetteville, North Carolina, Amarillo, Texas, and Martinsville, Virginia. HEW told the districts that they must prove that the presence of heavily black schools is not discriminatory.

June 23. School officials and civil rights leaders in Jackson, Mississippi, the largest school district in the state, agreed on a plan for desegregating the city's elementary schools through busing and educational parks. Both parties, in the first such compromise they have ever reached, agreed that the plan would remain in effect for three years without a court challenge. Dr. Harry S. Kirshman, acting superintendent of schools, announced that the agreement would affect some 18,000 to 19,000 elementary school children, with some 8,000 to 9,000 being bused to classes. The educational park concept is built on clusters of modules around a common center. Each module is to accommodate the equivalent of four traditional classrooms with 30-1 pupil-teacher ratios. Black enrollments in the schools would range from 41-70 percent.

June 25. Federal agents arrested three black men in Columbus, Georgia, and charged them with possessing firebombs in the racially tense city. The agents said they confiscated enough material at the People's Panther Party headquarters to make more than 50 firebombs. Two of the three arrested men were soldiers stationed at nearby Fort Benning. The third was a former Army private. The Treasury Department agents arrested William Craig Garr, Jesse Reed, Jr., and Anthony L. Brewer less than a week after the outburst of new racial disorders, which included firebombings. Garr was identified as the president of the People's Panther Party, described by a federal official as a training group for the Black Panther Party. Meanwhile, white policemen in Columbus presented a petition to Mayor J. R. Allen urging him not to give in to black demands. The petition was prompted by black charges of racial discrimination in the city's police deparment and a subsequent announcement by the mayor that the department would be investigated. Earlier, black policemen had told the mayor, in response to his plea to them to help "cool" the black community, that they would protect the black community "from the white cops " (See Also Above).

June 28. The U. S. Supreme Court overturned the draft-evasion conviction of former heavyweight boxing champion Muhammad Ali. In a unanimous, 8-0 (Justice Thurgood Marshall did not participate.) opinion the Court ruled that the Justice Department had erred in contending that Ali's objection to military service was based on political rather than religious beliefs. The Court said it was "indisputably clear . . . that the Department was simply wrong as a matter of law in advising that Ali's beliefs were not religiously based and were not sincerely held." Ali, who is a Black Muslim, exclaimed "Thanks to Allah!" when he learned of the Court's decree. "I thank the Supreme Court for recognizing the sincerity of my belief in myself and my convictions," he said (See Also Above).

June 28-July 8. Court action and out-of-court settlements continued in an effort to desegregate the nation's schools. On June 28, a federal district judge in Nashville, Tennessee approved a cross-town busing plan designed to desegregate the Nashville-Davidson County public school system. Judge L. C. Morton adopted, with modifications, a plan drawn up by the U. S. Department of Health, Education, and Welfare which required the daily busing of about 47,000 students, an increase of some 13,500 over those bused in 1970-71. The number of black children required to ride buses would almost double while the number of whites to be transported would increase by only one-third. The Nashville-Davidson County school system had an enrollment of about 95,000 pupils. Judge Morton ordered the plan implemented in September, 1971. On July 8, the NAACP's Legal Defense Fund and the Mobile, Alabama school board agreed upon a school desegregation plan that would allow at least ten of Mobile's public schools to retain virtually all-black student bodies until the fall of 1972. Attorneys for the blacks said they accepted the school board's suggested course of action only to avoid another year of litigation before a federal district judge they regarded as hostile to desegregation (See Above and Below).

June 30-August 8. Throughout the summer of 1971, members of the Black Panther Party were continuously engaged in legal disputes of various kinds. On June 30, a jury in Detroit acquitted twelve party members of charges that they murdered a policeman and of conspiracy to murder in a gun battle with police at the party's local headquarters in October, 1970. Three party members, however, were convicted of felonious assault in the case. This trio, Erone D. Desansser, Benjamin Fandrus and David Johnson, faced a maximum penalty of four years imprisonment. The Detroit jury, consisting of ten blacks and two whites, returned its verdict after four and a half days of deliberations. On July 2, David Hilliard, the Black Panther Party's Chief of Staff, was sentenced to a one-to-ten-year prison term by an Oakland, California judge for assault in connection with a gun battle with police in April, 1968. Hilliard, who was convicted on June 12 (See Above) was denied a retrial and remanded to custody. On August 6, a bi-racial jury of ten blacks and two whites acquitted twelve Black Panther Party members of the attempted murder of five New Orleans policemen in a gun battle at a local housing project in September, 1970 (See Above). The bi-racial jury, which received its instructions from a black judge, Israel M. Augustine, reached its verdict after only thirty minutes of deliberation. If convicted, the blacks could have faced terms of twenty years in prison on each of five counts. During the trial nine of the black defendants participated in an uprising involving 34 inmates at the Orleans Parish Prison, where they were held. The uprising was staged to protest what the blacks called the prison's "corrupt judicial system." The protest, which was held on July 26, ended after almost eight hours as the inmates released two black guards they had been holding hostage. On August 8, Superior Court Judge Harold B. Hove declared a mistrial in the second manslaughter trial of Huey P. Newton, co-founder of the Black Panther Party, in Oakland, California. A lone white housewife held out for the acquittal of Newton who had been charged in connection with the killing of an Oakland policeman in October, 1969 (See Also Above).

July 5-6. Members of the National Conference of Black Lawyers and the Black American Law Students Association distributed leaflets accusing the American Bar Association of excluding blacks from its major policy making organs and of emphasizing the "order" side of the law and order issue. The leaflets also called for an end to bar exams which allegedly excluded blacks. Similarly, Judge Edward F. Bell, president of the black National Bar Association (NBA), speaking before his group's annual convention, urged the abolition of bar exams, claiming that they did not reflect the potential for a successful practice and that they discriminated against minority applicants (See Also Above and Below).

July 5-9. Bishop Stephen G. Spottswood, board chairman of the NAACP, remarked during the group's 62nd annual convention in Minneapolis that the Nixon administration had taken steps during 1971 to dispel the image that it was "anti-Negro." Spottswood, without being very specific, said that the President had taken certain steps and announced certain policies which had "earned cautious and limited approval among black Americans." A year before, at the NAACP's convention, Spottswood had portrayed the Nixon administration as anti-black. Some NAACP leaders apparently disagreed with Bishop Spottswood's new assessment of the Nixon policies. NAACP Labor Director Herbert Hill characterized the administration's racial policy as "criminal negligence," a posture even worse than "benign neglect." Hill specifically accused the administration of failure to enforce laws forbidding discrimination by federal contractors which resulted, in his view, in a high unemployment rate among blacks. Similarly, NAACP Executive Secretary Roy Wilkins told the delegates that President Nixon could increase his influence among black voters in the 1972 elections if he made more jobs available to black workers.

July 6. Louis (Satchmo) Armstrong, the black jazz trumpeter, died in New York. The seventy-one year old Armstrong had reshaped the development of American music by introducing the black folk music of New Orleans into the mainstream of American culture. His distinctive abrasive voice and innovative solos were trademarks of his long career which began in small Southern nightclubs at the close of World War I. President Nixon eulogized Armstrong as "one of the architects of the American art form."

July 7. Professional baseball commissioner Bowie Kuhn announced that veteran black player, Satchel Paige, who pitched for some 25 years in the "Negro leagues" and the major leagues, would be given full membership in baseball's Hall of Fame shrine at Cooperstown, New York. Originally it had been intended that Paige and other black players be honored in a separate division of the Hall of Fame which was established for players in the old "Negro leagues." In response to criticism by baseball fans of the separate division of the shrine, the decision was made to give Paige full honors.

July 11. President Nixon signed a five billion dollar education appropriation bill, the largest of its kind in history. Among the features of the bill was a provision which prohibited the use of any of the funds to force school districts considered already desegregated under the Civil Rights Act of 1964 to bus students, abolish schools, or to set attendance zones against parents' wishes or as a stipulation for receiving federal funds.

July 13. A coalition of civil rights groups, the 126-member Leadership Conference on Civil Rights meeting in Washington, attacked President Nixon's housing policy as insufficient to meet the needs of minorities and the poor. The President's policy, which had been outlined on June 11, 1971, was, according to the group's spokesman Bayard Rustin, disastrous and chaotic. The coalition urged the federal administration to require localities to provide for low-income housing needs or risk losing all federal aid. The civil rights groups also urged the Justice Department to take action against any local zoning laws erected to block housing for low and moderate income families (See Above).

July 18-20. U. S. District Judge Jack Roberts refused to accept a Department of Health, Education, and Welfare school desegregation plan for Austin, Texas schools which would have required extensive cross-town busing. Instead the judge accepted a desegregation plan filed by the local school board which established learning centers in fine arts, avocations, and social and natural sciences which would be open to elementary pupils of all races for a portion of the school day. Students could be bused, if necessary, to these learning centers. The plan also assigned black junior high school students to schools which were not "identifiably Negro." In a related matter, on July 20, HEW officials announced that they had told 64 school districts in southern and border states that they would have to alter their school desegregation plans for the fall of 1971 so as to achieve greater racial desegregation. An HEW representative said that most of the 64 districts were in small and rural areas and that each contained one or more all-black schools.

July 21. Blacks in Passaic, New Jersey began a long boycott against downtown merchants protesting alleged police brutality. The boycott grew out of a series of incidents of "police harassment" and "brutality" which culminated in an incident on the night of July 20 between police and eight blacks. During the altercation a black man was beaten and shots were fired. The Rev. Calvin McKinney, head of the black Urban Crisis Council, protested that the town's all-white City Council ignored black pleas for protection against police harassment. The FBI did, however, agree to investigate the blacks' charges.

July 26. Federal analysts studying the 1970 Census returns concluded that despite a decade of general progress, black Americans remained far behind whites in terms of economic prosperity, social gains, and educational advancement. The study, compiled by the U. S. Census Bureau and the U. S. Bureau of Labor Statistics and entitled "The Social and Economic Status of Negroes in the United States, 1970," found that 28.9 of every 100 black families were headed by women. Many analysts saw this proportion of female-headed households as an important indicator of black social progress. (That view was disputed immediately by Dr. Robert B. Hill, a research analyst for the National Urban League, as he appeared before the League's annual convention. See Also Above.) The percentage of fatherless white families in the 1960's remained at about nine percent. Other statistics showed that blacks increased their median income by 50% during the 1960's, but that their incomes were still only three-fifths of that earned by whites, and that about half of the all-black occupied housing units in rural areas were substandard in 1970 as compared with only eight percent of white rural housing.

July 27. Frank W. Render, second deputy assistant secretary of defense, announced that almost a dozen military officers had been relieved of command, transferred to new assignments, or reprimanded for failing to adequately enforce the Defense Department's guidelines for racial equality in the armed services. The unidentified officers were said to rank from general down to company grade.

July 28. Vernon E. Jordan, Jr., executive director designate of the National Urban League, told the closing session of his group's annual convention in Detroit that the Nixon administration had compiled a "record of ambiguity" toward black Americans. He accused the administration of allowing federal civil rights laws to "languish in dusty books." The remarks were a part of Jordan's first major address to the Urban League since he was named its director, succeeding the late Whitney M. Young, Jr. (See Above).

August 2. Reverend Jesse Jackson of Chicago, leader of the Operation Breadbasket unit of the Southern Christian Leadership Conference, accused the newly reorganized U. S. Postal Service of discriminating against blacks. Jackson, speaking to postal workers in Washington, D. C., said the Postal Service had begun laying off a number of workers as a part of its reorganization plan and that since the majority of the black postal employees were in the lower job categories, they were the first to be fired. The black civil rights leader also accused the Postal Service of discrimination by placing new postal service offices in all-white suburban areas, where blacks could not obtain services or jobs.

August 3-11. President Nixon disowned a school desegregation plan drawn up by the Department of Health, Education, and Welfare (HEW) which would have required extensive cross-town busing in Austin, Texas. The President also took the occasion to reaffirm his strong opposition to any busing designed to achieve a racial balance in the schools. The President further directed HEW Secretary Elliott L. Richardson to aid individual school districts as they attempted to "hold busing to the minimum required by the law." The President, however, reasserted the duty of his administration to enforce orders of the federal courts, including those calling for busing to achieve desegregation. On August 11, the White House announced that

President Nixon had warned administrative officials that they risked losing their jobs if they pushed for extensive busing as a means of desegregating the nation's schools. The President reaffirmed his stated policy (of August 3) that the busing of children for purposes of school desegregation should be kept to the "minimum required by the law."

August 3-12. In an August 3rd pronouncement, the U. S. Commission on Civil Rights (USCCR) charged that Air Force officials in southwest Texas were seeking to continue the "illegal busing" of school children on a military base to a predominantly white school nearby. The busing permitted 850 children to bypass the closer San Felipe school district that was largely Mexican-American in order to attend the mostly white Del Rio schools. In July, the Texas Education Agency had advised the Del Rio district that it could no longer accept the Air Force children because of a federal court ruling that the transfers were illegally perpetuating segregation. The Air Force, denying that it was seeking to perpetuate segregation, contended that the San Felipe school district did not have sufficient educational facilities to handle the 850 children from Laughlin Air Force Base and hence the plea for continued busing. In an August 12th announcement, the USCCR maintained that President Nixon's directives to keep busing for racial desegregation to a minimum would undermine efforts to desegregate the nation's schools. The transportation of students, according to the commission's unanimous report, "is essential to eliminating segregation."

August 4. The nation's black federal, state, and municipal judges, attending the 46th annual meeting of the black National Bar Association (NBA) in Atlanta announced the formation of a Judicial Council through which they would work for legal reform. Judge Edward F. Bell of Detroit, president of the NBA, said the new council would seek to return to the idea that the courts belong to all of the people, poor as well as rich, black as well as white. The judges also pointed to the absence of black federal judges in the South. At the time of the meeting, there were 285 black judges in the country, representing slightly more than one per cent of 20,000 jurists in the nation.

August 12. The U. S. Court of Appeals for the 9th District declined to grant a delay in the implementation of a citywide elementary school desegregation program scheduled to take effect in San Francisco on September 8, 1971. The desegregation program involved the transfer of 48,000 children and had been ordered into effect on April 28, 1971 by U. S. District Judge Stanley A. Weigel (See Below).

August 16. The school board of Richmond, Virginia told Federal District Court Judge Robert R. Merhige, Jr. that it was unable to reduce the large black majorities in many of its public schools without a merger with the Henrico and Chesterfield counties school systems. The board asked the court to order such a merger. The Richmond officials reported to the judges that they had not been able to fully comply with his previous desegregation orders which involved widespread cross-town busing. This feature of the desegregation plan had been offset because too many white families had moved to the suburbs. (The plight of the Richmond school board was typical of that of many urban school districts trying to desegregate with large black populations in the inner cities and predominantly or all-white suburban populations.) Suburban residents expressed strong opposition to the school board's proposal. Some even demonstrated outside the home of Judge Merhige, who was protected by United States marshals.

August 18. A Jackson, Mississippi policeman, Lieutenant W. L. Skinner, was killed in a gun fight which broke out when local policemen raided the headquarters of a black separatist group, the Republic of New Africa, to serve three of its members with fugitive warrants. An FBI agent and another Jackson policeman were also wounded in a twenty minute exchange of gunfire. On August 23, 1971 eleven members of the Republic of New Africa (RNA) were accused of murdering Lieutenant Skinner. The previous day (Aug. 22), the eleven blacks had been charged with treason for allegedly engaging in armed insurrection against the state of Mississippi. Among those arrested was Imari A. Obadele, president of RNA. Obadele expressed regret that Lieutenant Skinner had been killed, but criticized the Jackson police and the F. B. I. for raiding the office. He declared that his group would receive any warrant peacefully, provided one or two black lawyers were present.

August 18. Governor George C. Wallace of Alabama ordered two of his state's school boards to ignore federal court-ordered desegregation plans. Wallace directed the school boards in Calhoun County and the city of Oxford to disregard the orders of a federal judge that an all-black school in Hobson City be paired with two predominantly white schools in Oxford. Governor Wallace contended that his actions were consistent with President Nixon's anti-busing declaration of August 3rd. The governor's actions followed by only two days federal district judge Sam C. Pointer, Jr.'s declaration that such action was "legally meaningless." Mississippi Governor John Bell Williams was one of those, however, who announced immediate support of Wallace's anti-desegregation tactics. Wallace, Williams said, had "drawn a line in the dust and I stand fully with him."

August 18-September 8. As the fall school term approached, additional legal skirmishes concerning desegregation took place across the South. On August 18, the Justice Department filed a brief with Associate Supreme Court Justice Hugo Black which supported the Corpus Christi, Texas school board's request for a stay of a federal court order to desegregate the school district. The court-approved plan had called for massive busing of students. On September 2, Supreme Court Justice Potter Stewart refused to stay a court order requiring extensive busing to achieve desegregation in the Nashville-Davidson County, Tennessee school system. On September 4, U. S. Supreme Court Justice Warren E. Burger refused to halt the busing of students to achieve desegregation in Arlington, Virginia. On September 8, the Mobile, Alabama school board implemented a plan which called for the massive busing of students for desegregation purposes (See Also Above and Below).

August 20. U. S. Attorney General John Mitchell rejected a plan for reapportioning the legislative districts of Louisiana contending that the plan would discriminate against blacks.

August 23. The Internal Security Committee of the U. S. House of Representatives issued a report declaring that while the Black Panther Party posed a physical danger to the nation's law enforcement officers, they were totally incapable of overthrowing the U. S. government by violent means. The four Republican members of the committee, Reps. John M. Ashbrook (Ohio), John G. Schmitz (California), Fletcher Thompson (Ga.), and Roger H. Zion (Indiana), objected to the committee's findings, contending that the majority view did not give "a clear understanding of the Black Panther Party as a subversive criminal group using the facade of politics as a cover for crimes of violence and extortion."

August 24.   Fourteen law enforcement officials, including Illinois State Attorney Edward U. Hanrahan, chief prosecutor for Chicago, were named in a long-suppressed indictment handed down in Chicago on charges of conspiracy to obstruct justice by trying to suppress or thwart criminal prosecutions of the eight policemen who participated in the raid in 1969 on a Black Panther Party apartment. The indictment was made public on orders issued by the Illinois Supreme Court. Judge Joseph A. Power of the Illinois Criminal Court had kept the indictment sealed since April, 1971, when it was first prepared. Power had refused to accept the indictment, contending that the grand jury had not heard all the pertinent witnesses and that it had been pressured into returning the true bills. Among others named in the indictment were an assistant state attorney, Police Superintendent of Chicago James B. Conlisk, Jr., eight policemen who took part in the controversial raid on December 4, 1969, and four police officers who later conducted departmental investigations into the raid. (See Also Above).

August 26.   The Office of Civil Rights in the U. S. Department of Health, Education, and Welfare (HEW) reported that black student enrollment in the nation's colleges and universities had increased at a rate five times greater than white student enrollment since 1968. Black enrollment grew from 303,397 in 1968 to 379,138 in the fall of 1970, a 24% increase. According to the HEW report, 44% of all black undergraduates were enrolled in colleges with black minorities. The largest increase in black enrollment, 47% since 1968, came in the eleven deep South states. Nevertheless, blacks still represented only six percent of the undergraduates in the nation.

August 30-September 8. As the nation's schools reopened for their fall terms, the stiffest resistance to court-ordered racial desegregation in public education was seen in the North and the West. In Pontiac, Michigan, eight white students and one black pupil were injured on September 8 as fights erupted during protests against a school busing plan. On August 30, 1971, arsonists in Pontiac had set firebombs which destroyed ten school buses that were to be used for implementing desegrgation plans. The protests in Pontiac were among the most violent ever seen in the country. White parents, carrying American flags, marched in front of the school bus depot on September 8 daring bus drivers to run them down. Police arrested nine demonstrators. In San Francisco, Chinese-American spokesmen announced that they intended to resist a court-ordered busing plan scheduled to be implemented on Septembr 13, 1971. The Chinese-Americans acted in response to Supreme Court Justice William O. Douglas' rejection of their anti-busing appeal on August 29, 1971. Under the plan, upheld by the courts, some 6,500 Chinese-Americans were to be included among 48,000 students to be bused for desegregation purposes. In Boston, parents of about 300 children assigned to a new racially desegregated school refused to enroll their children there on September 8th. Instead the children were returned to their previous neighborhood schools. A similar defiance of court-ordered desegregation occurred in Evansville, Indiana. By contrast, in the South most newly desegregated schools reopened quietly, although many were faced with new busing plans.

August 31. Warren E. Burger, Chief Justice of the U. S. Supreme Court, announced that he was afraid that federal judges were misinterpreting the Court's decision on busing which was delivered on April 20, 1971. Burger feared that judges were assuming that the order required racial balance in every school. In a ten-page opinion (unusual in denying a stay), denying a stay of enforcement of a court-ordered busing plan for the schools in Winston-Salem-Forsyth County, North Carolina, Burger said the unanimous court ruling in

April did not require a fixed racial balance or quota in order to legally desegregate schools. A school district's racial balance could be used as a point of beginning to determine "whether in fact any violation (of law) existed." On the same day, Secretary of Health, Education, and Welfare (HEW) Elliott L. Richardson reported that he agreed with President Nixon's announced policy of limiting school busing to achieve racial desegregation. The HEW Secretary denied that he had considered resigning after the President repudiated a school desegregation plan which HEW had drawn up for the Austin, Texas school district, a plan requiring extensive cross-town busing (See Above).

September 13. More than 1,000 state troopers, prison guards and sheriff's deputies stormed the Attica, New York state prison to end a five-day strike by inmates. Forty-three persons, including nine guards held as hostages, were killed in the most disastrous prison tragedy in United States history. Most of the slain prisoners were black. Independent investigations revealed that the troubles at Attica were sparked by a misunderstanding between two inmates who were playing touch football and a guard who believed they were fighting. An altercation between the guard and the inmates led to the latter's solitary confinement amid rumors that the inmates (one black, one white) had been beaten. When the full-scale uprising developed, inmates submitted a long list of grievances citing unhumane treatment and conditions within the prison. New York's Governor Nelson Rockefeller refused to meet with the rebellious prisoners and finally approved the assault on the institution. The Attica uprising sparked similar outbreaks at other penal institutions around the nation. On Thanksgiving eve, 1971, inmates, mostly black, at the Rahway State Prison in New Jersey, displaying signs reading "Remember Attica," rioted. The inmates' list of grievances included lack of medical care, poor food, lack of religious freedom and white racism. Governor William T. Cahill went to the prison and assured the inmates that their demands would be given serious consideration. The inmates subsequently released Warden U. Samuel Vukcevich and four other hostages they had been holding (See Also Below).

September 13. Approximately 45% of the school children in San

Francisco refused to attend classes as a new school desegregation plan calling for the busing of 48,000 children was put into effect.

September 22. Alabama Governor George C. Wallace signed a bill passed by the Alabama Legislature which permitted parents to send their children to their neighborhood schools if they felt that busing to achieve desegregation would be harmful to their children. In December, 1971, U. S. District Judge Sam C. Pointer declared the anti-busing law unconstitutional. The judge ruled that the statute "is but a freedom-of-choice option dressed in slightly different colors," and such options, he said, were illegal.

September 23. Associate Supreme Court Justice John M. Harlan, citing reasons of health, retired from the Supreme Court after sixteen years of service. (He died on December 29.) Harlan's retirement and the retirement and death of Justice Hugo Black left two additional vacancies on the high court which were to be filled by President Richard M. Nixon. Cognizant of the widespread black protests over the President's previous nominations of reputed segregationists Clement Haynesworth and Harold Carswell, NAACP Executive Secretary Roy Wilkins, claiming that he was conveying the unanimous view of representatives of more than 100 civil rights and social groups, wrote the President urging that he not propose persons opposed to civil rights progress. In October, 1971 the President nominated William Rehnquist of Phoenix, Arizona and Lewis F. Powell of Richmond to the Supreme Court. The nominees were again generally opposed by blacks. Black Judge George W. Crockett of the Detroit Recorders Court assailed the President for his refusal to consult black lawyers on the appointments. The chief criticisms coming from blacks were that Rehnquist was a "rational reactionary" and that Powell had been associated with private clubs and law firms in Virginia which discriminated against blacks. Both nominees denied anti-black attitudes and practices. Rehnquist, at the time, employed a black secretary in his office of Assistant U. S. Attorney. The Senate subsequently confirmed both appointees with a minimum of difficulty.

September 25. Hugo L. Black, who retired from the U. S. Supreme Court as an Associate Justice after 34 years of service on

September 13, 1971, died. Black had participated in many of the historic decisions concerning civil rights and legal protection for minorities and the poor. During his last years on the Court, Justice Black was accused of inconsistency and "turning his back on blacks." But Black replied: "I haven't changed a jot or a tittle." The native Alabamian, a one-time Ku Klux Klansman, was eulogized by the popular black newsmagazine *Jet* as "a real American."

September 26. The United States Bureau of Labor Statistics released a study which showed that 27.9% of the blacks employed across the country held white collar jobs during 1970. In 1960, 16.1% of the white collar jobs were held by blacks.

October 6. A black man and a white woman were married officially for the first time in North Carolina history. Lorraine Mary Turner and John A. Wilkeinson took their vows in Durham County, North Carolina.

October 9. The Ford Foundation announced a six-year $100 million program to aid black private colleges and to provide individual study awards to various minority students. About twenty of the nation's better known black private colleges, including Hampton and Tuskegee Institutes, Benedict College, Fisk University, and the Atlanta University Center complex, were chosen to receive awards averaging as much as $300,000 annually. In a closely related matter, Morris Brown College announced that it might withdraw from the famous Atlanta University Center complex and reject the Ford funds. Morris Brown officials objected to a proviso in the Atlanta grants which called for a reorganization of the structure of the Atlanta University Center, so as to effect closer cooperation (See Above and Below).

October 15. Elton Hayes, a seventeen year old black youth was killed by policemen in Memphis, Tennessee. The slaying of Hayes was followed by five days of racial violence in Memphis. Nine local law enforcement officers, including a black police lieutenant, were later charged with murder in the brutal death of the youth.

October—. Ralph David Abernathy, president of the Southern Christian Leadership Conference (SCLC), returned to the country from a European tour which took him, among other places, to Russia and East Germany. Abernathy preached to some 7,000 persons in the Russian Orthodox Cathedral. In East Germany, the veteran civil rights leader was awarded the Peace Medal of the German Democratic Republic (East Germany).

October—. A lively controversy arose among black and white politicians after Senator Edmund Muskie (D. Maine), a likely candidate for the Democratic nomination for President in 1972, stated that a black vice presidential candidate, regrettably, would be a handicap to the Democratic ticket. (Muskie, himself, was the Democratic vice-presidential candidate in 1968.) Vice President Spiro Agnew, former black Assistant Secretary of Labor Arthur Fletcher, both Republicans, and black Democratic National Committeeman Hobart Taylor, Jr. were among those disagreeing with Muskie. Former Georgia Governor Lester Maddox claimed he would vote for the "right" black vice-presidential candidate, but Alabama Governor George C. Wallace, himself a presidential candidate, said that Muskie's position was "probably right."

November 2. In general elections across the country blacks were elected mayors in four additional American cities and were named to various other local and state offices. In Englewood, New Jersey, the Reverend Walter S. Taylor was elected the city's first black mayor. Gilbert H. Bradley, Jr. was elected mayor of Kalamazoo, Michigan. In Benton Harbor, Michigan, Charles Joseph became the town's first black mayor. Richard B. Hatcher was easily reelected to a four-year term as mayor of Gary, Indiana. Two blacks, Henry Owens and Saundra Graham, were elected to the City Council in Cambridge, Massachusetts. Another black, Charles Pierce, was selected for the school board. In Mississippi, Fayette's black mayor Charles Evers was defeated in his bid for governor, but state Representative Robert Clark, the only black legislator in Mississippi, was returned to his seat. Blacks also won seven county supervisor posts, one circuit court clerk's position, and about 20 other county offices. Almost 300 blacks campaigned for offices in Mississippi during the November elections. Ex-heavyweight champion Jersey Joe Walcott was elected sheriff of Camden, New Jersey. Blacks were elected to the City Council in Indianapolis, Indiana; Davenport, Iowa; Burlington, Iowa; Memphis, Tennessee; and Miami, Florida. In Memphis, black councilman Fred Davis was elected chairman of the 13-member city legislature, the first black ever elected to that post. In Miami, the Rev. Edward Graham managed to retain his seat on the City Council, although black mayoral candidate Tom Washington was defeated. Defeated for the state legislature in Mississippi were veteran civil rights activists Fannie Lou Hamer and Aaron Henry. Voters in Cleveland, Ohio rejected a second black mayor in Arnold R. Pinkney's candidacy. Although Thomas I. Atkins, a black city councilman in Boston was defeated in his bid for mayor, he was appointed Secretary of the Department of Communications and Development, the highest position held by a black in Massachusetts state government.

November 16. The United States Commission on Civil Rights (USCCR) again criticized the Nixon administration charging that it had failed adequately to enforce civil rights laws and regulations (See Also Above).

November—. Alonzo G. Moron, the first black president of Hampton Institute in Virginia, died in San Juan, Puerto Rico. Moron had recently served as deputy director of the U. S. Department of Housing and Urban Development (HUD) office in San Juan.

December 15. Huey P. Newton, co-founder of the Black Panther Party, was declared free when charges that he had killed an Oakland, California policeman in 1967 were dismissed. Newton had been imprisoned for nearly two years and had been tried three times on the manslaughter charge. In his latest trial, charges were dismissed when the jury reported that it was "utterly unable to reach a verdict " (See Above).

December—. Two veteran champions of Negro rights died before the close of the year. Arthur B. Spingarn, the NAACP's president since 1940, succumbed at his home in New York at age 93. Spingarn, a white civil rights lawyer, once headed the NAACP's National Legal Committee. The NAACP's annual meritorious award, the Spingarn medal, was named in honor of the long-time civil rights leader. NAACP Executive Secretary Roy Wilkins eulogized Spingarn as one who had challenged "the sanctioned institutions of Jim Crow" and characterized his death as "a great loss to the Negroes in particular and the liberal social movement in general." Ralph J. Bunche, undersecretary general of the United Nations, Nobel Peace Prize winner, scholar, and civil rights activist, died at age 67 in New York. Bunche, who was a familiar figure in international councils as well as on civil rights battlefields (He was a key figure in Martin Luther King, Jr.'s Selma to Montgomery March in 1965.), was eulogized by United Nations Secretary General U Thant as "an international institution in his own right " (See Above).

1972

January 3. A U. S. District Court in Montgomery, Alabama ordered the implementation of a new reapportionment plan that would split the Alabama legislature into single-member districts. The decision could put as many as 20 additional blacks in the Alabama state legislature. There were, at the time, only two black members of the Alabama legislature. The new legislative districts would represent the decennial population count based upon the enumerated districts in the U. S. Census.

January 10. U. S. District Court Judge Robert R. Merhige, Jr. ordered the merger of the predominantly black schools of Richmond, Virginia with those of two suburban counties with nearly all-white enrollments in order to promote school desegregation. Judge Merhige directed that the new metropolitan school district be formed as the only "remedy promising immediate success" to end segregated education based upon separate housing patterns. The order required the merger of the 70% black Richmond city schools with the 90% white schools of Henrico and Chesterfield counties (See Also Below).

January 25. U. S. Representative Shirley Chisholm (D., N.Y.), the first black woman ever to serve in the U. S. Congress, announced that she would seek the Democratic presidential nomination. Representative Chisholm said her candidacy would help repudiate the notion that the American people would not vote for a qualified black or female candidate.

January 27. Mahalia Jackson, one of the world's foremost gospel singers, died at 60 in Evergreen Park, Illinois. Miss Jackson was largely responsible for spreading gospel music from black churches in the Deep South to concert halls throughout the world. Her 1946 recording of "Move on up a little higher" sold at least one million copies. President Nixon eulogized Miss Jackson as "an artist without peer."

February 11. About 50 members of the Congress of Racial Equality (CORE) went to the office of black U. S. Representative Augustus Hawkins (D., California) demanding that black opponents of busing to achieve school desegregation be given a voice in national black meetings. Victor A. Solomon, leader of the CORE contingent, said his group advocated separate but "really equal" schools under community control. The NAACP and other black organizations had supported busing as a necessary tool to achieve school desegregation.

March 24. Z. Alexander Looby, one of the first blacks elected to the Nashville, Tennessee City Council (1951-1971) and a veteran civil rights activist, died at 72 in Nashville (See Also Above).

March 27. An all-white jury in San Francisco acquitted Fleeta Drumgo and John Cluchette—the so-called Soledad Brothers—in the slaying of a Soledad Prison guard in 1970. Black communist Angela Davis had been charged with plotting to free these prisoners and the late George Jackson, her alleged lover, in the famous Marin County Courthouse shoot-out in August, 1970 (See Above and Below). In the Soledad Brothers trial, the prosecution was unable to produce witnesses who actually saw any fatal blows delivered or who had seen the defendants toss a guard over a third floor cell tier. The defendants had denied that they were present at the scene of the slaying.

April 4. Adam Clayton Powell, Jr., U. S. Representative from Harlem for more than 20 years (1945-1969) and one-time Chairman of the influential House Education and Labor Committee (1960-1967), died at 63 in Miami, Florida. Powell was surrounded with controversy in death, as in life, as two women fought over the disposition of his body and his estate. On April 10, the body was cremated and the ashes scattered over the island of Bimini in the Bahamas.

May 19. The National Education Association (NEA) reported that over 30,000 black teachers had lost their jobs in 17 Southern and border states because of desegregation and discrimination since 1954. Twenty-one percent of the teachers in these states were black in 1954, but by 1970 that percentage had dropped to nineteen. The percentage of black job losses was lowest in Alabama, and highest in Kentucky, Missouri and Delaware.

May 19. The National Black Political Convention issued a 58-page "Black Agenda" that had been adopted at its founding meeting in March in Gary, Indiana. Although a special committee had modified provisions on school busing and on black attitudes toward Israel, these statements continued to arouse opposition. Partly because of these provisions, the NAACP, as well as other black organizations and individuals, criticized that part of the report which called for the "dismantling" of Israel and which condemned that nation's "expansionist policy." The school provision which also provoked controversy called busing "racist" and "suicidal." In their modified forms, the Israeli statement embraced the condemnations of Israel contained in numerous resolutions of the Organization of African Unity and the United Nations Commission on Human Rights, while the school provision criticized the Nixon administration's busing policies and demanded that blacks retain control of any busing program. Despite the modifications, however, the NAACP announced its continued opposition and withdrawal on May 16. NAACP Assistant Executive Director John A. Morsell called the "Agenda's" Israeli and busing statements "particularly outrageous."

May 21. Professor David J. Armor, a white Harvard University teacher, released a study of school desegregation programs in six Northern cities in which he concluded that there was no improvement in either academic achievement among black students or racial cooperation. While no significant academic differences were found among black students who had been bused for desegregation purposes and those who remained in black ghetto schools, the desegregated students tended to show declines in educational and career aspirations and in self-esteem. Professor Armor did, however, recommend the continuation of "voluntary" programs of busing to achieve desegregation, because those bused students tended to get better opportunities for higher education. The study was conducted in Boston, Massachusetts, White Plains, New York, Ann Arbor, Michigan, Riverside, California, and Hartford and New Haven, Connecticut.

May 23. The annual convention of the National Congress of Parents and Teachers adopted a resolution requesting governmental and educational authorities "to search for solutions that would by rational means reduce racial isolation through transportation." The resolution passed by a vote of 303-296. The National Congress has eight and one-half million members.

May 24. The U. S. Senate passed and sent to the House of Representatives a final version of an omnibus higher education-desegregation aid bill with an anti-busing provision. The bill would delay all new court-ordered busing until appeals had been exhausted, or until January, 1974. Federal funds could not be used to finance busing to achieve desegregation unless specifically requested by local authorities. Federal officials would be prohibited from encouraging or ordering school districts to spend state or local funds for busing in cases where such busing endangered the health or education of students involved, "unless constitutionally required." John Ehrlichman, President Nixon's chief assistant for domestic affairs described the bill as falling "far short" of what was necessary to control busing to achieve desegregation.

June 2. Former SNCC head, H. Rap Brown was resentenced to five years in prison and fined $2,000 for a 1968 conviction on a federal weapons charge by U. S. District Court Judge Lansing L. Mitchell in New Orleans. Brown had been flown to New Orleans from New York City where he had been held since his capture by New York police during an alleged robbery attempt in October, 1971. Brown was wounded by police in that altercation and his attorneys protested against the trip to New Orleans, claiming that it endangered their client's health (See Above).

June 3. U. S. District Court Judge Alfonso J. Zirpoli of San Francisco ordered David Hilliard, Chief of Staff of the Black Panther Party, cleared of perjury charges after the Justice Department refused to disclose wiretap evidence requested by the jury. Chief of Staff Hilliard had been accused of filing false declaration of poverty in 1971. At the time of his latest trial he was serving a prison sentence for assaulting a policeman.

June 4. Black communist Angela Davis was acquitted on all charges of murder, kidnapping, and conspiracy by a Superior Court Jury in San Jose, California. An all-white jury deliberated for 13 hours before announcing their verdict. Miss Davis reacted to the acquittal by at first proclaiming that the "only fair trial would have been no trial," but later added that the verdict had been a victory for the people. Praise for the verdict was generally heard in the black and white "liberal" communities of the nation and in foreign capitals, including Moscow.

June 6. U. S. Senator James O. Eastland (D.) of Mississippi was renominated for a sixth term with 70% of the vote over two challengers, including James H. Meredith, the first black to enroll at the University of Mississippi in recent times (See Above). Eastland had earned a reputation for supporting anti-Negro policies.

June 6. The 4th U. S. Circuit Court of Appeals in Richmond, Virginia overruled a federal district court order that called for the merger of the school districts of Richmond and two suburban counties, which would have involved the busing of thousands of children to achieve desegregation. The court held that U. S. District Court Judge Robert R. Merhige, Jr. had excessively interpreted the 14th Amendment when he earlier ordered the "metropolitan desegregation" plan into effect. The Richmond Board of Education announced that it would appeal the Court's 5-1 ruling to the U. S. Supreme Court where it, with a similar case from Denver, Colorado, was expected to bring a new crucial ruling in the annals of school desegregation (See Also Above). The appeal to the 4th Circuit Court had been sponsored by suburban Henrico and Chesterfield counties and co-sponsored by the U. S. Department of Justice. The NAACP, the National Education Association (NEA), and the American Civil Liberties Union (ACLU) opposed the appeal to the Circuit Court.

June 8. The U. S. House of Representatives approved and sent to President Nixon for his signature an omnibus higher education-desegregation aid bill which would, among other things, delay all court-ordered busing to achieve desegregation until all appeals were exhausted or until January 1, 1974. (The U. S. Supreme Court had held since 1969 that busing to achieve desegregation had to be implemented immediately when ordered by federal district courts.) The bill also prohibited federal funds for busing unless requested by a community and where there was no danger to pupils "health, safety, or education." Federal officials were not to require or encourage busing to achieve desegregation "unless constitutionally required." The bill further appropriated $2 billion over a two-year period to aid school districts with the desegregation process. Although the Nixon administration had criticized the bill as inadequate, HEW Secretary Elliott Richardson announced that it embodied "the heart" of the President's "higher education initiative." The President signed the bill into law on June 23.

June 12. The U. S. Supreme Court ruled, in a 6-3 decision that a state could grant a liquor license to a private club which practiced racial discrimination. The Court ruled against the petition of K. Leroy Irvis, black majority leader of the Pennsylvania House of Representatives. Irvis had been denied service in the restaurant of the lodge of the Loyal Order of Moose in Harrisburg, Pennsylvania. Justice William H. Rehnquist wrote that the authority to grant liquor licenses did not "sufficiently implicate the state in the discriminatory guest policies" of private clubs. Justices Douglas, Brennan, and Marshall dissented from the majority view.

June 14. U. S. District Court Judge Stephen J. Roth ordered a massive busing program to desegregate the city and suburban schools in the Detroit, Michigan area. It was the most extensive desegregation plan ever ordered by a federal court. Under the plan, 310,000 of 780,000 students in Detroit and 53 suburban school districts would be bused to achieve desegregation. The Detroit schools had, at the time, 290,000 students, 65% black, while 29 of the 53 suburban districts had all-white enrollments and the rest were predominantly white. On June 22, President Nixon voiced complete disagreement with the court's decision and reiterated his appeal for congressional action on a strong anti-busing law. The President called the Detroit order "perhaps the most flagrant example that we have of all the busing decisions, moving against all the principles that I, at least, believe should be applied in this area." On July 21, the Sixth U. S. Circuit Court of Appeals issued an order delaying the implementation of Judge Roth's order until it could hear the merits of the case on August 24, 1972.

June 26. A bloc of black delegates to the Democratic National Convention led by Representative Walter E. Fauntroy (D., D. C.) endorsed the presidential candidacy of Senator George McGovern (D., S. D.). Fauntroy announced that 96 previously uncommitted black delegates would now vote for McGovern. The Democratic contender, McGovern, predicted that the black bloc might be enough to give him the nomination on the first ballot. A later recount by all parties confirmed that the black bloc really numbered only about 60 votes, not enough to assure McGovern a first ballot victory. Senator McGovern had won favor among blacks for his "positive" attitude as exhibited in his support of parts of the programs of the Black Congressional Caucus, the Black National Convention, and his pledge to appoint blacks to high-ranking positions in any administration which he should head.

June 29. The U. S. Supreme Court, in a 5-4 decision, ruled that the death penalty as it was usually enforced violated the eighth amendment prohibition against cruel and unusual punishment. The high Court order overturned the conviction of two Georgia blacks, Henry Furman, a convicted murderer, and Lucius Jackson, a convicted rapist, and a Texas black, Elmer Branch, also a convicted rapist. All of the victims in the crimes were white. Of the 600 men and women awaiting execution at the time of the ruling, 329 were black, while 14 belonged to other minority groups. Justice William O. Douglas wrote that the disproportionate number of minority and poor persons sentenced to death were victims of unconstitutional discrimination.

July 3-7. The annual convention of the National Association for the Advancement of Colored People (NAACP) again criticized the Nixon administration for its attitude toward blacks. The 2,632 delegates, meeting in Detroit, Michigan, passed an emergency resolution condemning the administration for its school busing policies. On July 6, NAACP Labor Director Herbert Hill reiterated his criticisms of the administration record on black employment. Black administration officials, including Assistant Secretary of Housing and Urban Development Samuel Jackson defended the Nixon program and claimed support for the President even among NAACP board of directors members.

July 6. James E. Baker, a career black foreign service officer, was appointed economic and commercial officer at the U. S. embassy in Pretoria, South Africa, the first black American diplomat to gain a permanent assignment in that nation. The U. S. Department of State expressed confidence that Baker would be accepted in South Africa without restrictions despite that nation's racist apartheid policy.

July 12. South Dakota Senator George S. McGovern, with widespread support from black delegates, won the Democratic presidential nomination on the first ballot in Miami Beach, Florida. U. S. Representative Shirley Chisholm of New York, the first black woman ever to seek a presidential nomination, received 151 votes of the more than 2,000 cast.

August 2. The U. S. Circuit Court of Appeals for the 5th District countermanded desegregation orders of lower courts for the school districts in Austin and Corpus Christi, Texas. In Austin, the lower court had rejected plans for crosstown busing of students, but the appeals court counselled against the total rejection of the busing tool and ordered new plans from all of the concerned parties. In the Corpus Christi case, the appeals court itself overturned a crosstown busing plan, telling the lower court to try all neighborhood-oriented tools before resorting to busing to achieve desegregation.

August 3-8. In fall primary elections, State Senator James O. Patterson, Jr. was nominated for a congressional seat in the new 8th Congressional District (Memphis) of Tennessee. Patterson thus became the first black to win a major party congressional nomination in the state's history. In Georgia, a former aide to Dr. Martin Luther King, Jr., Hosea Williams of Dekalb County placed a distant third in the Democratic race for U. S. Senator and, in the same state, another ex-aide to Dr. King, Andrew Young of Atlanta won the Democratic nomination from the 5th U. S. House District. Five blacks were also elected to the 10-man City Council in Selma, Alabama, scene of violent voting rights controversies in the 1960's. This group, elected from predominantly black wards rather than at-large, were the first of their race to win seats on the local council.

August 25-October 28. Black civil rights and political leaders campaigned in behalf of the presidential nominees of both parties. On August 25, Georgia State Representative Julian Bond told an audience at Columbia University in New York that black Americans ought to "come together to drive Richard Nixon from the White House." Bond predicted that Nixon's opponent, Sen. George McGovern (D., S. D.), would capture 90 percent of the nation's black vote. On October 28, Floyd McKissick, former National Director of the Congress of Racial Equality and developer of the new town of Soul City, North Carolina, told an Atlanta audience that he supported the re-election of President Nixon because blacks should belong to both political parties and because Nixon had done more for blacks than Senator McGovern had. Veteran Atlanta civil rights leader William Holmes Borders, another Nixon supporter, cited the administration's aid to Howard University in Washington, Tuskegee Institute in Alabama, and to the sickle-cell anemia and job retraining programs as evidence of the President's concern for blacks.

August 26. U. S. District Judge L. Clure Morton ordered the Nashville, Tennessee school board to obtain 30 additional school buses in order to meet the court's desegregation requirements. Nashville's mayor and city council had hesitated to release the necessary funds for the new buses. Judge Morton, however, told city officials that they must acquire the additional buses immediately so that his year-old busing order could be made effective.

August 26. Dr. Thomas A. Shaheen, an advocate of busing to achieve racial desegregation in the public schools, resigned under board pressure as superintendent of schools of San Francisco. Shaheen directed the first massive busing to achieve desegregation in a major Northern or Western city in September 1971 when more than half of San Francisco's 40,000 elementary school children were ordered bused by the federal courts. Shaheen predicted that "rocky days" were ahead for proponents of desegregation in American education. He was succeeded by Dr. Stephen Morena, Assistant Chancellor of the San Francisco Community College District (See Also Above).

August 26. John LeFlore, a veteran civil rights leader and newspaperman in Mobile, Alabama, was officially certified as the first black candidate for the United States Senate in Alabama since the Reconstruction era. LeFlore was certified by Alabama Secretary of State Mabel Amos under the banner of the mostly black national Democratic party of Alabama (NDPA). Other candidates in the senate race were Democratic incumbent John Sparkman and Republican W. M. Blount, former postmaster general of the United States.

August 30. Three Meridian, Mississippi whites were freed from a federal prison after serving slightly more than two years of their three-year sentences on charges of slaying three civil rights activists in Neshoba County, Mississippi in 1964. Jimmy Arledge, Jimmie Snowden, and Horace Doyle Barnette had been convicted in 1967 on conspiracy charges following the deaths of Andrew Goodman, Michael Schwerner, and James Chaney near Philadelphia, Mississippi. Chief Deputy U. S. Marshal Charles T. Sutherland said the convicted trio were approved for release in the spring of 1972 after receiving time off of their sentences for "good behavior " (See Above).

September 1. A group of black parents asked for federal protection for their children attending desegregated schools in Oklahoma City, Oklahoma. The blacks vowed not to return their children to the schools—scenes of continued outbursts of racial violence—without protection. The black parents presented their requests to the local school board and to the offices of the U. S. Attorney and U. S. Marshal. They suggested that federal officers board school buses and patrol the schools.

November 2. Racial tensions flared in Lavonia, Georgia after a black man was slain in a gunbattle with police. Police Chief Joe Foster said Ollis Hunter was killed after he opened fire on officers attempting to serve him with a peace warrant at his home. Lavonia patrolman Freddie Smith was wounded in the exchange of gunfire. Blacks contended that the slaying of Hunter could have been avoided. Almost immediately blacks in Lavonia began a boycott of downtown merchants, demanding, among other things, that better streets be provided in their communities, more black school bus drivers and policemen, and the firing of Chief Foster. Mayor Herman Ayers and the city council took the demands under advisement. On December 8, 1972 a gunman rode through the black residential area of Lavonia firing shotgun blasts into two homes, two restaurants, and a church. Police said one of the homes belonged to the head of the local chapter of the Southern Christian Leadership Conference. There were no injuries in the incident and no immediate arrests.

November 7. Richard M. Nixon was re-elected President of the United States by one of the largest majorities in the nation's history. As in 1968, the President failed to win substantial support from black voters. Preliminary estimates gave the President only about 30% of the black votes cast in the Presidential Election.

The fall elections also saw the selection of two additional black women for seats in the U. S. Congress and the election of the first black congressman from the South since Reconstruction days. The new black congresswomen are Yvonne Braithwaite Burke from California and Barbara Jordan from Texas. Andrew Young, formerly a top aide to the late Dr. Martin Luther King, Jr., was elected congressman from Georgia's Fifth District (Atlanta).

November 11. Black syndicated columnist Carl T. Rowan was elected to membership in the Gridiron Club, a prestigious organization of Washington newsmen. Rowan became the first black member of the Club, which was established in 1885.

November 14. Thirteen blacks, members of the Dallas, Texas chapter of the Southern Christian Leadership Conference were arrested on charges of disrupting a public meeting after they sat-in at the chambers of the Dallas City Council. George Holland, spokesman for the SCLC group, read a list of demands which included the resignation of Dallas mayor Wes Wise, Police Chief Frank Dyson, and city attorney Alex Bickley; the arrest of three officers who were recently cited, but exonerated, in the slaying of blacks; and a percentage (24) of city jobs commensurate with the black ratio of the city's population. Policemen arrested the blacks before Holland could finish reading his demands.

November 15. Private Billy Dean Smith, a black soldier, was acquitted by a courts-martial in San Francisco of the "fragging" slaying of two officers in South Vietnam. Smith later told a news conference, which was attended by black communist Angela Davis, that "the system of military justice is still riddled with injustice." Smith said the only fair trial in his case would have been "no trial at all."

November 15. The black National Bar Association announced that it will co-sponsor a federal court suit protesting the failure of all black applicants in the last semi-annual Georgia Bar examination. Atlanta City Councilman (Alderman) Marvin S. Arrington, deputy regional director of the NBA said that none of the 51 black applicants received a passing grade and charged that "there is conscious and invidious discrimination" on the part of the bar examiners in Georgia. He pledged to call on the U. S. Department of Justice and Georgia Governor Jimmy Carter to conduct investigations into allegations of discrimination. Georgia Bar Examination Board Chairman

Trammell Vickery denied that discrimination existed against black applicants and cited the fact that applicants are not identified by color (See Above and Below).

November 16. The Reverend Theodore Hesburgh, chairman of the U. S. Civil Rights Commission (USCCR) since 1969 and a member since its inception in 1958, resigned. Hesburgh, President of Notre Dame University, had led the USCCR in a constant stream of criticism of the Nixon administration's commitment to civil rights progress. Maurice Mitchell, Chancelor of the University of Denver also announced his resignation. Mitchell had charged that President Nixon ignored the commission and its work (See Above).

November 16. Two black students at Southern University, Baton Rouge, Louisiana were killed during a confrontation between black students and law enforcement officers. High ranking police officials denied, in the first statements following the shooting, that their men had fired the fatal shots. Some suggested that there might have been accidental firing. Black student spokesmen charged intentional shooting by law enforcement units. Louisiana Governor Edwin Edwards immediately requested State Attorney General William J. Guste, Jr. to investigate the incidents. The Attorney General subsequently appointed a bi-racial committee consisting of police officers, university administrators, students, elected officials, and private citizens. Some blacks expressed distrust of the official committee and vowed to assemble a group of their own to look into the altercation.

Southern University, one of the nation's largest all-black colleges, has been the frequent scene of student protests. The students have generally charged the school's administration, backed by the power of the state government, with being unresponsive to academic and social change.

November 17. U. S. District Judge John H. Pratt ruled in Washington, D. C. that efforts made by the U. S. Department of Health, Education, and Welfare (HEW) to obtain voluntary compliance with the 1964 Civil Rights Act had been largely unsuccessful and that HEW should withhold funds from school districts still practicing segregation. U. S. Attorneys announced that they would appeal the ruling, claiming that there appeared to be serious errors in the judge's decision. They did not specify the errors.

November 18. Fayette, Mississippi Mayor Charles Evers called for a federal investigation into problems faced by small southern cotton farmers. The black mayor told Secretary of Agriculture Earl Butz, in a telegram message, that many farmers, black and white, had come to him with their problems.

November 18. U. S. District Judge Edward T. Ginoux set a limit on the contempt-of-court sentence that may be ordered for the "Chicago 7" defendants and their lawyers and ordered contempt charges against Black Panther Leader Bobby Seale entirely dropped. The contempt charges arose from the actions of the defendants and the lawyers in the courtroom of Judge Julius J. Hoffman, who heard the case after disturbances during the 1968 Democratic National Convention in Chicago. The charges against Seale were dropped at the government's request. An Appeals Court had earlier ruled that if Seale were prosecuted, the government would have to reveal the contents of eavesdropping logs. The prosecution refused, claiming such disclosures would "endanger the national security" (See Above and Below).

November 22. The Louis Harris Poll, a major survey of public opinion, announced that the sharpest division in the 1972 presidential election was according to race, with blacks going 79-21% for Senator McGovern while whites voted 67-33% for President Nixon. The Survey went on to say that both in terms of their political inclinations and in their outlook on American issues, blacks and whites have rarely been so far apart. The Survey cited such examples as the blacks' overwhelming preference for racially desegregated schools (78-12%) as against a plurality of 46-43% among whites. While roughly 50% of the black population endorsed busing to achieve school desegregation, only 14% of the nation's whites endorsed this tool to dismantle separate schools. Also nearly 80% of the nation's blacks sympathized with the plight of the poor, while no more than 46% of whites supported increased federal assistance for poverty-stricken Americans. The Harris Survey reflected racial attitudes as of Thanksgiving Day, 1972.

November 27. H. Rap Brown, former secretary of the Student Non-Violent Coordinating Committee (SNCC), went on trial on charges of robbery, attempted murder and possession of an illegal weapon. There was speculation, however, that the trial might be further delayed by legal arguments over the effect of a magazine article dealing with one of the arresting officers. Brown was arrested, following his wounding, after a New York robbery on October 16, 1971. The trial finally got under way after Brown's lawyers, William Kunstler and Howard Moore, Jr., both famed civil liberties attorneys, failed in an effort to have the case transferred to the federal courts.

November 29. President Nixon nominated Peter J. Brennan, the president of the Building and Construction Trades Councils of New York, to be his new secretary of labor. Many blacks voiced opposition to the nomination claiming that Brennan was a representative of a segment of organized labor which had been desegregated "minimally" and, generally, at government insistence.

December 4. Black poet Imamu Amiri Baraka (Leroi Jones) told the representatives at the triennial general assembly of the National Council of Churches that the nation's major religious organizations must support the "revolution" of the poor or cease to exist. Baraka, an influential resident of Newark, New Jersey, called for the destruction of capitalism, claiming it was part of a "cruelly primitive social system" subjecting the poor to misery in this country and abroad. Observers of the American Jewish Committee, Rabbi A. James Ruden and the Rev. Gerald Strober, voiced "deep chagrin" at Baraka's appearance and accused him of "anti-white racism and vicious anti-Semitism." Many other delegates stood to applaud the black poet.

December 7. The Reverend W. Sterling Cary, the black administrative officer for some 90 United Church of Christ congregations in New York City, was unanimously elected president of the National Council of Churches at the group's annual meeting in Dallas, Texas. Cary, the first black American, to head the group was originally a

Baptist minister, then he preached in Presbyterian, Congregational, and interdenominational churches in a ministerial career spanning 24 years. The newly elected president of the "liberal" religious group told his fellow delegates at Dallas that American churches preach but do not practice integration. He said that as president of the National Council of Churches he would promote efforts to achieve decent housing for the poor, better employment opportunities for racial minorities, and an overhaul of the welfare system.

December 9. Lieutenant Edward Kerr, a black policeman with 15 years of service, was nominated as director of the Newark police department, the largest in the state of New Jersey. Kerr, a native of Willacoochee, Ga. and a student at Rutgers University, was slated to succeed John Redden, a white policeman, who resigned after becoming embroiled in a controversy over whether a black sponsored housing project ought to be built in a white community. The white members of Newark's bi-racial city council asked black mayor Kenneth Gibson not to accept Redden's resignation. Gibson refused to heed their plea.

December 11. Soul singer James Brown was arrested and charged with disorderly conduct in Knoxville, Tennessee. The arrest of Brown, an idol of rock and soul fans and a political supporter of President Nixon, sparked a heated controversy in which lawyers for the soul singer threatened to sue the city of Knoxville for one million dollars. Brown said he was talking with a group of children about drugs and the importance of school attendance when he was arrested by Knoxville police. The police charged Brown with disorderly conduct by creating a scene and failure to move on. On December 12, Knoxville Mayor Kyle Testerman said the arrest of Brown apparently resulted from a misunderstanding. The Mayor promised to meet with Brown's attorney, Albert G. Ingram, in an effort to resolve "differences brought about by this incident." Following his meeting with the Mayor on December 18, Attorney Ingram announced that the matter still had not been satisfactorily resolved.

December 14. The U. S. Supreme Court, in a unanimous opinion, ruled that the Civil Rights Act of 1964 authorized the residents of "white ghettos" to file lawsuits aimed at ending racial discrimination in their own apartment developments. The opinion, which was written by Justice William O. Douglas, said residents of both races, who lived in discriminatory housing developments could sue because they may suffer specific "individual injury" when deprived of the social, professional, and business "benefits" available in integrated communities. The decision was rendered in a San Francisco case involving an apartment complex formerly owned by the Metropolitan Life Insurance Co. The NAACP applauded the court decision because it said it lacked the personnel and resources to fight widespread housing discrimination.

December 14. Black Communist Angela Davis announced plans to form a national defense organization to help "black and brown political prisoners of the government." Miss Davis told a Harlem news conference that the new group would provide legal aid to the oppressed.

December 15. Fifty special sheriff's deputies and policemen patrolled the Escambra High School in Pensacola, Florida after a day of fighting between black and white students which left several persons injured and 47 arrested. All of these 38 whites and 9 blacks were subsequently released when school officials dropped trespassing charges against them. The fighting apparently began in the school's cafeteria and spread to other parts of the large school (3,400 students). Sheriff's deputies who broke up the melee said they seized bicycle chains, belts, and knives used as weapons by the students.

December 17. George Wiley, black director of the National Welfare Rights Organization (NWRO) since 1965, announced his resignation in Washington, D. C. Wiley said he was leaving the NWRO, the nation's leading group of welfare recipients, to form a broader-based organization to help the nation's poor. Wiley had headed the NWRO since its founding in 1965.

December 21. Horace Mann Bond, formerly Dean of the School of Education at Atlanta University and ex-president of Fort Valley

(Ga.) State College and Lincoln (Pa.) University, died in Atlanta. The 70 year-old educator was a pioneer in black scholarship, publishing distinguished books and articles in the fields of black education and history. He was the father of Ga. State Representative Julian Bond, whose name was placed before the 1968 Democratic Convention as a vice-presidential candidate. The *Atlanta Constitution*, the city's white daily newspaper, eulogized the black scholar as one who had "a full and fruitful life of achievement."

CHAPTER

XI

A Return to the Mainstream?

1973-1976

1973

January 4. U. S. Attorney General Richard Kleindienst announced that the Civil Rights Division of the Justice Department would have to conduct a careful examination of a report by the FBI on the killings of two students at black Southern University in Baton Rouge, Louisiana before deciding whether to call a federal grand jury into the case. The two black youths were slain by law enforcement officers on the Southern campus during student protests in November, 1972 (See Also Above and Below).

January 29. U. S. District Court Judge Jon O. Newman ordered the city of Bridgeport, Connecticut to hire blacks and Puerto Ricans to fill fifty percent of the vacancies on the police force until the two minority groups constituted at least fifteen percent of the force. The judge's order was designed to correct racial imbalances in Bridgeport's law enforcement.

May 29. Thomas Bradley, a veteran Los Angeles city councilman, was elected mayor of the city of Los Angeles. Bradley defeated incumbent mayor Sam Yorty who was seeking a fourth four-year term. The new black mayor, who lost to Yorty in 1969, won about 56% of the vote cast, although the city's total black population was about 18%. Yorty's campaign rhetoric had pictured Bradley as a fellow-traveler of left-wing radicals. Bradley assessed his victory as a rejection of racism in the election.

July 1. Alonzo A. Crim, formerly superintendent of schools in Compton, California, assumed his duties as the first black superintendent of Atlanta's public schools, one of the deep South's largest predominantly black school systems. Crim's selection resulted from a compromise desegregation plan worked out between local white and black business and political leaders in which the blacks agreed to desist from further pressures for busing to achieve desegregation and the whites agreed to the hiring of a black superintendent and other black school administrators. The plan, reminiscent of the famous "Atlanta Compromise" of 1895, in which Booker T. Washington urged blacks to shun social equality for economic advancement, was denounced by the National NAACP. NAACP leaders in New York felt the agreement set a bad precedent and would hamper future efforts to achieve massive desegregation of the nation's schools. Although local NAACP leaders who assented to the pact argued that massive desegregation was impossible in Atlanta, a city with a 55% black population and an 80% black school-age population, they were suspended and eventually expelled from office for their support of the desegregation agreement.

July 2. The National Black Network (NBN), the nation's first black-owned and operated radio news network, began operations with hourly newscasts to forty affiliated stations. Although based in New York City, the NBN planned to provide news stories of interest to blacks everywhere.

July 29. The U. S. Bureau of the Census released a report of six Northern urban areas which showed that Southern-born black males living in those areas were more likely to be employed and living with their wives than Northern-born blacks living in the same areas. The study, which was based upon data from the 1970 Census, reported that about 65% of the black men born in New York City were employed. The figure rose to 78% for Southern-born blacks who migrated north before 1965 and to 85% for those who moved north since 1965. The study also revealed that 70% of Southern-born black men were living with their wives as compared with 51% of the blacks born in Illinois. Robert Hill, the National Urban League's research director, said the report refuted the widely held view that Southern blacks migrated to the North to obtain higher welfare benefits.

August 15. The National Black Feminist Organization (NBFO) was founded in New York City, with chapters in several other localities, including Chicago, Cleveland and San Francisco. Eleanor Holmes Norton, a member of the New York City Human Rights Commission and a founder of the feminist group, accused the nation of expecting black women to suppress their aspirations in deference to black males. Another founder, Margaret Sloan, said the new group would remind "the black liberation movement that there can't be liberation for half a race."

August 15. Ralph David Abernathy announced that he would remain as president of the Southern Christian Leadership Conference (SCLC) after the civil rights group's board of directors refused to accept his resignation, during the SCLC's sixteenth annual convention in Indianapolis, Indiana. The board, however, agreed to try to remedy some of the complaints which led Abernathy, successor to Martin Luther King, Jr., to offer his resignation—inadequate financing and insufficient staff. The board pledged increased fund raising efforts, the hiring of more full-time staff, and the creation of five regional offices to assist in administration.

September ———. Henry C. Ponder, vice-president for Academic Affairs at Alabama A and M College, assumed the presidency of Benedict (S. C.) College. W. Clyde Williams, acting president of Miles College (Ala.) since 1971, was inaugurated as the tenth president of the Birmingham institution.

October 10. Richmond Hill, a 68-year-old black mortician and mayor pro tem of Greenville, Georgia (Hill had previously worked as a farmer before entering business and politics.), was elected mayor of his city and became the first black mayor in Georgia's history. Hill defeated a white opponent in a town with a population of about 1,500, forty percent of whom were black. Greenville, county seat of Meriwether County in southwest Georgia, had two blacks on its three-man police force and one black on its four-man city council. During the election Hill said he did not feel voters were thinking much about color, "but about us as men who could get something done."

October 14. The famed blues singer B. B. King was awarded an honorary doctor of humanities degree from Tougaloo College (Mississippi), making him the first blues musician ever to receive an honorary doctorate for his contribution to the music world. Dr. George A. Owens, president of the college, conferred the degree during the celebration of the 104th anniversary of the founding of Tougaloo, the state's most prestigious private black college.

October 16. Maynard H. Jackson, a 35-year-old attorney and vice mayor of the City of Atlanta, was elected mayor of the deep South's largest city. Jackson, who led a field of eleven candidates in the primary balloting, defeated incumbent mayor Sam Massell. In a campaign marred by Massell's injection of the race issue, Jackson ousted the city's first Jewish mayor to become Atlanta's first black mayor. The new black mayor was descended from a distinguished Georgia middle class family which included black Republican leader John Wesley Dobbs; the mayor's father, Reverend Maynard Holbrook Jackson; and opera star Mattiwilda Dobbs. Educated at Morehouse College and North Carolina Central University Law School, Jackson had run unsuccessfully for the U. S. Senate in 1968 before being elected vice mayor in 1969 (See Above). Jackson's election signalled a swing of political power from white to black in Atlanta as blacks achieved equality on the 18-man city council and a slight majority on the 9-man board of education. Slightly more than fifty percent of the population of Atlanta was black at the time of Jackson's election, but whites held a slight edge in voter registration. Although opposed by many whites for his forthright opposition to alleged police brutality in Atlanta, Jackson appealed to voters of both races and captured at least twenty percent of the white vote cast in the final election.

October 26. Vernon Jordan, Executive Director of the National Urban League, told an audience at Clark College in Atlanta that the Nixon Administration left "unfinished" the economic improvement of black Americans after a decade of advancement in civil rights. Jordan said the steady flow of congressional action, executive orders, and federal court decisions in the 1960's did for blacks what the New Deal had done for whites and organized labor, but the Nixon Administration allowed this "Second Reconstruction" to expire uncompleted. Jordan's remarks reiterated a continuing theme among black American leadership—criticism of President Nixon's failure to recognize the legitimate needs of black citizens.

October ———. Seven members of the Republic of New Africa (RNA), including president Imari A. Obadele, were convicted in the U. S. District Court in Biloxi, Mississippi on charges resulting from a shootout at RNA headquarters in Jackson, Mississippi in 1971. Two black women and five men had been charged with illegal possession of weapons and assault on a federal officer. Two of the defendants, Wayne M. James and Thomas E. Norman, were already serving life sentences for convictions in state courts. In the federal trial president Obadele received a twelve-year sentence; others received sentences ranging from three to twelve years. Attorneys for the blacks indicated that they would file for a rehearing of the cases (See Also Above).

October ———. Robert Threatt, president of the Georgia Association of Educators, assumed duties as president of Atlanta's Morris Brown College. Threatt succeeded John A. Middleton, a black member of the Atlanta Board of Education, who resigned because of the school's deteriorating financial condition, a situation which appeared to worsen as the school withdrew from the Atlanta University Center complex (See Also Above). Threatt, a graduate of Morris Brown and the University of Oklahoma, had been professor of education at Fort Valley (Ga.) State College prior to becoming, at 46, the youngest president in the history of Morris Brown.

October ———. As the 1973 professional baseball season closed, black centerfielder Willie Mays ended his long, outstanding career. Mays won national acclaim for his fielding heroics and his powerful bat during almost twenty years of play with the New York and San Francisco Giants and with the New York Mets. New York City honored Mays in special ceremonies at Shea Stadium on September 25. Mayor John Lindsay issued a proclamation of celebration and 55,000 fans cheered the black star. Alabama's Miles College presented Mays with an honorary LL.D. degree during the ceremonies. Mays was born in Alabama.

The Atlanta Braves' black star Henry (Hank) Aaron completed the season with 713 career home runs, just one short of the long held record of 714 set by baseball's immortal slugger, Babe Ruth.

Reggie Jackson of the world champion Oakland Athletics was unanimously selected as the American League's Most Valuable Player. Four other blacks had won the award in previous years—Dick Allen (Chicago), 1972; Vida Blue (Oakland), 1971; Frank Robinson (Baltimore), 1966; and Elston Howard (New York), 1963.

October ———. Jesse W. Lewis, a founder and former director of Industrial Bank, one of the nation's first black banks (opened during the Great Depression), died in Washington, D. C. Lewis was born in 1902 in Richmond, Virginia and was educated at Shaw University (N. C.) and New York University. He began his career as a teacher at Howard University, where he taught for nineteen years. In 1934, he joined with Jesse H. Mitchell and other black financial leaders to form the Industrial Bank. He was also a lawyer, a real estate broker, and a trustee of Virginia Union University.

November 6. Michigan State Senator Coleman Young was elected mayor of Detroit. With only about ten percent of the while blue-collar votes going to him, Young won with an overwhelming vote in black precincts. Young defeated former white police commissioner John F. Nichols in becoming the "Motor City's" first black mayor. The new mayor, a native of Tuscaloosa, Alabama, was to preside over the nation's fifth largest city, a city seriously plagued with crime. Black political power in Detroit was also measurably increased by the election of State Representative James Bradley as the first black city clerk, the second highest elective position in the city, and by the fact that four of the nine city councilmen were black. By the end of 1973, blacks would hold mayoral positions in almost 100 of the nation's 18,000 local governments, including major cities like Los Angeles, Washington, Newark, Cincinnati, and Atlanta.

November 9. An eight member biracial committee, including Georgia's Secretary of State Ben Fortson and Clarence A. Bacote, veteran professor of history at Atlanta University, met to select the portraits of three outstanding black Georgians to be hung in the rotunda of the Georgia State capitol in Atlanta. Georgia Governor Jimmy Carter, viewed by many as the state's most progressive governor on racial matters, ordered the selection of the black honorees after one of his black aides, Rita J. Samuels, made the suggestion. The selection committee was said to be certain to choose Martin Luther King, Jr. among its trio of greats. Tennessee had previously honored blacks by placing the portraits of blues musician W. C. Handy and Memphis political leader George Lee in its capitol building at Nashville.

November 23. U. S. Representative Yvonne Braithwaite Burke (D. Calif.), one of the first black women to serve in the U. S. Congress, gave birth to a baby girl in Los Angeles to become the first member of Congress to give birth while in office. Ms. Burke had been granted maternity leave by House Speaker Carl Albert.

November 26. The U. S. Department of Justice filed fifteen civil rights suits to desegregate 24 bars, liquor stores and pool halls in seven Southern states—Arkansas, Florida, Georgia, Louisiana, South Carolina, Tennessee and Texas. The civil suits charged the owners and operators of the establishments with violating the public accommodations section of the 1964 Civil Rights Act (See Above). Assistant Attorney General J. Stanley Bottinger, head of the Civil Rights Division, said all of the suits would seek federal court injunctions against racial discrimination and orders directing the defendants to correct the effects of past discrimination. The suits also asked the courts to require the defendants to post notice that they will serve all persons without regard to race. A Justice Department Representative said it was the largest number of civil rights suits filed in one day within memory.

November ———. George Washington Carver, the famed black scientist from Tuskegee Institute who won acclaim for developing hundreds of uses for the peanut, was elected to the Hall of Fame of Great Americans at New York University. Carver's bust will be placed in the Hall of Fame along with 100 other great Americans, including one other black, Tuskegee's Booker T. Washington who was elected in 1945. Candidates for election to the Hall of Fame must have been deceased for at least 25 years and must have been American citizens who made significant contributions to the nation. Carver's selection was sponsored in the Hall of Fame by black educator Benjamin E. Mays, an Elector since 1958.

December 2. Two U.S. District Court judges, in separate decisions, ordered the city of San Francisco to implement quota systems for the employment of minorities in its police and fire departments. Judge Robert F. Peckham directed the police department to hire three minority persons (defined by Peckham as blacks, "Latinos," and "Asians") for every two whites at the patrolman's level until minority representation reached 30%. The department was also instructed to adopt a one-to-one ratio in appointments to the rank of sergeant until 30% of those officers were from minorities. The judge outlawed a hiring and promotion test which had been used by the city's Civil Service Commission. He found the test to be discriminatory and ordered that any future tests be submitted to him for approval. In the second decision, Judge William T. Sweigert ordered the San Francisco Fire Department to fill half of its more than 200 vacancies with members of racial minorities.

December 3. The U.S. Supreme Court refused to overturn the contempt convictions of 81 Columbus, Georgia blacks who were convicted of violating a city ordinance prohibiting the gathering of more than twelve people in a group. The blacks were part of a larger movement formed to protest local police hiring policies in June, 1971 (See Above). Justices Brennan, Douglas, and Marshall dissented from the majority view.

December 4. The U.S. Court of Appeals for the Sixth Circuit upheld a desegregation plan for Memphis, Tennessee schools. Although the plan involved some crosstown busing, the NAACP opposed it because it allowed too many all-black schools. In rejecting the NAACP's contentions, the Court said there was a "necessity of tolerating some one-race schools because minority groups concentrate in urban areas." The Court also agreed with a lower court that the city of Memphis had acted improperly by cutting its transportation budget in an attempt to circumvent an order for busing to achieve desegregation.

December 19. U.S. District Court Judge Frank Gray, Jr. ruled that the Department of Health, Education and Welfare's (HEW) refusal to consider applications for transportation aid had "impeded" a court-ordered busing plan for the public schools in Nashville, Tennessee. Gray called the action illegal and ordered HEW to review within 30 days its earlier refusal to grant the city of Nashville funds to purchase buses to transport about half of Nashville's 95,000 students.

December 20. The U.S. Department of Labor announced that it had prepared and presented a plan to increase the employment of minorities on federally-aided construction projects in the Chicago area. The plan set goals and timetables and provided for penalties, including contract cancellations and ineligibility for future contracts, if companies failed to demonstrate "good faith" efforts to comply. The Labor Department imposed its plan in Chicago after voluntary efforts to end bias failed.

1974

January 7. The U.S. Department of Justice announced that it had obtained a consent decree whereby the state of Maryland agreed to hire more blacks and women for the state police and assign them on a nondiscriminatory basis. The state police stipulated that it would set a goal for a force which would be 16% black within a five-year period and that it would no longer use a pre-employment test that had been adjudged discriminatory to blacks and women. The Maryland agreement was made in response to a suit filed by the Justice Department on January 4, 1974.

January 8–February 8. Agencies of the federal government continued their efforts to end job bias against minorities and women. The Equal Employment Opportunity Commission (EEOC) obtained an agreement on January 8 from the El Paso (Texas) Gas Company in which that corporation pledged to increase job opportunities for minorities and women. The agreement provided back pay and salary increases for all employees whose current wages were below the norm of white males of similar experience and training. The company also pledged that within the next seven years it would seek to hire specific percentages of women, blacks, Spanish-surnames, and American Indians, according to the population make-up in the company's geographically defined operation areas. On February 8, a federal judge ruled in behalf of the Justice Department in a suit involving black and female employees of Eastex, Inc., a paper manufacturing subsidiary of Time, Inc., of Beaumont, Texas. Eastex was ordered to pay $325,000 in back wages and transfer bonuses, modify its seniority system to allow black and women employees to transfer to jobs previously denied them without losing seniority rights, and adopt percentage goals for hiring and job assignments (See Also Above and Below).

January 11. Senator William Proxmire (D., Wis.), Chairman of the Congressional Appropriations Subcommittee which oversees funds for the National Aeronautics and Space Administration (NASA), ordered the space agency to double the fiscal 1975 budget of its equal employment office and to report to his subcommittee every three months on progress in hiring minorities and women. Proxmire's action was prompted by reports that NASA, as of mid-1973, had the lowest percentage of minority and female employees of any federal agency, and that two-thirds of these workers were in lower level jobs. NASA officials also admitted that the agency had failed to act against project contractors who had not met minority employment goals.

January 11. The U.S. Bureau of the Census reported that as of July 1, 1973 the black population in the country had increased to 23.8 million, up 1.2 million from the 1970 census. The Bureau also reported a continuing pattern of black youthfulness, in comparison to the general population. According to the latest statistics, the median age of blacks was 22.9 years; the median age for the total population was 28.4 years.

January 15. The U.S. Supreme Court, in a 6 to 3 decision, ruled that a group of 17 blacks and 2 whites from Cairo, Illinois could not obtain injunctions against local judges and prosecutors who, the plaintiffs had claimed, were engaged in a pattern of setting excessive bail and meting out harsher punishments for blacks than whites. The Court held that the complaints did not constitute a real case or controversy, hence they did not meet the necessary test for receiving relief from the federal courts. Five members of the six-justice majority also ruled that the plaintiffs would not have been entitled to injunctions even if they had been able to prove discrimination, for such a procedure would be tantamount to "an on-going audit of state criminal proceedings" in violation of the principle of federalism—federal-state harmony. The majority opinion was supported by Justices Burger, White, Powell, Stewart, Rehnquist, and Blackmun. In a dissent, Justice William O. Douglas said that the record of the case demonstrated "a more pervasive scheme for suppression of blacks and their civil rights than I have ever seen." The majority's decision, Douglas added, "will please the white superstructure, but it does violence to the conception of even-handed justice envisioned by the Constitution." Cairo had been the scene of angry clashes between blacks and whites since 1969 (See Above and Below).

January 17. The Department of Health, Education, and Welfare (HEW) reported that racial discrimination still existed in the Topeka, Kansas school system. The Board of Education of Topeka was a defendant in the landmark Supreme Court decision, *Brown* vs *Board of Education*, which outlawed school segregation in 1954. HEW said that it found a substantial number of schools which had disproportionate minority enrollments and that attendance zone transfers had impeded desegregation. Most of the black junior high and elementary pupils, HEW discovered, attended schools where the facilities were generally inferior to those at predominantly white schools. The department began its investigation of Topeka's schools in December, 1973 after being named a party in a new suit against the city. As a result of its inquiry, HEW ordered Topeka school officials to submit corrective plans.

January 20. Dr. Peggy Sandy, a University of Pennsylvania anthropologist, released a study which indicated that whites scored higher than nonwhites on intelligence tests because of environmental factors rather than genetic differences between races. The study was conducted in the Pittsburgh public school system and financed by a grant from the U.S. Department of Health, Education, and Welfare (HEW). Dr. Sandy concluded that test score differences were a function, among other factors, of "middle-class social integration" and that her study, combined with data from other investigations, suggested that I.Q. differences between racial groups were "exclusively a matter of environment" while differences within racial groups were determined by both genetics and environment. These findings ran counter to the theories of Dr. William B. Shockley, a Nobel Prize winning physicist at Stanford University, who had held that intelligence was largely inherited and that the disadvantaged social position of American blacks was caused more by heredity than environment. Shockley's views had become increasingly controversial by late 1973, when he was prevented from speaking on several college campuses by protesters who contended that giving him a public forum would lend dignity to racist theories.

January 21. The U.S. Supreme Court upheld a lower court ruling approving a school desegregation plan for Knoxville, Tennessee. Under the approved plan, 59% of the city's black students would be placed in nine schools where the black enrollment would be 64% or more. Justices Powell and White dissented. Justice Marshall did not participate (See Also Above).

January 24. The U.S. Department of Justice filed a suit in the federal court in Boston accusing the city of Boston of discrimination in the hiring of black and Spanish-surnamed as firemen. The Justice Department cited that out of 2,100 firemen in Boston, only sixteen were black and three had Spanish-surnames, although these minorities constituted 16% and 4% of the city's population, respectively. These facts demonstrated, the department said, that the city had failed or refused to hire minorities on an equal basis with whites, and had employed tests and other qualifications that had "not been shown to be required by the needs of the fire department or predictive of successful job performance." The suit asked the District Court to order city officials to begin an active recruiting program and to hire enough black and Spanish-surnamed firemen to compensate individuals who had taken fire department examinations but had been unfairly denied positions. In a closely related matter, the Justice Department also reported that a job-bias suit against Montgomery, Alabama had been resolved by a consent decree filed on October 3, 1972. This action, the department said, substantially expanded job opportunities for blacks in Montgomery's city government.

January 28. U.S. District Judge Jack B. Weinstein of New York City ordered federal, state, and local housing authorities, along with the city departments of police, parks, and transportation, to cooperate with city school officials in formulating plans to desegregate a junior high school in Brooklyn. As of 1973, the school in question had an enrollment of 43% black, 39% hispanic, and only 18% white. In his order, Weinstein told housing officials to develop a joint plan "to undo the racial imbalance" in the public housing near the school. He said all levels of government had failed to take appropriate and available steps to counter trends toward segregation in both housing and education and ruled that "federal complicity in encouraging segregated schooling through its housing programs" was unconstitutional. In his order Weinstein directed housing authorities to include in their plan "advertisements and inducements" directed at the white middle class so as to "stabilize" the district's population. He also directed the city's department of transportation to develop busing plans for the immediate balancing of the school's enrollment. The police department was ordered to submit plans for the adequate protection of children in the area and the parks department, whose facilities were used frequently by the school, was directed to develop a desegregation plan. The judge set a March 1, 1974 deadline for submission and a September deadline for implementation of the joint desegregation program. The ruling, said to be the first decision of its kind, resulted from a suit filed by attorneys for the NAACP.

January 31. A federal court in Atlanta ordered the Georgia Power Company, the state's largest utility corporation, to pay retroactive wages and pension benefits amounting to almost 2.1 million to black employees who had been denied equal job rights. The ruling also required the company to increase black employment to 17% of the total work force within five years. At the time of the court's decision, 9.3% of the company's 8,278 workers were black. The ruling resulted from a suit filed by the U.S. Department of Justice in 1969.

February 4. The Voter Education Project (VEP) reported that 363 blacks had won elective offices in the South in the 1973 off-year elections. Of these victories, 253 were in elections for local councils and commissions, 63 were for school boards, 19 were new black mayors, 14 were election commissioners, and two were selected to state legislatures. The VEP, a privately-funded political study group, reported from its headquarters in Atlanta.

February 13. The American Association of University Professors (AAUP) issued a statement condemning both students and faculties at American colleges who prevented research and debate on the race-intelligence issue which recently had been brought into focus by Stanford University's William P. Shockley. The AAUP accused some of its own members of "undermining the integrity of the academic community by attempting to suppress unpopular opinions." Nevertheless, on February 18, the student-controlled Political Union at Yale University cancelled a scheduled debate between Shockley and Roy Innis, national director of the Congress of Racial Equality (CORE), after protest from various student groups.

February 15. The San Francisco *Chronicle* reported that two black escaped convicts had been identified as leaders of the Symbionese Liberation Army (SLA). The head of the interracial group of radical revolutionaries which received notoriety for their alleged kidnapping of newspaper heiress Patricia Hearst was said to be Donald D. De Freeze, age 30. De Freeze, who called himself Field Marshall Cinque on tapes sent to the Hearst family, was listed as an escapee from the minimum security area of the Soledad State Prison in California on March 5, 1973. The other black SLA leader was identified as Thero M. Wheeler, 29, an escapee from the medical facility at Vacaville State Prison in August, 1973. The report traced Wheeler and De Freeze's association with the SLA to their member- ships in the Black Cultural Association (BCA) at Vacaville State Prison. The BCA was described as an inmate group which sponsored cultural activities, educational programs, and pre-release preparation projects for prisoners. Russell Little, Jo Ann Little, and William Wolfe, all white, reportedly gained control of the BCA while working as tutors at the prison. De Freeze was listed as a teacher of a BCA course entitled "Unsight" which was designed to increase the racial consciousness of black inmates.

March 15–17. The second National Black Political Conven- tion met in Little Rock, Arkansas. The 1,700 delegates approved several resolutions, including (1) the creation of a black "united fund" of about $10 million to further convention agenda items, local organization within the United States, and to develop projects to aid African nations; (2) the condemnation of black congressmen who had voted for military aid to Israel, "ignoring" the plight of Arab Palestine refugees; and (3) support of African "liberation move- ments." The delegates rejected a resolution calling Israel a "major instrument" of an American supported "world strategy of monopoly," and another which sought to establish an all-black political party. Opponents of the latter resolution argued that the convention had not done enough local organizational work to effectively build such a party. The convention was seriously split, as it had been in 1972, between those arguing for a black separatist approach to political organization and those who favored a continuation of ties with exist- ing political structures. Black elected officials, such as Mayor Richard B. Hatcher of Gary, Indiana and Congressman Ronald V. Dellums (D.,Calif.), led those who urged the convention to remain an "inclu- sive" organization, embracing and tolerating different ideologies. Black separatist spokesmen, lead by Newark's Imamu Baraka, ac- cused the more conservative delegates of espousing "neocolonialism" and "opportunism." Baraka said blacks should build an anti-capitalist "revolutionary ideology" and operate as a separate political force. NAACP leaders again boycotted the convention and drew the ire of the co-chairman Mayor Hatcher. Many black elected officials, includ- ing veteran Congressman Charles C. Diggs of Michigan (Co-Chairman of the 1972 convention), were also criticized for being conspicuously absent.

March 16. Excerpt from the keynote address delivered by Mayor Richard Hatcher of Gary, Indiana at the National Black Political Convention, March 16, 1974, Little Rock, Arkansas:

After two years of wandering through the wilderness of Watergate, thank God we're together again.

After two years of reading the last rites over civil rights, thank God we're together again.

After two years of living in a land without a leader, thank God we're together again.

After two years of milk deals rather than fair deals, thank God we're together again.

After two years of cutting back on wheat and meat and heat, thank God we're together again.

After two years of grieving while West Africa filled with corpses, thank God we're together again.

After two years of watching white minorities oppress black majorities in Rhodesia and South Africa, thank God we're together again.

After two years of waiting in the wings while women's movements, and Indian movements, and ecology movements and youth movements took center stage and precedence over black liberation, thank God we're together again.

We have come to Little Rock tonight to recommit ourselves to a common purpose.

We have come to Little Rock tonight to heal our wounds.

We have come to Little Rock tonight to tell this country that our cries for justice will not be denied or turned aside.

We have come to Little Rock to demand a new era of black unity and leadership.

We have traveled more miles than any map will show from Gary, Indiana to Little Rock, Arkansas.

We were sure of ourselves, and of our new-born plans, in Gary. We must deal with deepening doubts and divisions today.

We challenged the heavens with visions in Gary. We hoped the sun would stand still until our cries for justice and equality were heard. We prayed that the red sea of racism would part and let us through to the promised land.

I am here tonight to tell you, to tell those incurable optimists among you that the age of miracles is over. The age of slogans is over. The age of progress without a plan is over. The age of striding without a strategy, of running without a reason and flying without a flight plan is OVER! The waters of reaction are not going to turn into the wine of justice. Not today. Not tomorrow. Not ever. If we do not come together.

What we must understand here tonight, what our long struggle and suffering should have told us, is that if we are to survive as a people, we must save ourselves. Others can help, but we must assume the leadership in this struggle.

March 17. U.S. District Court Judge Luther L. Bohanon ordered an end to racial segregation at the Oklahoma State Prison at McAlester, Oklahoma. Observing that he had "no idea of the deep cruelty inmates were subjected to," the judge also ordered prison officials to stop mistreating convicts. Bohanon found that since the riots that had occurred at the prison in the summer of 1973, inmates had not been provided with proper food, bedding, or heat, and that they had been punished arbitrarily with chemical mace and tear gas. The judge noted that black inmates had received worse treatment than whites.

March 20. The U.S. Department of Justice announced that it had obtained a consent decree under which seven large trucking companies agreed to adopt percentage hiring goals for blacks and Spanish-surnames. The seven companies were the Arkansas-Best Freight System. Inc., of Fort Smith, Arkansas; Branch Motor Express Co. of New York City; Consolidated Freightways Inc., of Menlo Park, California; I.M.L. Freight Inc., of Salt Lake City, Utah; Mason and Dixon Lines Inc., of Kingsport, Tennessee; Pacific Intermountain Express Co., of Oakland, California; and Smith's Transfer Corporation of Staunton, Virginia. Under the agreement, 50% of all vacancies would be filled by blacks and Spanish-surnamed applicants in each community where those groups made up more than 25% of the work force. In areas where the minority groups made up less than 25% of the work force, the hiring goal would be set at 33⅓%. These quotas would be subject only to the availability of qualified applicants in a particular locality. The decree also allowed the inclusion of American Indians and Asian-Americans in certain areas. The far-ranging agreement came on the same day that the Justice Department filed a suit against the seven companies, 342 smaller trucking firms, the International Brotherhood of Teamsters, the International Association of Machinists, and Trucking Employers, Inc. A spokesman for the Justice Department said that his agency believed that the remaining defendants would follow the pattern set by the seven firms involved in the consent decree.

March 31. The U.S. Department of Justice announced that it had reached an agreement with the city of Jackson, Mississippi calling for an increase in the number of blacks on municipal jobs and granting back pay up to $1,000 for blacks currently employed who had been denied promotion opportunities. The five-year plan set a goal of a 40% black work force, approximately the same percentage of blacks as in the city's population. At the time of the agreement, about 800 of Jackson's 3,000 municipal workers were black, most of these serving in the lowest-paying job classifications. Both the police and fire departments were affected by the accord.

April 8. Atlanta Braves baseball star Henry (Hank) Aaron hit his 715th career home run, thus becoming the all-time leading home run slugger. Aaron broke the record, previously held by the immortal Babe Ruth, at Atlanta Stadium. The Braves star had tied Ruth's record on April 4, 1974 in Cincinnati (See Above). The record-breaking pitch was thrown by a Los Angeles Dodgers pitcher, Al Downing.

April 8. U.S. Circuit Court Judge William E. Doyle ordered the desegregation of 70,000 students in the Denver public school system during the 1974–75 school year. The desegregation was to be accomplished mostly through the redrawing of attendance boundaries or zones and the pairing of black, white and Mexican-American pupils so that they might share classrooms on a half-day basis. The order further provided that elementary schools would have between 40% and 70% white enrollment and that white enrollment in high schools would be between 50% and 60%. Judge Doyle rejected the school board's plan to close twelve of the public schools. He saw this move as a tactic "to avoid adoption of a desegregation plan." He also ordered the merger of two high schools and the introduction of bilingual programs in schools with large numbers of Mexican-American pupils. The U.S. Supreme Court had first ordered a desegregation plan to be drawn up by Denver in 1973.

April 8. The Reverend C. Shelby Rooks was named the first black president of the predominantly white Chicago Theological Seminary, an affiliate of the United Church of Christ. Rooks, 49, was executive director of the Fund for Theological Education in Princeton, New Jersey at the time of his new appointment.

April 15. The U.S. Department of Labor and Justice and the Equal Employment Opportunities Commission (EEOC) announced that nine major steel companies had agreed to a five-year plan for ending job discrimination against women and minorities, and would grant back pay of more than $30 million to the victims of such bias. The companies directly involved were the Allegheny-Ludlum Industries, Inc., Amco Steel Corporation, Bethlehem Steel Corporation, Jones and Laughlin Steel Corporation, National Steel Corporation, Republic Steel Corporation, United States Steel Corporation, Wheeling-Pittsburgh Steel Corporation, and Youngstown Sheet and Steel Company. Together, they employed 347,000 employees in 249 plants, at the time of the agreement. The steel companies vowed to restore more than $30 million in back pay to 34,000 black and Spanish-surnamed male employees and to 5,599 women who were adjudged to be victims of job bias. The back pay settlements ranged from $250 to $3,000 per person, depending upon length of service. The agreement also called upon the companies to set first-year goals for hiring women at 20 per cent of all vacancies in production and maintenance jobs and hiring of members of racial minorities at 15 per cent of all vacancies in clerical and technical jobs. The companies were also required to select minorities and women for 25 per cent of vacancies in supervisory jobs and management training. The governmental agencies of Justice and Labor and EEOC, which sponsored the action, said it was the largest anti-discrimination agreement ever reached with an industry. Attorney General William B. Saxbe said the accord marked "a new day," and Labor Secretary Peter J. Brennan predicted that it would "prove a milestone in the federal government's effort to assure full equality in employment."

April 18. Peter Holmes, Civil Rights Director of the Department of Health, Education, and Welfare (HEW), reviewed the progress of school desegregation in the nation on the eve of the 20th anniversary of the historic *Brown* vs *Board of Education* decision and the 10th anniversary of the enactment of the Civil Rights Act of 1964. He told a group of Washington journalists that there were virtually no blacks in school with white students in the eleven Southern states in 1964. By 1968, he noted, a total of 18.4 per cent of the black pupils in the South were in majority white schools. This rose to 39.1 per cent in 1970, and to 44.4 per cent in 1972. Perhaps of greater significance, Holmes said, was the fact that the black pupils in all-black schools decreased in the South from 68 per cent in 1968 to 14.1 per cent in 1970, and to 9.2 per cent in 1972 (See Also Table Below). On the other hand, Holmes noted, while current school year figures were not available, there was likely to be an increase in segregation in Northern metropolitan school districts.

TABLE A   Percentage of Southern Blacks in Majority White Schools

Year	Percentage
1968	18.4
1970	39.1
1972	44.4

TABLE B   Percentage of Southern Blacks in All-Black Schools

Year	Percentage
1968	68
1970	14.1
1972	9.2

Source: U.S. Department of Health, Education, and Welfare *(Office of Civil Rights)*

April 20. The *New York Times* reported a sixth anniversary assessment of black studies in predominantly white colleges and universities. Since the student protests in the 1960's, which helped to give impetus to black studies as a legitimate academic enterprise, 1,272 institutions of higher learning have offered at least one course in the area. Although the tumult which surrounded the initiation of the black studies movement has ceased, the controversy over the validity, viability, and aims of the programs continues. One of the more vocal critics of the programs has been Professor Martin Kilson, a black political scientist at Harvard University. He has called them "distinctly anti-intellectual and anti-achievement in orientation." Others see them differently. Professor Barbara A. Wheeler, of the City University of New York, supported black studies as different from traditional studies in that they are organized around the black experience rather than around the subject matter. This allows the black person to see the impact of the event on his own life. Professors Elias Blake, head of the Institute for Services to Education; Henry Cobb, dean of Southern University at Baton Rouge; and Tobe Johnson, director of undergraduate Afro-American studies programs for the Atlanta University Center, completed an analysis of 29 black studies programs for the U.S. Office of Education just prior to the *Times* report. Blake told the *Times* that the ideological questions had been settled. "God knows," he said, "we need more study on black Americans. The issue is how do you build a good program." The Blake-Cobb-Johnson team found that only carefully structured programs were likely to survive in an era when colleges were undergoing financial retrenchment.

April 22. The Joint Center for Political Studies, a privately funded research organization, reported from Washington that 2,991 blacks held political office in 45 states and the District of Columbia, a gain of more than 300 over 1973 and a jump of more than 1,000 over 1969 (See Table Below). The Center noted that most of the gains during 1973 had resulted from municipal elections. For example, 1,080 out of the latest total were city councilmen, and 108 were mayors. Michigan led in the number of black elected officials with 194, followed by Mississippi with 191. Others with 150 or more included New York, New Jersey, Illinois, Alabama, Arkansas, and Louisiana.

TABLE C Black Elected Officials, 1969, 1973, 1974

Year	Number
1969	1,185
1973	2,621
1974	2,991

Source: Joint Center for Political Studies

April 25. U.S. District Court Judge Alfonso J. Zirpoli in San Francisco ruled that the San Francisco police had violated the constitutional rights of 600 black men they had stopped for questioning in their investigation of the so-called "Zebra" killings. ("Operation Zebra" was the police code used in the dragnet which officers conducted in their probe of the random slayings of twelve whites.) Zirpoli issued an injunction prohibiting their profile of the Zebra killer, a slimly built, young black man, as the sole basis for stopping men for questioning. The suit was filed by the American Civil Liberties Union (ACLU).

April 26. The U.S. Department of Justice rejected a Mississippi act eliminating party primaries and replacing them by a single open primary in which no candidate could be elected with less than a majority vote. The Justice Deartment said that such a system would discriminate against independent candidates, and thus against blacks, since most of the successful black candidates in recent general elections had run as independents. The Mississippi legislature was seeking to repeal current statutes which required a majority vote to win the separate party primaries, but which allowed independents to run in the general election and win with only a plurality. Under the Voting Rights Act of 1965, states like Mississippi, where a pattern of voter discrimination had been found, were required to submit changes affecting the suffrage to the Justice Department for approval.

April ———. The U.S. Circuit Court of Appeals for the 4th District ordered the Nansemond County, Virginia School Board to rehire 56 black teachers who the court said were arbitrarily discriminated against in the administration of a national teaching test. The Appellate Court directed the U.S. District Court in Norfolk to re-examine the circumstances surrounding the dismissal of the teachers, a practice which was begun in 1971. The Court also enjoined the school board from any further discrimination.

May 1. U.S. District Court Judge Albert Henderson in Atlanta ruled that the city's school system had done all it could to desegregate public education. Attorneys for the American Civil Liberties Union (ACLU) and the NAACP had argued for increased desegregation in the system, which has only 18% white enrollment. ACLU argued for more desegregation through a merger of the Atlanta city schools with surrounding suburban systems. The NAACP wanted more desegregation within the bounds of the current Atlanta system. Judge Henderson rejected both appeals and allowed previous court decisions approving the "Atlanta Compromise" school desegregation plan to stand. That controversial program required a minimum of school integration (See Also Above). Attorneys for the ACLU and NAACP filed notices of appeal to the 5th Circuit Court of Appeals in New Orleans.

May 7–14. In Spring primary elections, Southern blacks continued to increase their numbers in major posts in state governments and blacks continued to hold the mayor's office in major American cities. Fourteen blacks were assured election to the Alabama House of Representatives in the May 17 primary. Those victories could mean a total of 17 black representatives. Two blacks were assured election to the Alabama State Senate, with the possibility of one other also being selected. In North Carolina, three blacks won state house seats and one a post in the state senate in the May 7 primary. A black was elected to a municipal judgeship in Nashville, Tennessee. Another was elected a constable in Cleveland, and still another won an alderman's seat in Ripley, all in Tennessee. Three blacks led in contests for seats in the Texas legislature. Kenneth A. Gibson won an easy victory in his second bid for mayor of Newark, New Jersey on May 14. Gibson, the first black mayor of a major northeastern city, claimed that his victory showed that "Newark has come up from its past." He noted that the racial issue which divided the city during the 1970 mayoral election was not a major factor in the current campaign. Gibson won the support of about 65% of the

118,000 registered voters in defeating State Senator Anthony Imperiale. Also, in the May 7 Alabama primary, Alabama Governor George Wallace, for the first time, made a direct appeal for black votes. Estimates of the number he actually received ranged from about 10 per cent to as much as 30 per cent. Wallace won important backing from several black Alabama politicians, including Mayor Johnny Ford of Tuskegee. Despite criticism from fellow blacks throughout the nation, Ford stood by his support for Wallace. The young mayor justified his actions on the ground that Wallace had been responsive to the economic problems of Tuskegee and had aided the city in receiving state and federal grants. In connection with the spring elections, a joint report issued by the Voter Education Project in Atlanta, the Joint Center for Political Studies, and the Lawyers Committee for Civil Rights Under Law in Washington, showed that implementation of the 1965 Voting Rights Act led to a 169 per cent increase in the number of black elected officials in the South between 1969 and 1974 alone (See Also Table Below). According to the report, there were 299 black elected officials in the six Southern states entirely covered by the act—Alabama, Georgia, Louisiana, Mississippi, South Carolina, and Virginia—in 1969. By 1974 the number had risen to 815, a 169 per cent increase (See Also Above).

TABLE D Black Elected Officials in the South, 1969, 1974

Year	Number	Increase
1969	299	
1974	805	169%

Source: Voter Education Project, Atlanta.

May 8. Southern Democratic Congressmen, reportedly concerned about a major increase in black registered voters, joined with Republicans to defeat 204 to 197 a bill which would have allowed voters to register for federal elections by postcard.

May 16. Four young black men were indicted in the random "Zebra" killings of whites which left the city of San Francisco tense for five months. Indicted on various charges of murder, robbery, and assault with a deadly weapon were Manuel Moore, 29; J. C. Simon, 29; Larry C. Green, 22, and Jessie Cooks. All but Cooks were arrested during a massive manhunt by police on May 1, known as "Operation Zebra." Cooks was already serving a prison term for murder. Twelve murders and six assaults were attributed by police to the Zebra killers. During "Operation Zebra" San Francisco police blanketed the city stopping and searching young black males. A federal judge subsequently ruled the searches unconstitutional (See Also Above).

May 16. The United States Senate approved a bill to limit court-ordered busing to achieve school desegregation, but allowed judges to issue such orders as they see fit. The principal new limitation provides that pupils should not be bused beyond the next nearest school to their homes. The legislation also requires the consideration of alternatives to achieve desegregation before any busing can be required. These include such things as construction of new schools, revision of attendance zones, and permission for students to transfer to schools in which their race is a minority. Yet the bill also states that the new limitations are not intended to inhibit the courts from ordering busing if such measures are necessary to enforce the equal rights provisions of the U.S. Constitution. The new legislation, viewed as a compromise between pro- and anti-busing forces in the Senate, was co-sponsored by Republican leader Hugh Scott and Democratic leader Mike Mansfield. It was approved by a vote of 47 to 46.

May 17. In a speech at Emory University in Atlanta, Dr. Alvin Poussaint, a black Harvard University psychiatrist, gave a major assessment of the growing incidence of homicide among blacks. Poussaint said that 23 per cent of the deaths among black males aged 17-25 were the result of homicide, and that the matter should be treated as a health problem. Among the causes of homicide among blacks, according to Poussaint, is "black racism" or low self-esteem which is evidenced by the use of frequent racial epithets before a homicide is committed and by an inner battle by black men to preserve their self-respect in a racist society. Another contributing factor is that "black life has not been valued." Because of this, Pouissaint said, some police officers do not follow up on solving crimes in black neighborhoods and the media fail to give much attention to homicide unless it involves whites. Poussaint contended that the American black community was "in a state of despair and demoralization," partly because of its failure to realize some of the dreams of the civil rights era and partly because of governmental corruption. When official corruption goes unpunished, he said, a "jungle mentality is created and people begin to believe that they can do whatever they can get away with." Reduction of crime among blacks, Poussaint suggested, required the development of new values and psychological as well as political approaches. He called for the regulation of violence depicted in the media, particularly as portrayed in black "exploitation" films; the establishment of homicide prevention centers to help potential criminals before they commit murder; the control of handguns; increased black employment, particularly among youth; and the promotion of black pride or black consciousness programs. Although the matter was defined by Poussaint as a black health problem, he concluded that it would take interracial cooperation to solve it. Poussaint is the author of the book, *Why Blacks Kill Blacks*.

May 17. The twentieth anniversary of the historic Supreme Court decision, *Brown* vs *Board of Education*, which outlawed school segregation was observed in the nation. In assessing the impact of the decision, the editors of the Atlanta *Constitution*, the South's leading daily newspaper, admitted that even after a generation, racial prejudice and discrimination have not been eliminated. This fact gave credence, in the editors' opinion, to the view that one cannot legislate morals. Yet, the *Constitution* said, "there is no denying that tremendous progress has been made in race relations in our country since 1954 . . . The progress, the vast changes in education, in employment, in housing, in politics, was the result of a struggle for civil rights that was given a decisive impetus on the day the Supreme Court ruled in the case of *Brown* vs *Board of Education of Topeka* in 1954." The noted black syndicated columnist Carl Rowan, in his assessment of *Brown* twenty years later, found that "we are still a racist society," and that the historic school decision did not deliver justice to the black plaintiffs of 1954, or even to their children. "Some of the litigants in that 1954 decision," he said, "never saw a day of desegregated education. They saw evasion, circumvention, massive resistance and a generation of litigation." One of the plaintiffs, Linda Brown Smith (the "Brown" in the famous 1954 case) is now a grown woman with children of her own. Before a meeting of the Association of Social and Behavioral Scientists (ASBS), a mostly black professional group, in Atlanta in April, 1974, she recalled her family's motivations for permitting her to become a plaintiff. The family was incensed by the fact that their children had to wait in ofttimes inclement weather to be taken to black schools in Topeka when a white school was within walking distance from their home. Ironically, Mrs. Smith said she now opposes crosstown busing to achieve racial desegregation in the schools.

May 18. Benjamin L. Hooks, the only black member of the Federal Communications Commission (FCC), called for increased participation by whites in the NAACP. Although Hooks acknowledged that there was a difference between being born black and being born white, in that those "born black live in the valleys while those born white live on the mountain tops," he also said, "We made a mistake when we close the doors on our white brothers." Hooks also urged more blacks to join the organization as he spoke to the 38th annual NAACP Freedom Banquet at Port Huron, Michigan. Hooks was appointed to the FCC by President Nixon in 1972. Other blacks, including the late Harlem Congressman Adam Clayton Powell, Jr., had repeatedly asked the NAACP to purge itself of white influence.

May 22. U.S. District Court Judge Frank M. Johnson, Jr. in Montgomery, Alabama rejected crosstown busing as a remedy for the desegregation of some predominantly black schools in Montgomery County and instead ordered a new desegregation plan, one which allows, with some exceptions, elementary school children to attend neighborhood schools. He sanctioned the creation of a biracial committee to help the school board carry out the program. In approving the new plan, Johnson rejected proposals submitted by blacks and the federal government. He said those plans would require crosstown busing which would not "accomplish any effective and realistically stable desegregation." Even though he acknowledged that some schools in virtually all-black neighborhoods would have high percentages of black pupils, Johnson said all students would "attend a substantially desegregated school for the majority of their school careers." At the time of the decision, the county had a public school enrollment of about 38,000; almost 35 per cent of these pupils were black. Under the court order, it was projected that more than 80 per cent of the black children would attend a substantially desegregated school for at least six grades, and that all black pupils would attend desegregated classes in high school. Some observers, including the editor of the Atlanta *Constitution*, saw the Johnson decision as possibly prophetic and historic, for Johnson has been called "the best judge in America" and had achieved a reputation for stern orders upholding the constitutional rights of blacks. These observers saw in the Montgomery County ruling a possible future direction for the federal courts—one that would move irrevocably away from crosstown busing as a means of achieving racial desegregation in the schools.

May 24. Edward Kennedy "Duke" Ellington, one of America's greatest musician-composers died in New York at age 74. Described as a musical genius, Ellington began playing the piano at age seven, composed his first song at 17, and began playing professionally at 18. He wrote more than 1,000 compositions, including "Take the A Train," "Don't Get Around Much Anymore," "Satin Doll," and "Caravan." In later years he composed several orchestral pieces; tone poems; jazz masses; movie, television, and ballet scores; and several operas. His orchestra was one of the few of the "big bands" to thrive after the 1940's. Some of the members of his orchestra remained with him for more than forty years. Among Ellington's numerous awards were the NAACP's Spingarn Medal, the French Legion of Merit (France's highest honor), and America's highest civilian honor, the Medal of Freedom, bestowed upon him in 1970 by President Nixon. The President had told Ellington in February, 1974 that "There'll never be another you." The NAACP responded to Ellington's death by noting that "Few composers have attained the greatness of stature that was the Duke's at the time of his death.

Prolific, versatile and popular, the Duke claimed the hearts of a wide range of followers, black and white, rich and poor. He was indomitable." Although sometimes criticized for not taking on active role in the civil rights movement, Ellington himself claimed that "protest and pride in the Negro have been the most significant themes in what we've done." His composition of "My People" was a musical salute to blacks.

May 25. A federal grand jury paid a personal visit to Southern University at Baton Rouge, Louisiana to inspect the site where two students, Denver Smith and Leonard Brown, were shot to death on November 16, 1972. The jury was investigating the slaying of the youths by law enforcement officers during a student demonstration in an effort to determine whether or not their civil rights had been violated (See Also Above).

May 26. Housing segregation declined in many Southern cities during the 1960's according to a report cited by the Atlanta *Constitution*. Although in most cases the changes were slight, a prominent demographer, Karl E. Taeuber, said the study indicated that a long-term trend toward more rigid segregation was reversed during the past decade. In virtually every Southern city examined, the investigators found that in 1970 there were more blocks containing homes with both whites and nonwhites than there were in 1960. The changes were greater, however, in Southern cities that had large groups of Spanish-surnamed families than in areas where there were large numbers of blacks. The study was conducted at the University of Wisconsin's Institute for Research on Poverty.

May 27. About 1,000 orderly demonstrators marched through downtown Atlanta demanding the ouster of the city's controversial police chief, John Inman. The marchers were led by veteran protester Hosea Williams, formerly a top aide to slain civil rights leader Martin Luther King, Jr. Many Atlanta blacks had labeled the white police chief a racist and had long sought his removal. Atlanta's black mayor, Maynard Jackson, attempted to fire Inman on May 3, 1974 for administrative inefficiency and insubordination, but was prohibited from doing so by edicts from a Dekalb County Superior Court judge. The marchers reaffirmed their support of the efforts to oust Inman.

June 1. The Georgia Department of Offender Rehabilitation (DOR) completed a study which showed that blacks serve substantially longer sentences than whites in Georgia prisons. The report did not ascribe the longer sentences to racism, but suggested a further study involving some 24,000 convicts (the present study was based upon 7,000 inmates), to determine "whether the judiciary is responding not only to the facts of a crime but also to the race of the defendant in meting out justice." Many blacks had long contended that they received unequal justice in the courts of Georgia as well as elsewhere in the nation (See Also Table Below).

TABLE E   Prison Terms by Race in Georgia

Sentence	No. of Whites	% of Whites	No. of Blacks	% of Blacks
0-2	411	14.8	388	9.5
2-3	569	20.5	619	15.2
4-5	480	17.3	678	16.6
6-7	238	8.6	323	7.9
8-10	337	12.8	587	14.4
11-15	228	8.2	419	10.3
16-20	161	5.8	344	8.4
20	64	2.3	128	3.1
Life	281	10.1	594	14.5
Death	4	0.1	5	0.1
	2,773	99.9	4,085	100.0

Source: Atlanta *Constitution*, June 1, 1974

June 4. James Meredith, the first officially recognized black student to attend the University of Mississippi, led a field of five candidates for the Democratic Congressional nomination in the Fourth District of Mississippi. The forty-three–year old businessman had previously run unsuccessfully for the U.S. Senate in 1972 and for the Jackson City Council in 1973. Meredith announced immediately that he would bypass the Democratic run-off election, because it "is a senseless and useless election for me since the Mississippi regular

Democratic party will not support me if I win," and instead, launched a massive registration drive among blacks so that he might achieve victory in the November general elections. Forty-four per cent of the population of the Fourth District was black at the time of the election. In the Democratic primary, Meredith gained thirty-one per cent of the total vote. His closest opponent was Jackson television executive Kenneth Dean. Meredith assessed his primary victory as a milestone in the black struggle for "self-determination and full freedom." He said it proved what a determined people could do and boasted that he won without "white folks' money" and without "white folks' niggers, white folks' colored people, and white folks' Negroes " (See Also Above).

June 6. The Washington *Star-News* reported that President Nixon called the U.S. Supreme Court's only black justice, Thurgood Marshall, a "jackass" in a tape recording of a White House Conference with then-Counsel John W. Dean III on February 28, 1973. In the same conversation the president reportedly made other racial and ethnic slurs, particularly against Jews. The tape recording was one of many released to the public during the Watergate controversy (See Above).

June 16. The Reverend Lawrence W. Bottoms, a Decatur, Georgia minister, was elected as the first black moderator of the General Assembly of the Presbyterian Church of the United States at its 114th general meeting in Louisville, Kentucky. Bottoms, a 66 - year old native of Selma, Alabama, had had long experience as a pastor and leader of Georgia's black Presbyterians. A strong supporter of racial integration and toleration, Bottom's election placed him at the head of that portion of the Presbyterian Church that broke with its national body to defend slavery before the Civil War.

June 17. A tour guide in the Georgia State Capital at Atlanta reported that the portrait of slain civil rights leader Martin Luther King, Jr. had been defaced with a red ink pen. Although the portrait was only slightly damaged, it was removed immediately and placed with the artist, Paul Mandus, for repairs. Two days later, Georgia Governor Jimmy Carter announced that a black woman who had a history of mental illness had marred the King portrait. The woman told state officials that she scribbled on the painting to show her respect for Dr. King. The incident was reminiscent of the stabbing which King suffered at the hands of a crazed black woman in 1958 (See Above). The King portrait was the first of a black Georgian to hang at the state capital. Two other black Georgians (selected by a biracial commission appointed by Governor Carter), clergyman-politician Henry McNeal Turner and educator Lucy Laney, were also slated to be honored by having their portraits placed in the Georgia capital (See Also Above).

June 21. The U.S. Department of Health, Education, and Welfare (HEW) accepted university system desegregation plans from nine states, eight of them in the South. The HEW action stemmed from an order issued in February, 1973, by U.S. District Court Judge John H. Pratt in Washington which required the department to increase efforts to assure that the states were in compliance with the Civil Rights Act of 1964. States winning approval of their desegregation plans were Arkansas, Florida, Georgia, Maryland, North Carolina, Oklahoma, Pennsylvania, and Virginia. HEW rejected Mississippi's plan and announced that it would initiate a separate law suit against that state. Louisiana refused to submit a plan and was promptly sued by HEW. Louisiana officials had protested attempts by federal authorities to force a merger of the state's black and white universities. In a letter to HEW Secretary Caspar Weinberger on May 17, 1974, James Boyce, the chairman of the Louisiana Republican Party, had warned that such a merger "would destroy these fine (black) institutions (Southern University and Grambling College) of higher learning in our state." Other state officials had announced that they would lose federal grants for education in the state rather than accept the forced mergers. Black educators and civil rights leaders across the country had beome increasingly divided over the question of desegregation in higher eduation. Many blacks feared losses of jobs, social status, and aspects of their cultural heritage through desegregation plans which involved merger. Black students, particularly those in state-supported institutions, formed a nation-wide coalition called "Save Black Schools" to protest school mergers which might destroy the racial identification of their colleges. On the other hand, many civil rights leaders continued to clamor for desegregation at all costs. Joseph L. Rauh, Jr., an attorney for the plaintiffs in the 1973 Pratt decision, announced that he and his associates were undecided as to whether they would challenge in court any or all of the plans accepted by HEW. A typical plan was that submitted by Georgia. It left the state's three identifiably black colleges intact, but called for an increase in cooperative programs with nearby white schools. A faculty "clearing house" was to be established so that institutions in the state could draw on a central pool of faculty applicants in their efforts to increase teacher integration. In approving the new desegregation plans, HEW Civil Rights Director Peter E. Holmes remarked, "We have seen the development of consciousness, a sensitivity and an awareness to the problems of predominantly black institutions and minority students that was absent in these states in previous years " (See Also Above).

June 21. U.S. District Court Judge Robert McRae, Jr. began a preliminary hearing in Memphis, Tennessee to determine whether or not James Earl Ray, the confessed assassin of Martin Luther King, Jr., should receive a new trial. Ray was sentenced in 1969 to a term of 99 years for the slaying of King on April 4, 1968. He has been serving his time in the Tennessee State Prison at Nashville. Ray has sought a new trial on the ground that he was pressured into pleading guilty by his original attorneys, Percy Foreman and Arthur Haynes, Sr. because of their alleged financial relationships with William Bradford Huie, author of one of the first books to be published on King's slaying. Ray's new attorney, Robert Livingston, had also charged that his client was innocent of King's murder and that, in fact, two professional gunmen hired by four "wealthy, socially prominent Americans" had killed the Nobel Prize winning civil rights leader in 1968 (See Also Above).

June 21. U.S. District Judge W. Arthur Garrity, Jr. ruled in Boston that the Boston public school system was "unconstitutionally segregated" and ordered the implementation of a desegregation plan, including the busing of several thousand school children, in the fall of 1974. The order prohibited enrollments of fifty per cent or more nonwhites in any school. There were 95,000 pupils attending Boston public schools at the time of the decision. The Boston edict stemmed from a suit filed on behalf of black parents by the NAACP in the spring of 1972. The blacks contended that Boston operated a dual school system and asked the court to dismantle it.

June 22. U.S. Senator Hubert H. Humphrey (D., Minn.) introduced a bill in Congress providing for the placing in the U.S. Capitol of the portraits and statues of individuals from minority groups who have made significant contributions to the nation's history. Humphrey said that the statues and paintings now existing in the Capitol building "do not properly reflect the ethnic, cultural and racial diversity of the people of the United States who have made outstanding contributions to our country." Humphrey's concurrent resolution required the Senate and House of Representatives to appoint an advisory committee composed of nine distinguished Americans to nominate individuals whose likenesses would be obtained for permanent exhibit in the Capitol. This committee would receive suggestions from the public and then determine the number to be selected in accordance with the available space. The resolution, Humphrey said, aimed at allowing the United States "to show the world that we were able to create out of the diversity of our people a sense of common purpose without in any way destroying individuality of cultural heritage." Immediately following Humphrey's move, Senator Walter F. Mondale (D., Minn.) and Rep. Jonathan Bingham (D., N.Y.) co-sponsored a resolution to commission a statue of slain civil rights leader Martin Luther King, Jr. for the U.S. Capitol. Preliminary reports revealed that twelve Southerners were also co-sponsors of the resolution. Even though a portrait of Dr. King was hung in the Georgia State Capital at Atlanta amid some controversy, the only Georgia representative or senator supporting the resolution was black Congressman Andrew Young of Atlanta, a former key aide to King.

June 22. The U.S. Navy reported that its investigation showed no basis for accusations of racial discrimination made by a group of black sailors who refused to return to the aircraft carrier USS *Midway* when it left Japan the previous week. Eight of the fifty-five sailors who refused to return to the *Midway* when it left the Yokosuka Naval Base near Tokyo called for the U.S. Congress to investigate conditions aboard the ship and demanded replacement of the ship's captain, Richard J. Schutte. They complained of torture in the brig, long duty hours, and dangerous work, which they said they were forced to perform. Naval authorities reported that twenty-two of the absentees had returned to their base by June 22 and that the remaining thirty-three were listed as "unauthorized absentees." The Navy reasoned that since the complaint of racial bias was found to be unsubstantiated, the men were "being misled by private organizations" trying to exploit them for "their own purpose." There was no further elaboration. The *Midway* incident was the latest in a series of racially related events involving black armed forces personnel. Although Naval officials had announced new and far-reaching policies to combat bias as early as 1971, this branch of the service has also continued to experience racial problems (See Also Above).

June 26. Atlanta police armed with clubs broke up a march of about 250 blacks and arrested fourteen persons including the demonstration leader Hosea Williams, president of the local chapter of the Southern Christian Leadership Conference (SCLC). Seven persons, including three policemen, were injured in the disturbance. The violent conflict, the first in Atlanta since the urban riots of the 1960's, came as the marchers sought to protest the killing by police of a 17-year-old black youth the previous weekend and to continue their demand that the city's police chief, John Inman, be ousted. The blacks were charged with parading without permits. The controversial police chief defended the force used against the marchers, but the city's black mayor, Maynard Jackson, described it as excessive. The latest incident occurred as the Georgia Supreme Court was considering whether the city of Atlanta could legally fire Inman, viewed by many of the city's whites as a staunch defender of "law and order," but by many blacks as a racist.

June 29. Robert Livingston, the Memphis, Tennessee attorney handling the legal appeals of James Earl Ray (the convicted assassin of Dr. Martin Luther King, Jr.), told newsmen that he was convinced a conspiracy existed in the slaying of the civil rights leader. The attorney said he had been contacted on March 22, 1974 by an intermediary for the gunmen actually hired to kill King. This intermediary and two other men were prepared to testify before a grand jury that they were hired to kill Dr. King by four prominent black and white men, according to Livingston. The theory of a conspiracy in the assassination of the famed civil rights leader had been previously discounted by law enforcement officials. However, the Southern Christian Leadership Conference (SCLC), which was headed by King until his death, long subscribed to a belief in a conspiracy. In its latest statement on the subject, issued by its national communications director Tyrone Brooks, the SCLC official said that "powerful forces" were involved in the slaying. According to Brooks the rationale for the assassination was that "the tremendous following developing for Dr. King was a threat to the racism, militarism, and economic exploitation by the powerful forces who control and run this country."

June 30. The Atlanta *Journal-Constitution* reported that the state of Alabama was moving toward total compliance with a federal court order issued in 1972 which required that racial discrimination in hiring be eliminated. When the suit was filed in 1970, only a few blacks were on the state's payroll, most of these in janitorial and other low-paying jobs. As of June 30, 3,000 of the state work force of 21,000 were black. At that rate of hiring, the state was about four years away from reaching the court-assigned goal of a 25% black work force. At the upper levels, a black executive assistant had been hired by the head of the Public Service Commission and the Attorney General had selected several black assistants. Alabama Governor George C. Wallace, according to the report, had named several blacks to positions on various governmental boards, commissions, and committees, but had not hired a single black to an administrative position. The report quoted an unidentified "black leader" as saying that Alabama "will someday have the most model race relations program of any state in the Union."

June 30. A young black man interrupted the worship services at Ebenezer Baptist Church in Atlanta with gunfire, killing Mrs. Martin Luther King, Sr., mother of the slain civil rights leader, and church deacon, Edward Boykin. Another worshipper, Mrs. Jimmie Mitchel, was wounded. The alleged gunman, identified as Marcus Chenault of Dayton, Ohio, was subdued by other worshippers including Derek

King, grandson of the slain woman. Chenault told Atlanta police that he had orders from "his god" to go to Atlanta and kill the Rev. Martin Luther King, Sr., father of the Nobel Prize winning civil rights leader. Instead he allegedly fired upon Mrs. King and others as the 69-year-old matriarch of the King family played "The Lord's Prayer" on a church organ. The accused slayer was described as an Ohio State University dropout who had become deeply involved in a small religious cult which claimed that blacks were descendants of the original Jews. Chenault was said to have taken the name "Servant Jacob" and discarded his original name. The cult reportedly believed that Christian black ministers deceived black people and hence were the cause of many of the black people's woes. Mrs. King, born Alberta Williams, was the daughter of one of the founders of the historic Ebenezer Baptist Church, the Reverend Adam Daniel Williams. Her husband, a powerful religious and political figure in Atlanta for more than 25 years, succeeded Rev. Williams as pastor of the church. Dr. Martin Luther King, Jr. was serving as co-pastor of the church with his father when he was slain by an assassin on April 4, 1968 in Memphis, Tennessee. The tomb of the famed civil rights leader is located several feet from the edifice. Atlanta Mayor Maynard Jackson likened the recurring tragedies in the King family (another son, the Rev. A. D. King drowned in 1969) to that of the late President Kennedy's and remarked: "Never have I seen a family suffer so much for so long and yet give such brilliant leadership."

July 1. The Atlanta University Center Digest reported that the largest single gift ever donated by a black organization had been received by the United Negro College Fund (UNCF). UNCF Executive Director Christopher F. Edley announced that the $132,000 gift came from the Links, Inc., a national black women's organization. The Links have more than 130 chapters in 35 states across the nation. In the past the organization had contributed to the NAACP, the National Urban League, and the medical colleges of Meharry and Howard universities. Dr. Helen G. Edmonds, Distinguished Professor of History at North Carolina Central University and National President of the Links, presented the group's check to Director Edley during the Links' 19th General Assembly in Washington, D.C. She said that her organization, in making the donation, "recognized the absolute importance of higher education to black people at this point in history and agree wholeheartedly with the UNCF's slogan, "A Mind is a Terrible Thing to Waste." Edley responded that "the significance of the Links' contribution goes beyond even the generous amount of money given. Theirs is a superb example of the black community giving its substantial support to these black schools."

July 3. More than 600 persons, including Mrs. Gerald Ford, Mrs. Nelson Rockefeller, Georgia Governor Jimmy Carter, and Atlanta Mayor Maynard Jackson, attended the funeral services for Mrs. Martin Luther King, Sr., mother of the slain civil rights leader, in Atlanta. Mrs. King had been, herself, slain by a gunman on June 30, 1974 (See Above and Below).

July 4. Several thousand protesters, led by the avowed black communist Angela Davis and SCLC head Ralph David Abernathy, marched on the North Carolina state capitol at Raleigh to call for an end to the death penalty in North Carolina. The march, which was organized by the National Alliance Against Racist and Political Repression, was called, by its organizers, "a rebirth of the civil rights movement of the 1960's, but on a higher level." During the march, twelve picketers representing the American Nazi Party, the Ku Klux Klan, and similar groups stood alongside the route holding signs urging segregation forever and support for Governor George Wallace of Alabama as President. Raleigh police kept the two groups apart. Although there was jeering, no major incidents or arrests resulted. The crowd of four to five thousand protesters were welcomed to Raleigh by the city's black mayor, Clarence Lightner.

July 5. Some 200 blacks marched about seven miles on Georgia Highway 41 in Talbot County to protest the shooting of a young black man by the white police chief of Woodland. Willie Gene Carraker, a 25-year-old black resident of Woodland, died from gunshot wounds on June 29, 1974. The black man's family accused Police Chief Doug Watson of aggravated assault and murder in the slaying of Carraker. These charges were subsequently dismissed by a local Justice of the Peace. In the march on July 5th, black protesters, led by SCLC Field Secretary Tyrone Brooks, demanded the prosecution and removal of the Chief. During the demonstration Brooks told the crowd: "We are sick and tired of white folks shooting down our young men every weekend. We are sick and tired of being treated like second class citizens." Woodland City Attorney George R. Jacobs defended the dismissal of charges against Chief Watson and advised that the matter could be considered by the county Grand Jury in November, or by a specially called grand jury.

July 6. The *Atlanta Constitution* reported that the United Methodist Church had abolished districts which were racially segregated. According to the report, the last all-black districts, ones in Mississippi and South Carolina, were abolished in June, 1974. At the same time, Methodist officials announced that 37 of its 530 districts in the United States are now headed by ethnic minority persons including 34 blacks.

July 7. In a special supplement to *Time Magazine*, fifteen blacks were among 200 persons named who seem destined to provide the country with a new generation of leadership. *Time* said the principal criterion for inclusion on its list was that the persons selected have the capability to achieve "significant civic or social impact." Eligibility was restricted to persons 45 years old and younger. The blacks named included: State Senator Julian Bond of Georgia; Congresswoman Yvonne Brathwaite Burke of California; Congressman Ronald V. Dellums of California; Marian Wright Edelman of the Children's Defense Fund; Mayor Kenneth A. Gibson of Newark, New Jersey; Earl G. Graves, founder of *Black Enterprise Magazine*; Mayor Richard Hatcher of Gary, Indiana; Mayor Maynard Jackson of Atlanta, Georgia; Congresswoman Barbara C. Jordan of Texas; Vernon E. Jordan of the Urban League; John Lewis of the Voter Education Project; Eleanor Holmes Norton, Chairman of the New York City Commission on Human Rights; Congressman Charles Rangel of New York; Bill Russell, coach of the Seattle Supersonics; and Congressman Andrew Young of Georgia.

August 19. The Joint Committee on Congressional Operations, which handles hiring requests for members of Congress, began an investigation to determine whether one Senator and 19 Congressmen were duped or actually have been practicing racial or religious discrimination in seeking staff personnel. The Fort Worth *Star Telegram* reported on August 18, 1974 that it had obtained copies of the hiring forms with varying discriminatory requests from Senator William Scott (R.Va.) and 19 members of the House of Representatives. Senator Lee Metcalf (D. Montana), Chairman of the Joint Committee, said that some of the request forms contained such notations as "no minorities," or "white only," or "no Catholics," or "no Blacks." While most of the congressmen disclaimed responsibility for the biased forms, Senator Metcalf said it was "possible that (discriminatory) limitations expressed were those of the staff persons placing the request or a misunderstanding by the office staff."

August 20. The *Atlanta Constitution* reported that the unemployment rate among nonwhites in Georgia was three times as high as among white persons during 1973. The report cited statistics, furnished by Brunswick A. Bagdon, assistant regional director of the U.S. Bureau of Labor Statistics, which showed that the jobless rate among nonwhites was 7.6 percent last year against 2.9 percent for white workers. The highest unemployment was among nonwhite females (See Also Table Below). This report, coming at a time when the nation's economy continued in a slump, helped to confirm a commonly held belief that "blacks are the last hired and first fired."

TABLE F   Employment By Race and Sex in Georgia, 1973

	Total Unemployment	Total White-Collar Unemployment	Total Blue-Collar Unemployment	Total Service Unemployment
Whites	2.9%	54.6%	36%	6.8%
Blacks	7.6%	22.1%	49.1%	24.8%
White Males	2.1%			
Black Males	4.5%			
White Females	4.3%			
Black Females	11.1%			

Source: U.S. Bureau of Labor Statistics

August 23. Franklin W. Morton was elected chief legal Advisor for the Veterans of Foreign Wars (VFW). He is the first black person to hold a national leadership position in the organization.

August 25. Robert C. Weaver, former Secretary of Housing and Urban Development (HUD) and the first black Cabinet officer, told a news conference in Atlanta that the federal government had a "laissez-faire attitude" that threatened efforts for equal opportunity in housing. Weaver said the attitude was based on the revenue-sharing policy of allowing federal funds to be allocated at the local level and the lack of responsibility for social issues on the federal level. He said: "Federal funds (for housing) without strings attached are used for other things. . . . Sophisticated and concerned people must be watchful and vigilant to see that there is equitable participation and involvement in access to housing. . . . The federal government can make an impact." Weaver, president of the National Committee Against Discrimination in Housing (NCADH) made his remarks as he prepared to address the Southern Regional Conference of the NCADH.

August 29. The U.S. Department of Labor announced that in 1973 the unemployment rate in poverty areas of metropolitan centers was almost twice that in the non-metropolitan poverty areas, 9% as opposed to 4.7%. The report also revealed that 70% of the blacks living in poverty areas were in metropolitan centers. The total unemployment for blacks in all poverty areas was 10.8% as opposed to 4.6% for whites. The Labor Department defined a poverty area as a census tract in which at least one-fifth of the residents had income at or below $4,540 (based upon a non-farm family of four).

September 7. Owners of the Black National Network (BNN), the nation's first black oriented, owned, and operated radio network, announced plans to expand its coverage with a black news service. The 24-hour-a-day service was expected to be fully operational by March 1, 1975; employ 25 reporters; and use the resources of the networks' 68 affiliates in 68 major cities (See Also Above).

September 7. Public officials and spokesmen for civil rights groups criticized Secretary of Health, Education, and Welfare Casper Weinberger's latest pronouncement on school desegregation. On September 6, during an interview, Weinberger said that the cutoff of federal funds for education, which had been used in the past to coerce recalcitrant southern school districts into compliance, would serve to increase segregation in the North. Secretary Weinberger denied that his department was "footdragging" on the question of desegregation, but admitted that "we are dealing with a very fierce public opposition to desegregation." Mrs. Ruby Hurley, Southeastern Regional Director of the NAACP, disagreed with Weinberger's assessment that a cutoff of funds would be counterproductive. According to Mrs. Hurley, "Public school systems are often poor even without federal money. Officials who run segregated school systems will think twice if they are faced with a cutoff. . . . If you wait for people to change their minds on a problem like this without leverage, you'll wait a long time. . . . It's a lot easier to clean up somebody else's back yard than your own," Mrs. Hurley said, as she compared the conciliatory approach to northern school desegregation with the more forceful tactics in the South.

Atlanta School Superintendent Alonzo Crim responded to Weinberger's statement by declaring that: "The law should be applied with equal force in all parts of the country . . . quite often segregation is intensified by these delays."

Margie Hames, an attorney for the American Civil Liberties Union who has handled many desegregation cases, expressed the belief that "segregation in the South was more open and easy for us to deal with. I don't think the North has accepted the fact yet that they have more subtle forms of segregation." In defense of Weinberger, Peter Holmes, director of HEW's office for civil rights enforcement, pointed out that the cutoff of funds and other legal actions are more complex in the North than in the South since segregation was not legalized in the North.

September 12. Marcus Wayne Chenault of Dayton, Ohio was convicted and sentenced to death for the murder of Mrs. Martin Luther King, Sr., mother of the slain civil rights leader. Mrs. King was killed, along with Deacon Edward Boykin, during a worship service at the Ebenezer Baptist Church in Atlanta on June 30, 1974.

Chenault was identified as the gunman who interrupted that service with bullets. The Fulton County Court Jury rejected Chenault's plea of insanity in delivering their verdict (See Also Above and Below).

September 12-October 31. The city of Boston, Massachusetts began a program of busing to achieve school desegregation which sparked boycotts and demonstrations reminiscent of the early, vehement opposition to school integration in the South. In June, 1974, U.S. District Court Judge W. Arthur Garrity had ordered the busing of about 18,200 of the city's 94,000 public school pupils as part of a plan to dismantle Boston's dual school system. Opposition arose immediately.

On September 9, 1974, U.S. Senator Edward M. Kennedy (D. Mass.) was booed off a stage and splattered with a tomato as he tried to address an angry group of anti-busing demonstrators. The crowd, estimated at between eight and ten thousand persons, shouted insults, called for the impeachment of the Senator, and sang "God Bless America" when Kennedy stepped to a microphone. After preventing Senator Kennedy from speaking at the John F. Kennedy Memorial Building, the demonstrators—most of them white women—marched to the federal building. They stopped in front of the office of Judge Garrity and shouted, "Garrity must go." Kennedy, an advocate of peaceful school integration, said he was disappointed that he had not been able to speak, but assessed his treatment as milder than that received at the hands of anti-war demonstrators.

On September 11, 1974, Boston School Superintendent William Leary said that everything possible had been done in the time allowed to prepare for desegregation. Yet, he added, "I know there will be problems. I ask the public for patience." Boston Mayor Kevin White, on the eve of the scheduled desegregation, appealed for calm, but warned that "swift and sure punishment" would be meted out to those who resorted to violence. When the desegregation began on September 12, many white and black parents kept their children at home. Black children attending some of the schools, particularly in the white neighborhoods of South Boston, Hyde Park, and Dorchester, were subjected to jeers from angry white parents.

On September 16, a crowd of white teenagers and mothers clashed with policemen at South Boston High School. Twenty-two persons were arrested during the confrontation. Police ordered the closing of bars and liquor stores in the area for the next two days.

Violence continued in Boston for the next several weeks. Four white students were injured in skirmishes with black students at the Washington Irving Junior High School in Roslindale on September 18. None of them required hospitalization. After the incident, forty black children walked out of the school. Police made no arrests. Eleven persons, including three teachers, were injured on October 2 at the racially tense South Boston High School. A number of weapons were confiscated during the incident in which two black girls who allegedly pulled a knife on a policeman were arrested. Fighting broke out during an assembly of ninth graders at the Hart Deah Annex of South Boston High School on October 21. After this incident 30 of the 40 white pupils walked out of the school; most of the 130 black pupils remained.

On October 26, Matt Koehl, national commander of the American Nazi Party, demonstrated in front of the Boston federal building, protesting Judge Garrity's desegregation orders. He bore a sign reading, "White Power." Koehl was arrested and charged with impeding access to a federal building. Koehl's arrest followed by three days that of three other Nazi Party Members who were charged with attempting to incite a riot as they distributed anti-black literature in South Boston. Those charges were later reduced to disorderly conduct. John W. Roberts, Director of the Civil Liberties Union of Massachusetts, decried the arrests saying that the state charges were a violation of the Nazi's constitutional rights. In a final decree, issued on October 30, 1974, Judge Garrity told the Boston school committee to complete the total desegregation of its schools by the fall of 1975. The final order authorized Boston school officials to use "any known desegregation techniques," including busing (although this was to be minimized), changing school districts and voluntary transfers. The judge promised a new order at a later date dealing with minority recruitment and hiring of school teachers and administrators.

The traumatic experience of desegregating schools in Boston highlighted the growing manifestation of white opposition to massive school desegregation in the North. It also struck many observers as a sign of retrogression in American race relations (See Also Above and Below).

September 17. The U.S. Senate approved amendments to a $39.9 billion appropriations bill which prohibit the use of federal funds for busing to achieve school desegregation. According to the anti-busing amendment, which was approved by a vote of 45-42, federal funds could not be used for transporting students to achieve racial balance in schools. The practical effect of the bill, however, would be minimal, since very little federal money is used for such purposes.

September 21. White voters are reluctant to vote for black candidates for mayor in cities where blacks constitute a majority of the population, according to a study appearing in the September issue of *Psychology Today.* In comparing recent mayoral elections in Los Angeles (a white majority city) with Detroit and Atlanta (black majority cities), the article's author, Professor Howard Schuman of the University of Michigan Institute for Social Research, found that Los Angeles was the only major city where close to a majority of whites voted for a black candidate (Thomas Bradley) in preference to a white candidate (Sam Yorty). Los Angeles, Schuman said, apparently separated the question of the candidate's own race from the issue of which race would "control the city." By contrast, in Atlanta and Detroit where whites were becoming the minority population, the elections became "full scale battles over which race would run the city."

In a previous study, Professor Schuman had found that about 60% of the whites in 15 cities which had been surveyed said they would be willing to vote for a qualified black mayoral candidate of their own party. Yet, he pointed out, successful black mayoral candidates like Maynard Jackson of Atlanta and Coleman Young of Detroit received far less than half of the white vote.

Schuman concluded that while whites are becoming more liberal, they are still opposed to basic, structural changes in society. At the same time, he observed, blacks are becoming more open in their criticism of whites and are more distrustful of whites than in the past.

Schuman's study is entitled: "Are Whites Really More Liberal?"

September 27.   U. S. District Judge Albert V. Bryan, Jr., in Richmond, Virginia ordered the American Tobacco Company and Local 182 of the Tobacco Workers' International Union to allow blacks and females to "bump" white employees with less seniority. Having found Local 182 and the American Tobacco Company's two Richmond plants guilty of racial and sexual discrimination in violation of the Civil Rights Act of 1964, Judge Bryan directed the company to freeze hiring and promoting white male supervisors and adjust retirement and pension plans in order to halt discrimination. Any white employees who were displaced would be allowed to retain their present rates in the lower classifications. Litigation in the case began in March, 1973. It is believed to be the first instance in which a court has sanctioned "bumping" in a civil rights case. At the time of the decision, the tobacco company employed more than 1,000 production workers at its two plants in Richmond. Of that number 239 were black and 441 were female.

September 28.   The *Atlanta Inquirer* reported a study by the Southern Regional Council (SRC) which showed that the South, the historic home of black Americans, was going through a whitening process despite increasing black concentrations in the urban areas of the region. All Southern states, except Texas, were losing more blacks than were being replaced by the birthrate and the "reverse migration" of young blacks from the North. According to the study, the black exodus from the South continued at such a steady pace that the region's black population, as shown in the 1970 Census, was down to 20%—the same percentage recorded in 1790. The loss of black populations was particularly acute in the rural areas. In Georgia, two-thirds of the state's 152 counties were losing blacks; in Mississippi 90% of the counties had declining black populations. A similar story was told for Alabama, South Carolina, and Arkansas, all of which had 80% or more of their counties losing blacks. Conversely, 51% of the population of Atlanta was black. Augusta, Georgia had a 50% black population, and New Orleans, Charleston, and Savannah boasted black populations of 45% or more. In sum, the study reports, there were ten metropolitan areas in the 11 southern states where the black population was 40% or more.

The SRC report's authors, Jack Tucker of Atlanta University and Everett S. Lee of the University of Georgia, concluded that:

The growth of the black population lags behind that of whites. So year by year, the South becomes increasingly white. Losses of black population are frequent and heavy in rural counties, so Southern blacks are increasingly concentrated in metropolitan areas. And within the metropolitan areas, blacks are clustered in central cities with relatively few making their way into the more affluent suburbs.

"Generally," the report says, "people move from one area to another for one of two reasons, either the attractiveness of destination outweighs that of origin or there are so many negative features at the point of origin that any place seems better." Migration thus becomes a movement of the upper socio-economic classes to seek better opportunities and of the lower economic classes to escape oppression that can no longer be endured.

October 3. Frank Robinson, the only man in baseball history to be named Most Valuable Player in both the American and National leagues, was named baseball's first black manager by the Cleveland Indians. During a press conference held to announce the appointment, Robinson said: "To say that this is a proud day for me would be an understatement. . . . If I had one wish in the world today, that wish would be to have Jackie Robinson here to see this happen. . . . I don't think I could have stood the pressure or have gone through what Jackie had to. . . ." Jackie Robinson (no relation to Frank) became the major league's first black baseball player in 1947. He died in 1972 (See Also Above). Frank Robinson, as a professional player, had accumulated nearly 3,000 hits, including 574 home runs, before breaking the 105-year-old managerial color-line.

October 3. A simple bronze plaque was placed upon the unnoticed and unattended grave of ragtime composer Scott Joplin, who died in 1917. Joplin began composing ragtime in 1899, with "The Maple Leaf Rag." Ragtime music, however, was largely ignored until it regained popularity through the soundtrack of a 1974 film, *The Sting.* The plaque on the grave in St. Michael's Cemetery in Queens was purchased by the American Society of Composers, Authors, and Publishers (ASCAP).

October 4. Money for research dealing with blacks has diminished, according to an assessment given by Professor Charles Hamilton of Columbia University. Although Hamilton decried the lack of money "for research on blacks or for blacks to do . . . research," he added, "it may affect our budgets, but never our integrity or our legitimacy." Hamilton, co-author of the widely acclaimed book, *Black Power*, spoke to more than 400 black professors and students at the W.E.B. DuBois Conference on the American Black in Atlanta.

October 12. Frank L. Stanley, Sr., owner and publisher of the Louisville *Defender* and veteran civil rights activist, died in Louisville, Kentucky at age 68. Stanley, the son of a butcher, was born in Chicago. At the age of six, his family moved to Louisville. He attended Atlanta University, where he was an All-American quarterback and captain of the football and basketball teams, and the University of Cincinnati. He received honorary doctorate degrees from several universities, including the University of Kentucky. In 1933, Stanley went to work for the Louisville *Defender* as a reporter. Three years later he became editor, general manager, and a part owner. During the years that he published the *Defender*, it received more than 35 awards in journalism, including the President's Special Service Award of the National Newspaper Publishers' Association (NNPA) in 1970, and the coveted Russwurm Award in 1974. He was a co-founder of the NNPA and was elected its president on five separate occasions.

Stanley drafted the legislation which led to the desegregation of state universities in Kentucky by its General Assembly in 1950. Ten years later he wrote the bill that created the Kentucky Commission on Human Rights, and was one of the original members of that body. His influence on race relations in Kentucky was noted by the Louisville *Courier Journal* on the occasion of the 25th anniversary of the *Defender* in 1950. "Much of the credit," the newspaper said editorially, "for the even and amiable pace Kentucky has maintained in its working out of race relations problems must be given the *Defender*." Stanley was the force behind the *Defender's* role in that achievement.

October 16. Dr. Berkeley G. Burrell, president of the National Business League (NBL), told the 74th Annual Convention of the NBL in Atlanta that black businessmen must develop hard strategies in this time of economic turmoil. "If we do not come out of this 74th convention with a sound assessment of the situation and a unified front of committed allies to guarantee the continued survival of the black community and its economic resources," Dr. Burrell said, "a severe blow will be dealt to the potential economic independence of our people." The whole range of minority businesses, from the black capitalists to the Black Muslims, were represented at the 74th Annual NBL Convention.

October 26. Three black-owned businesses in the heart of downtown Sparta, Georgia were set aflame. Police suspected arson in the blazes which destroyed a furniture store and damaged an adjacent warehouse and barber shop. Police also reported some attempted burglaries during the three-hour fight to bring the fires under control. On October 30, 1974, the *Atlanta Constitution* reported that the records of the furniture store burned on October 24 had been subpoenaed by a federal grand jury investigating the affairs of Hancock County's foremost black political leader, John McCown. Local investigators, however, were unable to say whether the subpoenaed records were destroyed in the fire (See Also Below).

October 26. The *Atlanta Inquirer* quoted a report from the U.S. Department of Commerce which cited a trend of larger black insurance companies to purchase or merge with smaller ones to keep them from passing out of the hands of blacks. Lonnie Murray, spokesman for the Department of Commerce, said this development was strengthening the industry. Overall the number of black insurance companies has declined to 39, but the assets of these firms have increased. Within the past five years these assets have risen by $73 million. One of the larger black insurance companies engaged in the purchase and consolidation with smaller ones has been the Atlanta Life Insurance Company. In its most recent action, Atlanta Life, with assets of $84 million, purchased the People's Insurance Company, the largest black owned insurance company in Louisiana, to insure its retention in black hands. The People's Company had assets of $4 million which placed it 15th among the 39 black insurance firms. Since 1937, when there were 60 black insurance companies, four have passed out of black hands, seventeen have been purchased by or merged with other black firms (See Also Table Below).

TABLE G   Black Owned Insurance Companies in the United States, 1974

State	Number of Firms
Alabama	6
California	1
Florida	2
Georgia	3
Illinois	3
Louisiana	12
New York	1
North Carolina	2
Pennsylvania	2
Tennessee	3
Virginia	2

Source: U.S. Department of Commerce

October 29.   James Earl Ray, convicted assassin of Dr. Martin Luther King, Jr., told a federal court hearing in Memphis, Tennessee that he did not slay the Nobel Prize-winning civil rights leader. Ray admitted that he purchased the gun which killed King and that he rented the room in the building from which the shot was fired, but said he did not pull the trigger. Ray referred to a mysterious figure called "another party" as the possible slayer in a conspiracy to murder the civil rights leader. Prosecuting attorneys faced difficulties in their efforts to elicit further details from Ray because of a ruling from presiding judge Robert McRae that only questions about what he told his previous lawyers and not about what he failed to tell them could be admitted. Ray was seeking either his freedom or a new trial on the grounds that his original lawyers misled him into a guilty plea at the time of his 1968 trial. Those lawyers, Ray now contended, conspired with author William Bradford Huie for such a plea, so that Huie could write a financially profitable book on the assassination (See Also Above and Below).

October 29.   Muhammad Ali regained the heavyweight boxing championship by defeating George Foreman in Kinshasa, Zaire. Ali, a 32-year-old Black Muslim, knocked out the title holder, Foreman, in the eighth round of a scheduled fifteen round match. Ali had been stripped of his title in 1967 after being convicted for draft evasion. Four years later that conviction was overturned by the U.S. Supreme Court. The Zaire title fight was the richest contest in history, with both Ali and Foreman receiving $5 million each (See Also Above).

October 30.　A bi-racial group of citizens in Sparta, Georgia requested that the State Elections Board send officials to observe the conduct of the November General Elections in Hancock County. A committee of three persons sent to Hancock County under court order for the August primary elections reported widespread election abuses. That report, however, was ignored by the Hancock County Grand Jury in its September presentments. In the report on the August elections, the committee had said that the balloting was conducted in a "tense and undesirable atmosphere" caused partially by the presence of armed men in the polling places. Hancock County is the only county in Georgia with a black-run government. It has often been the scene of racial and political strife (See Also Above).

October 31.　The Voter Education Project (VEP) in Atlanta reported a record number of 118 blacks were seeking major public office in the November 5th General Elections in nine southern states. Seven blacks were seeking congressional seats, 14 were candidates for state senate seats, and the remaining 97 blacks were candidates for state houses. The VEP predicted that at least 31 of the candidates for state legislative seats would be successful. In 1962, when the VEP first began monitoring and promoting black political participation in the South, there were no black members in any Southern legislature. The black political progress continued despite "repulsive national political scandals and severe economic problems," according to VEP Executive Director John Lewis. "The black gains in state legislative posts in 1974, and the possible addition of at least one black member of Congress from the South will be yet another milestone in a steady progression of black political gains in the past few years," Lewis concluded.

November 2.　Huey P. Newton, co-founder of the Black Panther

Party, was being sought for murder. Newton was accused of shooting 17-year-old Kathleen Smith in the head during a dispute in an Oakland street on August 6, 1974. She never regained consciousness. The results of the police investigation as to the cause of the dispute were not released. Newton jumped a bail of $55,000 and disappeared on August 23, 1974. The accusation of murder was the latest in a long history of altercations between Newton and the law (See Also Above).

November 5-6. Controversial Atlanta civil rights activist Hosea Williams, who has had numerous encounters with the law, was acquitted on charges of simple battery on a police officer and of carrying a concealed and unlicensed pistol by two separate Fulton County Criminal Court juries. Williams had been accused of grabbing the genitals of Officer A.L. Bradfield during a demonstration at the Martin Luther King, Jr. Nursing Home on September 15, 1972 and of carrying a pistol into the Atlanta Hartsfield International Airport on March 9, 1974. Williams' attorneys claimed that he was the victim of political harrassment. Williams, himself, responded to the verdicts by declaring: "I carry only the love of God in my heart."

November 15. Robert Dancz, associate professor of music and director of the marching band at the University of Georgia, announced that the University of Georgia Redcoat Band would not play "Dixie" at future university football games. In a campus referendum, held several days before Dancz's statements, students had approved the playing of the song by a margin of 3,567 to 1,270. Despite this vote, however, Dancz said that his band would "under no circumstances play the song." It "brought out the worse in some people," he said, and "black people feel like it is a slap in the face. This isn't the same school it was 20 years ago and not many southern schools play 'Dixie' anymore." Dancz also said that the playing of the Civil War melody exposed his band members to physical dangers.

December 8. The 6th U.S. Court of Appeals in Cincinnati upheld a lower court ruling that the Grand Rapids, Michigan schools were not segregated. The Court said that "a review of the evidence and statistics in this case makes it clear not only that Grand Rapids was not guilty of acts of intentional segregation, but that much progress has been made toward elimination of the de facto segregation resulting from housing patterns." The court rejected the contentions of black plaintiffs that discriminatory acts of other individuals and governmental agencies were sufficient to support a finding of *de jure* segregation.

December 21. Five black women were named among the 40 most highly respected women in the United States according to a poll appearing in the January edition of *Good Housekeeping* magazine. The blacks were: Congresswomen Yvonne Braithwaite Burke (D. Calif.), Shirley Chisholm (D.N.Y.), Barbara Jordan (D.Texas); Mrs. Coretta Scott King, widow of the slain civil rights leader; and actress Cicely Tyson. The blacks were selected from a slate of 47 prominent women presented to the readers of *Good Housekeeping* in the sixth annual Most Admired Women's Poll. In the poll, Mrs. King ranked 19th (her name has been among the winners since 1970); Representative Chisholm ranked 24th (she has been represented five times); Ms. Tyson ranked 25th; Congresswomen Jordan and Burke ranked 38th and 39th respectively. The total number of black women named for 1974 was three more than in 1973.

1975

January 1. Samuel DuBois Cook assumed the presidency of Dillard University in New Orleans, Louisiana. Cook earned his bachelor's degree from Morehouse College and his master's and doctor's degrees from Ohio State University. Previously he had taught at Atlanta University and Duke University and had been a consultant to the U.S. Office of Education and the Ford Foundation. He is a trustee of the Martin Luther King, Jr. Center for Social Change and a former president of the Southern Political Science Association. Cook succeeded Dr. Broadus Butler as president of the 105-year-old predominantly black college.

January 2-26. Several reports appeared in the nation's newspapers revealing a history of Central Intelligence Agency (CIA) and Federal Bureau of Investigation (FBI) spying on black individuals and organizations. The *New York Times* reported on January 2 that the CIA had been collecting data on singer Eartha Kitt since 1956. According to the CIA files, Miss Kitt had danced, at the age of 20 with a group whose leader allegedly had "served as a sponsor or endorser of a number of Communist-front activities"; she had been involved in "escapades overseas and her loose morals were said to be the talk of Paris" in 1956; she had "a very nasty disposition" and was "a spoiled child, very crude," with "a vile tongue"; she "often bragged that she had very little Negro blood." The CIA file also revealed that Miss Kitt had, in 1960, signed an advertisement in support of the civil rights activities of the late Dr. Martin Luther King, Jr. which had also been signed by "a number of persons identified in the past with the Communist party." However, the CIA report concluded that there was no evidence of any foreign intelligence connections on the part of Ms. Kitt. The detailed investigation of Ms. Kitt, according to the *Times*, was possibly prompted by remarks which she made during a luncheon hosted by Mrs. Lyndon B. Johnson in January, 1968. At that time Miss Kitt shouted that the nation's youth were in rebellion because they were being "snatched off to be shot in Vietnam." Both Mrs. Johnson and the President were reportedly upset by the remarks.

In responses to the news of the investigation of Ms. Kitt, the *Atlanta Constitution*, on January 6, 1975, editorialized that: "Nobody in today's world should deny our government the right to protect itself and us by keeping a close eye on potential threats, foreign or domestic. The question is, who should do it and under what kind of controls and guidelines? The pursuit of national security should not lead us to a place where we jettison the Bill of Rights." Ms. Kitt, herself, responded, "I don't understand this at all. I think it's disgusting. . . . I've always lived a very clean life and I have nothing to be afraid of and I have nothing to hide."

On January 25, 1975, the *Washington Post* reported that the FBI had wiretapped the conversations of Dr. Martin Luther King, Jr., and other civil rights leaders during the 1964 Democratic Convention at Atlantic City, New Jersey. The reports from the wiretaps, according to the *Post*, were delivered to President Lyndon Johnson.

These reports of government spying on blacks came in the wake of the Watergate scandals and newer accusations that governmental agencies had illegally invaded the privacy of American citizens (See Also Above and Below).

January 3. The Swope Parkway National Bank, the only black operated bank in Kansas City, was declared insolvent by the Federal Deposit Insurance Corporation (FDIC). Officials, however, said that the bank, with total assets of $10.6 million, would be reopened on January 4 as the Deposit Insurance National Bank under FDIC receivership. The Deposit Insurance Bank stood ready to assume all of Swope's "insured and fully secure deposits." An FDIC spokesman said these moves were being taken "in recognition of both the practical and symbolic importance of the Swope Parkway National Bank to [Kansas City's] black community."

January 5. Professor Moses W. Vaughn of the University of Maryland-Eastern Shore announced that he was studying the nutritive value of some types of soul food—the popular name for a number of items, including chitterlings, pigs' ears, pig knuckles and feet, hog maws, neck bones and pigs' tails, said to be particularly favored by blacks. Vaughn said the study is expected to fill a gap in nutritional knowledge, for even the official U.S. Department of Agriculture handbook contains no mention of soul food pork products. Yet, according to Vaughn, consumer research organizations and the Agriculture Department have received numerous requests for information on those foods. Vaughn received a $175,000 federal grant for his two-year study.

January 8. The Federal Communications Commission (FCC) denied the Alabama Educational Television Commission license renewals for all eight of its television stations because of racial discrimination. The FCC also denied the Alabama agency's application for a license to cover a construction permit for a proposed ninth station at Demopolis. According to the FCC, the Alabama Commission had, between 1967 and 1970, failed to meet the high standards the FCC expects broadcast licenses to maintain. The Alabama Commission, the FCC found, had followed a racially discriminatory policy in its over-all programming practices and, through its "pervasive neglect" of Alabama's black population, had failed to meet adequately the needs of the public it served. However, the FCC held that because there have been improvements in its operations since 1970, and because of the pressing need for public TV in the state, the Alabama Commission would be allowed to operate the eight stations on an interim basis until their future is determined. The denial of license renewal is one of the FCC's most severe and most rarely used actions.

January 8. Students returned to school in South Boston, Massachusetts for the first time in four weeks as more than 400 policemen kept watch on the arrival and departure of school buses. Four schools in the South Boston area had been closed since December 11, 1974 when a white student was stabbed at South Boston High School. As the students returned to school, school officials announced a first day attendance of 876 out of a total of 3,000 pupils enrolled in the four affected buildings. Meanwhile, the Boston School Committee appeared before U.S. District Court Judge W. Arthur Garrity, Jr. with a new desegregation plan. The new plan, which omitted busing, was the means by which the committee hoped to avoid punishment for contempt of court for three of its five members.

The continuing racial tensions over desegregation in Boston was assessed in a syndicated column by Vernon E. Jordan, Executive Director of the National Urban League, in the January 22, 1975 edition of the *Atlanta Constitution*. Excerpts from Jordan's essay are quoted below:

> It struck in its sickest form around New Year's when a home owned by a respectable, hard-working black family was dynamited in a previously all-white neighborhood in Queens.
>
> It struck in its currently accepted form when Boston's School Committee, defying a contempt of court citation, refused to submit a desegregation plan for the city's troubled schools.
>
> And it struck in its most hidden form—the accumulated hurts and pain of a black lifetime—when a Chicago police detective died of heart attack, leaving behind a letter revealing the toll prejudice and discrimination took. "Mine is a wasted life," he wrote, "full of degradation, muted feelings and not belonging. This is one hell of a world for a black man."

It is instructive that racism's victims in these instances—an innocent black family, black school children, and a lone black man—all lived in the North, in cities that were vocal in their support for black civil rights in the South.

Doubtless, instances of racism could be drawn from the South, perhaps even more. But that would only prove that racism, that peculiarly national disease, is an infection that's spread across the length and breadth of this land.

The stupid thing about it is that the victims include hater and hated, alike. Psychologists could probably explain the twisted mental mechanisms that result in racism, but the social costs of that behavior are plain for all to see.

Boston is a good example of this. White parents are tearing up their town just to prevent busing that will integrate the school. They can't even claim they want to preserve the excellence of their school system because, if anything, the schools of Boston's white ghetto are even worse than those in Roxbury.

If nothing else, integration could break down the defensive barriers of white and black school kids alike and better prepare them for our multi-racial world. At best, it could galvanize white and black parents to go after the real enemy—the forces that keep the city's schools inferior for all.

The anti-busing hysteria has provided a convenient cover for overt racist feelings. In Boston, the facts are very clear: the all-white School Committee has persistently and consciously maintained a segregated school system, they have done so in defiance of the laws of their State and their country, and they have persisted in this in the face of court orders to remedy the situation.

Desegregation in Boston has been made more difficult by the failure to comply with the law and by the failure to prepare parents and school officials for the change. Desegregation has worked elsewhere—even in the most segregation-ridden Deep South towns —and there is no reason why mob rule should prevent it from working in Boston. What's needed in Boston and in the nation is firm leadership.

The President has been asked to assert leadership in a number of areas, from energy to the economy, but he should realize that true leadership in our multi-racial society must be based on an idealistic goal that transcends the transient problems of the day. By leading the nation in the fight for racial equality, he will be better able to lead it in the fight against inflation, recession and the many other problems pressing in upon us.

January 10. A crowd of 3,000 persons, most of them young blacks, rushing to apply for 225 new public service jobs, crashed into the glass doors at the Atlanta Civic Center Auditorium. The job seekers had gathered in the pre-dawn hours in search of employment. In December, 1974, the unemployment rate in Atlanta had been 7.5%, but the jobless rate among blacks was 9.2%. The spectacle at the Civic Center Auditorium pointed up again the growing economic desperation of blacks during the current recession.

January 11. A committee of the Governor's Minority Affairs Council of Mississippi reported that it is investigating reports that highway patrolmen have been beating blacks. The council, composed of 15 black citizens, met with Governor Bill Waller to inform him of its plans for the investigation.

January 15. Celebrations were held throughout the nation commemorating the 46th birthday of slain civil rights leader, Martin Luther King, Jr. Much of the activity was focused in King's hometown, Atlanta, Georgia.

On January 12, King's widow, Coretta Scott King, gave a major new assessment of the current civil rights struggle from her Atlanta office. Excerpts from her statements are quoted below:

What we are seeing in the South is a transformation. . . . You don't have the tensions in the South that you had 10-15 years ago. The battleground is definitely in the North now. . . . Detroit, Chicago, New York—most of these cities are sitting on a powder keg because of neglect. Urban America is where it's going to happen in the 70's and 80's. The problems in the major cities across the country are the problems of America in miniature. Every city is beset by problems of poverty, crime and housing. . . . Blacks always suffer more than any other group. . . . With 7 per cent unemployment, you can multiply that twice for blacks. The black community is most times in a continuous recession and depression. It's just worse now. . . . It is going to take an act of Congress to deal with poverty and hunger, not only in this country, but throughout the world. We have the resources but we don't have the will. The wealthy people and big corporations that don't pay any taxes are going to have to start paying taxes.

[The Nixon administration was] totally unresponsive to the basic human needs of blacks and whites. . . . [In the Ford Administration] the only thing is the climate is a little less oppressive. . . . I think that the people were so relieved to get rid of Nixon that they set Ford up as a kind of saviour. I don't think he's really a leader. . . .

In some instances as we still have to march but not as much as we once did. . . . I think the movement has reached a more sophisticated state. Marches, picketing and boycotting are part of it, but we are at the stage now where we have some political power. We are the balance of power in many areas. . . .

President John F. Kennedy wasn't going to do anything about civil rights in 1963. . . . He [Kennedy] told him [King] so. President Lyndon Johnson wasn't going to do anything about voting rights in 1964. He [Johnson] told him [King] so. Martin went on with the movement. He dramatized Birmingham and got the people to saying, 'You've got to do something about Birmingham and those fire hoses and dogs.' Most people then sat back and said, 'That's reasonable.' Those people just want accommodations. . . .

We do have a lot to work on but I do believe that Martin Luther King left us a great legacy and told us how we can achieve the American dream—a just and peaceful society.

Mrs. King made her remarks during an interview with Walt Smith of United Press International.

Also in connection with the birthday celebration, a summit meeting of national civil rights and political leaders was held in Atlanta on January 13. The meeting, called to discuss the Voting Rights Act of 1965 and its possible extension or renewal, was sponsored by the Martin Luther King, Jr. Center for Social Change. Participants included U.S. Senators Hugh Scott (R. Mich.) and Birch Bayh (D.

Ind.); Representatives Ronald Dellums (D. Calif.) and Andrew Young (D. Ga.); Former U.S. Attorney-General Nicholas Katzenbach; National Urban League Director Vernon E. Jordan; Bayard Rustin, Executive Director of the A. Philip Randolph Institute; John Lewis, Executive Director of the Voter Education Project; Georgia State Senator Julian Bond; and Atlanta Mayor Maynard Jackson.

In his remarks at the conference, Senator Bayh said that other minorities needed the extension of the Voting Rights Act to foster their causes, because there was substantial evidence that the protection provided by the act could aid Mexican Americans, especially. Bayh also cited statistics showing that blacks hold only two percent of the elected offices in the South while making up 20 percent of the population. The Nixon administration, according to Bayh, tried to "gut" the Voting Rights extension bill in 1970, but said he doesn't anticipate that the Ford administration will try to do the same.

Former Attorney-General Katzenbach expressed the opinion that the Voting Rights Act freed southern white politicians from campaigns of "race, race, race" and enabled them to seek office without reference to race. It also enabled, he said, blacks to seek national office for the first time in 40 years.

According to Jordan, four levels of black leadership have grown up since the passage of the 1965 Voting Rights Act. He said the "metamorphosis of black leadership" had broadened beyond the very few to thousands of black elected officials, administrators in federal and private agencies, the "unseen but important" black members of corporation boards, and a whole spectrum of black community leaders which did not exist when the act was first passed. Jordan added, "I think Martin (Luther King, Jr.) would be pleased to see the kind of development that has taken place among us. Jordan also called upon President Ford to publicly support legislation to extend the Voting Rights Act." He said "We need to hear from a President whose credentials are dubious in the black community—based on past record and six months in office—a firm commitment to the Voting Rights Act. . . . on Wednesday [the anniversary of King's birth]."

In his remarks, Rustin said that the issues of the turbulent 1960's were black issues—equality under the law and the end of segregation. Today, he continued, the issues are broader and include blacks, other minorities and women, and are economic and political in nature. The agenda, he said, has now changed from getting the rights whites had to the things whites want—"a job, a house, a decent education."

John Lewis of the Voter Education Project predicted a renewal of the Voting Rights Act, but added that the law needed to be broadened to include the whole nation in its protection of minority voting rights.

In his extended remarks, Senator Bond said the 1965 Voting Rights Act had produced the greatest civil rights advances ever and that it must be extended to prevent minorities from becoming victims of a complacent majority. Excerpts from Bond's statement are quoted below:

> There can be no doubt that simple justice calls for the Voting Rights Act to be extended by five years at least . . . and that it be enforced more vigorously. . . . As we have reaped the benefits of social activism of the 1960's, we have been lulled to sleep in the 70's. . . .

> [The election of President Nixon in 1972] was a victory for a mighty coalition of the comfortable, the callous and the smug, who closed their ranks, their minds, and their hearts against the claims and calls to conscience put forward by the forgotten and unrepresented elements in American society. Human problems are now placed on a balance sheet and forced to add up; to pay for themselves. The new administrators in Washington run the programs they direct with all the solicitude of a hungry mortician at an old folks home. . . .

> While the nation waltzed into the 70's believing that its black problem had been blown or burned away, infant mortality rates remained twice as high for us as for everyone else; nearly half of all black families in the U.S. earned less than $5,000 a year, and the average black American was dying seven years earlier than his white counterpart. . . .

> [Some black youths] now seem bowled over by bugaloo and Boone's Farm (Wine). . . . [Some black politicians are] political pimps. They endorse candidates not because they're good but because they'll win; they respect no party or principle, but owe

allegiance only to themselves; you cannot engage them in a battle of wits for they are all unarmed men. . . .

[The Voting Rights Act enfranchised] millions of black men and women, [elected] thousands more, [eliminated] gerrymandered districts and restrictive voting practices, and [granted] political rights and representation to black people outside the southern region. It must be renewed.

On January 15, an ecumenical service was held at the Ebenezer Baptist Church, where King pastored, with the Reverend Theodore Hesburgh, president of Notre Dame University and former chairman of the U.S. Commission on Civil Rights as the principal speaker. Other activities in King's hometown during the day included breaking ground for the Martin Luther King, Jr. Memorial Center buildings, dedication of the King birthplace as an official Historic Place, and a "people's march" in the downtown area of the city.

January 15.   John Lewis, Executive Director of the Voter Education Project (VEP), was awarded the Martin Luther King, Jr. Nonviolent Peace Prize for 1975. The award is the highest prize of the Martin Luther King, Jr. Center for Social Change. The presentation was made by Mrs. Coretta Scott King, widow of the slain civil rights leader, who said of Lewis:

We feel that this man exemplifies the life, the teachings, and the contributions of Martin Luther King, Jr., and certainly has brought about in his efforts the kind of non-violent social changes in our society that have moved us forward and will continue to move us toward the dream. . . . This young man is a very humble man, a deeply committed man, and a man whom I respect, admire, and love very deeply.

Lewis began his civil rights career as a member, and later Executive Secretary, of the Student Non-Violent Coordinating Committee (SNCC). He participated in the first Freedom Rides in 1961 and was a principal speaker at the March on Washington in 1963. He was a leader of the Selma-to-Montgomery Voting Rights Marches. It was during the first of these marches in 1965 that Lewis received a fractured skull after Alabama law enforcement officers charged the crowd of peaceful demonstrators. As head of the VEP, Lewis directs programs to advance, through nonpartisan action, minority political participation.

In receiving the award, Lewis said, "I am deeply moved and I hope that in the days, months, and years to come I will be worthy of this honor. As Dr. King said so many times, "We've come a distance, but we still have a distance to go.""

January 16-February 22. Blacks in DeKalb County, Georgia staged a number of demonstrations protesting what they called "the racist" DeKalb school system. On January 15 (the anniversary of the birthday of Dr. Martin Luther King, Jr.), 60 black parents and pupils picketed at the Columbia High School in Decatur. They accused the school system of, among other things, dishonoring the memory of Martin Luther King, Jr. by refusing to declare a holiday on his birthday. However, Joe Renfroe, an assistant superintendent of schools, said that special programs, rather than a holiday, would "make all students more aware of his (King's) contributions better than closing down which we do not do for the birthdays of other great men."

On February 20, about 100 black students at Columbia High School were arrested after they refused to obey an order from school authorities to leave the campus. The arrested students were part of a group of 170 blacks who had been suspended the previous week for staging a sit-down and walkout because the school failed to hold an assembly during Black History Week.

On February 22, more than 100 black students and parents marched from Columbia High School to the DeKalb County Courthouse in the continuing protest. According to one parent: "Our children have been coming home all this time telling us how bad the situation is and some of the things that the school officials up there do to them. . . . We see what they've been telling us is true."

Also on February 22, Columbia High School readmitted nearly all of the black students suspended during earlier demonstrations. DeKalb County, whose seat is the city of Decatur, is a part of the Metropolitan Atlanta area.

January 16. Muhammad Ali, heavyweight boxing champion, was named the Associated Press' Athlete of the Year for 1974. In winning the award, as a result of a nationwide poll of sportswriters and sportscasters, Ali edged out another black, baseball's Hank Aaron, by a margin of 162 to 110. Ali became only the third fighter to win the AP award since it was initiated in 1931. Joe Louis won it in 1937 after he had knocked out heavyweight Jim Braddock for the title, and Ingemar Johansson was selected in 1959 after he defeated Floyd Patterson for the heavyweight championship.

Although Ali fought only twice in 1974, one of these was the eighth round knockout of George Foreman in Zaire in October which gave him the world championship. The AP Award signalled a new acceptance of Ali by Americans. The champion had incurred widespread disfavor and was forced to take a 3½-year layoff from the ring when he refused induction into the Armed Forces in 1968. Ali began his comeback to the ring in 1971, after the U.S. Supreme Court overturned his conviction for draft evasion. The comeback fight was a third round knockout of Jerry Quarry in Atlanta. Coincidentally, Ali was in Atlanta at the time of his selection as Athlete of the Year to participate in ceremonies surrounding the anniversary of the birth of Martin Luther King, Jr., and to stage a mock fight with Atlanta Mayor Maynard H. Jackson (See Also Above and Below).

January 17. Stanley Scott, President Ford's chief black White House aide, told a seminar on mass communications at the John F. Kennedy Center in Atlanta that "fast buck operators" were threatening America's remaining black-owned newspapers. He said wealthy whites were "buying out black owned newspapers and franchising them like McDonald's hamburgers." "The black press should survive," Scott said, because the "majority white press" does not cover adequately all aspects of life in the black community. "I believe in integration," he continued, "but I think we should maintain and save some of our old institutions too." Scott estimated that of the 500 black-oriented newspapers in the country, "only about 30 or 35 are still black-owned." One of these is the Atlanta *Daily World,* a pioneer black daily, published by Scott's uncle, C. A. Scott. (See Also Above).

January 22. In its latest report, the U.S. Commission on Civil Rights said that President Ford must exert leadership to insure "vigorous and effective enforcement" of school desegregation laws. The commission was also, again, highly critical of the civil rights enforcement of several governmental agencies. Noting the continued resistance to school desegregation in Boston and elsewhere, the Commission said: "We are at a dangerous crossroads in connection with school desegregation. . . . We cannot afford—because of organized resistance in Boston or any other community—to turn back." The Commission called for "extraordinary actions," including appointment by the President of "an appropriate federal official" who would have the responsibility of making certain federal agencies fully enforce civil rights laws.

In the new report, the Commission charged that the Department of Health, Education, and Welfare (HEW), the Internal Revenue Service (IRS), and the Veterans Administration (VA) have failed to use existing federal laws to guarantee equal educational opportunities for racial minorities, non-English speaking persons, and women.

HEW, according to the Commission, has "diminished its over-all effectiveness and credibility" by interminable negotiations with segregated school districts, rather than cutting off their federal funds. The Commission also accused HEW of failing to tell school districts what they must do to comply with civil rights laws, including the degree of busing required to desegregate schools.

The IRS, the Commission contended, has taken little action to make sure that private schools which receive exemptions from federal taxes, are operated without racial bias.

The VA, which is responsible for enforcing anti-bias laws regarding profit-making schools, apprenticeship programs and on-the-job training programs "remains deficient in several areas," according to the Commission. The VA, for example, has refused to examine possible discrimination in the hiring of faculty.

The latest Commission document was the third in a series of reports assailing the degree of civil rights enforcement under the Nixon and Ford administrations.

January 22. The Voter Education Project (VEP) rendered an assessment of the political progress of blacks in the 1974 general elections. Georgia, according to the VEP report, led the South in the number of blacks elected and reelected to public office. In elections from coroner to Congressman, Georgia had 101 blacks elected out of the 525 successful black candidates. That state's black office holders now include a U.S. Congressman, two state senators, twenty state representatives, forty-seven city council persons, nineteen school board members, ten county commissioners, two mayors, a coroner, and a justice of the peace. Among the new black officeholders in Georgia were John White, the first black to represent Daughtery County in the state legislature; and Henry Dodson and J. O. Wyatt, the first black commissioners of Fulton County.

Elsewhere, Harold Ford was elected to the U.S. Congress from Memphis, Tennessee; 46 blacks were elected to state legislatures in Alabama, Georgia, and South Carolina alone; and blacks were elected to 226 city councils and commissions (See Also Table Below). In the end, however, according to VEP Executive Director John Lewis, "the election of 525 blacks in a single year is a small but important step in the long march toward equity of representation in Southern politics."

TABLE H   Black Officials Elected in Eleven Southern States, 1974

Office	Number
U.S. Congress	3
State Senates	9
State Houses	74
Municipal Legislatures	226
County Legislatures	55
School Boards	101
Mayors	8
Judges	4
Magistrates	14
Coroners	4
Justices of the Peace	10
Vice Mayors	3
City Recorders	1
Tax Collectors	1
Constables	3
Law Enforcement Officers	9

Source: Voter Education Project

January 24.   J. Mason Brewer, possibly the best known writer of Negro folklore in America, died in Commerce, Texas, at age 78.

Brewer wrote some of his stories and poems in black dialect, "so ancient" that it was difficult for most persons to read. Others were written in standard English. Prior to his death, Brewer had served as a vice-president of the American Folklore Society, and a member of the Texas Institute of Letters and the Texas Folklore Society. He had been a lecturer at Yale University, the University of Southern California, and the University of Texas, and a Distinguished Visiting Professor at East Texas State University. The late J. Frank Dobie, himself a distinguished folklorist, once called Brewer the best storyteller of Negro folklore anywhere in America.

January 25. Nannie Mitchell, founder of the *St. Louis Argus* and a veteran black business and civic leader, died in St. Louis, Missouri at age 88. In 1905, Mrs. Mitchell, her late husband William and her brother-in-law J. E. Mitchell, founded the We Shall Rise Insurance Company in St. Louis and began publishing a newsletter to be distributed to black churches in the area. This newsletter eventually became the *Argus*, a newspaper which has been published weekly since 1915.

January 25-February 15. George C. Wallace, a perennial symbol of resistance to civil rights for blacks, began his third term as Governor of Alabama. At his most recent inauguration, Wallace observed that social changes had been effected so smoothly in Alabama that other states might want to emulate it. Fifteen black state legislators and the state's first black cabinet officer, Jesse Lewis, witnessed the ceremonies. Wallace had received more black support than ever before in his recent successful reelection campaign and his subsequent recognition by black organizations had been the source of considerable controversy in the black communities of the nation. John Lewis, Director of the Voter Education Project (VEP), who was assaulted during the famous Selma to Montgomery March, is one of those who oppose black support for Wallace. In an interview with Boyd Lewis of the *Atlanta Inquirer*, John Lewis said: "Black people giving Wallace an award is like the Anti-Defamation League giving a posthumous award to Hitler." Other excerpts from the interview are quoted below:

George Wallace, in spite of his condition remains a symbol of the most brutal forms of violence inflicted against poor and black people in Alabama. . . . There is no way you can erase that from the psyche of black people. . . . As we celebrate Black History Week, we must not forget. . . . I am troubled by this newly found admiration of a man like Governor Wallace (See Also Above).

January 29. Former Georgia State Senator Leroy R. Johnson was convicted in the U.S. District Court in Atlanta of submitting a false statement to the Internal Revenue Service (IRS) in connection with his 1969 and 1970 income tax returns. Johnson was acquitted of two other charges of willfully evading some $40,000 in taxes for 1969 and 1970. Johnson's lawyers announced that they would appeal the verdict. Johnson became the first black person elected to a Southern state legislature since Reconstruction days when he won a seat in the Georgia legislature in 1962. During his twelve years in the state legislature, he became one of the most powerful black politicians in Georgia and the South. He was defeated for reelection in 1974, after an unsuccessful campaign for mayor of Atlanta, and with the tax charges against him still pending. (See Also Above).

January 29. Atlanta Mayor Maynard H. Jackson appointed the first full-time black Municipal Traffic Judge and the first black Municipal Court Solicitor in the city's history. Edward L. Baety, a 30-year-old attorney who graduated from Morris Brown College and Harvard University, was named judge. Ms. Mary Welcome, a 31-year-old attorney who graduated from the Howard University Law School, was named Municipal Court Solicitor.

February 1. The results of a study of the public schools of Philadelphia, Pennsylvania were released which showed that whether the race of the pupil and teacher was the same appeared unrelated to learning. Other parts of the report dealing with race concluded that counseling and remedial education—given current rates of expenditure—had "no particular value" in increasing learning. The report also showed that optimal learning growth at the elementary level occurred in classes that were about half black and half white. In junior high schools, the achievement among blacks increased as the percentage of blacks increased. On the other hand, white junior high school students experienced a decline in learning in schools that were more than half black. The study, sponsored by the Federal Reserve Bank of Philadelphia, was co-authored by Anita Summers and Barbara L. Wolfe.

February 2. Sam Beard, head of the Development Council, announced in New York that minority-owned companies were moving into the economic mainstream and doing business with the industrial giants of the nation. According to Beard, "There was almost no history of minority business ownership prior to the Sixties," but in the last three years, his nonprofit organization had arranged 1,003 contracts totaling $141 million between minority-owned businesses and major corporations. Included among the Council projects are the financing of a health center in South Jamaica, a section of Queens, New York, where thirty black doctors had tried unsuccessfully for 18 months to raise money for a medical facility to treat the community of 150,000; the funding of Soul City, the multi-racial town under construction in North Carolina; assistance to the Black Feet Indian Writing Company in Montana which now supplies pens to Atlantic-Richfield Company; and assistance to the black-owned Baldwin Ice Cream Company of Chicago which sells food to United Airlines. The Council, according to Director Beard, is not a charity organization. Instead, he said, "We're building long-lasting business relationships that will feed hundreds of thousands of dollars back into minority communities and create jobs."

February 3. Georgia State Representative Hosea Williams, head of the Atlanta chapter of the Southern Christian Leadership Conference, and three other men, including Socialist Workers Party presidential candidate, Peter Camejo, were arrested during a demonstration in Atlanta outside of a hotel where President Ford was speaking. Williams and fifty other demonstrators demanded to see the President to ask for jobs for the poor. A presidential aide told them that Ford's schedule did not permit such a meeting. Amid jeering from hotel guests, the demonstrators were arrested and charged with trespassing and disorderly conduct.

February 4. The Opportunities Industrialization Centers (OIC) held its 11th Annual Convention in Atlanta. The OIC, a black self-help organization, was founded in Philadelphia in 1964 by the Reverend Leon Howard Sullivan. Sullivan, the pastor of Philadelphia's Zion Baptist Church, first received national attention in 1963 when, after increasing his church's membership from 600 to 5,000, establishing a day care center, a federal credit union, a community center, an employment agency, adult education reading classes, several athletic teams, choral groups, and a family counseling service, he was cited by *Life* Magazine as one of the 100 outstanding young adults in the United States. During this same period he was named one of the ten outstanding young men in America and the outstanding young man of Philadelphia. He also won the City of Philadelphia Good Citizenship Award, the Silver Beaver Award of the Boy Scouts of America, the West Virginia State College Outstanding Alumnus Award, the Freedom Foundation Award and the Russwurm Award.

In 1964, at the age of 41, Sullivan established the first OIC in an abandoned jailhouse in Philadelphia. Starting with almost nothing, Sullivan built OIC into a $4.5-million-a-year enterprise which has trained and found jobs for more than 200,000 people. A comparison of OIC's expenditures with the number of people it has successfully trained over the past 10 years shows that the organization has been able to put trainees through its programs at an average cost of only $1,500 each. Secretary of Health, Education, and Welfare Caspar Weinberger has said that OIC is more effective at training people and finding jobs for them than the vocational educational programs in the nation's high schools.

During the 11th Annual Convention, President Ford addressed the delegates and praised the work and enthusiasm of Sullivan. The OIC head responded: "Mr. President, we are glad you came. It is time someone came to us to give the poor and those who work with the poor, some encouragement and some hope. It is refreshing to know that now, at last somebody in the White House seems to care."

Also on February 4th, the OIC presented a State Government Award to Alabama Governor George Wallace, for his support of OIC. The award, along with a kiss on the cheek, was given to the handicapped governor by Connie Harper, executive director of the Central Alabama OIC. A week later, Tyrone Brooks, public information officer for the Southern Christian Leadership Conference, resigned from the

Board of Directors of the Atlanta OIC in protest of the award to Wallace. Brooks called the presentation "an insult to all of black Atlanta and black America."

February 12. U.S. District Court Judge Wilbur Owens, Jr., in Macon, Georgia, approved the Georgia State Board of Regents plan for the desegregation of predominantly black Fort Valley State College. The thrust of the plan calls for upgrading academic programs, especially in agriculture, in order to attract more whites to Fort Valley State. Special education courses and a master's degree program in education were also parts of the plan. The suit against Fort Valley was filed in 1972 by a group of white citizens of the town who objected to a black, state-run school existing in their midst while their children had to attend other state schools. It was also contended, by blacks, that the plaintiffs opposed the influence which the blacks at Fort Valley were exerting on local politics.

Judge Owens, in his ruling, said "there is no magic way whereby this college can be transformed overnight." Yet, he continued, "the court feels the plan is real and it is designed to do what is necessary. The court believes the plan is evidence of an intention to attempt to do what the court says."

Black faculty members and students at Fort Valley announced that they may appeal the judge's ruling. Some of them had joined the case with a contention that the desegregation suit was in reality an attempt by whites to take control of the school. Thomas M. Jackson, attorney for the blacks, said the plan contained some provisions which were commendable, but asserted that the "concept is most suspect that a college must be controlled or operated by whites in order to attract white students." One of the attorneys for the Board of Regents told Judge Owens that a "reading of the plan" indicated that there was no justification for Jackson's fears. In his ruling, Owens, himself, noted that "there are some who will say the plan will result in the demise of this college but the court feels that those fears are unfounded. . . . If the plan is carried out by everyone involved the end result will be that students who attend—be they black, white or any other race—will get a good college education that they need, want, and ought to have!"

Even before Judge Owens' ruling, some white faculty members had been transferred to the school and some white students had enrolled. About 25 percent of the faculty and student body were white at the time of the decision.

The issues involved in the desegregation of Fort Valley State College are similar to that which have faced a number of predominantly black colleges in the past decade. Federal law has dictated the dismantling of dual school systems. In most instances white controlled State Boards of Regents or Trustees have recommended closing, merger, or transformation of the predominantly black colleges as a principal means of accomplishing these objectives. Blacks, while not opposed to the principle of desegregation, have often contended that the plans for achieving it would destroy essential elements of their cultural heritage and place them at an unfair disadvantage in competition for positions in the newly desegregated schools (See Also Above).

February 13. Dr. Peter T. Singleton, Jr., of Atlanta, Georgia was awarded the Commendation for Excellence in Clinical Medicine and Human Relations at the Walter Reed General Hospital and Medical Center, Washington, D.C. The young black cardiologist was graduated from Morehouse College and the Howard University Medical College.

February 15. Alameda County, California Superior Court Judge Lyle Cook ordered the city of Berkeley to promote eight white firemen who were passed over in favor of minority race candidates. Judge Cook ruled that the city's "affirmative action" program, introduced in 1972, was unconstitutional because it amounted to discrimination in reverse. According to the 1972 act, persons of minority races should be represented in the fire department in proportion to their population in the city. Whites, however, complained that they were discriminated against because non-whites were hired and promoted ahead of them on the basis of quota rather than merit. Judge Cook agreed that ignoring competitive examinations to hire and promote minority persons violated the Berkeley Charter, the Civil Rights Act of 1964, and the Fourteenth Amendment of the U.S. Constitution.

February 16. The Anacostia Neighborhood Museum, a branch of the Smithsonian Institution, announced that a travelling exhibit on black history will tour the country as part of the bicentennial celebration. The exhibit will include 46 illustrated panels, along with artifacts and a written text. Among the characters and events in the exhibit are York, William Clark's slave; Mary Fields, a colorful Western pioneer; Benjamin "Pap" Singleton, an early black migrationist; Bill Pickett, a pioneer black cowboy; and Mary Ellen Pleasant, a pioneer civil rights leader.

York was a strapping, six-foot interpreter for the Lewis and Clark expedition of 1804-1806. His fluency in French and Indian dialects as well as English made him indispensable to the Lewis and Clark exploration. He was, in fact, seen as the leader of the expedition by the Indians. Because of his services, he was granted his freedom in 1805.

"Black Mary" Fields was born in slavery, but migrated to Montana after emancipation. She became a friend and confidante of the nuns of Cascade, a restaurant owner, and a mail woman, who often walked through the snow, when it was too deep for horses, to insure that the mail got through.

Benjamin "Pap" Singleton, one of the earliest "Black Moses," led an exodus of blacks from the South to the West in 1879. Between 1870 and 1890, a number of these Western migrations took place as blacks sought to escape racial oppression in the Post-Reconstruction South. Men like Singleton organized "colonies" to help the blacks move West, where they often faced legal and extra-legal moves to keep them out of the frontier territories. Once in the West blacks founded all-black towns, worked on the railroads and in cattle drives. It is estimated that there were at least 8,000 black cowboys during this pioneer era.

Among the most famous of the black cowboys was Bill Pickett, "the Dusky Demon" of the rodeo circuit. Pickett lost his life at age 71, when he tried to make a comeback to the rodeo by roping and taming a wild horse.

Mary Ellen Pleasant was born a slave in Georgia, but also became a migrant to the West. She was one of San Francisco's first civil rights leaders and helped to finance the raid of John Brown at Harper's Ferry, Virginia in 1859 (See Also Above).

February 25. Georgia Governor George Busbee urged his state legislature to pass a bill dictating increased state employment for blacks and women. Busbee told leaders of the House and Senate that an affirmative action plan was needed to prevent mandatory hiring quotas imposed by the federal government. In May, 1974 the Equal Employment Opportunities Commission had accused eleven state departments and agencies of racially and sexually discriminatory hiring practices. The federal government had earlier imposed hiring quotas on the states of Alabama and Mississippi (See Also Above).

February 25. Elijah Muhammad, leader of the Black Muslims, died in Chicago at age 77. Muhammad was born as Elijah Poole, near Sandersville, Georgia in 1897. He moved to Detroit in the 1930's and there met W. D. Fard, Founder of the Temple of Islam (Black Muslims). Muhammad himself erected a temple in Detroit, then, in 1934, moved to Chicago. Subsequently, 79 temples were erected in 70 cities. Jesse Jackson, head of Operation PUSH and one of the nation's most articulate black civil rights leaders, eulogized Muhammad as "the single most powerful black man in this country. . . . His leadership extended far beyond his membership. He was the father of black self-consciousness during our 'colored' and Negro days." Muhammad was succeeded by his son, the honorable Wallace D. Muhammad.

During the height of the Civil Rights Movement, Muhammad and his Muslims provoked the ire of white and black leadership alike for their preachings of racial separatism, racial pride, and self-defense. The increasing popularity of those teachings among blacks, however, was demonstrated in the scope of philosophies represented in the eulogies for Muhammad. Civil rights leaders, including Jackson and Tyrone Brooks (SCLC), joined politicians such as Julian Bond of Georgia, and traditional black Baptist ministers in extolling the virtues of the Black Muslim patriarch.

Quoted below are excerpts from one of Muhammad's major statements, as it appeared in the January 22, 1971 edition of the Muslim newspaper, *Muhammad Speaks.*

> The so-called American Negro needs self-education and the education of others in order to get the respect and recognition of others. He is not independent. He does not own any land that he can call his own.

HE DOES NOT have an organized government of his own; he needs even more than equal education. He needs superior education to that which is ruling the nations of the earth today.

IT IS ESSENTIAL for a nation—if they want recognition—to be united and to enjoy self-control and in a country of their own.

We call this independence. Now, we do not have self-education, self-control, or a country—not even some of this earth that we can call our own. We need a superior education or teaching in order to achieve the respect of others who are now enjoying such recognition.

THE MOST ESSENTIAL qualification is the art of practicing that which we need in order to be accepted.

Cleanliness, inwardly and outwardly, is number one on the list. Manners, along with general moral aspects, are second. The so-called American Negroes' warped minds and disrespect of self is one of the main objections of the self-respected societies.

There are no members of an educated and clean self-respecting society who want their society disgraced by a member who has ill and disrespecting morals.

THE SO-CALLED American Negroes (the majority of us) have been reared by southern white people who have the most profound hatred and dislike for us. And, this being true, they have made us (just as they did our foreparents) a degree below nothing for the last 400 years.

At the same time, they frightened the so-called American Negro slaves to such a degree, they have no hope of ever being recognized authorities among themselves.

They try to please the same white people as did our fathers under servitude and slavery. Whether this 'please' is for or against them, they will do it, because they fear the white man. We must remember that the Bible closes with announcing this fear in Rev. 21:8.

OUR PEOPLE are afraid of the slavemaster and his children, afraid to displease them in their dislike of the salvation that has come to the slave, and God (Allah) has not offered the same to them (the slavemaster and his children).

THE SO-CALLED Negro, who tries to please his master, displeases himself. He would love to see Hereafter and live in a kingdom (a government) of peace and security, but he would not like to accept any such glory if this acceptance is not liked by the slavemaster.

Therefore, he suffers the consequence of the slavemaster's children, which is referred to in Rev. 19:20 under the name, beast (clearly symbolized as human beings in Rev. 19:19).

DESTRUCTION

Those who refuse (of the so-called NEGROES) TO ACCEPT God (Allah) as their King, and the people of God (Allah) as their brothers and nation, will suffer the destruction of hell-fire with the enemies.

YOU MUST WASH and be clean as Isaiah 1:16 warns you. Proverbs 30:12 specifies us as a generation not washed. Hebrew 10:22 makes mention that it is necessary that our bodies be washed with pure water to enter into the recognition and respect of God (Allah).

Revelations 1:5 reads in a parable of Jesus, who will wash us inwardly but from our sins. I want you to remember that this does not mean the Jesus who was here 2,000 years ago.

It means a Jesus at the end of the time. One whom Jesus prophesied God would send under the title of a Comforter (in the Bible) and as Ahmad in the 61st Chapter of the Holy Qur'an.

Elijah Malachi had to first come and wash and clean up a people and make them self-respecting so that God would accept them in His presence.

So if we want white or Black to respect us, we must clean and wash ourselves of the filth in and out. No self-respecting nations will accept you as you are today, because of your ill-mannered behavior.

HURRY AND JOIN ONTO YOUR OWN KIND. THE TIME OF THIS WORLD IS NOW AT HAND!

Quoted below are excerpts from the Black Muslim Creed:

What the Muslims Want

This is the question asked most frequently by both the whites and the blacks. The answers to this question I shall state as simply as possible.

1. We want freedom. We want a full and complete freedom.

2. We want justice. Equal justice under the law. We want justice applied equally to all, regardless of creed or class or color.

3. We want equality of opportunity. We want equal membership in society with the best in civilized society.

4. We want our people in America whose parents or grandparents were descendants from slaves, to be allowed to establish a separate state or territory of their own—either on this continent or elsewhere. We believe that our former slave masters are obligated to provide such land and that the area must be fertile and minerally rich. We believe that our former slave masters are obligated to maintain and supply our needs in this separate territory for the next 20 to 25 years—until we are able to produce and supply our own needs.

Since we cannot get along with them in peace and equality, after giving them 400 years of our sweat and blood and receiving in return some of the worst treatment human beings have ever experienced, we believe our contributions to this land and the suffering forced upon us by white America, justifies our demand for complete separation in a state or territory of our own.

5. We want freedom for all Believers of Islam now held in federal prisons. We want freedom for all black men and women now under death sentence in innumerable prisons in the North as well as the South.

We want every black man and woman to have the freedom to accept or reject being separated from the slave master's children and establish a land of their own.

We want that the above plan for the solution of the black and white conflict is the best and only answer to the problem between two people.

6. We want an immediate end to the police brutality and mob attacks against the so-called Negro throughout the United States. We believe that the Federal government should intercede to see that black men and women tried in white courts receive justice in accordance with the laws of the land or allow us to build a new

nation for ourselves, dedicated to justice, freedom and liberty.

7.   As long as we are not allowed to establish a state or territory of our own, we demand not only equal justice under the laws of the United States, but equal employment opportunities. NOW!
We do not believe that after 400 years of free or nearly free labor, sweat and blood, which has helped America become rich and powerful, that so many thousands of black people should have to subsist on relief, charity or live in poor houses.

8.   We want the government of the United States to exempt our people from ALL taxation as long as we are deprived of equal justice under the laws of the land.

9.   We want equal education—but separate schools up to 16 for boys and 18 for girls on the condition that the girls be sent to women's colleges and universities. We want all black children educated, taught and trained by their own teachers.
Under such schooling system we believe we will make a better nation of people. The United States government should provide, free, all necessary text books and equipment, schools and college buildings. The Muslim teacher shall be left free to teach and train their people in the way of righteousness, decency and self respect.

10.   We believe that intermarriage or race mixing should be prohibited.
We want the religion of Islam taught without hinderance or suppression.

These are some of the things that we, the Muslims, want for our people in North America.

February 28.   U.S. District Court Judge Robert M. McRae, Jr. in Memphis, Tennessee denied James Earl Ray's motion to withdraw his guilty plea and face a new trial on the charge that he murdered Dr. Martin Luther King, Jr. in 1968. McRae said Ray's original plea of guilty was "cooly and deliberately" submitted and that he found no violation of Ray's constitutional rights that would warrant a reversal of the plea and a full trial in state court. McRae rejected Ray's contention that he came to believe he had no choice but to plead guilty because of his former attorneys' actions and rejected Ray's allegations that famed criminal lawyer Percy Foreman of Houston,

Texas and attorney Arthur Hanes, Sr. of Birmingham, Alabama failed to take adequate steps to prepare a defense because they were more interested in promoting their royalties on the Ray story under contracts with Alabama author William Bradford Huie. McRae ruled groundless Ray's argument that Foreman, specifically, coerced him into the guilty plea. The judge said there was no "impermissible pressure" from the attorney. "On the contrary, the matter was discussed on numerous separate occasions over almost one month, at the least. . . . Ray carefully considered and partially amended the lengthy stipulation of facts that formed the basis for accepting his guilty plea . . . and entered the plea in an open court where he spoke to correct the record as he thought appropriate," according to Judge McRae. Robert I. Livingston, one of Ray's new attorneys, announced an imme diate appeal to the U.S. 6th Circuit Court of Appeals (See Also Above).

February. The Free Southern Theater presented the play, *If the Opportunity Scratches, Itch It* in Eutau, Alabama· It was the first time ever that live theater, other than high school plays, had been performed in this predominantly black farm community in central Alabama. The occasion also marked the first time since 1969 that the Free Southern Theater had taken a show on the road, although this was its original purpose when it was established in 1962 as a cultural arm of the Student Non-Violent Coordinating Committee (SNCC).
The Free Southern Theater has been seen by some as the beginning of a modern renaissance of black culture that grew out of the civil rights and black consciousness or black awareness movements of the 1960's and 70's. The idea of a theater to dramatize the concept of black liberation has spread rapidly across the country, and most cities with a sizeable black population now have some form of organized cultural activity. These include The Fire Company in Birmingham, Alabama; the New African Company, the National Center of Afro-American Artists, and the Museum of Afro-American History in Boston; the Ku Mba Workshop in Chicago; the Karamu House Theater in Cleveland; the Rapa House in Detroit; Opera South in Jackson, Mississippi; Bodacious Buggerilla, the Mafandi Institute, and the Performing Arts Society in Los Angeles; the Black Theater Troupe and Umba Ujaama in Phoenix; and the Kahero Cultural Gallery of Richmond.

The aim of all of this activity is to allow blacks, who feel that they have been generally left out or misrepresented in America's cultural media, to interpret their own history, thoughts, ideas, strengths, weaknesses, and aspirations. In addition to theater, blacks are engaged in community writing, dancing, directing, designing, sculpturing, singing, and photography.

In interviews with the *New York Times* in February, 1975, Kenneth E. Snipes, executive director of the Karamu House Theater and Gilbert Moses, one of the founders of the New Orleans based Free Southern Theater, assessed the new movement. According to Snipes, "Blacks have more needs for certain kinds of programs to provide them with a sense of self-worth, more of the things that are appreciative of black people." "There is a need to appreciate black people, to appreciate the role of blacks in the history of this country, to appreciate the work of the black playwright or the black dancer is doing today to eventually attain self-worth and self-esteem." Moses said, "It was more important that we develop our own artists, our own image. It had to happen."

March 2.   The nation's leading black tennis player Arthur Ashe won the singles finals of the World Championship Tennis Green Group Tournament in Rotterdam. He defeated Tom Okker of the Netherlands 3-6, 6-2, 6-4, in a 95-minute match at the Ahoy Sports Palace.

March 14.   U.S. District Court Judge John H. Pratt in Washington, D.C. ordered the U.S. Department of Health, Education, and Welfare (HEW) to quickly enforce school desegregation laws in 125 school districts in 16 states where voluntary desegregation was in effect. The judge told HEW to begin proceedings against the school systems within two months and said that in the future only seven months would be granted for systems to formulate voluntary school desegregation plans. HEW, itself, had found within the past 15 months that the school districts, included in the order, were "substantially disproportionate" in their racial composition. The affected districts were located in Arkansas, Delaware, Florida, Kentucky, Louisiana, Maryland, Mississippi, Missouri, North Carolina, Oklahoma, South Carolina, Tennessee, Texas, Virginia, and West Virginia. The ruling came as a result of a suit filed by the NAACP's Legal Defense Fund in 1971. Failure of any district to comply with HEW requirements could mean a cut off of federal funds.

March 17. The American Civil Liberties Union (ACLU) released documents indicating that the Federal Bureau of Investigation (FBI) had fabricated a threatening letter in order to persuade a black civil rights worker to leave Mississippi in 1969. A month after Muhammad Kenyatta received the letter, he returned with his family to Pennsylvania. The ACLU said that Kenyatta (formerly Donald W. Jackson) had come under the scrutiny of Countelpro, the FBI's counter intelligence unit, which the Bureau operated between 1956 and 1971 in an effort to disrupt groups it considered subversive. The letter in question, allegedly written by a group of Tougaloo (Mississippi) college students, warned Kenyatta to leave Mississippi or "we shall consider contacting local authorities regarding some of your activities or take other measures available to us which would have a more direct effect and which would not be as cordial as this note." The ACLU obtained the FBI documents in connection with a suit filed against the Bureau by Kenyatta, alleging a violation of his constitutional rights.

March 17. The Reverend Jesse Jackson of Chicago, head of People United to Save Humanity (Operation PUSH), told a press conference in New York that the National Collegiate Athletic Association (NCAA) was "racist" and warned that a black boycott of the college football bowl games may be the next target of civil rights groups. Jackson remarked that "the NCAA is not fair. . . . The colleges don't have black head coaches. They will select an assistant coach grudgingly but they don't consider the black man to be head coach or athletic director. . . . We found that the selection committees for the various bowl games are almost totally white. This is a situation we intend to change."

Earlier the same day, Jackson had met with Michael Burke, president of Madison Square Garden, and Peter Carlesimo of Fordham University on the issue of giving black colleges a role in the National Invitational Basketball Tournament (NIT). Jackson's organization had threatened to picket the NIT unless changes were made. Under an agreement reached with Burke and Carlesimo, two athletic directors from black colleges would be elected to the NIT Selection Committee (Jackson suggested the names of Earl Banks of Morgan State College and Eddie Robinson of Grambling University), at least one black institution would be invited to compete in future NIT events, and the New York branch of Operation PUSH would play a supportive role in the promotion of future tournaments. Jackson said that the pressure on the NIT was part of a national program to break down racial barriers which extended beyond the playing field.

March 20. The April issue of *Redbook* listed four black women among the 44 American women qualified for top governmental positions, including cabinet officers, in the United States. The blacks include U.S. Representative Barbara Jordan (D. Texas), who was suggested as eminently qualified for Attorney-General of the United States; Mrs. Martin Luther King, Jr., listed as qualified for chairperson of the Equal Employment Opportunity Commission; Eleanor Holmes Norton, Commissioner of Human Rights for New York City, listed as qualified for Secretary of Housing and Urban Development; and C. Delores Tucker, Secretary of State of Pennsylvania, seen as qualified for Ambassador to the United Nations. The list of qualified women was drawn up by Frances "Sissy" Farentold, chairperson of the National Women's Political Caucus, because she became convinced that women's abilities are underestimated when selections for high level jobs are made.

March 20. Kenneth Ivory, a 17-year-old black youth from Milwaukee, Wisconsin, was installed as national "Boy of the Year" in a White House ceremony, attended by President Gerald R. Ford. Ivory, a senior at Lincoln High School in Milwaukee, was president of his student body and captain of the football, basketball, and baseball teams at the time of his selection as Boy of the Year.

March 24. Heavyweight boxing champion Muhammad Ali defeated Chuck Wepner in the final round of a 15-round title fight to retain his crown. Wepner went down in the last round from a right to the head and referee Tony Perez stopped the fight at the count of eight.

March 28. The *Washington Star* reported new evidence of governmental spying on black individuals and organizations. These included investigations of Marion Barry, a former SNCC official and an ex-president of the Board of Education of Washington, D.C.; Walter Fauntroy, Washington, D.C.'s delegate to the U.S. House of Representatives; the Reverend David Eaton, pastor of Washington's All Souls Unitarian Church; and Absalom Frederick Jordan, chairman of the Black United Front. Of Barry, according to the *Star*, one file read, "Subject referred . . . by FBI due to activities in SNCC, active in civil rights movement. Dislikes police." (See Also Above and Below.)

April 1. The Black Christian Nationalist Church (BCN) opened its third biennial national convention in Atlanta. The BCN is a movement dedicated to changing the condition of black people by changing their life-styles. According to the creed of the BCN, "Jesus, the Black Messiah, was a revolutionary leader, sent by God to rebuild the Black Nation, Israel, and to liberate Black people from powerlessness and from the oppression, brutality and exploitation of the white gentile world." The national chairman of BCN, Jaramazi Abebe Agyeman (formerly Reverend Albert Cleage) was lauded by Atlanta Mayor Maynard Jackson as "a master teacher." Coleman Young, mayor of Detroit, presented Agyeman with a certificate from his city's Council. Young said that, "BCN is a force to be reckoned with, not only in Detroit but in the nation."

April 1. Poppy Cannon White, widow of the late NAACP Executive Secretary Walter Francis White, died after a plunge from the terrace of her apartment in New York. White, himself, died in 1955. His marriage to the white author in 1947 created a mild controversy in the ranks of the NAACP. The NAACP issued an official statement of sorrow, however, upon the death of Mrs. White.

April 2. Judge Dennis Jones of the DeKalb County, Georgia Juvenile Court dismissed charges against 80 black students arrested during a demonstration in February, 1975 at the Columbia High School in Decatur. Judge Jones did not specify his reasons for dismissing the charges. Assistant School Superintendent Joe Renfroe, who had brought charges against the blacks, said he was "shocked" by the judge's ruling. He said the demonstrating blacks had disrupted the instructional and academic process at Columbia. Defense Attorney Roger Mills praised the judge's decision, calling it "amazing." The blacks had been brought into court accused of juvenile delinquency by violation of public disturbance statutes, during a series of protests aimed at what they called the "racist administration" of DeKalb County schools (See Also Above).

April 8. The last remaining barrier in professional sports fell as Lee Elder, a black golfer, began competition in the famed Masters Tournament at Augusta, Georgia. Elder was invited to participate in the prestigious Masters after winning the Monsanto Open in 1974. The black golfer had been officially welcomed to Georgia by the state's governor, George Busbee. In the tournament, itself, Elder was disqualified in the preliminary rounds.

April 9. The Georgia Supreme Court upheld the murder conviction and death sentence of Marcus Wayne Chenault for the slaying of Mrs. Martin Luther King, Sr. and Deacon Edward Boykin at the Ebenezer Baptist Church in Atlanta on June 30, 1974. Chenault had been convicted by a Fulton County Court Jury on September 12, 1974. Like the trial jury which convicted him, the State Supreme Court rejected Chenault's plea of insanity. Chenault's attorney, Randy Bacote accused the high court of "overlooking the essence of a fair trial," and of being "very lax and lenient in addressing itself to the question of whether he (Chenault) had competent psychiatric tests and evaluations." He promised to explore other avenues of defense (See Also Above).

April 12. Josephine Baker, for half a century one of the most popular American singers in France, died in Paris at age 69. Ms. Baker began dancing as a small child. She left her hometown of St. Louis at the age of 15 with a dance troupe and began regular performances at the Music Hall and the Plantation Club in Harlem. After Broadway rejected her as being "too ugly," she went to Paris, where in 1925 she became an instant success in the all-black "Blackbird Revue" at the Champs-Elysees theater. In the 1920's and 1930's, she also starred in the Folies-Bergère and the Casino de Paris. She became a French citizen in 1937. During the Second World War, she won the Croix de Guerre and Resistance Medal for her dangerous assignments with French intelligence units. Ms. Baker announced numerous retirements, but kept coming out of them in order to raise money for the orphan home which she set up in the French countryside for children of all races and nationalities. Two days before her death, she celebrated the 50th anniversary of her first appearance in Paris with a gala performance of "Josephine." Princess Grace of Monaco was one of the celebrities in the audience. French President Valery Giscard d'Estaing sent a congratulatory telegram. During this performance, Ms. Baker said, "I have two loves, Paris and my own country." She collapsed two days later prior to going onstage. She, herself, had once said, "The day I no longer go on stage will be the day I die."

April 14.   Preliminary legal motions were presented in the Beaufort County, South Carolina Superior Court in the celebrated murder case of Joanne Little, a 20-year-old black woman charged with murder after a Beaufort County Jailer, Clarence Alligood, was found dead in her cell on August 27, 1974. Ms. Little pleaded self-defense on the grounds that the semi-nude jailer had attempted to rape her. In the preliminary legal skirmishes, Ms. Little's attorneys, Jerry Paul and Karen Galloway, sought a change of venue and a delay of the trial. They argued that racist feelings and pretrial publicity had made it impossible for Ms. Little to get a fair trial in Beaufort County.

The Little case became a cause célèbre when civil rights groups and feminist organizations rallied to the young black woman's defense, claiming that the case typified the abuses which the Southern criminal justice system has long heaped upon blacks and women. By early April, thousands of dollars had been raised in behalf of the defense effort. Also, U.S. Representative Shirley Chisholm (D. N.Y.) had asked U.S. Attorney General Edward Levy to intervene in the case on Ms. Little's behalf. Rep. Chisholm said: "There are very few black people of either sex called to serve on juries in these eastern North Carolina counties. So this can really hurt Joanne, who lives in a region where many, many Caucasian people hold the worst sort of prejudices against black women."

April 15.   The Georgia Institute of Technology (Georgia Tech) announced that it had hired the first black assistant football coach in its history. Bill McCullough of Atlanta, a graduate of Fort Valley State College (Ga.) and Georgia State University, resigned from his position as Education Program Coordinator with the Georgia Department of Public Safety to accept the position at Tech.

April 23.   Thirteen persons, including self-avowed Communist and Black Panther Party leader Ron Carter, were arrested during a demonstration outside the office of Georgia State Labor Commissioner Sam Caldwell. The protest centered on demands for an extension of unemployment benefits, a minimum $75 per week payment, and reduction of "red tape" in connection with unemployment aids. The arrests came after the demonstrators refused to clear the halls outside of Caldwell's office. Labor Department officials had told the protesters that they could picket on the sidewalk outside the building.

April 23.   Racial fighting erupted at the Boca Raton High School in Boca Raton, Florida. Three students and a policeman were injured. Two white students were arrested on charges of disorderly conduct. Police said the melee began about 7 a.m., when several busses carrying black students from Delray Beach arrived at the school. The blacks discovered a "racial slur" on the wall, became incensed and the fight was on. The school, located in a resort area for millionaires, was first desegregated in 1971. At the time of the racial incident, it had 225 black and 1,050 white students.

May 1.   A new U.S. 10-cent commemorative stamp honoring the black poet Paul Laurence Dunbar went on sale. Dunbar, the son of ex-slaves, was born on June 27, 1872 in Dayton, Ohio, and the first day issue of the stamp was sold there. Dunbar, best known for his humorous poems in black dialect, published several volumes of verse, three novels, and five collections of short stories. He died in 1906.

Coincidentally with the issuance of the Dunbar stamp, the U.S. Postal Service opened a special exhibit called "Black Americans on U.S. Postage Stamps" at the Museum of African Art in Washington, D.C. At the conclusion of the special showing in Washington, the exhibit will tour various post offices throughout the nation (See Also Above).

June 5. Attorneys for Joanne Little, accused of murder in the slaying of a North Carolina jailer, announced that they were filing a $1 million damage suit against the estate of the man who she accused of attempting to rape her in a Beaufort County jail when she stabbed him to death. The suit claims that the deceased jailer Clarence Alligood, acting under the color of North Carolina law, inflicted cruel and unusual punishment on Ms. Little and invaded her privacy in the alleged sexual attack. Ms. Little was being held in the Beaufort County jail on a charge of breaking and entering at the time of the alleged assault. The suit, sponsored by the Southern Poverty Law Center in Montgomery, Alabama, also asked the Federal District Court in New Bern, North Carolina to protect all female inmates from sexual abuse by male attendants at the Beaufort County jail. The class-action portion of the suit claims that women prisoners are largely supervised by males who can see them as they bathe, undress or use restroom facilities; that women inmates "are confined in such a manner that male trusties, jailers, and other male persons given free run of the jail expose their genitalia . . . and make vulgar and obscene remarks and gestures against the will and beyond the control" of the female inmates; that bail bondsmen are allowed access to the women's cells to conduct bonding business and at times have "made lewd and vulgar sexual propositions" to the female prisoners; and that prior to the slaying of Alligood, the women inmates were under 24-hour surveillance by closed-circuit television cameras which all persons in the jailer's office could watch and although the camera was removed after Alligood's death, it could be reinstalled. Ms. Little's suit was filed as she awaited trial for the murder of Alligood (See Also Above).

June 6. New reports of FBI spying on black individuals and organizations appeared in the *Atlanta Constitution*. According to the newspaper, the FBI had spied on the Afro-American's Patrolmen's League since its founding in Chicago in 1968. The report quoted the Patrolmen's League founder, Renault Robinson, as saying that the FBI shared its information with Army intelligence units and with the intelligence division of the Chicago Police Department. The Afro-American Patrolmen's League was organized to voice the particular racial grievances of black policemen.

June 10. Harvard University announced that it had negotiated an agreement under which 20 percent of the University's $228 million in group life insurance is to be insured by the North Carolina Mutual Life Insurance Company and the Atlanta Life Insurance Company, the two largest black-owned insurance companies in the nation. The total amount involved in the deal is approximately $45 million, with one half going to each company. A spokesman for Harvard, Walter J. Leonard, said, "the agreement is a mutually beneficial one. . . . Our joint venture will not only enhance North Carolina Mutual Life Insurance Company's and the Atlanta Life Insurance Company's images as growing and strong companies, but it will, simultaneously, radiate Harvard's concern for the development and growth of stable and strong black business enterprises."

June 12. Judge Dan M. Russell of the U.S. District Court in Jackson, Mississippi declared a mistrial in the tax evasion trial of Fayette, Mississippi Mayor Charles Evers after an Internal Revenue Service (IRS) agent suggested from the witness stand that Evers might have "pocketed" campaign contributions. The questionable remarks were made by IRS agent William Jack Sykes when asked about possible sources of taxable income Evers allegedly failed to report. Sykes said, "Well, he did run for Congress." Defense Attorney Michael Fawer objected to the agent's remarks on the grounds that the government's attorneys had agreed not to bring up the 1968 campaign as a source of more than $161,000 in taxable income that Evers allegedly concealed between 1968 and 1970. Although he declared a mistrial, Judge Russell refused to agree to a defense motion to dismiss the indictment against Evers.

Evers, a native of Mississippi, returned to his home state in 1963 following the murder of his brother, civil rights leader Medger Evers. He succeeded his brother as state field secretary of the NAACP, and later entered politics. He was closely identified, for example, with the presidential campaign of the late Senator Robert F. Kennedy in 1968. In 1969, he was elected Mayor of Fayette, the first black mayor of a bi-racial town in Mississippi in modern times. In 1971, he ran an unsuccessful campaign for governor and subsequently became Democratic national committeeman from Mississippi. The IRS contended that Evers' total assets jumped from $58,457 at the beginning of

1968 to $222,013 by the end of 1970, but that he had failed to report $161,409 in taxable income during these years and had actually evaded taxes of $48,177. The defense retorted that Evers' assets did not actually increase during the period because he had about $160,000 in undisclosed cash at the time—money earned from bootlegging, gambling and other illegal operations in Chicago in the 1950's and 1960's (See Also Above).

June 14. The U.S. Department of Justice announced in Washington that it has asked a federal court in Mississippi to order that state to adopt a new reapportionment plan for its legislature that meets federal standards prior to the 1975 elections. The Justice Department asked the court specifically to prohibit the use of a reapportionment plan drawn up by the Mississippi legislature during its 1975 session and to forbid the implementation of any plan that is not cleared in advance, as having met federal standards. The Voting Rights Act of 1965 requires that such advanced clearance be obtained either from the U.S. Attorney-General or the U.S. District Court in Washington, and that any political change in an affected Southern state must meet the test of whether it would have the intent or effect of diminishing the voting rights of minorities.

June 22. In an interview on the second anniversary of his election to the mayoralty of Los Angeles, California Tom Bradley said that race was not a factor in his administration. Excerpts from Bradley's statements are quoted below:

I don't think that race is a significant factor in my administration. In part this is because I have tried to serve all the people of the city in the best way I know how. We've tried to bring in the advice of all segments of the city: the business community, homeowner groups and just grassroots citizens. That kind of openness has created the atmosphere of acceptability that has made possible the view of my service without regard to color. I have not run across a single incident of bigotry. In fact, the usual expression I hear is: "Well, I didn't vote for you, but I think you're doing an excellent job and commend you and I'd like to help." . . .

Bradley's remarks were in response to a question from Paul Finch of the Associated Press (See Also Above).

July 3. Attorneys for the National Association for the Advancement of Colored People (NAACP), the NAACP Legal Defense and Educational Fund (LDEF), and the Center for National Policy Review (CNPR) filed a suit in the U. S. District Court in Washington to compel the federal government to require northern and western states to end school segregation or to face termination of their school aid, as had been done in the South. The suit was filed on behalf of children in 18 families in eight northern and western school districts and as a class action representing the interests of minority children in 33 states outside the South. The suit charged that Secretary of Health, Education, and Welfare (HEW) Caspar W. Weinberger had not performed his legal obligation to be certain that no federally funded school system segregates teachers by race or national origin. The complaint also charged that HEW had failed to act even when evidence came to its attention suggesting segregation, and that protest proceedings tended to drag on indefinitely. The suit said that 24 of 58 pending investigations of school systems in the North and West were six or seven years old. The suit asked that HEW make findings of noncompliance, seek voluntary compliance on a prompt basis, and then cut off federal aid if all else failed. On August 13, 1975, officials of HEW responded to the suit by calling for a meeting in Cleveland, Ohio, to plan stepped-up enforcement of school desegregation in northern districts.

July 24. The U.S. Senate voted 77 to 12 to extend the Voting Rights Act of 1965 for an additional seven years. The act of 1965 allowed federal registrars and the U.S. Department of Justice to assist thousands of blacks to register and vote in the South. The new law was even supported by a few southern senators. The southerners had failed earlier in an attempt to extend the coverage of the law from the South to the entire nation (See Also Above and Below).

July 28. The U.S. House of Representatives voted 346 to 56 in favor of an extension of the 1965 Voting Rights Act. Earlier, the U.S. Senate had approved the same measure, allowing the law to remain in effect for seven additional years. Scores of southern representatives, including seven out of ten of the congressmen from Georgia, supported the measure in the House.

July 30. U.S. District Court Judge James F. Gordon ordered the full desegregation of the Louisville, Kentucky, public schools. The judge's order called for the busing of 22,600 pupils to achieve the desegregation. Judge Gordon's ruling climaxed four years of litigation by civil rights groups. Since the Louisville and Jefferson county schools were merged, the order affected a system of 140,000 pupils, including about 20,000 blacks. Judge Gordon said that all of the Louisville-Jefferson county schools would be desegregated and each would have a black enrollment of at least twelve percent. No school could be more than forty percent black. Gordon also warned those "who would resort to public disorder and violence" to oppose the desegregation to "think twice."

August 6–15. Racial violence continued in Boston, scene of sporadic incidents ever since busing to achieve school desegregation was ordered in the city in 1974. On August 6, racial fighting erupted at the Charles Street jail and 150 police officers were called in to put down the disturbance involving 75 to 100 inmates. Martin Whitkin of the Sheriff's Office said the trouble apparently started in the lunchroom with a fight between a white inmate and several blacks, then escalated into a full scale brawl throughout the jail. On August 10, black and white swimmers threw rocks and bricks at one another on South Boston's Carson Beach. About 500 blacks were at the beach in this predominantly white section in response to a request by black leaders who urged them to "reassert the rights of all Boston residents to use all public facilities." There were no reports of injuries. On August 13, police patrols were increased in the Roxbury section of Boston after young blacks had made sporadic attacks on passing whites for three days. On August 15, three persons were slightly injured during incidents of stone throwing in the city. A sixteen-year-old black youth was arrested during the melee in the largely black Roxbury section. Meanwhile, black U.S. Senator Edward Brooke, R. Mass., joined local leaders in an attempt to ease racial tensions. Brooke said: "I think the polarization in the community is unfortunate, but it seems to be building."

August 8. Julian "Cannonball" Adderley, a "prophet of contemporary jazz," died in Gary, Indiana. Adderley was born in Tampa, Florida, in 1928, the son of a jazz cornetist. Known primarily as an alto saxophonist, Adderley also played tenor sax, trumpet, clarinet, and flute. He studied brass and reed instruments in a Tallahassee, Florida, high school from 1944 until 1948 and formed his first jazz group there with the school's band director as advisor. Because of his hearty appetite, fellow students nicknamed him "cannibal," which later became "Cannonball." From 1948 until 1956, Adderley was music director at the Dillard High School in Fort Lauderdale, Florida. At the same time, he directed his own jazz group in southern Florida. He served for three years as a member of the 36th Army Dance Band and later studied at the Naval School of Music in Washington, D. C. Adderley's first big break came in New York in 1955 when he appeared with Oscar Pettiford. The next year he signed his first recording contract with EmArcy Records. He later recorded for Capitol Records and other companies, and became famous for such albums as *Black Messiah*, *Country Preacher*, *Fiddler on the Roof*, *Walk Tall*, and *Quiet Nights*. His last album was *Phenix*. Until 1957, Adderley toured with his brother, Nat, a cornetist. In 1957, he joined the Miles Davis group. After a tour with George Shearing, he formed his own quintet, including brother Nat, in 1959. Charles Suber, publisher of *Down Beat* magazine, which named Adderley New Alto Sax Star of the Year in 1959, described the "Cannonball" as "a helluva musician. . . . He was one of the best alto players in recent years." During his eulogy of Adderley before 2,000 persons in Tallahassee, Florida, the Reverend Jesse Jackson, Director of People United to Save Humanity (PUSH), said the "Cannonball" had "his greatness and his fame, but he did not use it, abuse it, or lose it. He expanded it. . . . When he blew his saxophone you felt a little ease in the troubled world and the savage beast had to hold his peace."

August 10. Emory O. Jackson, editor of the Birmingham *World*, was laid to rest in Birmingham, Alabama. Jackson was born on September 8, 1908, in Buena Vista, Georgia. He moved with his parents to Birmingham in 1919. He was graduated from Morehouse College in 1932, after which he taught school in Dothan and Jefferson counties, Alabama. After serving in World War II, Jackson became managing editor of the Birmingham *World*—a position he held from 1943 until his death. Jackson was one of the founders of the Alabama Conference of NAACP Branches and a leader of several other political and civil rights organizations. In his eulogy of Jackson, the Reverend Samuel Pettagrue of the Sardis Baptist Church of Birmingham proclaimed that "the presses in heaven have stopped. A new edition was on the street and its headline read: 'The paper's top foreign correspondent, Emory O. Jackson, after serving 67 years away has returned home to serve out his assignment eternally.' " In another eulogy, Benjamin E. Mays, president of the Atlanta, Georgia, Board of Education and president-emeritus of Jackson's *alma mater*, said the late editor was "born a free man. He walked like one; talked like one and looked like one."

August 15. A jury of six whites and six blacks in Raleigh, North Carolina, acquitted Joan Little of murder in the August 27, 1974, icepick stabbing death of white jailer, Clarence Allgood. The murder case of the twenty-one-year-old black woman became a *cause celebre* for feminist and civil rights groups after she claimed she stabbed Allgood while defending herself against a sexual attack (See Above and Below).

August 16. U.S. District Court Judge Robert DeMascio rejected the busing of students to achieve school desegregation in Detroit, Michigan. He ordered the Detroit Board of Education to seek an alternate plan to better balance the races in the schools. C. L. Golightly, president of the city's school board, called the judge's decision "a victory for the school-children of Detroit." Lawrence Washington of the Detroit branch of the NAACP expressed disappointment. He said: "We're right back to where we started five years ago."

September 1. Lieutenant General Daniel "Chappie" James, Jr., became the first black man to be promoted to the rank of full four star general. The Pentagon announced that James, a veteran of nearly 200 combat missions in Korea and Vietnam, was also appointed Chief of the North American Air Defense Command (NORAD). James, 55, was born in Pensacola, Florida, and graduated from Tuskegee Institute. He was one of the original black pilots in the U.S.

Army Air Corps, predecessor to the Air Force. He achieved a great deal of notoriety for his speeches on Americanism and patriotism. With the appointment of James, there are now twenty-one black generals and admirals in the Army, Air Force, and Navy out of a total of about 1,200 in the U.S. Armed Services.

November 19.   James B. Adams, associate deputy director of the FBI, told the U.S. Senate's Intelligence Committee that there was no legal justification for the 25 separate attempts by the Bureau in the 1960s to discredit the late Dr. Martin Luther King, Jr., as a civil rights leader. The FBI, he continued, was led to investigate King because of the possibility that Communist influences were being brought to bear on him and the civil rights movement. No such evidence, however, was ever uncovered. Public evidence revealed that the FBI installed a total of 16 electronic bugs and eight wiretaps on King and even sent him and his wife an anonymous letter and tape which King reportedly interpreted as a suggestion for suicide.

November 19.   Former Black Panther Party leader Eldridge Cleaver arrived in California in federal custody to face charges of attempted murder. Cleaver, 40, was to be charged in connection with a shootout with police on April 6, 1968, in which Panther Bobby Hutton, 17, was killed and a police officer was wounded. Cleaver had earlier ended his seven years of exile abroad to have his "day in court." After having lived in Cuba, Guinea, Algeria, North Korea, and France, Cleaver said his voluntary return was prompted by his belief that the United States "had changed" to the extent that he could now receive a fair trial. Cleaver's *Soul on Ice*, revealing intimate details of his life and thought in the ghetto, has become a minor classic in revolutionary literature.

November 21.   John Calhoun, 38, a former Foreign Service Officer and Deputy Special Assistant to President Gerald R. Ford, was appointed Special Assistant to the President for Minority Affairs. Calhoun succeeded Stanley Scott, another black man, who resigned. Calhoun, at the time of his new appointment, had been a member of the White House Staff since 1973.

1976

January 20. The U.S. House of Representatives voted by voice vote to authorize an appropriation of $25,000 for the creation of a bust of the late Martin Luther King, Jr., and to install it in the Capitol. King will be the first black person ever so honored, if the bill is passed by the U.S. Senate. The House measure noted King's contribution to the civil rights movement and his winning of the Nobel Peace Prize. The House's Administration Committee had said that the tribute was appropriate "because of Dr. King's prominence in American history and because of all the black Americans who have done so much to contribute to this country's greatness, [yet] not one is now honored among the 681 works of art in the Capitol."

January 21. Black and white students fought with fists and chairs at the Hyde Park High School in Boston, Massachusetts, and, across the city in East Boston, whites tried to block a major Boston harbor tunnel during the morning rush hour as protests against school desegregation continued. At least seventeen persons were arrested in the two incidents. Five persons, including a Boston policeman and the mother of a student, received minor cuts and bruises at Hyde Park. (See Also Above and Below).

January 31. A plan that involved a limited amount of busing to achieve school desegregation was begun in the Detroit, Michigan, school system—the nation's fifth largest. The implementation of the desegregation plan climaxed a court battle that began in 1970. The NAACP filed suit against the Detroit system in 1970 after the Michigan legislature overruled the city's first desegregation plan. In 1972, a federal district court ordered the integration of the primarily black schools of Detroit with those of surrounding, predominantly white suburbs. But in an important decision in July, 1974, the U.S. Supreme Court struck down the provision relating to suburbs and ordered the district court to draw up a plan relating to Detroit only.

The Detroit plan, which was ordered by U.S. District Court Judge Robert De Mascio, permitted a total of 21,800 pupils in kindergarten through eighth grades to be bused. Another 4,700 were transferred to schools within walking distance. In addition, 1,500 ninth and tenth graders were transferred to other schools, but they had to provide their own transportation.

In sum, some 160 schools exchanged pupils in order to achieve enrollments of about half black and half white. The city's remaining 140 schools remained all black.

The NAACP opposed the Detroit plan on the grounds that it did not go far enough, but yet urged compliance with the court order. (See Also Above).

June 16.   The Reverend Richard Allen Chapelle of Jacksonville, Florida, was elected General Conference Secretary of the African Methodist Episcopal (AME) Church during the Fortieth Quadrennial General Conference of the Church in Atlanta, Georgia. Chappelle succeeded the Reverend Russell S. Brown of Chicago who, at 78, was at the age of retirement. More than 30,000 participants, representing more than one million members of the denomination from eighteen districts in the United States, Africa, Central America, and the Caribbean attended the meeting.

June 25.   The U.S. Supreme Court voted 7–2 to prohibit private schools from excluding blacks on the basis of their race. The private school case stemmed from a suit filed by the parents of two black children who were turned away from the Fairfax-Brewster School and Bobbe's Private School, both in the Virginia suburbs of Washington, D.C. The two schools had denied that they discriminated and said they had not had previous black applicants. They contended, however, that they had a right to discriminate if they chose.

The Council for American Private Education, which represents about 90 percent of the nation's private school enrollment, and the U.S. Department of Justice supported the black children in their suit, but the Southern Independent Schools Association, which represents 395 schools, and President Gerald R. Ford opposed judicial relief for the blacks. President Ford did say that he personally disapproved of discrimination against blacks by such schools. According to the Court, racial discrimination by private schools was a "classic violation" of the Civil Rights Act of 1866 which prohibited, among other things, discrimination in the enforcement of contracts. The Court continued: "It may be assumed that parents have a First Amendment right to send their children to educational institutions that promote the belief that racial segregation is desirable, and that the children have an equal right to attend such institutions. . . . But it does not follow that the practice of excluding racial minorities from such institutions is also protected by the same principle."

In reacting to the ruling, Andrew Lipscombe, an attorney for the Fairfax-Brewster, Virginia, schools, said: "Parents are not going to be able to have the associations for their children that they wish, even in private situations which in small, private schools are intimate."

The Court's majority opinion was written by Justice Potter Stewart. In their dissents, Justices Byron R. White and William H. Rehnquist said the Act of 1866 prohibited only discrimination imposed by state law; hence the majority had gone too far in outlawing bias in the private schools.

A Selected Bibliography

Major Repositories

The major collections of materials in Afro-American History are the Amistad Collection at Fisk University, the Moorland Collection at Howard University, the Slaughter Collection at Atlanta University, the James Weldon Johnson Collection at Yale University, the Washington Collection and the Records and Research Center at Tuskegee Institute, the Schomburg Collection at the New York Public Library, and the Hampton Institute Library.

Bibliographical Aids

For a long time the best aid in the study of black Americans was Monroe N. Work, *A Bibliography of the Negro in Africa and America* (1928). It continues to have some value, especially for the pre-20th century periods, but has been largely supplanted, particularly with respect to the United States, by James M. McPherson, et al., *Blacks in America: Bibliographical Essays* (1971). Other useful bibliographical aids are: Dorothy B. Porter, *A Selected List of Books by and about the Negro* (1936) and *A Working Bibliography on the Negro in the United States* (1969); Erwin A. Salk, *A Layman's Guide to Negro History* (1966); Loren Katz, *Teacher's Guide to American Negro History* (1968); Elizabeth W. Miller, *The Negro in America, A Bibliography* (1966), mainly on the period since 1954; African Bibliographic Center, *Black History Viewpoints* (1969).

General Surveys and Collections of Sources

The standard Afro-American history text is John Hope Franklin, *From Slavery to Freedom* (3rd ed., 1969). Other general surveys are Saunders Redding, *They Came in Chains* (1950); Lerone Bennett, *Before the Mayflower* (Rev. ed., 1966), a well illustrated journalistic text; August Meier and Elliott M. Ruddwick, *From Plantation to Ghetto* (1966), a reasoned interpretive study, despite some errors in fact; E. Franklin Frazier, *The Negro in the United States* (1957); Rayford Logan, *The Negro in the United States* (1957); Eli Ginzberg and Alfred S. Eichner, *The Troublesome Presence*; *Democracy and the Negro.* The pioneer general works include: George Washington Williams, *History of the Negro Race in America, 1619-1880* (2 vols., 1883); James W. Pennington, *Text Book of the Origin and History of the Colored People* (1841); William T. Alexander, *History of the Colored Race in America* (1887); Harold M. Tarver, *The Negro in the History of the United States from the Beginning of the English Settlements in 1607 to the Present Time* (1905); E. A. Johnson, *School History of the Negro Race* (1893); Booker T. Washington, *The Story of the Negro* (1909); Willis D. Weatherford, *The Negro From Africa to America* (1924); Charles S. Johnson, *The Negro in American Civilization* (1930); Benjamin Brawley, *The Negro Genius* (1937); Benjamin G. Brawley, *A Short History of the American Negro* (1913); Carter G. Woodson, and Charles H. Wesley, *The Negro in Our History* (10th ed., 1962); and Edwin R. Embree, *Brown Americans* (1945). Thomas F. Gossett, *Race: The History of an Idea in America* (1963) and Winthrop Jordan, *White Over Black* (1968) as well as Louis Ruchames, *Racial Thought in America: From the Puritans to Abraham Lincoln* (1969) are reputable surveys of American racial attitudes. The best biographical compilation is Richard Bardolph, *The Negro Vanguard* (1961 ed.). Other useful biographical compilations are Benjamin Brawley, *Negro Builders and Heroes* (1937); Russell L. Adams, *Great Negroes Past and Present* (1963); and Langston Hughes, *Famous Negro Heroes of America* (1965). The better general studies in the intellectual and social history of Afro-Americans include: Horace Mann Bond, *The Education of the Negro in the American Social Order* (1934); Alain Locke, *Negro Art* (1936); Carter G.

Woodson, *History of the Negro Church* (1921); Benjamin E. Mays and Joseph Nicholson, *The Negro's Church* (1933); E. Franklin Frazier, *The Negro Church in America* (1963); Joseph R. Washington, *Black Religion* (1964); Benjamin Brawley, *The Negro in Literature and Art in the United States* (1921); Hugh M. Gloster, *The Negro in American Fiction* (1948); Robert Bone, *The Negro Novel in America* (1958); Frederick G. Detweiler, *The Negro Press in the United States* (1922).

There are a number of collections of essays and readings in Afro-American history. The better and more recent ones include: Talcott Parsons and Kenneth Clark, eds., *The Negro American* (1966); Howard Brotz, *Negro Social and Political Thought 1850-1920: Representative Texts* (1966); Dwight Hoover, ed., *Understanding Negro History* (1968); Langston Hughes and Milton Meltzer, *Pictorial History of the Negro in America* (1968), especially valuable for young readers; Melvin Drimmer, ed., *Black History* (1969); August Meier and Elliott M. Rudwick, eds., *The Making of Black History* (2 vols., 1969); Allen Weinstein and Frank O. Catell, eds., *The Segregation Era, 1863-1954* (1970); William G. Shade and Roy Herrenkohl, eds., *Seven on Black* (1969); Eric Foner, ed., *America's Black Past* (1970).

Useful collections of sources are Encyclopedia Brittanica's *The Negro in American History* (3 vols., 1969); Herbert Aptheker, ed., *A Documentary History of the Negro People in the United States* (1951), an especially good treatment of the 19th century; Gilbert Osofsky, ed., *The Burden of Race* (1967); William Loren Katz, ed., *Eyewitness: The Negro in American History* (1967); Leslie H. Fishel and Benjamin Quarles, eds., *The Negro American: A Documentary History* (1967), replacing Aptheker as the standard documentary work.

Involuntary Servitude, 1619-1860

The slave period in Afro-American history is exhaustively treated. Some of the more useful works include: Oscar and Mary Handlin, "Origins of the Southern Labor System," *William and Mary Quarterly* (1950); Carl Degler, "Slavery and the Genesis of American Race

Prejudice," *Comparative Studies in Society and History* (1959); Winthrop D. Jordan, "The Influence of the West Indies on the Origins of New England Slavery," *William and Mary Quarterly* (1961); Eugene Sirmans, "The Legal Status of the Slave in South Carolina, 1670-1740," Winthrop D. Jordan, "Modern Tensions and the Origins of American Slavery," *Journal of Southern History* (1962); Eugene D. Genovese, "The Legacy of Slavery and the Roots of Black Nationalism," *Studies on the Left* (1966), a controversial essay which can best be read in conjunction with the criticisms of Herbert Aptheker and C. Vann Woodward in the same issue. See also Robert C. Twombly and Robert H. Moore, "Black Puritan: The Negro in Seventeenth Century Massachusetts," *William and Mary Quarterly* (1967); Edward R. Turner, "Slavery in Colonial Pennsylvania," *Pennsylvania Magazine of History and Biography* (1911); Don B. Kates, "Abolition, Deportation, Integration: Attitudes Toward Slavery in the Early Republic," *Journal of Negro History* (1968); Ernest J. Clarke, "Aspects of the North Carolina Slave Code, 1715-1860," *North Carolina Historical Review* (1962); Harold D. Woodman, "The Profitability of Slavery: An Historical Perennial," *Journal of Southern History* (1963); John H. Moore, "Simon Gray, Riverman: A Slave who was Almost Free," *Mississippi Valley Historical Review* (1962); John B. Cade, ed., "Out of the Mouths of Ex-Slaves," *Journal of Negro History* (1935), E. O. Settle, "Social Attitudes During the Slave Regime: Household Servants Verus Field Hands," *Publications of the American Sociological Society* (1934); and J. Ralph Jones, ed., "Portraits of Georgia Slaves," *Georgia Review* (1967), all good collections of the reminiscences of ex-slaves. For an excellent analysis of slave songs and folk beliefs see Sterling Brown, "Negro Folk Expression; Spirituals, Secular, Ballads, and Songs," *Phylon* (1953). Other noteworthy works on slavery are Kenneth Scott, "The Slave Insurrection in New York in 1712," *New York Historical Society Quarterly* (1961); T. W. Clark, "The Negro Plot of 1741," *New York History* (1944); Ferenc M. Szasz, "The New York Slave Revolt of 1741: A Re-examination," *New York History* (1967); Raymond and Alice Bauer, "Day to Day Resistance to Slavery," *Journal of Negro History* (1943); Richard Wade, "The Vesey Plot Reconsidered," *Journal of Southern History* (1964), a controversial analysis of the famous South Carolina conspiracy; Marion D. Kilson, "Toward Freedom: An Analysis of Slave Revolts in the United States," *Phylon* (1964); George M. Frederickson and Christopher Lasch, "Resistance to Slavery," *Civil War History* (1967).

The best books on American Negro slavery include: Lorenzo Green, *The Negro in Colonial New England* (1942); Ulrich B. Phillips, *American Negro Slavery* (1918), solid scholarly research, though it reflects the racism of the time; Kenneth M. Stampp, *The Peculiar Institution* (1956), a major revisionist work; U. B. Phillips, *Life and Labor in the Old South* (1929); Stanley Elkins, *Slavery* (1959), a controversial historical-psychological study; Matthew T. Mellon, *Early American Views of Negro Slavery* (1934); Charles Sydnor, *Slavery in Mississippi* (1933); Edward J. McManus, *A History of Negro Slavery in New York* (1966); Joe Gray Taylor, *Negro Slavery in Louisiana* (1961); James C. Ballagh, *A History of Slavery in Virginia;* Guion G. Johnson, *Ante-Bellum North Carolina* (1937); Frank J. Klingberg, *An Appraisal of the Negro in Colonial South Carolina*; Ralph B. Flanders, *Plantation Slavery in Georgia*; Staughton Lynd, *Class Conflict, Slavery, and the United States Constitution* (1967); Frederic Bancroft, *Slave Trading in the Old South* (1931); Richard C. Wade, *Slavery in the Cities* (1964); Eugene D. Genovese, *The Political Economy of Slavery* (1965); Alfred H. Conrad and John R. Meyer, *The Economics of Slavery* (1964); Frederick Douglass, *My Bondage and My Freedom* (1955), autobiographical reminiscensces; Gilbert Osofsky, ed., *Puttin' On Ole Massa* (1969), Arna Bontemps, ed., *Great Slave Narratives* (1969), the latest of the ex-slave narratives; Benjamin Botkin, ed., *Lay My Burden Down* (1945), the largest of the ex-slave reminiscenses; Frank Tannenbaum, *Slave and Citizen* (1946), a comparative work.

Abolitionists and abolitionism are well treated in Arthur Zilversmit, *The First Emancipation* (1967); Frederick Douglass, *The Life and Times of Frederick Douglass* (1881); Miles M. Fisher, *Negro Slave Songs in the United States* (1953); Herbert Aptheker, *American Negro Slave Revolts* (1943), one of the most controversial works on the subject; John Lofton, *Insurrection in South Carolina* (1964), a study of Denmark Vesey's plot; William Freehling, *Prelude to Civil War* (1966), another account of the Vesey conspiracy; Herbert Aptheker, *Nat Turner's Slave Rebellion* (1966), like most of Aptheker's works, perhaps a bit exaggerated; Louis Filler, *The Crusade Against*

Slavery, an excellent study (1960); Dwight Dumond, *Anti-Slavery* (1961); Benjamin Quarles, *Black Abolitionists* (1969), a long overdue work; Philip S. Foner, *The Life and Writings of Frederick Douglass* (4 vols., 1950-1955); Philip Foner, *Frederick Douglass* (1964); Benjamin Quarles, *Frederick Douglass* (1948); Herbert Aptheker, ed., *One Continual Cry* (1965); Larry Gara, *The Liberty Line* (1961), a study of the Underground Railroad; Herbert Aptheker, *To Be Free* (1948); Martin Duberman, ed., *The Anti-Slavery Vanguard* (1965); Aileen Kraditor, *Means and Ends in American Abolitionism* (1969), weakened by its tendency to avoid controversy; Eugene H. Berwanger, *The Frontier Against Slavery* (1967); Eric Foner, *Free Soil, Free Labor, Free Men* (1970); Henrietta Buckmaster, *Let My People Go: The Story of the Underground Railroad and the Growth of the Abolition Movement* (1941); David B. Davis, *The Problem of Slavery in Western Culture* (1958); Nicholas Halasz, *The Rattling Chains: Slave Unrest and Revolt in the American South* (1959), a novelistic treatment; Joseph C. Carroll, *Slave Insurrections in the United States, 1800-1860* (1938); Lorenzo J. Green, "Mutiny on the Slave ships," *Phylon* (1944), a fascinating, but little studied subject; Ann Petry, *Harriett Tubman* (1955); Herbert Aptheker, *The Negro in the Abolitionist Movement* (1941); David Walker, *Appeal in Four Articles* (1830), a militant, contemporary anti-slavery pamphlet.

On the Ante-Bellum Free Negroes, the better works are Charles S. Sydnor, "The Free Negro in Mississippi Before the Civil War," *American Historical Review* (1927); Horace Fitchett, "Origin and Growth of the Free Negro Population of Charleston, South Carolina," *Journal of Negro History* (1941); Dorothy B. Porter, "The Organized Educational Activities of Negro Literary Societies, 1818-1846," *Journal of Negro Education* (1936); Robert Ernst, "The Economic Status of New York City Negroes, 1850-1863," *Negro History Bulletin* (1949); Lee Calligaro, "The Negro's Legal Status in Pre-Civil War New Jersey, *New Jersey History* (1967); Richard C. Wade, "The Negro in Cincinnati, 1800-1830," *Journal of Negro History* (1954); Benjamin Quarles, *The Negro in the American Revolution* (1961); Shirley Graham, *The Story of Phyllis Wheatley* (1949); William Nell, *The Colored Patriots of the American Revolution* (1855); William Wells Brown, *The Negro in the American Revolu-*

tion (1867); Howard H. Bell, "The Negro Emigration Movement, 1849-1854: A Phase of Negro Nationalism," *Phylon* (1959); H. H. Bell, "Expressions of Negro Militancy in the North, 1840-1860," *Journal of Negro History* (1960); H. H. Bell, "Negro Nationalism: A Factor in Emigration Projects, 1858-1861," *Journal of Negro History* (1962); Hollis R. Lynch, "Pan-Negro Nationalism in the New World Before 1862," *Boston University Papers on Africa* (1966); L. Mehlinger, "The Attitude of the Free Negro Toward African Colonization," *Journal of Negro History* (1916); H. N. Sherwood, "Paul Cuffe," *Journal of Negro History* (1923), the story of New England's most noted free black; Leon Litwack, *North of Slavery* (1961), the standard account on the subject; John Hope Franklin, *The Free Negro in North Carolina, 1790-1860* (1943); John H. Russell, *The Free Negro in Virginia* (1913); Carter G. Woodson, *Free Negro Heads of Families in the United States in 1830* (1925); Emma Lou Thornbrough, *The Negro in Indiana Before 1900* (1957); Charles H. Wesley, *Richard Allen* (1935), still the best biography of the founder of the A. M. E. Church; Philip J. Staudenraus, *The African Colonization Movement, 1816-1865* (1961): Roger W. Shugg, "Negro Voting in the Ante-Bellum South," *Journal of Negro History*, XXI (October, 1936); John H. Russell, "Colored Freemen as Slave Owners in Virginia," *Journal of Negro History* (1916); Carter G. Woodson, *Free Negro Owners of Slaves in the United States in 1830* (1925).

The role of free blacks in abolitionist activities appears in William Brewer, "John B. Russwurm," *Journal of Negro History* (1928); Monroe Work, "The Life of Charles B. Ray," *Journal of Negro History* (1919); Dorothy Porter, "David Ruggles, An Apostle of Human Rights," *Journal of Negro History* (1943); Ray A. Billington, "James Forten, Forgotten Abolitionist," *Negro History Bulletin* (1949), an excellent, though perhaps exaggerated, account of this wealthy and influential black abolitionist; Larry Gara, "The Professional Fugitive in the Abolitionist Movement," *Wisconsin Magazine of History* (1965); Charles H. Wesley, "The Negro in the Organization of Abolition," *Phylon* (1941), "The Participation of Negroes in Anti-Slavery Political Parties, *Journal of Negro History* (1944), and "The

Negro of New York in the Emancipation Movement," *Journal of Negro History* (1939); William and Jane H. Pease, "Anti-Slavery Ambivalence: Immediatism, Expediency, Race," *American Quarterly* (1965); Leon F. Litwack, "The Abolitionist Dilemma: The Anti-Slavery Movement and the Northern Negro," *New England Quarterly* (1961); Benjamin Quarles, "The Breach Between Garrison and Douglass," *Journal of Negro History* (1938); William and Jane H. Pease, "Boston Garrisonians and the Problem of Frederick Douglass," *Canada Journal of History* (1967); Eric Foner, "Politics and Prejudice: The Free Soil Party and the Negro, 1819-1852," *Journal of Negro History* (1965).

War and Freedom, 1861-1876

Significant works on blacks during the Civil War and Reconstruction include: Herbert Aptheker, "Negro Casualties in the Civil War," *Journal of Negro History* (1947); Edgar A. Toppin, "Humbly They Served: The Black Brigade in the Defense of Cincinnati," *Journal of Negro History* (1963); Richard H. Abbott, "Massachusetts and the Recruitment of Southern Negroes, 1863-1865," *Civil War History* (1968); N. W. Stephenson, "The Question of Arming the Slaves," *American Historical Review* (1913); Harvey Wish, "Slave Disloyalty Under the Confederacy," *Journal of Negro History* (1938); Charles H. Wesley, "The Employment of Negroes as Soldiers in the Confederate Army," *Journal of Negro History* (1919); Charles H. Wesley, "Lincoln's Plan for Colonizing the Emancipated Negro," *Journal of Negro History* (1919); Bernard Weisberger, "The Dark and Bloody Ground of Reconstruction Historiography," *Journal of Southern History* (1959); W. E. B. DuBois, "Reconstruction and its Benefits," *American Historical Review* (1910); Joseph A. Barome, ed., "The Autobiography of Hiram Revels," *Midwest Journal* (1952-53); A. E. Perkins, "Oscar James Dunn," *Phylon* (1943); Robert H. Woody, "Jonathan Jasper Wright," *Journal of Negro History* (1933); Edward F. Sweat, "Francis L. Cardozo-Profile of Integrity in Reconstruction Politics," *Journal of Negro History* (1961); LaWanda Cox, "The Promise of Land for the Freedman," *Mississippi Valley Historical Reivew* (1958); Patrick W. Riddleberger, "The Radical's Abnadonment of the Negro During Reconstruction," *Journal of Negro History* (1960); Leslie H. Fishel, "Northern Prejudice and Negro Suffrage, 1865-1870," *Journal of Negro History* (1954), "The Negro in Northern Politics, 1870-1900," *Mississippi Valley Historical Review* (1953), and "Repercussions of Reconstruction: The Northern Negro, 1870-1883," *Civil War History* (1968); Benjamin Quarles, *The Negro in the Civil War* (1953); Dudley Cornish, *The Sable Arm* (1956); James McPherson, ed., *The Negro's Civil War*; Thomas Wentworth Higginson, *Army Life in a Black Regiment* (1870), relating the experiences of a white officer with black troops; John Hope Franklin, *The Emancipation Proclamation* (1962) and *The Militant South* (1964); Benjamin Quarles, *Lincoln and the Negro* (1962); James M. McPherson, *The Struggle for Equality* (1964); Bell I. Wiley, *Southern Negroes, 1861-1865* (1953); V. Jacque Voegel, *Free But Not Equal* (1967); C. L. Wagandt, *The Mighty Revolution: Negro Emancipation in Maryland* (1965); Charlotte L. Forten, *The Journal of Charlotte L. Forten* (1961), diary of a black teacher in the South during the Civil War; Irvin H. Lee, *Negro Medal of Honor Men*; W. E. B. DuBois, *Black Reconstruction* (1935), the pioneer revisionist work; Kenneth Stampp, *The Era of Reconstruction* (1965), the leading modern revisionist survey; John Hope Franklin, *Reconstruction After the Civil War* (1961); Lerone Bennett, *Black Power USA, The Human Side of Reconstruction, 1867-77* (1967), a slightly exaggerated account; LaWanda and John Cox, *Politics, Principle, and Prejudice* (1963), a revisionist study of national politics in the Reconstruction period; Henry L. Swint, *The Northern Teacher in the South* (1965); Robert Cruden, *The Negro in Reconstruction* (1969); Theodore Wilson, *The Black Codes of the South* (1965); Henderson Donald, *The Negro Freedman* (1952), not a wholly satisfactory work; Joel Williamson, *After Slavery* (1965), and Willie Lee Rose, *Rehearsal for Reconstruction: The Port Royal Experiment* (1964), both fine studies of South Carolina; Joe M. Richardson, *The Negro in the Reconstruction of Florida* (1966); Vernon Lane Wharton, *The Negro in Mississippi, 1865-1890* (1947); A. A. Taylor, *The Negro in the Reconstruction of Virginia* (1926); Otis A. Singletary, *Negro Militia and Reconstruction* (1957); Samuel Smith, *The Negro in Congress, 1870-1901* (1940); John M. Langston, *From the Virginia Plantation to the Na-*

tional Capitol (1894), and John R. Lynch, *The Facts of Reconstruction* (1913), reminiscences of black reconstruction politicians; Walter C. Fleming, *Documentary History of Reconstruction* (3 vols., 1906-1907); Harry Hyman, ed., *New Frontiers of the American Reconstruction* (1966); James P. Shenton, ed., *The Reconstruction* (1963); E. Merton Coulter, *Negro Legislators in Georgia During the Reconstruction Period* (1968) and *The South During Reconstruction* (1948), both warrant caution for anti-Negro bias; George Bentley, *A History of the Freedmen's Bureau* (1955), the standard work, although not entirely satisfactory; William Mcfeeley, *Yankee Stepfather: General Oliver O. Howard and the Freedmen* (1968), a recent work that tells much about the workings of the Freedmen's Bureau as well as the life of its federal commissioner. A good supplement for Bentley's older work on the Bureau; Martin Abbott, *The Freedman's Bureau in South Carolina* (1967); Walter L. Fleming, *The Freedmen's Savings Bank* (1927).

The Nadir, 1877-1900

Studies of black life in the post-Reconstruction era include: Clarence A. Bacote, "Negro Proscription and Proposed Solutions in Georgia, 1880-1908;" *Journal of Southern History* (1959); John Hope Franklin, "The Negro Goes to School: The Genesis of Legal Segregation in Southern Schools," *South Atlantic Quarterly* (1959); Jack Abramowitz, "The Negro in the Populist Movement," *Journal of Negro History* (1953); Charles Crowe, "Tom Watson, Populists, and Blacks Reconsidered," *Journal of Negro History* (1970), a new article which offers, perhaps, the best summary on the subject; Edwin S. Redkey, "Bishop Turner's African Dream," *Journal of American History* (1967); C. Vann Woodward, *Origins of the New South* (1951) Thomas Clark and Albert Kirwan, *The South Since Appomattox* (1967); Charles Wynes, ed., *The Negro in the South Since 1865* (1965); George B. Tindall, *South Carolina Negroes, 1877-1900* (1952); Frenise Logan, *The Negro in North Carolina, 1876-1894* (1964); Albert D. Kirwan, *Revolt of the Rednecks* (1951), a good work on Mississippi politics; Stanley P. Hirshon, *Farewell to the Bloody Shirt* (1962); Vincent P. DeSantis, *Republicans Face the*

Southern Question (1959); Rayford Logan, *The Negro in American Life and Thought: The Nadir* (Also titled *the Betrayal of the Negro*) (1954), an excellent study of the entire period; C. Vann Woodward, *The Strange Career of Jim Crow* (3rd. ed., 1966), the standard account of the origins of segregation; Horace Mann Bond, *Negro Education in Alabama* (1939); Louis R. Harlan, *Separate and Unequal* (1958); Henry Bullock, *A History of Negro Education in the South* (1967); Edwin S. Redkey, *Black Exodus* (1969); Charles E. Wynes, *Race Relations in Virginia, 1870-1902*; (1961); Everett L. Jones, *The Negro Cowboys* (1965); Shirley Graham and George D. Liscomb, *Dr. George Washington Carver, Scientist* (1965); Arthur F. Raper, *The Tragedy of Lynching* (1933); David M. Chalmers *Hooded Americanism: The First Century of the Ku Klux Klan* (1965).

The Age of Booker T. Washington, 1901-1917

Noteworthy studies on the Washington era in Afro-American history include August Meier's works, "Booker T. Washington and the Negro Press," *Journal of Negro History* (1953), "Booker T. Washington and the Rise of the NAACP," *Crisis* (1954), and "Toward a Reinterpretation of Booker T. Washington," *Journal of Southern History* (1957); Daniel Walden, "The Contemporary Opposition to the Political Ideas of Booker T. Washington," *Journal of Negro History* (1960); Donald J. Calesta, "Booker T. Washington: Another Look," *Journal of Negro History* (1964); Louis R. Harlan, "Booker T. Washington and the White Man's Burden," *American Historical Review* (1966); Vincent Harding, "W. E. B. DuBois and the Black Messianic Tradition," *Freedomways* (1969); Mary L. Chaffee, "W. E. B. DuBois' Concept of the Racial Problem in the United States," *Journal of Negro History* (1956); Elliott M. Rudwick, "The Niagara Movement," *Journal of Negro History* (1957); Thomas R. Cripps, "The Reaction of the Negro to the Motion Picture *Birth of a Nation*," *Historian* (1963); Dewey W. Grantham, "The Progressive Movement and the Negro," *South Atlantic Quarterly* (1955); Kathleen Wohlgemuth, "Woodrow Wilson and Federal Segregation," *Journal of Negro History* (1959); Nancy J. Weiss, "The Negro and the New Freedom: Fighting Wilsonian Segregation," *Political Science Quarterly* (1969); Bernard Mandel, "Samuel Gompers and the Negro Workers, 1886-1914," *Journal of Negro History* (1955); Hugh Hawkins, ed., *Booker T. Washington and his Critics* (1962); August Meier, *Negro Thought in America, 1880-1915* (1963); Samuel R. Spencer, *Booker T. Washington and the Negro's Place in American Life* (1957); Booker T. Washington's own works, *The Future of the American Negro* (1899), *Up From Slavery* (1900), *The Negro in the South* (1907), and *Selected Speeches* (1932); Francis Broderick, *W. E. B. DuBois: Negro Leader in a Time of Crisis*; Elliott M. Rudwick, *W. E. B. DuBois, Propagandist of the Negro Protest* (1961); DuBois' own autobiographies, *Dusk of Dawn* (1940) and *Autobiography of W. E. B. DuBois* (1968), as well as his penetrating *The Souls of Black Folk* (1903); Kelly Miller, *Race Adjustment* (1908); Charles Kellogg, *NAACP* (1967); Langston Hughes, *Fight For Freedom; Story of the NAACP* (1962); Robert L. Jack, *History of the NAACP* (1943); Ray Stanndard Baker, *Following the Color Line* (1908); I. A. Newby, *Jim Crow's Defense: Anti-Negro Thought in America, 1900-1930* (1965); Charles Wesley, *Negro Labor in the United States 1850-1925* (1927); Elliott M. Rudwick, *Race Riot at East St. Louis, July 2, 1917* (1964); Emmett J. Scott, *The American Negro in the World War* (1919); Ullin W. Leavell, *Philanthropy in Negro Education* (1930); W. E. B. DuBois, *Atlanta University Studies* (1898-1901).

Between War and Depression, 1918-1932

The better works for this period include: Emmett J. Scott, ed., "Letters of Negro Migrants," *Journal of Negro History* (1919); Charles S. Johnson, "How Much is the Migration A Flight From Persecution?," *Opportunity* (1923); Gilbert Osofsky, *Harlem: The Making of a Ghetto* (1966); James Weldon Johnson, *Black Manhattan* (1930); Seth Scheiner, *Negro Mecca* (1965); Claude McKay, *Harlem: Negro Metropolis* (1940); Allan Spear, *Black Chicago* (1967); St. Clair Drake and Horace Cayton, *Black Metropolis* (1940), also on Chicago, a classic; Emmett J. Scott, *Negro Migration During the War* (1920); Thomas J. Woofter, *The Negro Problem in*

Cities (1928); Louise V. Kennedy, *The Negro Peasant Turns City-ward* (1930); Claude V. Kiser, *Sea Island to City* (1932); Carter G. Woodson, *A Century of Negro Migration* (1918); Arna Bontemps and Jack Conroy, *Anyplace But Here* (1966); Robert Kerdin, ed., *Voice of the Negro* (1919) (1920); Edmund D. Cronon, *Black Moses* (1955), the standard biography of Marcus Garvey; Amy Garvey, *Garvey and Garveyism* (1968); Charles S. Johnson, *The Economic Status of Negroes* (1933); Arthur Fauset, *Black Gods of the Metropolis* (1944), John Hoshor, *God in a Rolls-Royce* (1936); Sara Harris, *Father Divine: Holy Husband* (1953), all on Father Divine, leader of a pseudo-religious cult; Milton Meltzer and August Meier, *Time of Trial, Time of Hope: The Negro in America, 1919-1941* (1966); Roi Ottley, *The Lonely Warrior: The Life and Times of Robert S. Abbott* (1955), biography of the publisher of the militant Chicago *Defender*; Arthur I. Waskow, *From Race Riot to Sit-In* (1966), traces black protest from the riots of 1919 to the 1960's. Works treating the Harlem Renaissance are John A. Emanuel and Theodore Gross, eds., *Dark Symphony* (1968); John Henrik Clarke, ed., *American Negro Short Stories* (1966); Langston Hughes ed., *The Best Short Stories by Negro Writers* (1967); Abraham Chapman, ed., *Black Voices* (1968); Sterling Brown, *The Negro in American Fiction* (1937); Saunders Redding, *To Make a Poet Black* (1939); Stephen Bronz, *Roots of Negro Racial Consciousness* (1969); Mercer Cook and Stephen Henderson, *The Militant Black Writer in Africa and the United States* (1969); Alain Locke, ed., *The New Negro* (1925), the best collection, a contemporary account; Blanche Ferguson, *Countee Cullen and the Negro Renaissance* (1966); James Weldon Johnson, *Along This Way* (1933), an autobiographical treatment, as is Langston Hughes, *The Big Sea* (1940); Benjamin Brawley, "The Negro Literary Renaissance," *The Southern Workman* (1927).

A New Deal — A New Life?, 1933-1940

The Negro in the New Deal era is still an inadequately treated subject. There are, however, some good studies; among them are James A. Harrell, "Negro Leadership in the Election Year 1936," *Journal of Southern History* (1968); John A. Salmond, "The CCC and the Negro," *Journal of American History* (1965); Leslie H. Fishel, "The Negro in the New Deal Era," *Wisconsin Magazine of History* (1964-65); Bernard Sternsher, ed., *The Negro in Depression and War* (1969); Arnold Hill, *The Negro and Economic Reconstruction* (1937); Abram Harris, *The Negro as Capitalist* (1936); Charles S. Johnson, et. al., *The Collapse of Cotton Tenancy* (1938); Charles S. Johnson, *Shadow of the Plantation* (1934); John Dollard, *Caste and Class in a Southern Town*, a sort of classic, an in-depth study of black life and race relations in a Mississippi town (1937); Harold Gosnell, *Negro Politicians*, a standard account, focusing on Chicago (1935); Wilson Record, *The Negro and the Communist Party* (1951); E. Franklin Frazier, *Negro Youth at the Crossroads* (1949); Drake and Cayton, *Black Metropolis* (cited above); James W. Ford, *Hunger and Terror in Harlem* (1935), the story of that year's Harlem riot; Roi Ottley, *New World A-Coming* (1943), treats FDR's Black Cabinet; Robert C. Weaver, *Negro Labor* (1946); Marian Anderson, *My Lord, What A Morning* (1956), an autobiography of the well-known contralto; Catherine O. Peare, *Mary McLeod Bethune* (1961).

War Again, 1941-1945

The most noteworthy works on Afro-Americans during the War years are Richard M. Dalfiume, "The Forgotten Years of the Negro Revolution," *Journal of American History* (1968); Dan T. Carter, *Scottsboro* (1969), the story of the multifaceted Alabama rape case; Alfred M. Lee, *Detroit Race Riot* (1943); Ulysses Lee, *The Employment of Negro Troops* (1966); Herbert Garfinkel, *When Negroes March* (1959), the story of A. Philip Randolph's proposed March on Washington; Rayford Logan, ed., *What the Negro Wants* (1944); Loren Miller, *The Petitioners* (1968), treats the legal assaults of the NAACP; Walter White, *A Rising Wind* (1945), a fine account of blacks on the fighting front; Louis Ruchames, *Race, Jobs and Politics: the Story of FEPC* (1953); Gunnar Myrdal, *An American Dilemma* (1944), a classic study of American race relations; Louis Kesselman, *The Social Policies of FEPC* (1953); B. R. Brazeal, *The Brotherhood of Sleeping Car Porters* (1946); Carl N. Degler, "The Negro in America — Where Myrdal Went Wrong," *New York Times Magazine* (1969); Poppy Cannon, *A Gentle Knight* (1956), biography of the NAACP leader Walter White by his wife; Richard Wright, *Black Boy* (1945), an autobiographical novel; John D. Silvera, *The Negro in World War II* (1946); Seymour J. Schoenfield, *The Negro in the Armed Forces* (1945); Earl Brown, "American Negroes and the War," *Harper's Magazine* (1942); John Temple Graves, "The Southern Negro and the War Crisis," *Virginia Quarterly Review* (1942).

The Attack Against Segregation, 1945-1954

The most useful studies of the post-war years include: Elliott M. Rudwick, "How CORE Began," *Social Science Quarterly* 1969); Thurgood Marshall, "An Evaluation of Recent Efforts to Achieve Racial Integration Through Resort to the Courts," *Journal of Negro Education* (1952); L. D. Reddick, "The Negro Policy of the United States Army, 1775-1945," *Journal of Negro History* (1949); Walter F. White, *A Man Called White* (1948), autobiography of the second executive secretary of the NAACP; Henry L. Moon, *Balance of Power: The Negro Vote* (1948), examining the role of the black vote in the election of 1948; Richard J. Stillman, *Integration of the Negro in the United States Armed Forces* (1968); Richard Dalfiume, *Desegregation of the U. S. Armed Forces* (1969); Harry S. Ashmore, *The Negro and the Schools* (1954); Abram Kardiner and Lionel Ovesey, *The Mark of Oppression* (1951), a classic, cites the psychological effects of discrimination; J. Alvin Kugelmann, *Ralph J. Bunche, Fighter for Peace* (1952); Robert Penn Warren, *Who speaks for the Negro?* (1954); Rayford W. Logan, *The Negro and the Post-War World* (1945); Robert C. Weaver, *The Negro Ghetto* (1948).

The Era of Civil Rights, 1954-1964

A flood of articles and books has appeared on the Civil Rights Era; the better studies include: August Meier, "On the Significance of

Martin Luther King," *New Politics* (1965); Edward A. Leonard, "Nonviolence and Violence in American Racial Protests, 1945-1967," *Rocky Mountain Social Science Journal* (1969); Lerone Bennett, "The South and the Negro: Martin Luther King, Jr., *Ebony* (1957); Lerone Bennett, Jr., "Daisey Bates: First Lady of Little Rock," *Ebony* (1958), on the Little Rock NAACP leader who spearheaded school integration in her town; Benjamin Muse, *Ten Years of Prelude* (1964) and *The American Negro Revolution* (1968); Lerone Bennett, *What Manner of Man?* (1964), a rather uncritical biography of Martin Luther King, Jr.; David L. Lewis, *King: A Critical Biography* (1970); Martin Luther King's own works, *Stride Toward Freedom* (1958); *Why We Can't Wait* (1964), *Where Do We Go From Here?* (1967), *The Trumpet of Conscience* (1969); James Peck, *Freedom Ride* (1962); James Farmer, *Freedom-When?* (1965); Waskow, *From Race Riot to Sit-In* (cited above); Merrill Proudfoot, *Diary of a Sit-In* (1962); Howard Zinn, *The New Abolitionists* (1964), mostly a story of SNCC; Elizabeth Sutherland, ed., *Letters From Mississippi* (1965), views of civil rights workers in Mississippi; Len Holt, *The Summer That Didn't End* (1965) and Sally Belfrage, *Freedom Summer* (1965), both detailing civil rights work in Mississippi during 1964; James Silver, *Mississippi, The Closed Society* (2nd ed., 1966); Louis Lomax, *The Negro Revolt* (1962); Charles Silberman, *Crisis in Black and White* (1964); Alan Westin, ed., *Freedom Now!* (1964); Lerone Bennett, *The Negro Mood* (1964); James Q. Wilson, *Negro Politics: The Search For Leadership* (1960); Jack Greenberg, *Race Relations and American Law* (1969), reflections of an NAACP lawyer; William Brink and Louis Harris, *The Negro Revolution in America* (1964); C. Eric Lincoln, *The Black Muslims in America* (1961); E. U. Essien-Udom, *Black Nationalism* (1962), also on the Muslims; E. Franklin Frazier, *Black Bourgeoisie* (1957), a classic on the black middle class; Robert F. Williams, *Negroes With Guns* (1962); Carl Rowan, *Go South to Sorrow* (1957); United States Commission on Civil Rights, *Freedom to the Free* (1963); Doris E. Saunders, *The Day They Marched* (1963), well illustrated, principally about the 1963 March on Washington; Vivian W. Henderson, *The Economic Status of Negroes* (1963).

An Age of Disillusionment, 1964-1973

The renewed interest in Afro-American history and the contemporary black revolt have produced a great outpouring of works. Much of the material is, regrettably, shoddy and hastily contrived, but among the most useful studies are: Robert Fogelson, "From Resentment to Confrontation: The Police, the Negroes, and the Outbreak of the 1960's Riots," *Political Science Quarterly* (1968); Nathan S. Caplan and Jeffrey M. Paige, "A Study of Ghetto Rioters," *Scientific American* (1968); Ulf Hannerz, "What Negroes Mean by Soul," *Trans-Action* (1968); Martin Kilson, "Black Power: Anatomy of a Paradox," *Harvard Journal of Negro Affairs* (1968); A. J. Gregor, "Black Nationalism: A Preliminary Analysis of Negro Radicalism," *Science and Society* (1963); Stokely Carmichael, "What We Want," *The New York Review of Books* (1966); David Danzig, "In Defense of Black Power," *Commentary* (1966); Kenneth Clark, *Dark Ghetto* (1965); Thomas F. Pettigrew, *A Portrait of the Negro American* (1964); Alphonso Pincney, *Black Americans* (1969), a compact interdisciplinary study; Karl E. Taeuber, and Alma F. Taeuber, *Negroes in Cities* (1965); Paul Jacobs, *Prelude to Riot: A View of Urban America From the Bottom Up* (1967); Lee Rainwater and William Yancey, *The Moynihan Report and the Politics of Controversy* (1967); Robert Conot, *Rivers of Blood, Years of Darkness* (1967), on the Watts Riot; Fred Shapiro and James Sullivan, *Race Riot, New York, 1964* (1964); Tom Hayden, *Rebellion in Newark* (1967); Robert Shoggin and Tom Craig, *The Detroit Race Riot* (1969); Ben W. Gilbert, *Ten Blocks from the White House* (1969); on the Washington riot; John Hersey, *The Algiers Motel Incident* (1968), a novelistic treatment of one aspect of the Detroit riot; Louis H. Masottli and Don R. Bowen eds., *Riots and Rebellion* (1969); William H. Grier and Price M. Cobbs, *Black Rage* (1968), a psychological study; Ulf Hannerz, *Soulside* (1969); Claude Brown, *Manchild in the Promised Land* (1965), a well received autobiography of ghetto life; Malcolm X, *Autobiography* (1965), has become somewhat of a classic; George Brietman, *Malcolm X Speaks* (1965); also by Brietman, *The Last Year of Malcolm X* (1967); John Henrik Clarke, ed., *Malcolm X: The Man and His Times* (1969); Floyd Barbour, ed., *The Black Power*

Revolt (1968), a documentary collection; Stokeley Carmichael and Charles Hamilton, *Black Power* (1967), a political definition of the controversial slogan by one of the originators of the concept; H. Rap Brown, *Die, Nigger, Die* (1969), the story of, and by, the exiled SNCC leader; Whitney M. Young, Jr., *Beyond Racism:Building an Open Society* (1969), views of the moderate head of the National Urban League; Floyd McKissick, *Three-Fifths of a Man* (1969), views of the militant CORE leader; Nathan Wright, *Black Power and Urban Unrest* (1967); Lewis M. Killian, *Impossible Revolution? Black Power and the American Dream* (1968); Chuck Stone, *Black Political Power in the United States* (1968); Eldridge Cleaver, *Soul on Ice* (1968), *Eldridge Cleaver* (1969), *Post-Prison Writings and Speeches* (1969), writings of the exiled Black Panther leader; Harold Cruse, *The Crisis of the Negro Intellectual* and *Rebellion or Revolution* (1968); S. Eric Lincoln, ed., *Is Anybody Listening to Black America?* (1968), essays on the contemporary black mood; Gary T. Marx, *Protest and Prejudice* (rev. ed., 1968); Robert Allen, *Black Awakening in Capitalist America* (1969); Elijah Muhammad, *Message to the Black Man in America* (1965), words from the head of the Muslim sect; Calvin Hernton, *Sex and Racism in Ameirca* (1967), an interesting, though slightly exaggerated, work; Floyd B. Barbour, *The Black Power Revolt* (1968); Charles E. Fager, *White Reflections on Black Power* (1967); William Bradford Huie, *Three Lives for Mississippi* (1965), a well told story of the 1964 murders of civil rights workers; Fred Powledge, *Black Power, White Resistance: Notes on the New Civil War* (1967); *Report of the National Commission on Civil Disorders* (1968); Thomas F. Gossett, *Race: The History of An Idea in America* (1963); Vincent Harding, *Black Radicalism in America* (1970); Hanes Walton, *The Negro in Third Party Politics* (1969) and *The Political Philosophy of Martin Luther King* (1970); C. Eric Lincoln, ed., *The Negro Pilgrimage in America* (1969); Hubert G. Locke, *The Detroit Riot of 1967* (1969); Robert H. Brisbane, *The Black Vanguard* (1970), traces the origins of the Negro "social revolution"; Lee Rainwater, *Behind Ghetto Walls* (1970); and Theodore Draper, *The Rediscovery of Black Nationalism* (1970); the book is not entirely satisfactory, but tries to give a basic general treatment of the subject; Debbie Louis, *And We are Not*

Saved: A History of the Movement as People (1970) contains much first-hand data from a young white CORE worker; C. Eric Lincoln, ed., *Martin Luther King, Jr.: A Profile* (1970) includes selections from King's own writings as well as the assessments of others; James Boggs, *Racism and the Class Struggle*, a radical essay on the conditions of black Americans; Peter Goldman, *Report from Black America* (1970), a study of contemporary black public opinion. New works on religion and racism include Joseph C. Hough, *Black Power and White Protestants* (1968), Charles F. Sleeper, *Black Power and Christian Responsibility* (1969), and Robert S. Lecky and H. Elliott Wright, eds., *Black Manifesto: Religion, Racism, and Reparations* (1969). Important critical studies of black capitalism include Robert L. Allen, *Black Awakening in Capitalist America* (1969) and Earl Ofari, *The Myth of Black Capitalism* (1970). The latest noteworthy writings on the era which began in 1964 include: Donald Freed, *Agony in New Haven: The Trial of Bobby Seale, Ericka Huggins and the Black Panther Party* (1973); John Henry Cutter, *Ed Brooke: Biography of a Senator* (1972); Edwin K. Norton, *Juror Number Four* (1973), the story of the trial of thirteen Black Panthers as seen by one of the jurors; Peter Goldman, *The Death and Life of Malcolm X* (1973); Stephen Henderson, *Understanding the New Black Poetry* (1972) and Huey P. Newton, *Revolutionary Suicide* (1973).

Index

NOTES

NOTES

NOTES

NOTES

NOTES

NOTES

NOTES

NOTES

NOTES

NOTES

NOTES

NOTES